AdvancED CSS

Joseph R. Lewis and Meitar Moscovitz

friendsof

DESIGNER TO DESIGNER™

an Apress® company

AdvancED CSS

ISBN-13 (pbk): 978-1-4302-1932-3

ISBN-13 (electronic): 978-1-4302-1933-0

Printed and bound in the United States of America 9 8 7 6 5 4 3 2 1

Distributed to the book trade worldwide by Springer-Verlag New York, Inc., 233 Spring Street, 6th Floor, New York, NY 10013. Phone 1-800-SPRINGER, fax 201-348-4505, e-mail orders-ny@springer-sbm.com, or visit www.springeronline.com.

For information on translations, please contact Apress directly at 2855 Telegraph Avenue, Suite 600, Berkeley, CA 94705. Phone 510-549-5930, fax 510-549-5939, e-mail info@apress.com, or visit www.apress.com.

Apress and friends of ED books may be purchased in bulk for academic, corporate, or promotional use. eBook versions and licenses are also available for most titles. For more information, reference our Special Bulk Sales–eBook Licensing web page at http://www.apress.com/info/bulksales.

The source code for this book is freely available to readers at www.friendsofed.com in the Downloads section.

Credits

Lead Editors	**Production Editor**
Clay Andres and Douglas Pundick	Elizabeth Berry
Technical Reviewer	**Compositor**
Paul Haine	Diana Van Winkle
Editorial Board	**Proofreader**
Clay Andres, Steve Anglin, Mark Beckner,	Nancy Bell
Ewan Buckingham, Tony Campbell, Gary Cornell,	
Jonathan Gennick, Michelle Lowman,	**Indexer**
Matthew Moodie, Jeffrey Pepper,	Becky Hornyak
Frank Pohlmann, Ben Renow-Clarke,	
Dominic Shakeshaft,	**Artist**
Matt Wade, Tom Welsh	Diana Van Winkle
Project Manager	**Cover Image Designer**
Sofia Marchant	Bruce Tang
Copy Editor	**Interior and Cover Designer**
Liz Welch	Kurt Krames
Associate Production Director	**Manufacturing Director**
Kari Brooks-Copony	Tom Debolski

To Yingwen, Maxwell, Dylan, and the musicians
— Joseph R. Lewis

To Penn and Koll, for giving me glimpses of my own past;
and to all young people who don't yet know how to get from
where they are to where they want to be
— Meitar Moscovitz

CONTENTS AT A GLANCE

CONTENTS

PART THREE **CSS PATTERNS AND ADVANCED TECHNIQUES**

Chapter 7 **Semantic Patterns for Styling Common Design Components**

Chapter 8 **Using a Style Sheet Library**

ABOUT THE AUTHORS

Joseph R. Lewis is chief web architect at Sandia National Laboratories, and is a recognized expert in standards-based web development, information design, Semantic Web, and scientific collaboration. In an earlier life, Joe was a professional musician. A graduate of the New England Conservatory of Music in Boston, he has performed with orchestras and chamber ensembles in major concert halls and music festivals across North America and Europe.

Meitar Moscovitz is a freelancer specializing in front-end web development. He has worked as a technology professional in various roles for more than a decade at such companies as Apple and Opsware (now HP), and he has developed web sites for clients including Oxygen Media, Inc. and the Institute of Electrical and Electronics Engineers (IEEE). Meitar is also an outspoken blogger and sexual rights advocate who writes and speaks about the intersection of technology and sexuality.

A New York City native, Meitar spent a year in Sydney, Australia, and has recently returned to the United States to live in San Francisco. Meitar volunteers his technical talents to nonprofit organizations and other small groups, is an avid juggler, and has way too many profiles on social networking sites.

ABOUT THE TECHNICAL REVIEWER

Paul Haine is a client-side developer currently working in London for the Guardian newspaper. He is the author of *HTML Mastery: Semantics, Standards, and Styling* (friends of ED, 2006) and runs a personal web site at www.joeblade.com.

ABOUT THE COVER IMAGE DESIGNER

Bruce Tang is a freelance web designer, visual programmer, and author from Hong Kong. His main creative interest is generating stunning visual effects using Flash or Processing.

Bruce has been an avid Flash user since Flash 4, when he began using Flash to create games, web sites, and other multimedia content. After several years of ActionScripting, he found himself increasingly drawn to visual programming and computational art. He likes to integrate math and physics into his work, simulating 3D and other real-life experiences onscreen. His first Flash book was published in October 2005. Bruce's folio, featuring Flash and Processing pieces, can be found at www.betaruce.com, and his blog at www.betaruce.com/blog.

The cover image uses a high-resolution Henon phase diagram generated by Bruce with Processing, which he feels is an ideal tool for such experiments. Henon is a strange attractor created by iterating through some equations to calculate the coordinates of millions of points. The points are then plotted with an assigned color.

$$x_{n+1} = x_n \cos(a) - (y_n - x_n^p) \sin(a)$$

$$y_{n+1} = x_n \sin(a) + (y_n - x_n^p) \cos(a)$$

ACKNOWLEDGMENTS

My heartfelt thanks go out to my coauthor, Meitar Moscovitz, for his creativity, enthusiasm, and passion for the subject matter of this book. Thanks to the folks at friends of ED for helping produce this book and for putting up with our busy schedules and our picky behavior. Thanks to Molly Holzschlag for being an inspiration to us all—we owe you so much. There is no way to adequately thank my wife and children for putting up with the late nights and weekends, but I'll keep trying.

Joseph R. Lewis

It was my great pleasure to work with my coauthor, Joe Lewis, and I'd like to take this opportunity to first and foremost thank him for working so well with me on this book.

I'm also happy to say that this book was a combined effort on the parts of many individuals beyond Joe and myself. The efforts of the committed people who work at friends of ED and Apress publishers were exceptional, particularly our editorial staff: Clay Andres, for wholeheartedly believing our book proposal sound and for doing his best to help us in writing the highest-quality work we could despite the many challenges; Sofia Marchant, for her attention to detail; Liz Welch for her careful copyediting; Elizabeth Berry for her prompt production work; and Douglas Pundick for his thorough reviews. Thanks also and especially to Paul Haine, whose astute technical comments found their way into the manuscript at many points.

For personal reasons, it was a particular sort of challenge for me to write this book when I did. Therefore, I'd also like to acknowledge my many friends in New York City, Boston, and Providence, including Sarah Rauschelbach, Eugenia Van Bremen, Jessica Wray, Maria Halmo, Michael Gilbert, and—in particular—Sarah Cohen, Jennifer Salengar, and Zachary Bruner. I have no doubt that this book would not have been possible without their generous hospitality over the course of the many weeks I spent on their couches and in their guestrooms.

Finally, I'd also like to thank Emma Beth Gross for reminding me that I can safely be unhappy when I forget it, and my family for their unique and unending support.

Meitar Moscovitz

LAYOUT CONVENTIONS

To keep this book as clear and easy to follow as possible, the following text conventions are used throughout.

- Important words or concepts are normally highlighted on the first appearance in **bold type**.
- Code is presented in `fixed-width` font.
- New or changed code is normally presented in **`bold fixed-width font`**.
- Pseudo-code and variable input are written in *`italic fixed-width font`*.
- Menu commands are written in the form Menu ➤ Submenu ➤ Submenu.
- Where we want to draw your attention to something, we've highlighted it like this:

> *Ahem, don't say we didn't warn you.*

- Sometimes code won't fit on a single line in a book. Where this happens, we use an arrow like this: ➥.

```
This is a very, very long section of code that should be written all on ➥
the same line without a break.
```

Part 1

INTRODUCTION: DIGESTING THE WEB'S ALPHABET SOUP

Today's Web is quickly evolving from a collection of linked documents to a collection of things with relationships. Where we once only had the simplistic Hypertext Markup Language (HTML) to distribute web content, today we have a plethora of formats that include two different varieties of traditional web pages; HTML and XHTML; multiple syndication formats such as RSS and Atom; and many others. Even the content of web pages themselves—text, images, tables, charts and graphs, and movies—have multiple different de facto standard formats like Flash, SVG, and various other dialects of proprietary XML.

Modern browsers use JavaScript techniques such as Ajax to transform themselves into full-fledged application platforms. Thanks to the networked nature of web content, the browser-as-application-platform model is pushing the boundaries of technological innovation at an ever-increasing rate. Web developers have so many different technologies at their disposal that it's often difficult to discern the appropriate path you should take.

To get from today's web of linked documents to tomorrow's web of things with relationships, web developers need a way to describe these things flexibly, and they need a way to make each thing available in all the different ways it's going to be accessed. Now that's a tall order.

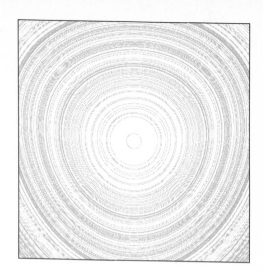

Chapter 1

MARKUP UNDERPINS CSS

They say that every journey begins with a single step. The journey we're on began in 1965 at Brown University, where the idea of *hypertext* was born.[1] Hypertext, or text in documents that enables nonlinear navigation (called *hypertextual navigation*), was eventually encoded as a markup language named the Hypertext Markup Language (HTML).

As the Web evolved, HTML was stretched and strained as it tried to be everything to everyone. Inside HTML documents there existed a mishmash of information, sometimes called "tag soup" by developers, which included display logic and code for user interaction. Somewhere in the middle of all of that metadata you could also find some content.

It didn't take very long for people to realize that this approach wasn't going to work in the future because it was fundamentally limiting. Rather than try to deliver one monolithic document to web browsers, it made a lot more sense to give browsers the building blocks of the content itself and then let the browser handle putting it all together. This principle is known as the *separation of concerns*.

---

1. More precisely, the idea of hypertext is generally credited to Vannevar Bush in 1945, when he wrote about an electronic desk he called the "Memex." For the most part, our personal computers are modern-day manifestations of this device. It was in 1965 that Ted Nelson first coined the term *hypertext* to describe this idea.

This simple idea is so fundamental to understanding how the Web works that it behooves us to take a closer look at the markup in documents upon which Cascading Style Sheets (CSS) acts. So let's first briefly examine the linguistics and semantics of markup languages.

The linguistics of markup languages

When you read the code of a markup language, you're reading a real language in much the same way as you are reading English when you read the words in this book.

As you know, when you view a web page you're asking your web browser to fetch a document. This document is just a text file that happens to be constructed in a special way. It's constructed according to the syntax and grammar of a particular markup language so that all the content it contains is represented in a structured format.

It turns out that this structure has some remarkable similarities to human languages. Put simply, when we construct sentences in human languages we often use a grammatical structure that begins with a subject, followed by a verb, and that then ends with an object. For instance, in the sentence, "The cow jumped over the moon," the *cow* is the subject, *jumped* is the verb, and *the moon* is the object.

Markup languages also have rules of grammar. There are *elements*, each a building block or component of the larger whole. An element can have certain properties that further specify its details. These properties are often *attributes*, but they can also be the element's own contents.[2] Finally, an element has a certain position within the document relative to all the other elements, giving it a *hierarchical context*.

In the following HTML code, we can see an example of these three concepts:

```
<blockquote cite="http://example.com/">
    <p>Welcome to example.com!</p>
</blockquote>
```

You can think of the `<blockquote>` element as our subject. It has an attribute, `cite`, which describes where the quoted paragraph came from, and you can think of it as our verb. The `<p>` element, which is the quote itself, can be considered our object. In English, this snippet of code might translate to something like, "This quote cites the page at http://example.com/."

There are already some noteworthy points to make about this simplistic example. For one thing, the document is all about *semantics*, or the code's *meaning*. (The important role that semantic markup plays on the Web is discussed in more detail in Chapter 7.) For another, *only* semantic information and actual content (in this case, text) are present in the example code. Nowhere do you see any information about the way this content is to be displayed to the user, or what options the user has for interacting with it.

---

2. Figuring out when to use which syntactical structures is a common question XML language developers have. In his article on the Principles of XML Design, Uche Ogbuji clearly articulates when and why to use one structure, such as elements, over another, such as attributes. The article can be found at http://www.ibm.com/developerworks/xml/library/x-eleatt.html.

This lack of presentational and behavioral information is an example of the *separation of concerns* principle at work. By delivering only the semantic content itself to the browser, you now have the flexibility to mix this *same* content with whatever other presentation or behavior you wish to give it. Lastly, of course, this example is written in XHTML, the markup language used to create traditional web pages.

HTML's semantics come from its history as a markup language originally intended to describe academic papers. It was derived from a subset of IBM's Standard Generalized Markup Language (SGML), which was used by large corporations and government organizations to encode complex industry papers.[3] This is why HTML has a relatively rich vocabulary for describing different kinds of textual structures often found in written resources, such as lists (<ul>, <ol>, and <dl>) and computer output (<code>, <samp>, <kbd>), but has such a dearth of other kinds of vocabularies.

Thankfully, a modern variation of generic SGML exists today that allows anyone, including individual developers like us, to create their own markup language with their own vocabulary. This technology is known as XML, and it is arguably the technology on top of which tomorrow's Web will be built.

XML dialects: the many different flavors of content

One of the Web's challenges is describing many different sorts of content. With HTML's limited semantics, describing all the different kinds of content available online is clumsy at best, impossible at worst. So, how is it done?

Early on, the World Wide Web Consortium (W3C), an organization that governs the publication of industry-wide web technology standards, realized that in order to thrive, the Web needed the capability to describe all kinds of content, both existing and yet to be created, in a way that could be easily interoperable. In other words, if Joe invented something new and made it available online, it would be ideal if he would do so in a way that Jane can access.

The solution the W3C developed is the Extensible Markup Language (XML). XML has two primary characteristics that make it exceptionally well suited for the Web. First, it's a generic document format that is designed to be both human and machine readable. This is accomplished by using a strict subset of the familiar syntax and grammar that HTML uses, so it's very easy for humans to learn and for machines to parse. Second, the marked-up documents double as a data serialization mechanism, allowing autonomous systems to easily exchange the data they contain among themselves.

What sets XML apart from the other standard document formats is that, much like SGML, it's not really any specific language at all, but rather a metalanguage. If someone or some system were to tell us that they "can speak XML," our first question would be, "What XML dialect do you speak?" This is because every XML document is some distinct kind of XML, which may or may not be a widely known standard, with its own vocabulary (set of valid elements) and semantics (things those elements mean).

As more disparate content emerged on the Web, various XML-based markup languages were developed to describe that content. The most famous of these is undoubtedly the Extensible Hypertext Markup Language (XHTML), which is simply an *application* (XML jargon for "specific instance") of XML that copies all the semantics from the SGML-derived version of plain-old HTML and defines them

---

3. Perhaps the most famous document marked up in SGML is the Oxford English Dictionary, which remains encoded in SGML to this day.

using XML's syntax. There isn't any meaningful distinction between HTML and XHTML beyond those restrictions imposed by the stricter XML syntax.

One of the other fundamental advantages of XML is its support for *namespaces*. An *XML namespace* is simply a formalization of this "multiple dialects" idea. Specifically, a namespace, defined using the xmlns attribute on the root element of an XML document, identifies each XML dialect with a unique string, thus enabling any XML-based markup language to mix and match the semantics of multiple XML applications inside a single document. This is important because it provides a means for application developers (including, theoretically, browser manufacturers) to design markup languages in a modular fashion, according to the principles and ideals of the age-old "software tools" approach that early UNIX systems took. Conceptually, this is not unlike a computerized version of the notion of multi-lingual humans.

Each application of XML can itself be described with another form of XML document called a Document Type Definition (DTD). DTD files are like dictionaries for markup languages; they define what elements are valid, what properties those elements have, and rules for where those elements can appear in the document. These documents are written by XML application developers, and most of their utility for typical web developers is simply as the authoritative (if sometimes cryptic) reference for the particular syntax of an XML application. Each XML document begins with a couple of lines of code that define the version of XML it uses, called an *XML prologue*, and what DTD the file uses, called a *document type (or DOCTYPE) declaration*.

Although CSS can be used in conjunction with a number of these user-facing technologies, the rest of this book focuses on a few specific XML applications that are in widespread use today. Let's now take a whirlwind tour of some of the ones we'll be styling with CSS in the remainder of this book.

RSS and Atom: content syndication formats

Possibly the most common XML-derived document format on the Web today that *isn't* a traditional XHTML web page are those formats used for syndicating content as "web feeds" or "news feeds." The two (reasonably equivalent) standards for this technology are RSS and Atom. These standards specify an XML-based format for documents that summarize the content and freshness of *other* resources, such as news articles, podcasts, or blog posts, on the Web.

Although there are several different versions of RSS, since they all have the same aim we will feature the use of RSS 2.0 throughout this book. Atom is really a term that refers to both an XML document format, called the Atom Syndication Format, and a lightweight HTTP protocol. When we use the term *Atom* in this book, we mean the Atom Syndication Format unless mentioned otherwise.

Since both RSS and Atom were designed for describing other content, their vocabularies consist almost entirely of element sets that describe document metadata. For example, each format has an element for encoding the URI (web address) of a given resource. In RSS this is the <link> element, and in Atom it is the <guid> element. Likewise, both formats have an element to encode the title, description, and other information about resources.

Both RSS and Atom feeds can appear as unstyled source code in browsers, though some browsers feature native feed reading capabilities. When these features are made active, these browsers apply some baked-in styles to the feed you load. For example, Figure 1-1 shows what Firefox makes of an RSS feed when viewed over HTTP. In contrast, Figure 1-2 shows the same feed in the same browser when accessed through the local filesystem.

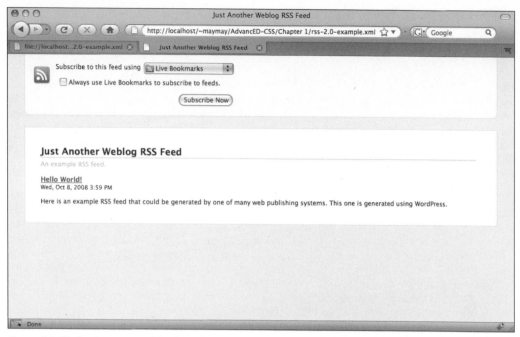

Figure 1-1. Firefox 3 uses a combination of XSLT and CSS to give web feeds some style.

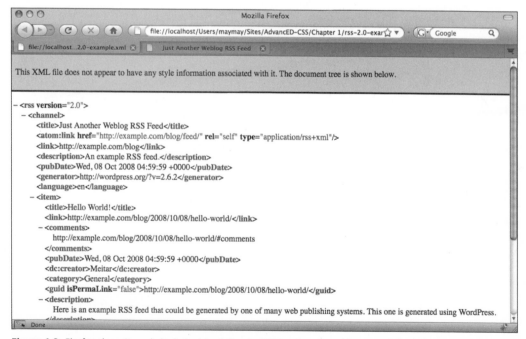

Figure 1-2. Firefox doesn't apply its baked-in styling to RSS feeds accessed by way of the `file:` scheme.

As you can see, the two screenshots look almost nothing alike. In Figure 1-1, Firefox displays the feed data using a friendly user interface, whereas in Figure 1-2 the (mostly) raw source code is shown. What's most interesting for our purposes in Figure 1-2 is Firefox's admission that, "This XML file does not appear to have any style information associated with it."

The style information Firefox is referring to is any `<?xml-stylesheet ... ?>` XML prologue. Like the XHTML `<link>` element, an `xml-stylesheet` can be given a type attribute whose value can be `text/css`. When this is so, Firefox will use the style information provided in the CSS file to change the presentation of the feed. Although the specific linking mechanism differs, adding a style sheet to a non-XHTML XML document is conceptually no different than doing so to a regular web page. Using the `xml-stylesheet` prologue to add style sheets to XML documents like this is covered in more detail in Chapter 9.

> *Intrepid explorers may have noticed that Firefox's style sheet used to style the feed in Figure 1-1 has selectors that target HTML and not RSS elements. Indeed, if you use Firebug[4] to inspect the source of most RSS feeds on the Internet in Firefox 3, you'll see HTML and no RSS in sight. How can this be? Where did the HTML come from?*
>
> *It turns out that in XML parlance a "style sheet" can actually mean two things. It can mean a CSS file in the way we already know and love, but it can also mean an Extensible Stylesheet Language Transformations (XSLT) file. These files are yet another form of XML document that, given an original XML-formatted file, are used to convert the markup from one kind of XML to another. Firefox uses an XSLT file to turn RSS and Atom feeds into an XHTML file on-the-fly, so the CSS file used to style this feed is linked to the result of the XSLT transformation (which is XHTML) instead of to the original feed.*
>
> *XSLT is beyond the scope of this book, but we heartily recommend that you take a closer look at it if you suspect you'll be doing any significant amount of XML document processing.*

SVG: vector-based graphics in XML

Vector graphics and 2D animation on the Web was popularized by Flash, a compiled binary format acquired by Macromedia (which since has merged with Adobe) and marketed under the name "ShockWave Flash." However, since 2001 (well before Flash made it big), there has been an XML-based open standard for defining these kinds of graphics. This standard is known as Scalable Vector Graphics (SVG).

SVG's history is an interesting one. Invented by Sun Microsystems and Adobe (which, ironically, now owns Macromedia), SVG was (and still is) used extensively in the Adobe Illustrator graphics editing application as a format to easily export and import vector graphics. In fact, the easiest way to make an SVG document these days is to simply draw something in Adobe Illustrator and choose to save it in SVG format from the Save As menu option.

---

4. Firebug is an excellent add-on for the Firefox web browser that gives users the ability to inspect and change the document loaded by the browser. We think it is a must-have tool for any serious web developer.

Unfortunately for Adobe, Microsoft created a competing markup language for vector graphics called the Vector Markup Language (VML) and implemented it in its Internet Explorer web browser. During the years of the browser wars due to rise of Flash and no cross-browser implementation of a vector graphics markup language, SVG fell by the wayside. SVG remained an unknown and untouched standard for a very long time.

Recently, however, thanks to renewed interest in web standards, there has been resurgence in native SVG implementations among browsers. Mainstream browsers, including Firefox, Safari, and Opera, all natively support a subset of the SVG specification to varying degrees today. In some cases, Adobe's own SVG plug-in adds even more support. Moreover, with the help of scripting and the hard work of JavaScript library developers,[5] it's now possible to reliably use vector graphics in a cross-browser fashion.

Thanks to its extremely visual nature, SVG provides an ideal environment for examining CSS more closely. Like all forms of XML, SVG documents begin with an XML prologue, followed by a DTD, followed by a root element containing the entirety of the document's content. This is the same pattern used by XHTML documents,[6] so it should be quite familiar. The only distinction is that in the case of SVG the root element is <svg> instead of <html>.

Therefore, an SVG document shell might look like the following code snippet:

```
<?xml version="1.0"?>
<!DOCTYPE svg PUBLIC "-//W3C//DTD SVG 1.1//EN"
    "http://www.w3.org/Graphics/SVG/1.1/DTD/svg11.dtd">
<svg xmlns="http://www.w3.org/2000/svg" version="1.1">
    <!-- Here is where the SVG elements will go. -->
</svg>
```

Since SVG was designed to describe visual objects as opposed to textual objects, the vocabulary available to SVG developers differs quite radically from the one that is available in XHTML. For example, in SVG, there are no <p> or <div> elements. Instead, to create text on the screen you use the <text> element, and to group elements together, the <g> element.

Here's an extremely basic example of what an SVG image that contains the text "Hello world!" in red lettering would look like. All that is needed is to insert our <text> element into the document markup with the appropriate attributes, like this:

```
<?xml version="1.0"?>
<!DOCTYPE svg PUBLIC "-//W3C//DTD SVG 1.1//EN"
    "http://www.w3.org/Graphics/SVG/1.1/DTD/svg11.dtd">
<svg xmlns="http://www.w3.org/2000/svg" version="1.1">
    <text x="50" y="50" style="fill: red">Hello world!</text>
</svg>
```

---

5. One such noteworthy developer is Dmitry Baranovskiy, whose hard work on the Raphaël JavaScript library enables an SVG file to be translated to Microsoft's VML on the fly, so that SVG-based imagery works in both standards-compliant browsers and Internet Explorer.

6. In practice, most documents that use an XHTML DTD don't include an XML prologue. This is because including the prologue erroneously switches Internet Explorer into quirksmode (a standards-noncompliant mode). Further, despite the presence of an XML prologue, all browsers will still treat XHTML files as though they were plain-old HTML unless the web server that delivered it does so along with the appropriate HTTP Content-Type header of application/xhtml+xml instead of the default text/html. See http://hixie.ch/advocacy/xhtml.

This results in the image shown in Figure 1-3. The x and y attributes of the <text> element define the initial position of the text in the image. The style attribute uses CSS to make the element contents red.

Figure 1-3. A simple and minimally styled SVG "Hello world!" example

> Yes, you in the back with your hand raised. "Element attributes that define visual positioning? I thought that's what CSS is for," I hear you asking. Yes, that is what CSS is for, but remember that SVG is a language to describe graphics. It could therefore be argued that the positioning of the text is its metadata, and thus it makes sense to use the markup language's own semantics to define this. Moreover, as you'll see in the next chapter, CSS isn't merely or necessarily a visual styling language anyway. In fact, the style attribute that defines the fill property in this example could be entirely replaced by using the fill attribute as well.

So far, this is pretty straightforward. The interesting takeaway is in the way that CSS was used to color the text red. Instead of using the color property, we use the fill property. This is because SVG is graphical, and so our semantics have changed radically from those used to develop in XHTML.

Here is another illustrative example. To make the text seem as though it is a sort of pill-shaped button, you might use the following code:

```
<?xml version="1.0"?>
<!DOCTYPE svg PUBLIC "-//W3C//DTD SVG 1.1//EN"
    "http://www.w3.org/Graphics/SVG/1.1/DTD/svg11.dtd">
<svg xmlns="http://www.w3.org/2000/svg" version="1.1">
    <rect width="150" height="50" x="20" y="20" rx="15" ry="25"
        style="fill: teal; stroke: #000; stroke-width: 3;" />
    <text x="50" y="50" style="fill: red">Hello world!</text>
</svg>
```

The effect of this code is shown in Figure 1-4.

Figure 1-4. A rectangular shape, defined with the <rect> element, is all that's needed to create a background.

However, even with these visual semantics, structure is still important. If this were an actual button on a real interactive SVG chart, then both the text and the background could conceptually be treated as one logical object. It's for this reason that SVG defines the <g> element for specifying groups of elements to be treated as a single object.

Like XHTML, all elements can have class and id attributes to identify them, so we can use such an attribute to identify our example button. The grouped example looks no different on the screen, but now looks like this in code:

```
<?xml version="1.0"?>
<!DOCTYPE svg PUBLIC "-//W3C//DTD SVG 1.1//EN"
    "http://www.w3.org/Graphics/SVG/1.1/DTD/svg11.dtd">
<svg xmlns="http://www.w3.org/2000/svg" version="1.1">
    <g id="example">
        <rect width="150" height="50" x="20" y="20" rx="15" ry="25"
            style="fill: teal; stroke: #000; stroke-width: 3;" />
        <text x="50" y="50" style="fill: red">Hello world!</text>
    </g>
</svg>
```

As you can see, there are myriad formats of XML in common use today. Each XML application defines semantics that relate to its purpose. By using XML namespaces, developers can import the semantics of a XML application and use them within their own documents, creating endless possibilities for describing content in incredibly rich ways.

All these possibilities will remain mere potential, however, if we can't get these structured, semantic documents into the hands of users. To do that, we need to understand how the software tools users use to access our content work. These tools are called user agents, and for better or worse, they are the gatekeepers between our users and our content.

User agents: our eyes and ears in cyberspace

A user agent is nothing more than some entity that acts on behalf of users themselves.[7] What this means is that it's important to understand these users as well as their user agents. User agents are the tools we use to interact with the wealth of possibilities that exists on the Internet. They are like extensions of ourselves. Indeed, they are (increasingly literally) our eyes and ears in cyberspace.

Understanding users and their agents

Web developers are already familiar with many common user agents: web browsers! We're even notorious for sometimes bemoaning the sheer number of them that already exist. Maybe we need to reexamine why we do that.

There are many different kinds of users out there, each with potentially radically different needs. Therefore, to understand why there are so many user agents in existence we need to understand what the needs of all these different users are. This isn't merely a theoretical exercise, either. The fact is that figuring out a user's needs helps us to present our content to that user in the best possible way.

Presenting content to users and, by extension, their user agents appropriately goes beyond the typical accessibility argument that asserts the importance of making your content available to everyone (though we'll certainly be making that argument, too). The principles behind understanding a user's needs are much more important than that.

You'll recall that the Web poses two fundamental challenges. One challenge is that any given piece of content, a single document, needs to be presented in multiple ways. This is the problem that CSS was designed to solve. The other challenge is the inverse: many different kinds of content need to be made available, each kind requiring a similar presentation. This is what XML (and its own accompanying "style sheet" language, XSLT) was designed to solve. Therefore, combining the powerful capabilities of CSS and XML is the path we should take to understanding, technically, how to solve this problem and present content to users and their user agents.

Since a specific user agent is just a tool for a specific user, the form the user agent takes depends on what the needs of the user are. In formal use case semantics, these users are called actors, and we can describe their needs by determining the steps they must take to accomplish some goal. Similarly, in each use case, a certain tool or tools used to accomplish these goals defines what the user agent is in that particular scenario[8].

A simple example of this is that when Joe goes online to read the latest technology news from Slashdot, he uses a web browser to do this. Joe (our actor) is the user, his web browser (whichever one he chooses to use) is the user agent, and reading the latest technology news is the goal. That's a very traditional interaction, and in such a scenario we can make some pretty safe assumptions about how Joe, being a human and all, reads news.

---

7. This is purposefully a broad definition because we're not just talking about web pages here, but rather all kinds of technology. The principles are universal. There are, however, more exacting definitions available. For instance, the W3C begins the HTML 4 specification with some formal definitions, including what a "user agent" is. See http://www.w3.org/TR/REC-html40/conform.html.
8. In real use cases, technical jargon and specific tools like a web browser are omitted because such use cases are used to define a system's requirements, not its implementation. Nevertheless, the notion of an actor and an actor's goals are helpful in understanding the mysterious "user" and this user's software.

Now let's envision a more outlandish scenario to challenge our understanding of the principle. Joe needs to go shopping to refill his refrigerator and he prefers to buy the items he needs with the least amount of required driving due to rising gas prices. This is why he owns the (fictional) Frigerator2000, a network-capable refrigerator that keeps tabs on the inventory levels of nearby grocery stores and supermarkets and helps Joe plan his route. This helps him avoid driving to a store where he won't be able to purchase the items he needs.

If this sounds too much like science fiction to you, think again. This is a different application of the same principle used by feed readers, only instead of aggregating news articles from web sites we're aggregating inventory levels from grocery stores. All that would be required to make this a reality is an XML format for describing a store's inventory levels, a bit of embedded software, a network interface card on a refrigerator, and some tech-savvy grocery stores to publish such content on the Internet.

In this scenario, however, our user agent is radically different from the traditional web browser. It's a refrigerator! Of course, there aren't (yet) any such user agents out crawling the Web today, but there are a lot of user agents that aren't web browsers doing exactly that.

Search engines like Google, Yahoo!, and Ask.com are probably the most famous examples of users that aren't people. These companies all have automated programs, called spiders, which "crawl" the Web indexing all the content they can find. Unlike humans and very much like our hypothetical refrigerator-based user agent, these spiders can't look at content with their eyes or listen to audio with their ears, so their needs are very different from someone like Joe's.

There are still other systems of various sorts that exist to let us interact with web sites and these, too, can be considered user agents. For example, many web sites provide an API that exposes some functionality as web services. Microsoft Word 2008 is an example of a desktop application that you can use to create blog posts in blogging software such as WordPress and MovableType because both of these blogging tools support the MetaWeblog API, an XML-RPC[9] specification. In this case, Microsoft Word can be considered a user agent.

As mentioned earlier, the many incarnations of news readers that exist are another form of user agent. Many web browsers and email applications, such as Mozilla Thunderbird and Apple Mail, do this, too.[10] Feed readers provide a particularly interesting way to examine the concept of user agents because there are many popular feed reading web sites today, such as Bloglines.com and Google Reader. If Joe opens his web browser and logs into his account at Bloglines, then Joe's web browser is the user agent and Joe is the user. However, when Joe reads the news feeds he's subscribed to in Bloglines, the Bloglines server goes to fetch the RSS- or Atom-formatted feed from the sourced site. What this means is that from the point of view of the sourced site, Bloglines.com is the user, and the Bloglines server process is the user agent.

Coming to this realization means that, as developers, we can understand user agents as an abstraction for a particular actor's goals as well as their capabilities. This is, of course, an intentionally vague definition because it's technically impossible for you, as the developer, to predict the features or capabilities present in any particular user agent. This is a challenge we'll be talking about a lot in the remainder of this book because it is one of the defining characteristics of the Web as a publishing medium.

---

9. XML-RPC is a term referring to the use of XML files describing method calls and data transmitted over HTTP, typically used by automated systems. It is thus a great example of a technology that takes advantage of XML's data serialization capabilities, and is often thought of as a precursor to today's Ajax techniques.
10. It was in fact the much older email technology from which the term *user agent* originated; an email client program is more technically called a mail user agent (MUA).

Rather than this lack of clairvoyance being a problem, however, the constraint of not knowing who or what will be accessing our published content is actually a good thing. It turns out that well-designed markup is also markup that is blissfully ignorant of its user, because it is solely focused on describing itself. You might even call it narcissistic.

Why giving the user control is not giving up

Talking about self-describing markup is just another way of talking about semantic markup. In this paradigm, the content in the fetched document is strictly segregated from its ultimate presentation. Nevertheless, the content must eventually be presented to the user somehow. If information for how to do this isn't provided by the markup, then where is it, and who decides what it is?

At first you'll no doubt be tempted to say that this information is in the document's style sheet and that it is the document's developer who decides what that is. As you'll examine in detail in the next chapter, this answer is only mostly correct. In every case, it is ultimately the user agent that determines what styles (in which style sheets) get applied to the markup it fetches. Furthermore, many user agents (especially modern web browsers) allow the users themselves to further modify the style rules that get applied to content. In the end, you can only influence—not control—the final presentation.

Though surprising to some, this model actually makes perfect sense. Allowing the users ultimate control of the content's presentation helps to ensure that you meet every possible need of each user. By using CSS, content authors, publishers, and developers—that is, you—can provide author style sheets that easily accommodate, say, 80 percent of the needs of 90 percent of the users. Even in the most optimistic scenario, edge cases that you may not ever be aware of will still escape you no matter how hard you try to accommodate everyone's every need.[11] Moreover, even if you had those kinds of unlimited resources, you may not know how best to improve the situation for that user. Given this, who better to determine the presentation of a given XML document that needs to be presented in some very specific way than the users with that very specific need themselves?

A common real-life example of this situation might occur if Joe were colorblind. If he were and he wanted to visit some news site where the links in the article pullouts were too similar a color to the pullout's background, he might not realize that those elements are actually links. Thankfully, because Joe's browser allows him to set up a web site with his own user style sheet, he can change the color of these links to something that he can see more easily. If CSS were not designed with this in mind, it would be impossible for Joe to personalize the presentation of this news site so that it would be optimal for him.

To many designers coming from traditional industries such as print design, the fact that users can change the presentation of their content is an alarming concept. Nevertheless, this isn't just the way the Web was made to work; this is the only way it could have worked. Philosophically, the Web is a technology that puts control into the hands of users. Therefore, our charge as web designers is to judge different people's needs to be of equal importance, and we can't do this if we treat every user exactly the same way.[12]

---

11. As it happens, this is the same argument open source software proponents make about why such open source software often succeeds in meeting the needs of more users than closed source, proprietary systems controlled solely by a single company with (by definition) relatively limited resources.
12. This philosophy is embodied in the formal study of ethics, which is a compelling topic for us as CSS developers, considering the vastness of the implications we describe here.

Abstracting content's presentation with CSS

Up to this point, we've talked a lot about content, markup, and user agents. So how does CSS fit in? CSS is the *presentation layer* for your content.

CSS leverages existing markup to create a presentation. It can also reuse the same elements to present content in specialized ways depending on the type of user agent consuming it. CSS is not limited to presenting content visually. Separating the presentation of content from the content itself opens many doors. One of these is being able to restyle the same content later. Another is to simultaneously create different presentations of the same content.

This is important because different user agents will interpret your CSS to render your content in whatever way is appropriate for them. Since content may be conveyed by user agents to people or other machines in a variety of ways, CSS abstracts the specific mechanisms, or "media," by which this occurs. This is how one piece of content, with the same underlying markup, can be rendered on media, including the screen connected to your computer, the printer on your desk, your cell phone, a text-to-speech screen reader, or in some other way.

CSS defines this abstraction based on the media being used, and provides a way to detect this. The way to do so is with the CSS media type construct, so let's start there. After that, we'll briefly describe an extension to this construct called CSS media queries.

The nature of output: grouping output with CSS media types

How a user agent renders content depends on the target media the content is destined for. CSS's purpose has always been to provide a way to describe the presentation of some content in a standard way. Despite its goal of remaining implementation agnostic, however, CSS still needs to have some notion of what the physical properties of the presentation medium are going to be.

To implement this, the CSS2.1 specification identifies ten characteristics of different interaction paradigms that together form four **media groups**. These characteristics are things like whether a document's content must be broken up into discrete chunks (such as printed pages) or whether it can be presented all at once, with no theoretical limit (such as inside a web browser's viewport with scroll bars). These two opposite characteristics are one of the media groups.

Each of the **media types** simply defines specific characteristics for each of the four media groups. Various CSS properties are therefore coupled to a particular media type since not all properties can be applied to all media types. For example, monochrome displays don't always make full use of the color property (although many try anyway). Similarly, purely visual user agents can't make use of the volume property, which is intended for aural presentation and is thus bound to the media types that incorporate audio capabilities.

The nine media types defined by CSS2.1 are braille, embossed, handheld, print, projection, screen, speech, tty, and tv. Table 1-1, taken from the CSS2.1 specification, shows the relationships between media groups and media types.

Table 1-1. Relationships between Media Groups and Media Types

Media Type	Continuous/ Paged	Visual/Audio/ Speech/Tactile	Grid/ Bitmap	Interactive/ Static
braille	Continuous	Tactile	Grid	Both
embossed	Paged	Tactile	Grid	Static
handheld	Both	Visual, audio, speech	Both	Both
print	Paged	Visual	Bitmap	Static
projection	Paged	Visual	Bitmap	Interactive
screen	Continuous	Visual, audio	Bitmap	Both
speech	Continuous	Speech	N/A	Both
tty	Continuous	Visual	Grid	Both
tv	Both	Visual, audio	Bitmap	Both

In addition to the continuous/paged interaction paradigm, we have

- A visual/audio/speech/tactile paradigm that broadly specifies which human senses are used to consume content
- A grid/bitmap paradigm that specifies two broad categories of display technology
- An interactive/static paradigm that defines whether or not the output media is capable of dynamically updating

It's up to individual user agents to implement support for the capabilities assumed to be present by a particular media group. Further, it's up to individual implementations to recognize a particular media type and apply its styles.

Briefly, the intent of each of the media types is as follows:

- screen is intended for your garden-variety computer screen, but certain newer web browsers found in mobile devices such as the Apple iPhone use this media type as well. Most of the time, it's this media type people are referring to when they talk about web design.
- print is intended for printers, or for print-to-file (that is, PDF, PostScript) output, and also shows up in the print preview dialogs of most browsers. We discuss the print media type in much greater detail in Chapter 4.
- handheld is intended for cell phones, PDAs, smartphones, and other devices that would normally fit in your hand or pocket. These devices generally share a set of characteristics, such as limited CPU and memory resources, constrained bandwidth, and reduced screen size, that make targeting them with their own media type handy. Notable exceptions come in the form of mobile versions of WebKit and more recent versions of Opera, which have elected to use the screen media type instead.
- aural is intended for style sheets that describe text-to-speech output, and is most often implemented by assistive technology such as screen reading software. In the current working draft of the CSS3 specifications, this media type is being deprecated in favor of a new media type called speech.

- braille is intended for Braille readers, currently the only form of tactile-feedback device CSS has been developed for use with.

- embossed is similar to braille as it's intended for *paged* (as opposed to *continuous*) Braille printers. This media type could theoretically be used to target Braille printers, although we know of no user agents that implement this capability.

- projection is intended for overhead projection systems, usually considered for things like presentations with slides. Like mobile devices, projection displays share a set of characteristics that make them unique, such as a lower screen resolution and limited color depth. If styles applying to this media type are specified, Opera switches from screen styles to projection styles when entering its full-screen or kiosk mode.

- tv is intended for television displays. We have yet to see this actually implemented in a user agent, although like handheld and projection, television hardware is another kind of device with unique display properties and it would be extremely useful if devices such as gaming consoles or smart TVs would adopt this.

- tty is intended for displays that use a fixed-pitch character grid, such as terminals and teletypes. Like embossed, we know of no user agents that support this media type, and its use is growing increasingly anachronistic.

- all is the default media type used when a media type is not specified, and any styles applied for this media type also apply for every other media type.

Media types are specified using the media attribute on a <link> or <style> element, or they may be applied using @media CSS rules within style sheets themselves. Here's an example using the <link> element to target a style sheet to all media types:

```
<link rel="stylesheet" href="default.css" type="text/css" media="all">
```

Here's one targeting an embedded style sheet to the handheld media type:

```
<style type="text/css" media="handheld">
    div.foo { color: red; }
</style>
```

Using @media screen applies styles to many traditional visual displays:

```
<style type="text/css">
    @media screen {
        div.foo { color: red; }
    }
</style>
```

The @import CSS rule also takes an optional media type parameter to import a style sheet for specific target media, print in this case:

```
<style type="text/css">
    @import url(print.css) print;
</style>
```

Considerations for targeting media types

When composing style sheets, most CSS developers still tend to think in terms of a few user agents used within one medium: web browsers on a traditional computer desktop. However, as we've just seen, CSS can be used in a much wider arena than is implied by this limited scope. Why limit yourself at the outset of a project? With a little planning and attention, you can make a far more usable, far-reaching, and successful web presence by considering possibilities for all media types from the very start.

> With the increasing influx of user agents in the market, it makes more sense to discuss the rendering engines user agents use rather than discuss the end-user products specifically, since each engine's ability to render markup and CSS are similar between the products that use it. The four mainstream rendering engines in the wild today are
>
> - **Trident**, which is used in all versions of Internet Explorer
> - **Gecko**, used in products based on Mozilla's code base (such as Firefox, Flock, Camino, and other derivatives)
> - **WebKit**, which was originally developed as KHTML for the Konquerer web browser on Linux and is now used in Safari and many Nokia smartphones, among other products
> - **Presto**, developed and used by the Opera family of products
>
> Therefore, in the remainder of this book, when we discuss a particular rendering engine you can safely assume we're talking about most of the user agents that use it. Conversely, when we discuss a particular user agent you can safely assume that the rendering behavior of the other browsers that use its rendering engine will be similar.

Targeting screens

The screen, handheld, and projection media types are somewhat similar in that they are intended to be presented visually using display technologies that emit light. The handheld media type is typically a smaller form factor of the screen version of a design, while the projection media type is usually—but not necessarily—intended for slideshow-style formatting. Though similar, there are still distinct differences among these media types, and examining them closely illustrates how the different media groups that a media type refers to influence design decisions and possibilities.

The screen media type

One characteristic of the screen media type is that it is *continuous*, meaning that the content will flow in an ongoing manner past the bottom of a given viewport. As a result of this behavior, it's the width of a layout that becomes the primary concern, and decisions as to how the site will be laid out in scenarios with different widths must be made. In contrast, you don't have to pay as much attention to the layout's height, since the page can be as long as is required for the contents to fit vertically within it.

The widths of screens can vary greatly from one user to the next. Moreover, a web browser's window can typically be resized to whatever width the user wishes, so it's best for your design to be as flexible as possible with regard to the resolutions and browser widths that it can accommodate. One way to accomplish this is with a variable-width, or "liquid," layout that expands and contracts to fill whatever space is made available. However, even if your design can be made flexible like this, it's often necessary for some elements (such as images) to maintain fixed-width dimensions, so certain judgments must eventually be finalized.

As display resolutions evolve, different widths have been used as the basis for layout grids. Recently, there's been a tendency toward using base widths of 960 pixels, which works well considering that most monitors out there today have display resolutions that are 1024 pixels wide and greater. This width not only accommodates browser chrome such as scroll bars but also is divisible by 3, 4, 5, 6, 8, 10, 12, 15, and 16, allowing for a number of possibilities for implementing various narrower grid-based layouts if needed.[13]

The projection media type

The projection media type is interesting in comparison to the screen media type because despite being intended for similar display technologies, it is considered *paged* as opposed to *continuous*. In other words, rather than having content continue to scroll endlessly past the bottom of the viewport, you can specify that content be chopped up into discrete chunks that are each, ostensibly, as tall as the projector's resolution allows them to be. Then, to navigate through the document contents, you page forward and backward between each chunk separately.

Of all the screen-related media types, projection is the least supported and least used. Opera is the one browser that has some support for this media type with a feature called Opera Show. When invoked by pressing Alt+F11, or by choosing View ➤ Full Screen from the menu, Opera Show will expand the browser's viewport to the full width of the display it's running in. This is more than just a "full screen" viewing mode, however, since with a simple CSS rule you can transform the continuous blocks of your existing document into paged items, resulting in presentation-style slides similar to what you'd see when using Microsoft PowerPoint or Apple Keynote:

```
.slide {
    page-break-after: always;
}
```

With this CSS rule applied, every block element with the .slide class will be rendered as a discrete chunk (a "slide") when viewed in Opera Show mode. Use your Page Down key to move forward in the resulting slide deck, and use Page Up to move back a slide. This creates the opportunity to give you an open, nonproprietary presentation tool that is easily portable and won't lock up your data—a nice feature we wish more browsers supported![14]

---

13. Cameron Moll made the case for 960 pixels in a blog post titled "Optimal width for 1024px resolution?" published at http://www.cameronmoll.com/archives/001220.html. Both the post itself and its comments are an interesting read for anyone wondering how the community standardizes these seemingly arbitrary numbers.
14. Thankfully, Eric Meyer has created the Simple Standards-Based Slide Show System (S5), which reproduces and even expands on the features of Opera Show for the rest of the standards-conscious browsers out there. S5 makes a great foundation for building platform-independent presentations using the XHTML and CSS that you already know. It can be found at http://meyerweb.com/eric/tools/s5/.

There are other possibilities in addition to presentation slides, too. Anything that works better on screen when presented in separate parts that you incrementally expose as opposed to all at once that you scroll through could make use of the projection media type. For instance, small form factor displays such as ebook readers could simulate the experience of "turning pages" with this media type while still taking advantage of *interactive* content and styling, which would not be possible if they used the print media type, which is considered *static*.

The handheld media type

In many ways the handheld media type is the most amorphous of the screen-related media types. It can be either continuous or paged; supports visual, audio, and speech interactions; can be based on either grid or bitmap display technology; and can present either static or interactive content. In reality, the handheld media type is mostly used to design for the small screens that are found on mobile devices, so its typical application to date has been to linearize and simplify a design's screen styles.

The handheld media type is also at the center of some heated arguments regarding media types in general, since Safari on the Apple iPhone and the latest versions of Opera Mobile have begun to ignore it in favor of the screen media type. Among other criticisms, Apple and Opera Software claim that most handheld style sheets don't provide an adequate user experience for the capabilities of their devices when compared to screen style sheets, and so they have introduced media queries as an extension to media types, discussed later in this chapter. Nevertheless, using the handheld media type is still prevalent and useful on many other cell phones and PDAs.

In previous years, designing for mobile devices was considered a nice-to-have, an optional add-on if time and expense permitted. This is no longer the case. Since mobile web use has begun to increase rapidly in recent years, we devote an entire chapter of this book to CSS development in a mobile context (see Chapter 5).

> *In his book* Mobile as 7th of the Mass Media *(2008, futuretext Ltd.), Tomi T. Ahonen makes the case that mobile media is nothing to be ignored: 31 percent of consumer spending in the music industry is spent on mobile purchases, while in the gaming industry the number is 20 percent. It has been deduced that—as of this writing—approximately one and a half billion Internet connections being generated from cell phones and 63 percent of the global population have a potentially Internet-capable cell phone. Over 60 countries around the world have cell phone penetration exceeding 100 percent of the population—which means many people own not one but two mobile devices. And finally, Nielsen in May 2008 reported that leading Internet sites increased their usage by 13 percent over desktop-based traffic alone, and in certain cases, such as for weather and entertainment, up to 20 percent. These are significant trend indicators for mobile web growth, which will undoubtedly continue to increase in the coming years.*

The print media type

The print media type is another familiar category of CSS work for most developers. This media type is implemented by user agents that are capable of physically printing to paper or of outputting electronic equivalents in formats such as PDF or PostScript.

Printing documents presents a set of significantly different issues from the screen output we are most commonly used to, since the paradigm of designing within a dynamic viewport is replaced by the notion of a static page box representing the physical printable area of the paper. Due to the static nature of printed media, designers lose many dynamic capabilities of CSS, such as the :hover pseudo-class, and need to consider alternative ways of displaying information to readers.

The reasons for printing web pages are usually readability (printing a long document to ease eyestrain), portability (taking print copies to read during a commute), or utility (such as when printing online forms that require physical signatures). Users rarely need portions of pages such as navigation since you obviously can't click a hyperlink on paper, so these should be excised. Additionally, supplemental information such as that commonly found in sidebars should also be removed. Much of these transformation concerns can be solved with CSS declarations like display: none and setting the main content's width to better fill the available space on the paper.

All the major modern web browsers support the print media type, so it's not only useful but also easy to implement and test. We discuss print media in detail in Chapter 4.

Aural media

When you read the text on a web site, do you hear a masculine voice or a feminine voice in your mind? Unbeknownst to many designers, the voice with which content is read aloud by text-to-speech-capable user agents, specified by the voice-family property, is one of the many aural properties that CSS offers you.

In fact, CSS offers a relatively rich set of auditory properties for a designer to use, including spatial audio properties to specify the direction where sound is coming from using the azimuth and elevation properties, aural emphasis with the stress and pitch properties, and even the reading speed using the speech-rate property. Moreover, different elements can be given audio cues using the cue-before or cue-after properties so that particular chimes or other sounds can precede links, licensing information, or an image's alternative text. This is an audio equivalent of the way certain icons depict an element's meaning in visual presentations.

The most common aural user agents are screen readers, but these are merely one class of potential implementations. As the name implies, screen readers literally need a screen from which to read aloud and it doesn't take a rocket scientist to figure out that requiring visually impaired people to use a visual interface is not an optimal solution for them. People who cannot see have no real use for a display that emits light, so devices that focus on other media such as sound make much more sense. Here is where aural style sheets could theoretically shine.

Of course, it's entirely feasible that aural web browsers will find use in other markets as well, such as in network-capable cars, home entertainment systems, and even in multimodal presentations of traditional web content.[15] We frequently use the text-to-speech features of our operating systems to listen to long blog posts and news articles while we do household chores, so it would be extremely useful to gain more control over this presentational transformation. For example, longer pauses between a headline and the subsequent text could be inserted to improve comprehension, since many headlines lack completing punctuation (like a period) and therefore run together too quickly when interpreted by most text-to-speech programs.

Browsers with aural CSS support are scarce. Opera with Voice (available only for Windows 2000 and XP) has the fullest support for the specification. However, we can envision a day not too far into the future when support will improve, opening up completely new possibilities that were once unimagined. For instance, perhaps whole blogs could be automatically turned into audio netcasts with the simple application of an RSS feed and an aural style sheet. Wouldn't that be something?

Feature detection via CSS media queries

Although CSS's notion of media types gives CSS developers some amount of control over which of their styles are applied in which rendering contexts, they are still very broad. Believe it or not, today's web-capable devices are even more heterogeneous than those of yesteryear. New form factors and new technologies have challenged some of the assumptions that the current CSS specifications have made about media types, particularly the handheld media type. CSS developers needed more precise ways to determine a user agent's capabilities.

This is precisely what **media queries**, introduced as part of the evolving CSS3 specification,[16] addresses. Media queries extend the notion of media types by defining a set of *media features* that user agents can purport to have. The CSS developer provides a set of conditions as an expression, of which a media type and one or more media features are a part. Here is an example of a media query you can use today that pulls in an external style sheet only if the user agent supports the screen media type and its physical screen is less than 481 pixels wide:

```
<link type="text/css" rel="stylesheet" media="only screen and (max-device-width:
480px)" href="webkit.css" />
```

Conveniently enough, this describes the width of an Apple iPhone in landscape orientation, as well as many of the other WebKit-based mobile devices on the market today. In the previous example, the media feature being queried is device-width. Other queries might be directed at color depth or capability, aspect ratio, and similar attributes. Here is another example, which links two style sheets for print. One is specifically for color printers while the other handles black and white printers:

```
<link rel="stylesheet" media="print and (color)" href="print-color.css" />
<link rel="stylesheet" media="print and (monochrome)" href="print-bw.css" />
```

---

15. These uses for aural web browsers were recognized by the W3C as early as 1999 and published as a technical note that suggested additions to the CSS1 specification to support aural style properties for such browsers to implement. See http://www.w3.org/Style/CSS/Speech/NOTE-ACSS.

16. The media queries specification is a W3C Working Draft as of this writing, and can be found at http://www.w3.org/TR/css3-mediaqueries.

Since color values sometimes look the same in black and white output, we now have a way to specifically set a higher contrast value on the black and white printers than the color ones. This way, the printed text will be easier to read for users printing in grayscale, but we can still retain the desired color range for users printing in full color.

As of this writing, the only major browsers supporting media queries are Safari 3, Konqueror 4, and versions of Opera greater than 7. The widest use of media queries is in targeting styles for mobile devices running Opera or WebKit-based browsers. As the CSS3 specification evolves and more implementations appear over time, we expect to see much wider adoption of media queries across the gamut of media types.

One document, multiple faces

In the past, it was very common for web sites to redirect their users to one version of a document or style sheet if they used certain web browsers and another way if they used others. This not only proved difficult to accomplish, but extremely expensive to maintain as well. Growing frustration on the part of web developers eventually led to the abandonment of these efforts in favor of advocating for web standards, where a single version of the code could be used across all user agents that conformed to those standards.

Ironically, today it's not uncommon for web sites to provide one version of their pages for online viewing with a desktop-based web browser, a different page for printing, and yet another version altogether for mobile device access. Once again, many use user agent detection schemes to try to route traffic accordingly—an exercise in futility considering the transient nature of user agent strings in HTTP headers. Many also place links and buttons on their pages that read "Print this page" or "View using mobile access."

As you would expect, all of this effort is largely unnecessary, redundant, and very costly to maintain. This functionality can be replaced simply by using the constructs that already exist in CSS in order to deliver the same underlying document to all the user agents. Moreover, doing so often increases the usability of the site because the transformation from one format to the next is seamless and automatic. There's no longer any reason to force your users to painfully navigate through a desktop-based design to find that "mobile access" link.

By leveraging the capabilities that CSS media types and media queries provide, content authors can design style sheets that are used by user agents based on the user agent's own environment. As we'll discuss in upcoming chapters, media queries are the recommended way to target styles for the Apple iPhone and iPod Touch, and they work wonderfully for the wide variances in mobile devices for the browsers that support them. For those that don't, JavaScript can sometimes be used to approximate these behaviors without resorting to user agent detection.[17]

---

17. A striking example of this can be found at Cameron Adams's site; Adams, who wrote about resolution-dependent layouts as early as 2004. His writings on the topic are available at http://themaninblue.com/writing/perspective/2004/09/21/.

Complementing semantics with CSS

CSS describes how elements are styled, but the *semantics* are defined in the markup itself. Nevertheless, CSS is a great way to highlight the semantic meaning, to explore semantic nuances, and to provide presentational confirmation of what an element is supposed to represent. For illustrative purposes, let's pretend to describe "Sarah" as a human being using CSS:

```
#Sarah {
    /* Sarah stands 166 centimeters tall. */
    height: 166cm;
    /* She has white skin and freckles. */
    background: white url(freckles.png);
}
#Sarah #hair {
    /* She has red hair */
    color: red;
    /* that's 150 centimeters long. */
    height: 150cm;
}
#Sarah .eye {
    /* Her eyes are blue */
    color: blue;
    /* and are each 2.2 centimeters across. */
    width: 2.2cm;
}
```

Of course, you cannot describe any concept, much less our friend Sarah, completely in CSS. Is her hair color an integral part of her being, of her identity? Perhaps. In part, it's up to the content author to determine which pieces of their publication are content and which are presentation. The totality of the experience is the structure *and* presentation. It's sometimes tough to distinguish between what should be one and what should be the other.

What we can do is use CSS to work in tandem with semantic markup to further enhance and illustrate the meaning of our content. As much as possible, our CSS should strive to be self-documenting, clear, meaningful, and supportive of the markup it is designed to represent.

Summary

In this chapter, we reviewed some of the basic principles and philosophies on which the World Wide Web was built, so at first we talked about markup languages. You learned why the idea of document semantics, popularized through hypertext, is at the core of most web technologies today. We showed examples of RSS and SVG, markup languages that highlight two very different document formats that are both based on Extensible Markup Language (XML).

The modularization that XML provides gives developers some important advantages over SGML-derived HTML for writing markup semantically. Creating entire special-purpose markup languages (XML applications) to describe things like news feeds, vector graphics, and other kinds of content makes it possible for the Web to house an entire information ecosystem that contains many different sorts of things. XML namespaces allow multiple XML applications to use differing semantics within a single XML document. When "multilingual" software tools see these additional XML dialects being used, they can do more for users.

Since different users have different needs, how software tools (user agents) actually behave may vary from one to the next, so developers need to recognize that they are limited to influencing—not controlling—their content's presentation. Thankfully, keeping ultimate control in the hands of users is a constraint that actually helps keep published markup semantic, encouraging an appropriate separation of concerns between content and presentation.

In this chapter, you learned why adding CSS as a presentational layer atop the underlying markup is valuable from a technical and semantic point of view. We discussed how CSS does this using its notion of media types, taking a single piece of content and presenting it in many different ways. Finally, you learned how this approach could increase the accessibility and the reusability (that is, repurposing) of the content itself.

With these conceptual fundamentals firmly in mind, let's next explore CSS itself in further detail. Just how much influence do you have over a document's presentation using CSS? As we'll see in the next chapters, you have much, much more than you might have previously thought.

Chapter 2

CSS FUNDAMENTALS FOR ADVANCED USE

In the previous chapter, we discussed many of the foundational concepts on which the Web as we know it today is built. Although some of that material is not directly involved with the minutia of day-to-day web development, all of it contributes to your awareness and skill when you are writing code. Similarly, it's important to have a strong understanding of certain foundations of CSS before you can build much on them.

We will therefore spend this chapter thoroughly exploring critically important aspects of how CSS works, such as the influence of user and user agent style sheets, and some of the more esoteric capabilities provided by CSS selectors and values. We will also discuss the foundations of CSS's visual rendering model, including the oft-over-looked concept of document flow and how it relates to the CSS box model. Readers with significant CSS development experience may find some of the material in this chapter familiar, but should still come away with an enhanced understanding of the intricacies of CSS-based design.

Origins of a style sheet and the CSS cascade

Like an army general, your success or failure as a CSS developer will depend on your ability to consider many variables at once. Perhaps the most underappreciated variable in professional front-end web development is the presence of other style sheets in addition to your own. These additional style sheets are applied to your markup *before* your style sheet has a chance to affect it, so it behooves you to be aware of how these other style sheets can help or hinder your own work.

知 彼 知 己 百 戰 不 殆

Know your enemy and know yourself, and you cannot lose.   —*Sun Tzu*, Art of War

User agent style sheets (default browser styles)

A user agent style sheet is a style sheet that is "baked into" the web browser your visitor is using. Every user agent has such a *default style sheet*, and this style sheet is the very first one applied to your markup. Being aware of it and how your own style sheets inherit from it means you'll be able to much more confidently create consistent-looking designs in a cross-browser fashion.

All CSS-capable user agents, such as web browsers, are actually required by the CSS specification to assign initial values to the elements in a document that they render. In many cases these default styles are literally coded as—you guessed it—a user agent's own style sheet. However, whether or not an actual CSS file exists, from the point of view of a CSS developer all conforming user agents behave as though such a style sheet were in effect.

It turns out that this initial styling is extremely beneficial, since it's the result of these default browser styles you are seeing when you load a document that doesn't have any CSS styling applied to it (a so-called "unstyled page"). However, if you are unaware of a user agent's style sheet or blatantly disregard it, it can because a source of confusion or, worse, a source of bugs. To illustrate this point, let's look at the following basic markup example and how it would be rendered in a couple of web browsers:

```
<!DOCTYPE html PUBLIC "-//W3C//DTD XHTML 1.0 Strict//EN"
    "http://www.w3.org/TR/xhtml1/DTD/xhtml1-strict.dtd">
<html xmlns="http://www.w3.org/1999/xhtml">
<head>
<title>Every Good Boy Deserves Fudge</title>
</head>
<body>
<h1>Every Good Boy Deserves Fudge</h1>
<p>The phrase <em>"Every Good Boy Deserves Fudge"</em> is
a <strong>mnemonic</strong> to help new music students
remember the names of the lines on the
<a href="http://en.wikipedia.org/wiki/Clef#The_treble_clef"
title="Clef - Wikipedia, the free encyclopedia">treble
clef</a> staff. The first line on the bottom is the note "E,"
```

and moving up from there we have G, B, D, and F at the top position. The following illustration shows the note name that each line represents:</p>
<a href="egbdf.png" title="View this image"><img src="egbdf.png" alt="Lines on the treble clef staff from bottom to top: E, G, B, D, F" /></a>
<p>The lines will change depending on the clef in question. Here are a few examples:</p>
<table summary="A table of musical clef line names and their mnemonics">
<caption>Clef Mnemonics</caption>
<thead>
<tr>
<th scope="col">Clef</th>
<th scope="col">Lines</th>
<th scope="col"> Mnemonic</th>
</tr>
</thead>
<tbody>
<tr>
<td>Treble Clef</td>
<td>EGBDF</td>
<td>Every Good Boy Deserves Fudge.</td>
</tr>
<tr>
<td>Bass Clef</td>
<td>GBDFA</td>
<td>Good Burritos Don't Fall Apart.</td>
</tr>
<tr>
<td>Alto Clef</td>
<td>FACEG</td>
<td>Felix After Christmas Eats Grapes</td>
</tr>
<tr>
<td>Tenor Clef</td>
<td>DFACE</td>
<td>Don't Fear Alligators Cruising East.</td>
</tr>
</tbody>
</table>
<p>See if you can come up with some mnemonics for some of the other clefs:</p>
<ul>
<li>Baritone Clef: <abbr title="Big Dogs Find Acting Comfortable">BDFAC</abbr></li>
<li>Mezzo-Soprano Clef: <abbr title="Anger Causes Eggs Great Breakage">ACEGB</abbr></li>
<li>Soprano Clef: <abbr title="Charlie Ellis Gets Big

```
Dollars">CEGBD</abbr></li>
</ul>
</body>
</html>
```

This basic example covers a few of the elements that would commonly be encountered in a standard web page. It begins with an <h1> element surrounding the title of the page, followed by a paragraph of content that contains some <a>, <em>, and <strong> elements, providing links and emphasis to a paragraph describing our subject. Following that, we see an <img> element supporting an illustration of our subject, a table, and an unordered list. A style sheet is conspicuously absent. Figure 2-1 shows how this appears in Firefox, and Figure 2-2 shows the result in Safari.

Figure 2-1. The Firefox web browser contains a user agent style sheet that defines its default browser styles, so even otherwise unstyled pages contain a modicum of basic styling.

Figure 2-2. The Safari web browser contains its own, different user agent style sheet, again resulting in a plain but somewhat-styled and readable page. Note the differences between the Firefox default styles and the Safari version.

It is actually Firefox itself that's applying the 14-pixel whitespace (padding in this case) around the edge of the document (technically, the <body>), that larger and bolder font size on the <h1> element, that blue color to the hyperlink's anchor text and the blue border around the hyperlinked image, the underlines appearing on the hyperlink's anchor text and <abbr> elements, as well as the various whitespace sprinkled about the rest of the page. As you can see, there are a number of styles already applied to these pages, and we have yet to write a single CSS rule.[1]

---

1. The default style sheet for many user agents is typically not hard to find. Using current versions of the Firebug add-on for Firefox, you can actually distinguish a user agent's styling from other styles by enabling the Show User Agent CSS option in the Style pane of the HTML tab.

Unfortunately, not all user agent style sheets are the same, as a comparison of these Firefox and Safari screenshots reveal. Vive la différence! Unlike in Firefox, there are no underlines for our <abbr> elements in Safari, nor is there a blue outline border on the hyperlinked image.

Thankfully, a user agent's style sheet is not magical; it is just a regular style sheet that happens to be first in line to be applied. That is, user agent style sheets always come first in the CSS cascade. This means that, somewhere in Firefox's user agent style sheet exists a CSS rule similar to the following one that is responsible for creating that blue border around the hyperlinked image:

```
a img {
    border: 5px solid blue;
}
```

Of course, since this is just ordinary CSS, we can do a lot to remove all this inconsistency by adding a little CSS of our own that would override what the browser's default styles specify. Here's an example of one such style sheet that overrides the styles we saw applied in the earlier screenshots:

```
<head>
<title>Every Good Boy Deserves Fudge</title>
<style type="text/css" media="screen">
    body * {
        margin: 0;
        padding: 0;
        list-style-type: none;
        text-align: left;
        text-decoration:none;
        border-bottom:none;
        display:inline;
        font-size:14px;
        font-weight:normal;
        font-style:normal;
        border:none;
        color:#000;
    }
</style>
</head>
```

This single CSS rule overrides most of the default styles that the browser provides, by selecting all elements (the * in the selector, described later) inside the <body> element. The result is shown in Figure 2-3.

By "zeroing out" the user agent's default style sheet with one of your own, you give yourself a known, more consistent point from which to begin styling elements.[2] Although you may not often need to completely zero out the default browser styles as this example does, you should always pay attention to what styles you have applied to a finished design and what styles the user agent itself has applied. One of the more common mistakes caused by a failure to do this is forgetting to specify the <body> element's color or background-color because these are often initialized to black and white, respectively.

---

2. This is a technique popularized by Eric Meyer, who called it "resetting CSS," and on which many CSS frameworks later built. We'll discuss resetting CSS in more detail when we discuss CSS frameworks later in this book.

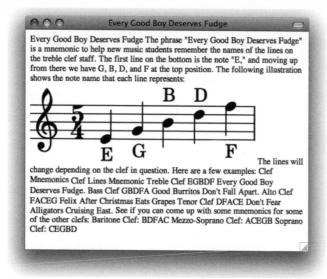

Figure 2-3. Our page with Firefox's and Safari's default browser styles "zeroed out"

One more example, less dramatic but more common in everyday development, is the discrepancy in list rendering. The whitespace used on <ul>, <ol>, and <dl> elements to indent them can be achieved either through the element's margin or padding properties. In order to ensure that list styling is consistent, it thus behooves us to zero out, or "reset," either margins or paddings and use the other for indentation to achieve more consistent rendering, which can be accomplished with CSS as simple as the following rule:

```
ul, ol, dl {
    padding-left:2em;   /* We'll use paddings */
    margin-left:0;      /* not margins. */
}
```

Additionally, with this in mind, one of the first rules we tend to write in a style sheet is

```
html, body {
    margin: 0;
    padding: 0;
    background-color: #fff;
    color: #000;
}
```

This rule ensures that no matter what element in the viewport (that is, the part of the browser window that renders content) is being given the default margin and/or padding in a user agent, it will always be zeroed out for consistency. A background-color and default text color is specified for consistency as well. It's good practice to set both background and foreground colors in the same place, just so you know you're not going to end up with, say, unreadable white text on a white background by mistake.

What we learn from all this is that the CSS developer must take into account default browser styles and be aware that there are a number of issues like these that could be potential challenges. Making discrepancies consistent such as in the previous examples will not only ensure a more consistent look, but can also ease debugging later on.

User style sheets

As we alluded to earlier, CSS fundamentally gives control of a document's presentation to the users of the document, or the consumers of its information. One of the most powerful mechanisms it has for doing this is the user style sheet. If you think of your markup as an API, then you can think of a user style sheet as a theme or template file.

Like user agent style sheets, user style sheets are not magic. Essentially, a user style sheet is a set of CSS rules created by a human visitor (a "user") of your site. Users compose style sheets themselves for a number of reasons, including usability and accessibility reasons as well as aesthetic preference. An individual with vision impairment issues might want to set text in a particular way, and may therefore specify a CSS rule that enlarges all the text on a page or prevents certain fonts from being used. Other individuals may simply want to give their favorite web application a face-lift, and using user style sheets, they can do that.[3]

A user style sheet will be applied immediately after the user agent style sheet is applied and immediately *before* any of your style sheets are. Once rules from these two sources are applied, the rules in your style sheets are applied to the markup. Then, after that, one last round of processing applies any so-called "important" declarations specified in user style sheets, overriding your rules.

Therefore, five stages of the CSS cascade exist that relate to the origin of a style sheet. In order of precedence from least to greatest, they are

- CSS declarations in the user agent style sheet
- CSS declarations in user style sheets of normal importance
- CSS declarations in author style sheets of normal importance
- CSS declarations in author style sheets that are !important
- CSS declarations in user style sheets that are !important

---

3. For a dramatic example of a user style sheet face-lift to Google Reader, be sure to check out Jon Hicks's impressive gReader Theme, which gives the web-based application the look and feel of a Mac OS X desktop application. Jon's gReader theme can be found at http://hicksdesign.co.uk/tag/googlereader/.

User style sheet support in web browsers

Support for user style sheets was dismal for a long time, but today most browsers support user style sheets, including Firefox, Internet Explorer 7, Safari, and Opera.

Opera has far and away the best native support for user style sheets, with an extensive feature set for selecting, managing, and even combining user styles. To have a look at what is in Opera, pull down the latest copy from http://www.opera.com/ and fire it up. Direct your attention to the View menu and then the Styles submenu. You should see selections for switching between Author mode and User mode—basically allowing the user to fully dispense with any author styles and work the site from their own style sheet. You'll also see a Manage Modes command, which brings up a rich dialog box for managing many of the ways Opera will behave when using custom style sheets, and even how author styles would be applied. This dialog box is also where you can set a file path to your own user style sheet.

Firefox disappoints here by not having a built-in interface to choose a user style sheet from its GUI. Instead, you have to go in to your Firefox profile directory (wherever that might be on your system) and look inside the chrome directory (that is, the directory that contains the Firefox browser chrome source files, not to be confused with the new Chrome browser from Google) where you'll find a file called userContent-example.css. Rename it to userContent.css and you can then use it as your user style sheet.

This is a real chore, so thankfully there is a better solution by way of an extension called Stylish (http://userstyles.org/stylish/). This extension does a wonderful job of letting the user create and manage user style sheets on a per-site basis. Stylish puts an icon in the lower-right corner of the browser's status bar, which provides a menu to create global or site-specific styles right from the browser GUI. The extension's companion web site at http://userstyles.org/ has an extensive repository of user-contributed user style sheets to explore, all of which import directly into the Stylish extension.

Both Internet Explorer 7 and Safari contain simple built-in style sheet selectors in their preferences windows. In IE7, this option can be found in Tools ➤ Internet Options ➤ General ➤ Accessibility. Then in the resulting dialog box, select the check box to format pages using your own style sheet and click the Browse button to locate a user style sheet CSS file.

In Safari, similar functionality can be found by navigating to Safari ➤ Preferences ➤ Advanced and then using the Style sheet drop-down menu to select or browse for a user style sheet. There is also a plug-in for Safari called SafariStand (http://hetima.com/safari/) that provides capability similar to the Stylish extension for Firefox.

What are the !important declarations?

CSS declarations can have one of two levels of importance—normal or important—which contributes to the declaration's overall specificity. Declarations are specified important by being flagged with the special keyword !important at the end of the declaration, just before the closing semicolon.

These important declarations are given a higher precedence than declarations of normal importance, and when used in user style sheets they will trump all conflicting declarations from other sources. Consider the following example, where #strings p has a higher specificity than .violas, and the result is that the paragraph directed at the violas has no visual differentiation from the rest of the document:

```
<!DOCTYPE html PUBLIC "-//W3C//DTD XHTML 1.0 Strict//EN"
    "http://www.w3.org/TR/xhtml1/DTD/xhtml1-strict.dtd">
<html xmlns="http://www.w3.org/1999/xhtml" xml:lang="en" lang="en">
<head>
<title>Rehearsal Notes</title>
<style type="text/css">
/*<![CDATA[*/
    #strings p { color:#400080;}
    .violas { color:#c71919; }
    #brass p { color: #b46417; }
/*]]>*/
</style>
</head>
<body>
<h1>Rehearsal Notes</h1>
<div id="strings">
<p>The string section as a whole was starting to get ahead of
the conductor. Please keep an eye on the tempo changes.</p>
<p class="violas">The violas really need a sectional or two
for the last movement of the Shostakovich. Try to get
together at least once before the next rehearsal.</p>
</div>
<div id="brass">
<p>Crescendos need to be more gradual throughout. We are
getting too loud too early in the last movement.</p>
</div>
</body>
</html>
```

However, it appears the conductor (who is not the author of this page) wants to print these notes and distribute them to the orchestra, but also wants to call the information for the violas out. To do this, they add the !important keyword to the .violas rule.

```
.violas {
    color:#c71919 !important;
}
```

Now, provided the viola section is not colorblind as well as deaf,[4] they will see the note directed toward them on the conductor's page highlighted in red.

Although this can sometimes be a handy shortcut for raising the specificity of a particular declaration, it is not often the best way to go in any circumstance. Having your style sheets polluted with a significant number of conflicting !important declarations can make debugging a style sheet a difficult proposition. As you will learn later in this chapter, using a CSS selector's implicit specificity is a far more flexible way to go.

---

4. It is usual and customary for orchestral musicians to continually poke fun at the viola section.

Attributes and characteristics of author style sheets

As a CSS developer, you cannot modify a user agent's baked-in style sheet, although you can override them because a user agent's style sheet is applied first in the CSS cascade. A visitor to your site may supply their own user style sheet to complement or override the CSS rules you've created to implement the design of your site. Therefore, the style sheets you write as a front-end web developer, called *author style sheets*, sit firmly within this middle ground.

It's this middle ground, the author style sheets, which are our domain. This is what we typically think of when we talk about CSS development, and indeed this middle ground is the majority of what the rest of this book is about. These author styles could be styles placed inline with the HTML markup as part of a style attribute (*inline styles*), embedded within an HTML document as part of a <style> element (an *embedded style sheet*), or linked to in one or more *external style sheets*. Each of these methods of applying CSS to page elements has its own characteristics.

External and embedded style sheets

An *external style sheet* is a separate CSS file paired with the document to be styled using one of two mechanisms. The more familiar mechanism comes from HTML and is the <link> element. A minimal example might look like this:

```
<link rel="stylesheet" type="text/css" href="foo.css" />
```

The rel, href, and type attributes are all required. Since HTML's <link> element can pair a document with more than just a style sheet, the rel attribute, which indicates a relationship between two things, must contain the value stylesheet (notice it is one keyword, not two separate words) to indicate that it is being used specifically to pair a style sheet with the document in which the <link> element resides. For the purposes of CSS, the type attribute must contain the single value text/css. This indicates that the linked style sheet is a CSS file. Finally, the href attribute indicates the location of the external style sheet by URI (*hyperlink reference*).

When linking CSS to XML documents that are not XHTML, however, we use a different construct. The equivalent of the previous HTML example would look like this in an XML document that isn't XHTML:

```
<?xml-stylesheet type="text/css" href="foo.css"?>
```

Notice that in the XML example, we use an XML processing instruction (tags that begin with <? and end with ?>) rather than an element, and that since the processing instruction is named xml-stylesheet, we don't need a rel attribute. Later in Chapter 9 of this book we'll discuss CSS in the context of non-XHTML XML documents in more detail.

An *embedded style sheet* is placed within a <style> element (itself placed within the document's <head> element) directly within a given document. As a result, this method is architecturally less flexible than using external style sheets because it can only affect the one document. On the other hand, embedded style sheets can be useful when developing prototypes, to avoid caching issues, or to reduce HTTP overhead to optimize performance in some situations. In HTML, a typical embedded style sheet might look like this:

```
<style type="text/css">
    .warning {
```

```
        background-color: #fffda4;
    }
    .error {
        background-color: #f0aeaf;
        font-weight: bold;
    }
</style>
```

With embedded style sheets, the relationship of the content to the document is obvious, so there is no need for a rel attribute.

> Sometimes, you'll see embedded style sheets in XHTML documents (and hopefully never in HTML documents) begin and end with a funny sequence of characters like this:
>
> ```
>     <style type="text/css">
>     <!--/*--><![CDATA[/*><!--*/
>         /* The embedded style sheet goes in here. */
>     /*]]>*/-->
>     </style>
> ```
>
> What you see here is a sequence of HTML and CSS comments and a special instruction for an XML parser. At the beginning of the embedded style sheet, the sequence is an opening HTML comment (<!--), an opening CSS comment (/*), a closing HTML comment (-->), the opening XML instruction (<![CDATA[), another opening CSS comment, another opening HTML comment, and finally a closing CSS comment (*/). Then, at the end of the embedded style sheet, there is another opening CSS comment, followed by the closing XML instruction (]]>), a closing CSS comment, and finally the closing HTML comment opened earlier.
>
> What a mouthful! So why is all this here? Well, briefly, jumping through this particular sequence of comments protects both legacy user agents that don't support XML and the XML parser in those that do from the raw CSS inside the embedded style sheet. For now, you need to be mindful that this is only a potential issue when you use XHTML, and you can avoid it by using HTML. Later, when we discuss styling proper XML documents with CSS, we'll examine the <![CDATA[...]]> construct in more detail.

External style sheets and embedded style sheets have the same level of precedence in the CSS cascade. It is the style sheets' ordering that resolves conflicts between CSS declarations, with style sheets declared earlier (closer to the opening <head> tag) having less precedence than those style sheets embedded or linked later (closer to the </head> tag). It is a widespread misunderstanding that embedded styles have a higher specificity than linked styles, and that any conflicts between CSS declarations in your external style sheets and your embedded style sheets will be overridden by the embedded ones, caused by the fact that many authors place embedded style sheets after externally linked ones in their HTML sources.

Naming and specifying media and character encoding details

In both the HTML and XML mechanisms are additional attributes we can use to specify the characteristics of the linked style sheet in more detail. The other possible attributes are media, title, and charset, and they are all optional. A more detailed example where we specify a number of additional details about the external style sheet at foo.css may look like this:

```
<link rel="stylesheet" type="text/css" href="foo.css" title="Foo"
    charset="utf-8" media="screen" />
```

Here, we've given this style sheet a more human-readable name using the title attribute. This is both more succinct and functional than, say, an HTML comment would be, since some browsers or browser extensions display this name to the user. In much the same way as a user style sheet can create a "theme" for a site for individual users, you've essentially created a named "theme" for all your site's visitors by titling your style sheet.

Since you can link more than one style sheet to the same document, you can now use this functionality to create multiple themes for your site by supplying different values in the title attribute. This example, similar to the previous one, provides both the "Foo" theme along with an additional "Bar" theme:

```
<link rel="stylesheet" type="text/css" href="foo.css" title="Foo"
    charset="utf-8" media="screen" />
<link rel="alternate stylesheet" type="text/css" href="bar.css"
    title="Bar" charset="utf-8" media="screen" />
```

Now, in user agents that support the capability, users will have the option of choosing either the Foo or Bar themes that you provide for viewing your site. This is accomplished by providing the supplemental keyword alternate in the rel attribute and providing a title of Bar in a second <link> element. This opens up some interesting possibilities and further demonstrates the power of using the same underlying markup with multiple different style sheets, so we'll return to explore this CSS functionality in more detail later in Chapter 6 of this book.

The screen value to the media attribute indicates that the linked style sheet is for use only in that rendering context. That is, it's not intended for printers, nor for aural reproduction, and it *may be* used for certain handheld devices.[5] The media attribute can have more than one value, so a single style sheet can apply to more than one media type. An example is media="screen projection", which might be used to link to a style sheet implementing a variable-width, so-called "liquid" layout.

Finally, the charset attribute specifies that the referenced CSS file is encoded in UTF-8. UTF is the Unicode Transformation Format, and UTF-8 is the most common variant of Unicode on the Web. Most user agents in HTML contexts don't worry tremendously about issues of character encoding, but character encoding becomes important when dealing with XML contexts. Therefore, we'll discuss the implications of the charset attribute as well as Unicode in CSS in more detail later in this book.

---

5. Handheld devices using WebKit such as Apple's iPhone or smartphones running Google's Android ignore the handheld media type and instead use the screen media type. The specifics of CSS for mobile devices are discussed in Chapter 5.

Inline styles

Whereas both external and embedded style sheets define whole style sheets, *inline styles*, which appear within the style attribute of a given element, are only declarations. The declaration is applied to that element possibly inherited by any its child elements. For instance, here is an inline style applied to a paragraph element that italicizes the entire paragraph, including the child <q> and <cite> elements:

```
<p style="font-style: italic">
<q>A table, a chair, a bowl of fruit and a violin; what else does a man
        need to be happy?</q>
    -<cite>Albert Einstein</cite>
</p>
```

The least flexible way to apply styles to a document, inline styles will have higher specificity than declarations in either embedded or external style sheets. It is generally best to avoid the use of inline styles whenever possible in production code, as they add unnecessary rigidity and nonsemantic clutter to markup, bloat the code, and make it more difficult to read.

Nevertheless, due to their high specificity, inline styles are useful for occasional debugging purposes, although using temporary !important declarations may provide another avenue for debugging. They are also useful in some situations where presentational markup is unavoidable or required by implementation details. In these instances, inline styles can be calculated on the server and inserted into the code of markup templates.

A common situation in which you might see inline styles used is in the creation of progress meters. A PHP template might dynamically change where a progress bar should be filled to with code like this:

```
<div class="progress-bar"
        style="width: <?php print getPercentComplete();?>%">
<span><?php print getPercentComplete();?> complete</span>
</div>
```

The PHP function in this example, getPercentComplete(), would return a number such as 100, which would indicate completeness. A value of 0, on the other hand, could indicate that the process has yet to begin, and other values in between could represent varying levels of progress. It's used in two places so that the progress is presented not only visually but also as textual content for accessibility reasons. The other visual styling required to render the progress bar, such as its height, a border, and so forth, would be applied in a CSS rule in an external style sheet that targets the progress-bar class.

Selectors: from simple to complex to surgical

Although the syntax of CSS is very simple, a single style sheet can contain theoretically infinite presentational information. This information is organized into a sequence of **statements**, each of which specifies one **rule** (sometimes also called a **ruleset**). A typical rule contains one **declaration block**, itself a series of **declarations** (composed of **property** and **value** pairs) and a **selector**. One of the keys to becoming a CSS surgeon, so to speak, is the intelligent and thoughtful use of CSS selectors.

Selectors allow us a great deal of flexibility and efficiency in how we apply presentational style to documents. Using selectors, you can **target** (or **select**) a single element or, with a **selector group**, a group of elements to apply styles to. These selected elements are known as **subjects** of the selector. CSS selectors are composed of two primary building blocks: **simple selectors** and **combinators**.

Simple selectors

CSS's simple selectors are the fundamental units with which you build a selector in a rule.[6] All CSS rules must contain at least one explicit simple selector written by you, and often contain at least one implicit simple selector (inserted by the browser's CSS parser) as well. Further, there are many different kinds of simple selectors that CSS makes available to you, and each one allows you to target elements in a slightly different way.

Multiple simple selectors can be grouped, or **chained**, together one after the other to create a **sequence of simple selectors**. Each simple selector in the sequence adds its own filter to the set of elements selected by the simple selector that came before it, adding specificity to the selector and narrowing the set of possible elements the selector will target. Here are a few examples of valid CSS selectors that are composed purely of simple selectors:

```
h1
div.vcard
img.logo[title]
```

The first selector is a single simple selector that targets <h1> elements, and is called a type selector, described in the next section. The second selector is a sequence of two simple selectors, the div type selector chained with the class selector .vcard, and therefore targets all <div> elements with a class name of vcard. Finally, the third is a sequence of three simple selectors, img chained with .logo chained with the attribute selector [title], so it selects all <img> elements whose class name is logo and who also have a title attribute.

From these examples you can see how chaining simple selectors together provides increased specificity and precision when targeting elements to style. You can also see that each kind of simple selector is slightly different in how it targets elements. Most important, note that creating a sequence of simple selectors is distinct from creating a selector group. The following two CSS rules are therefore not equivalent:

```
div.vcard    /* Single selector composed of two simple selectors. */
div, .vcard /* A selector group with two selectors each composed of
                one simple selector. */
```

The second example will potentially apply to many more elements than the first example, since it is a selector group composed of two individual simple selectors. It will target *any* <div> element, and it will also target any element with a class name of vcard, regardless of whether that element is a <div>. Next, let's take a tour of some of the basic as well as the lesser known simple selectors available to you as a CSS developer.

---

6. Note that the definition of a simple selector is slightly altered from CSS2.1 to CSS3. We use the CSS3 terminology because it is more precise. For details on the differences between the two specifications, see http://www.w3.org/TR/css3-selectors/#changesFromCSS2.

Type selectors

The most common simple selector is the **type selector**, which lets you specify CSS rules for a given type of element in your document markup. To use it, simply indicate the name of the element (sans the angle brackets) of the element you want to target. To target all <h1> elements, for instance, your type selector is merely h1. To target *all* headlines in an HTML document, simply create a selector group that contains each type of headline element: h1, h2, h3, h4, h5, h6.

You can use type selectors for any markup language. If there is an element in the markup, it can be targeted with a type selector. In some contexts such as XML and XHTML, where element names are case sensitive, so too are CSS type selectors. Therefore, in an XML document, the following two type selectors actually refer to two different types of elements:

```
DIV /* Selects elements like <DIV> */
div /* Selects elements like <div> */
```

You can do a lot with type selectors alone. In this next example, we have some very simple HTML elements—a few <li> elements, which are descendants of a single <ul> element, a couple of <p> elements, and a single <h1>. All of them are descendants of the <body> element. Styles are applied to each of these via CSS rules that make use of a single type selector.

```
<!DOCTYPE html PUBLIC "-//W3C//DTD XHTML 1.0 Strict//EN"
    "http://www.w3.org/TR/xhtml1/DTD/xhtml1-strict.dtd">
<html xmlns="http://www.w3.org/1999/xhtml" xml:lang="en" lang="en">
<head>
<title>2009-01-21 Concert Plan</title>
<style type="text/css" media="screen">
    body {
        font-family:Helvetica, Verdana, sans-serif;
        background-color:#E6E6E6;
        font-size:80%;
    }
    h1 {
        font-style:italic;
        color:#004080;
    }
    ul {
        margin:0;
        padding-left:2em;
    }
    li {
        list-style-type:circle;
        font-style:italic;
    }
    em {
        text-decoration:underline;
        background-color:#ccc;
        padding:1px;
    }
```

```
</style>
</head>
<body>
<h1>2009-01-21 Concert Plan</h1>
<p>The January 2009 chamber ensemble performance will be
based on the works of <em>Igor Stravinsky</em>. The program
will cover representative works from his three main stylistic
periods, the Russian Period (1908-1919), the Neoclassical
Period (1920-1954), and the Serial Period (1954-1968). Works
will include:</p>
<ul>
<li>L'Histoire du Soldat (The Soldier's Tale), for chamber
ensemble and three speakers (1918)</li>
<li>Octet for Wind Instruments (revised 1952)</li>
<li>Epitaphium, for flute, clarinet and harp (1959)</li>
</ul>
<p>There will be a 1/2 hour pre-concert lecture, and the
post-concert reception will be held at Moe's Tavern next door
to the performance hall.</p>
</body>
</html>
```

In our embedded style sheet, we have indicated that the <body> element should use a nice sans-serif font family and a light gray background color, and the overall font size will be reduced by 80 percent of the browser default. The <h1> gets a soothing, ocean-blue hue in an italic typeface. The <ul> element establishes a consistent model for how the left spacing will appear since we know that this will be interpreted differently between browsers, and the accompanying <li> elements will get circle markers and italics. Finally, our <em> elements will be treated with extra emphasis by giving the text an underline and giving the background a gray color and a bit of padding so that the background box looks a bit more comfortable around the content, as shown in Figure 2-4.

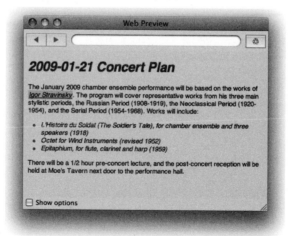

Figure 2-4. Even mere type selectors can be used to great effect to add a little style to our element types.

Universal type selector

We briefly saw this selector earlier when we were discussing user agent style sheets: the **universal type selector** is an asterisk (*). This selector targets all types of elements, as its name implies. When used by itself, it applies the specified styling to every single element in the document.

Using the universal type selector is distinct from inheritance, where child elements inherit the values of certain properties from their parent or ancestor elements, since in this case you explicitly apply certain styles to each and every element. Let's examine the same code that we used when examining type selectors, but this time we'll outline all of the elements with a one-pixel border using just one rule that takes advantage of the universal type selector:

```
<style type="text/css" media="screen">
    * { border:1px solid #400080;}
</style>
```

This one small CSS rule will place that border around every element in our page. Figure 2-5 shows that all our elements are now outlined.

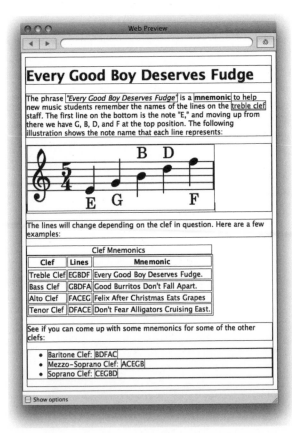

Figure 2-5. Using the universal type selector, we can target every type of element regardless of their names.

Since all CSS rules must be applied to elements in a document's markup, every CSS rule must begin with either a specific type selector or the universal type selector. If an explicit type or universal type selector is omitted from the start of a CSS selector, then the user agent assumes the presence of the universal type selector for the purpose of element selection. In other words, when you use a selector such as .vcard, the browser interprets this as *.vcard.

Attribute selectors

In many markup languages, a lot of information is codified as attributes with particular values. Such information might appear as the URI of an image (<img src="images/viola.gif">), supplemental information in a title attribute (<abbr title="firewood">), or as the destination of a hyperlink (<a href="http://en.wikipedia.org/wiki/Viola">). Using CSS's **attribute selectors**, we have powerful ways to target elements based on the attributes and attribute values they contain.

You delimit attribute selectors by placing an opening bracket ([) and a corresponding closing bracket (]) on either side of an expression. In the simplest case, the expression is merely the name of the attribute whose presence you'd like to target. For example, an attribute selector like [title] would select any elements that have a title attribute, regardless of its value.

You can also target elements based on an attribute's value using attribute selectors. If you specify [foo=bar], you'll target the elements that have the attribute foo where that attribute's value is exactly bar. For instance, using the selector [title=viola] would target an element like <abbr title="viola">vla</abbr> but not <abbr title="double bass">db</abbr>, despite the fact that both abbreviations have title attributes.

Many attributes can contain more than one individual value. For instance, you can assign multiple class names to a single element by separating each of the element's class names with a space. Another example is a situation wherein an attribute value contains human-readable text, which naturally contains spaces. Using the [foo~=bar] attribute selector syntax, you can target elements that have a foo attribute where at least one of the words in the attribute's value is bar.

With the [foo~=bar] attribute selector, the word can't be part of a longer word, so in this case it can't be "barcamp" or, say, "barbarella." Typically, this is exactly the behavior that you want in the real world. Another example could be [title~=bass], which would target <abbr title="double bass">db</abbr> but not <abbr title="bassoon">bs</abbr>.

A fourth and final kind of attribute selector defined by CSS2 is [foo|=bar]. This is less commonly used, but can be helpful in internationalization contexts since it targets elements whose foo attributes contain a hyphen-separated list of words and the first word is exactly bar. This sounds confusing at first, so let's take a look at an example.

The Chinese language code[7] is zh. Since it has a number of dialects spoken in different countries around the world, it can be suffixed with a hyphen and a country code. Often, however, these regional variances are tertiary to your goal for styling purposes, so using an attribute selector like [lang|="zh"] is sufficient for targeting all of the following paragraph elements: <p lang="zh"> (Chinese), <p lang="zh-cn"> (Chinese/China), <p lang="zh-hk"> (Chinese/Hong Kong), and <p lang="zh-tw"> (Chinese/Taiwan).

---

7. A language code is simply a standard way of representing human languages with succinct strings. The international community originally standardized language codes as the ISO 639 standard. As it is wont to do, Wikipedia has a detailed and thorough explanation of language codes at http://en.wikipedia.org/wiki/Language_code.

Since attribute selectors are a kind of simple selector, we can chain them in a single CSS rule to target elements whose attributes match all of our criteria. For example, if we wanted to target elements written in Chinese that had been cited from the Wikipedia article on *The Art of War*, we could use an attribute selector chain such as [lang|=zh][cite="http://en.wikipedia.org/wiki/The_Art_of_War"]. Note that quotations around the attribute value's portion of an attribute selector's syntax are optional, but could be used to improve readability for your fellow human beings.

In addition to these capabilities, CSS3 defines three new attribute selectors, called **substring matching attribute selectors**, that give us ways to match substrings within attribute values. The [title^=bass] syntax will match elements with a title attribute whose value begins with bass (such as <abbr title="bassoon">bs</abbr> but not <abbr title="double bass">db</abbr> in the earlier example). The attribute selector syntax of [title$=bass] will match elements with a title attribute whose value ends with bass, so this will again only match the double bass and not the bassoon. Finally, the [title*=bass] attribute selector will match elements with a title attribute in which any part of its value contains the string bass, which will match both of the abbreviations for the bassoon and the double bass.[8]

The substring matching attribute selectors work in many of the mainstream modern browsers today, such as Safari 3, Chrome, Opera, and Firefox. Internet Explorer is, of course, the notable exception.

ID and class selectors

IDs and classes are two attributes that can be used to identify certain chunks of content as well as group them together. Their importance to a document's structure and semantics and to CSS gives them special treatment that simplifies their selection model, making it unique. In XHTML and most other markup languages, the **ID attribute** is named id and the **class attribute** is named class, but the other markup languages are not required to stick to this convention.

Consider the following example XHTML document, which uses an attribute selector to target a specific <p> element that has been given a unique ID:

```
<!DOCTYPE html PUBLIC "-//W3C//DTD XHTML 1.0 Strict//EN"
    "http://www.w3.org/TR/xhtml1/DTD/xhtml1-strict.dtd">
<html xmlns="http://www.w3.org/1999/xhtml">
<head>
<title>Toscanini</title>
<style type="text/css" media="screen">
p[id="conductor"] {
        font: 1.2em Helvetica, sans-serif;
}
</style>
</head>
<body>
<p id="conductor">Arturo Toscanini referred to the orchestra as
"assassins" when he famously disagreed with their performance.</p>
</body>
</html>
```

---

8. Astute readers are likely to note that the syntax of these substring matching attribute selectors are based loosely on traditional Perl Compatible Regular Expressions (PCRE)–compatible regular expression syntax.

This CSS rule reads, "Select the <p> element with an id attribute whose value is exactly equal to conductor." However, since we have an ID attribute, the rule targeting the paragraph here could be written using CSS's **ID selector** instead:

```
p#conductor {
    font: 1.2em Helvetica, sans-serif;
}
```

The octothorpe symbol (#) precedes the value of the ID attribute, and in this case it replaces all that bracket-id-equals-quote-conductor-quote-bracket stuff. This change reads subtly differently than before since it now says, "Select the <p> element with the identifier of conductor." The difference is that you are no longer selecting the id attribute explicitly, but rather whatever attribute happens to be defined as that markup language's ID attribute.

Since element IDs are required to be unique among all the elements in a document, the ID selector also has higher specificity than attribute selectors. Moreover, for the same reason, you can make the selector even simpler and write the rule without the leading p type selector. This also makes our selector more compact and much more convenient to write:

```
#conductor {
    font: 1.2em Helvetica, sans-serif;
}
```

The same pattern follows for classes, with the single syntactic difference that a **class selector** uses the dot character (.) as its indicator instead of an octothorpe. Classes, in contrast to IDs, may appear multiple times within a document (so they have a lower specificity). Whereas IDs explicitly identify a single element, classes can be used to identify a "kind of" element.

For instance, in the following example we have a set of repeating semantic structures describing conductors, with their name and the orchestra they conduct marked up as children of the conductor "kind of" elements. In our CSS, we specify that the conductor class will outline each conductor's block with a gray border, a little padding inside the block, and a bit of margin below each one to separate them. The beauty of this approach is that defining the style for the conductor class is only necessary once, yet each instance of our conductor "kind of" elements receives the appropriate styling.

Additionally, since we can have as many classes in our markup as we like, we can use this construct to also specify a name class and apply bold type to it. We'll also have an orchestra class and place the orchestra's name in italics. These additions are shown here:

```
<!DOCTYPE html PUBLIC "-//W3C//DTD XHTML 1.0 Strict//EN"
    "http://www.w3.org/TR/xhtml1/DTD/xhtml1-strict.dtd">
<html xmlns="http://www.w3.org/1999/xhtml" xml:lang="en" lang="en">
<head>
<title>Conductors</title>
<style type="text/css" media="all">
    .conductor {
        border:1px solid #aaa;
        margin-bottom:1em;
        padding:1em;
    }
    .name {
```

```
                    font-weight:bold;
            }
            .orchestra {
                    font-style:italic;
            }
    </style>
    </head>
    <body>
    <h1>A few conductors</h1>
    <div class="conductor">
    <p class="name">Hans Graf</p>
    <p class="orchestra">Houston Symphony Orchestra</p>
    </div>
    <div class="conductor">
    <p class="name">Esa-Pekka Salonen</p>
    <p class="orchestra">Los Angeles Philharmonic</p>
    </div>
    <div class="conductor">
    <p class="name">Michael Tilson Thomas</p>
    <p class="orchestra">San Francisco Symphony</p>
    </div>
    <div class="conductor">
    <p class="name">James Levine</p>
    <p class="orchestra">Boston Symphony Orchestra</p>
    </div>
    </body>
    </html>
```

Pseudo-classes

Like attribute selectors, pseudo-classes are a way to target elements that have a particular character-istic. You use a colon (:) to delimit the beginning of a pseudo-class selector. However, unlike the attri-bute selectors we've just examined, the characteristics that pseudo-classes target are not *necessarily* the element's attribute and value pairs.

Pseudo-classes can, in fact, be used to target elements based on any sort of criteria. In some cases, such criteria may even be independent of the document markup itself. The most well known pseudo-classes are those that relate to the styling of links on a page, so let's look at these first.

Hyperlinks: the :link and :visited pseudo-classes

The :link pseudo-class, unsurprisingly, targets any elements that are **hyperlinks**. In XHTML, that means it targets any <a> element that contains an href attribute, but there's actually some subtlety in this as well. In particular, there is a distinction between **anchor elements** and hyperlinks.

First, note that <a> elements in XHTML without an href attribute are not targeted by the :link pseudo-class because these anchor elements are not defined as links in the HTML family of languages. Second, note that in many XML documents the :link pseudo-class may apply to elements other than the <a> element because many document languages can create links using different element types.[9] The key point is that the :link pseudo-class applies only to whatever combination of characteristics defines a hyperlink in the elements of a particular markup language you are styling.

In practice, this means that *for XHTML pages* the following two CSS rules are equivalent (albeit with slightly different specificities). The distinction is that if the same style sheet was later paired with a different XML application that didn't use <a> elements to define links, the first selector would no longer target any elements while the second one would. The latter is therefore preferred for reasons of reusability and portability.

```
a:link { color: blue; }
:link { color: blue; }
```

The :visited pseudo-class takes this concept one step further and targets hyperlinks that have been visited. More precisely, the :visited pseudo-class targets only the subset of elements that the :link pseudo-class targets and that are in the visited state. What the "visited state" means is up to the user agent to decide, although for web browsers it commonly means "links the user has previously clicked on and are now in the local browser cache."

These two pseudo-classes illustrate how a pseudo-class can target characteristics that can be any number of things, including element characteristics (links) and things other than the underlying document structure itself (whether or not a link was previously clicked). Other pseudo-classes can be used to target elements based on things like repetitive patterns within the document structure, what document fragment the user navigated to, and even user interaction. Let's look at user interaction next, since these pseudo-classes are also commonly used for styling links.

User interaction: the :hover, :active, and :focus dynamic pseudo-classes

User agents that render "interactive" media types, which include traditional web browsers, can take advantage of a few additional pseudo-classes. These pseudo-classes are collectively called the **dynamic pseudo-classes** because they apply to elements the user has acted upon in some way. For most of the Web's existence, the only really interactive part of a web page was its hyperlinks, so that's still where you'll still see the dynamic pseudo-classes used most often.

The dynamic pseudo-classes are relatively self-explanatory. The :hover pseudo-class targets rendered elements that that user's cursor is hovering over. This dynamic effect is the cornerstone of all CSS-based rollover techniques.

The :active pseudo-class targets elements that are currently "active," a state that user agents may interpret as they see fit. Common examples are the moment when a user clicks a hyperlink and has not yet released the mouse button or when the user clicks a button on a form. Another way a user might "activate" an element is by pressing the Return or Enter key on their keyboard while the element has keyboard focus.

Speaking of keyboard focus, you can use the :focus pseudo-class to target the element on a page that has it. Sometimes it makes sense to group the styles you declare for the :hover pseudo-class with the

---

9. A W3C recommendation called XLink defines a standard XML-based linking language that builds on the hyperlink concept introduced by HTML. In particular, it defines a set of attributes that can be used generically within elements of other XML applications to give those elements hyperlink-like properties.

:focus pseudo-class, too. Then there are other times—particularly when designing form interfaces—when styling focused elements independently makes sense.

Since all of the dynamic pseudo-classes are ordinary simple selectors, they can be used on any element you desire. Unfortunately, many older browsers do not apply some of these pseudo-classes to all elements. Frustratingly, Internet Explorer 6 only applies the :hover pseudo-class to <a> elements.

Selecting elements containing text in a particular language: the :lang() pseudo-class

Earlier, we mentioned that the [foo|=bar] attribute selector could be used to select elements based on their lang attribute's value. More commonly, the :lang() pseudo-class is used for this purpose since, like the :link pseudo-class, it targets elements of a particular human language regardless of the technical mechanism used to identify it.[10] It's also the first CSS construct we've shown that uses a new kind of syntax, called *functional notation*.

Functional notation gets its name from formal programming contexts, where function names are traditionally followed by a pair of parentheses that contain the arguments the function is intended to use. In CSS, functional notation is used when a specific number of arguments are required to construct a valid selector. In the case of the :lang() pseudo-class, a language code (such as en for English or zh for Chinese) must be specified; using the pseudo-class without specifying a language results in an invalid CSS rule.

Using the earlier attribute selector example of Chinese excerpts from Sun Tzu's *The Art of War*, the following two selectors are equivalent *when used in XHTML contexts*, as both of them will apply to elements whose contents are written in Chinese:

```
[lang|=zh]
:lang(zh)
```

Thanks to the document language-specific abstraction that the :lang() pseudo-class provides, it's generally considered good practice to use it in favor of the explicit attribute selector when your intent is to select human languages. You might use this in a generic user style sheet to highlight blocks of content in languages you are trying to pick up, for example, in which case the highlighting effect will work whether you're reading an RSS feed or a web page or any other kind of document. However, if your intent is to specifically target elements with a lang attribute, the first selector is preferred.

Selecting target elements via document fragment URIs: the :target pseudo-class

As mentioned earlier, individual elements within a document can be given a particular ID to uniquely identify them. These elements can then be selected with the CSS ID selector. Earlier, we showed a selector targeting a paragraph with an ID of conductor, and it looked like this:

```
#conductor {
    font: 1.2em Helvetica, sans-serif;
}
```

Conveniently, the octothorpe (#) is also the symbol used to specify **URI fragments**, or a particular element *within* a document. Therefore, any element that you assign an ID can be accessed directly by appending an octothorpe followed by that element's ID value to the document's URI.

---

10. It just so happens that in XHTML, the lang attribute is how human languages are declared; however, other applications of XML may have their own mechanism for doing so.

For example, if the previous code were excerpted from the page located at http://example.com/ orchestra.html, then to jump to the particular element with information about the conductor, the address in your browser's location bar would be http://example.com/orchestra.html#conductor. Not surprisingly, the end of this URI looks very similar to your ID selector rule. Coincidence? We think not.

When you access a page via a URI with a **fragment identifier** like this, the element identified by the fragment becomes known as the **target element**.[11] An element that is the designated target of a URI can be selected in a CSS rule using the :target pseudo-class. For instance, we could modify the previous ID selector by chaining the :target pseudo-class to it so that it only targeted the conductor element when accessed via a link with a fragment identifier:

```
#conductor:target {
    font: 1.2em Helvetica, sans-serif;
}
```

Being able to target elements in this way provides some interesting possibilities for user interaction. In particular, the :target pseudo-class makes it possible for web designers to provide the user with additional context *after* they follow a link. Sadly, neither Internet Explorer 6 nor 7 supports this CSS3 pseudo-class, even though other mainstream browsers, including Safari, Opera, and Firefox, all do.

Selecting the first or last element in a series using the :first-child or :last-child pseudo-classes

Using the :first-child or :last-child pseudo-classes, you can select the first or last occurrence of a particular element in a series, which often warrant special styling. One common example is a navigation list, where the first or last list item requires different surrounding whitespace or border widths. Without these pseudo-classes, you might have relied on special class names like "first" or "last" in your markup.

For example, many navigation lists on the Web today are marked up with code similar to this:

```
<ul id="GlobalNav">
<li class="first"><a href="/">Home</a></li>
<li><a href="/about/">About</a></li>
<li><a href="/contact/">Contact</a></li>
<li class="last"><a href="/register/ ">Register</a></li>
</ul>
```

Using the :first-child pseudo-class, you no longer need to use a first class name, and using the :last-child pseudo-class, you no longer need to use a last class name. Instead, a CSS selector such as #GlobalNav li:first-child or just #GlobalNav :first-child could be used. Here are some additional selector examples that use these pseudo-classes:

```
/* match only the first h2 element inside any div */
div h2:first-child
/* match the very last child of the body element */
body > :last-child
/* match all elements that are 1st children of their parents */
:first-child
/* match all the 1st table cells in the last row of any tables */
tr:last-child td:first-child
```

---

11. Perhaps it should also be noted that such a target element is distinct from the elements targeted by CSS selectors.

It's worth paying special attention to the fact that only the :first-child pseudo-class is defined as part of CSS2.1, while the :last-child pseudo-class is technically only available as of CSS3. Thankfully, in practice, many of the user agents that support the :first-child pseudo-class support the :last-child pseudo-class as well. The exception is Internet Explorer 7, which only supports the :first-child pseudo-class.

More pseudo-classes

There are even more pseudo-classes to cover, but instead of an exhaustive explanation of them in this chapter we'll examine them in more detail in future chapters where their use is directly relevant. In particular, take a look at Chapter 4 to examine the :left, :right, and :first pseudo-classes for selecting left- or right-hand or cover pages in a printed context.

Pseudo-elements

Pseudo-elements are similar to pseudo-classes in that they extend the capabilities of CSS selectors so styles can be applied to parts of a document with more precision. Unlike pseudo-classes, however, pseudo-elements select fictional elements that don't really exist in the markup. You can think of them as abstractions to target smaller parts of a larger element that would be impossible to style in any other way.

> *Be careful, four-eyes! There is a subtle but important distinction between the syntax of CSS2 and CSS3's pseudo-elements. In CSS2, pseudo-elements are written in exactly the same way as pseudo-classes, with a single colon followed by the name of the pseudo-class. Currently in CSS3, pseudo-elements are delimited by a double colon prefix (instead of one). As of this writing, the CSS3 Selectors Module is at Last Call stage on the way to standardization and is expected to be ratified with this difference intact. As a CSS developer, you may use either the older single-colon syntax or the newer double-colon syntax for the pseudo-elements present in CSS2.1, but you must use the double-colon syntax for pseudo-elements defined by CSS3.*

Selecting the first character in an inline box using the :first-letter pseudo-element

Traditional publishing scenarios often style the first character of a chapter in a book or an article in a magazine differently from the others. Drop caps are one example of this. Unfortunately, there is no way to select only the first letter in a paragraph using CSS selectors that solely rely on the document tree created by the markup unless the document authors explicitly added structural hooks for such styling ahead of time. Of course, coupling markup for the sake of presentation is the problem CSS was invented to resolve.

Therefore, in much the same way that the :first-child pseudo-class obviates the need for an explicit "first" class, CSS's :first-letter pseudo-element obviates the need for such structural markup around the first character in a paragraph. In other words, using the :first-letter pseudo-elements lets you turn markup like this:

```
<p>
  <span class="first-letter">I</span>t was a long and stormy night.
</p>
```

into markup like this:

```
<p>It was a long and stormy night.</p>
```

When conforming user agents encounter the following CSS, they will behave as though the `<span>` element in the first example exists in the second, even though it doesn't:

```
p:first-letter { font-size: 1.5em; }
```

Thanks to its typographic heritage and despite its name, the `:first-letter` pseudo-element will also select numerals if they are the first character in an inline box. Additionally, punctuation that precedes the first letter or numeral, such as quotation marks, will be also be selected by the `:first-letter` pseudo-element.

Matching the first inline box inside a block box using the :first-line pseudo-element

The `:first-line` pseudo-element behaves just like the `:first-letter` pseudo-element, but instead of selecting only the first character, it selects the entire first line. If the browser window is resized or if the dimensions of the targeted element change, the beginning and end of the `:first-line` pseudo-element is updated on the fly. Therefore, there is no possible markup equivalent for the `:first-line` pseudo-element like there is for the `:first-letter` pseudo-element.

More pseudo-elements

There are two additional pseudo-elements worthy of note: the `:before` and `:after` pseudo-elements. However, these pseudo-elements relate to CSS's capability to render "pseudo-content" that doesn't actually exist in a page's XHTML document structure. We cover this feature of CSS in greater detail in Chapter 3.

Additionally, CSS3 adds a `::selection` pseudo-element that targets any content currently selected (or highlighted) by the user. As of this writing, the forthcoming CSS3 specification states that only a restricted subset of CSS properties apply to the `::selection` pseudo-element, of which only color and background (except `background-image`) are required. Unfortunately, Opera at versions 9.5 and greater is the only browser as of this writing that supports the `::selection` pseudo-element.

Using combinators

In much the same way as simple selectors can be chained to create sequences that increase a selector's specificity and filter the selector's subjects to a more precise set of elements, **combinators** can be used to chain sequences of simple selectors together with a similar effect. When you combine these sequences of simple selectors with combinators, you're specifying that the subjects of the simple selectors on the right-hand side of the combinator have a particular relationship to the subjects of the simple selectors on the left-hand side. The kind of relationship specified is determined by the kind of combinator that's used to chain the two sequences together.

CSS2.1 defines three kinds of combinators, and CSS3 adds a fourth. In CSS2.1, the combinators available to you are descendant combinators, child combinators, and adjacent sibling combinators. CSS3 adds the general sibling combinator to the bunch. Each of these combinators is named for the relationship between the simple selectors that they specify.

As we discussed in the previous chapter, documents encoded in markup languages have a hierarchical structure known as the *document tree* (or DOM tree), wherein each element is "nested" within other elements. This gives each element a hierarchical context relative to the other elements in the tree. This is depicted in Figure 2-6, which shows a sample HTML document tree.

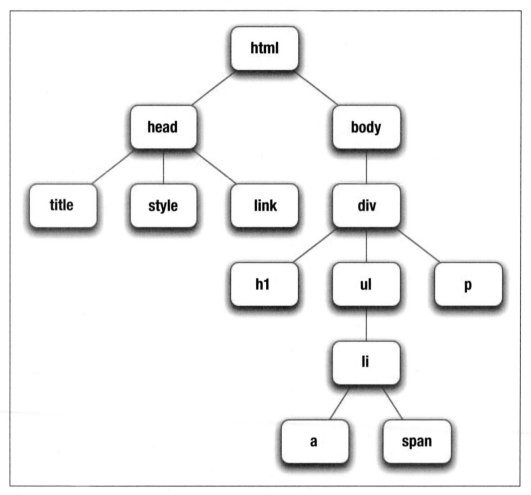

Figure 2-6. A chart depicting the hierarchical structure of HTML elements, known as the document tree, which intentionally looks very much like a family tree

As you can see, the ultimate ancestor of all the elements in the document is the <html> element, which is said to be the *root element*. Within the <html> element are two elements, <head> and <body>, which are said to be *children* of the <html> element (their *parent element*), and are therefore *siblings* of one another. These elements, in turn, each have additional child elements within them, each with their own children, populating the document with further descendant elements. It's these familiar—and familial—relationships that combinators describe.

Descendant combinator

The **descendant combinator** selects the elements targeted by the sequence of simple selectors on its right that are descendants of the elements targeted by the sequence of simple selectors on its left. Descendant combinators are written using any amount of whitespace (such as a space or tab character) between two sequences of simple selectors. In the following example, any `<p>` or `<a>` element that is nested within any `<div>` element will get the gray color treatment:

```
div p, div a { color: #777; }
```

The first selector in the selector group would select the `<p>` element in Figure 2-6 because it is descended from a `<div>`. The same is true of the `<a>` element inside the unordered list, even though it's not a direct child of the `<div>` like the `<p>` element is, so the second selector in the selector group also applies.

Just as you can chain any number of simple selectors into a sequence, so too can you chain any number of sequences of simple selectors with any number of combinators. This CSS rule has the same selector subjects as the previous one, but by explicitly including the body type selector we increase the selector's specificity:

```
body div p, body div a { color: #777; }
```

One challenging and instructional exercise you can try is to style all of the elements in your design that you currently select via ID and class selectors with descendant selectors instead. By constraining your available styling hooks to a document's hierarchical structure alone, you force yourself to think long and hard about the structure of your markup. It also instantly exposes areas of structural ambiguity that could possibly be candidates for refactoring.

Child combinator

The **child combinator** selects the subject on its right if that element is an immediate child (that is, not a grandchild, great-grandchild, or other descendant) of the subject on its left. The child combinator is denoted using a greater-than sign (>) and any optional amount of whitespace. Using the markup structure we've shown in Figure 2-6, this means that the following two CSS rules will have the same effect, since the `<p>` element is both a descendant *and* the child of the `<div>` element:

```
div p { color: #777; }
div > p { color: #777; }
```

This makes sense since children are also descendants, of course. However, because they are a specific kind of descendant, the child combinator's precedence is greater than the descendant selector's. Therefore, if our CSS rules had instead conflicted, as shown next, it's the CSS rule with the descendant selector that would override the other, despite its source order:

```
div > p { color: #F00; }
div p { color: #777; }
```

Whitespace is optional in all combinators except the descendant combinator you just saw in the previous section, so the selectors div > p, div> p, and div>p will all be interpreted in the same way. As a word of caution, the child combinator will not function in versions of Microsoft Internet Explorer prior to 7. While Internet Explorer 6's market share continues to wane over time, be sure to consider your audience and future usage trends when using the more advanced combinators. Other modern browsers such as Safari, Firefox, and Opera will have no trouble with these combinators.

55

Adjacent sibling combinator

The **adjacent sibling combinator** selects the subject on its right if that element is the sibling immediately following the subject on its left. An adjacent sibling combinator is indicated by a plus sign (+) and like the child combinator, the same optional whitespace rules apply. For an illustrative example, let's say that the document tree we've shown in Figure 2-6 is an abbreviated representation of the following XHTML code:

```
<!DOCTYPE html PUBLIC "-//W3C//DTD XHTML 1.0 Strict//EN"
    "http://www.w3.org/TR/xhtml1/DTD/xhtml1-strict.dtd">
<html xmlns="http://www.w3.org/1999/xhtml" xml:lang="en" lang="en">
<head>
<title>Adjacent Sibling Combinator Example</title>
<style type="text/css">
/* CSS will go here. */
</style>
</head>
<body>
<div>
<h1>Count <em>every</em> measure</h1>
<p>Some orchestral musicians have more to do than others.
Take for instance the difference between the string players
and the percussion sections. While the strings <em>almost
always</em> have to play frequently in every movement of a
given work, the percussion sections often have to sit back
and count measures. Often they <em>won't even have to play a
single note</em> in a given movement, and frequently they
must sit out an entire work during a performance if their
instrument isn't even needed.</p>
<p>Counting measures can be a difficult task. With tempos
changing throughout a work and the thought that really one is
just staring at a long chain of blank measures, it is easy to
get lost or distracted and miss an entrance. Some of these
musicians might be getting paid more to count measures than
to actually produce sound!</p>
<p>Missing an entrance during a performance can be quite an
embarrassing moment for an orchestral performer. Hopefully
this will never happen to you. To keep count, try writing in
musical cues into your parts and writing little reminders.
Practice the entire part along with a recording, being sure
to pay as much attention to the counting during practice as
you would during a performance. This will help you feel more
comfortable about how long you need to count measures and how
your entrance will sound.</p>
<div>2008-10-18@<em>4:43pm</em></div>
</div>
</body>
</html>
```

This structure gives us a number of sibling elements (an <h1>, several <p>, and a <div>), all children of the outermost <div> element. Using the adjacent sibling selector, we can target the first <p> element, the two <p> elements after it, or the final <div> element. Each of these selectors are shown here:

```
h1 + p  /* Selects only the first paragraph. */
p + p   /* Selects only the last two paragraphs. */
p + div /* Selects only the inner <div> element. */
```

Selecting siblings in this manner can be useful, as it provides a way to use a document's source order for styling hooks. It's common, for instance, to use the first paragraph after a top-level heading as a summary or introduction to a given piece. We can therefore use the adjacent sibling selector to present this introductory first paragraph specially, as we do here:

```
<head>
<title>Adjacent Sibling Combinator Example</title>
<style type="text/css">
    h1 + p { font-style: italic; }
    h1 + p em { font-weight: bold; }
</style>
</head>
```

In the first CSS rule, we use italics to make the first paragraph stand out. In addition to that, we further chain the adjacent sibling combinator with a descendant combinator in the second CSS rule in order to present the <em> elements within the first paragraph in bold type; otherwise, the emphasis would be missed with the default italic style. The results of these styles are shown in Figure 2-7.

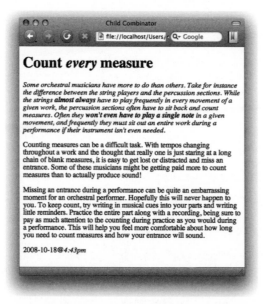

Figure 2-7. Using the adjacent sibling selector, you can present the leading paragraph after a heading as a summary.

General sibling combinator

The **general sibling combinator**, introduced in CSS3, is similar to the adjacent sibling combinator in that it selects the subject on its right if that element is a sibling that follows the subject on its left. However, whereas the adjacent sibling combinator requires that the subject on the right *immediately* follow the subject on the left, the general sibling combinator doesn't. The only requirement is that the two elements are siblings of one another and the subject on the left precedes the one on the right.

This combinator is written using a tilde sign (~). Using the same document structure used in the previous examples, this means you could use the general sibling selector to similar but not identical effect, and you have a few more ways you could write the selectors. Instead of targeting only the first <p> element, you would target *all* of the <p> elements:

```
h1 ~ p /* Selects all of the paragraphs. */
p ~ p /* Selects only the last two paragraphs. */
p ~ div /* Selects only the inner <div> element. */
h1 ~ div /* Also selects only the inner <div> element. */
```

Of particular illustrative interest is the last selector, h1 ~ div, which in this instance behaves the same way as p + div does. Note, however, that neither the adjacent sibling combinator nor the general sibling combinator allows you to construct a selector that targets the <h1> element, since that element is the first child of the outermost <div>. You could target it using any of the following selectors instead:

```
h1
h1:first-child
div h1
div > h1
body > div :first-child
```

These examples draw on much of the capability of CSS selectors you've learned about in this chapter. Notice how any number of any combinators can be used in conjunction with one another to create CSS rules that are ever more precise. In this way, CSS selectors provide extremely surgical accuracy when targeting elements to style.

However, this flexibility also begs an obvious question: which selector is best in which situation? Interestingly, there is no simple answer to this question because it often falls to the CSS developer to judge each situation appropriately. That said, we'll discuss this and similar issues in Chapter 6. In the meantime, let's continue exploring the fundamental concepts of CSS itself.

Property values and units

As you know, a single CSS declaration contains at most one property (although it may be a shorthand property that expands to more than one simultaneously) and at least one value. Learning which values can go with which properties is part of the process of becoming proficient in CSS. A value is composed of tokens that represent an amount of some unit.

Although a single value can only be described using one kind of unit, values of different units may be used together in the same declaration. Some units can be used in contexts where others cannot, such as temporal (time-based) units in aural style sheets. Moreover, using some units in certain situations can actually cause undesirable, or unintended, consequences despite being perfectly legal.

Broadly speaking, CSS units can be classified either by the type of tokenization they employ (how they're written and what they reference) or their characteristics, such as whether they are computed relative to some other value or used as specified. It's both illustrative of CSS's diverse capabilities as well as instructional to closely examine the different kinds of units that can be used in CSS declarations. These values are, both literally and figuratively, what ultimately give your designs dimension and color.

Keywords and font names

Keywords are extremely prevalent in CSS. These are specific tokens that are known by the user agent and always mean the same thing to that user agent. An example is font-style: italic. The value italic in this declaration is a keyword[12] that computes to a specific variation of typeface italicization.

Another place where you'll often see keywords used is in the color property's values, such as blue, yellow, or green. The CSS2.1 specification defines 17 color keywords (aqua, black, blue, fuchsia, gray, green, lime, maroon, navy, olive, orange, purple, red, silver, teal, white, and yellow), although these keywords may not always compute to the exact same color in different user agents. While not valid CSS2.1, all current major web browsers also support extended *SVG color keywords* (such as darkolivegreen), which are part of the CSS3 draft.

Although not technically a keyword, a font name is similar. To style text in a particular font, you use a declaration such as font-family: Helvetica to provide a comma-separated list of fonts to use. If the first font isn't available, each subsequent value in the list is attempted, defaulting to the standard system font if none are. Some keywords, such as serif, sans-serif, or monospace, can be used to generically refer to a particular class of fonts, allowing the user agent to automatically pick the first one in the class that is available for its use.

CSS3 also returns support for so-called "web fonts" that was removed in CSS2.1. With it, you can reference a downloadable font file as you might a background image and give it a name using the @ font-face at-rule. Once you've defined it, you can then reference the font name in a font-family declaration to use it.

> *An at-rule is a CSS rule that begins with the @ symbol. These are used to include special CSS instructions for a particular subject area or medium. Common uses include @import to import one style sheet into another, @page to define page-specific properties in print media, @media for rules directed at a specific media type, and @font-face for importing and generating fonts. We discuss the use of many of the various at-rules throughout this book, particularly when we discuss styling for print (Chapter 4), mobile (Chapter 5), and font importing (Chapter 11).*

Unlike the keywords for color, whose values can differ across implementations, some keywords are like shorthand for a different kind of value. Examples of this can be seen in common declarations like

---

12. Incidentally, the property font-style is also, technically, a keyword. Indeed, all property names are keywords to a certain extent.

`font-weight: bold`. Here, the `bold` value actually references a number, specifically 700, which represents a precise amount of typeface bolding.

Numbers

There are many kinds of numbers in computing, and CSS is no exception. CSS defines several categories of number values composed of ordinary **numbers** versus **non-negative numbers** and **numbers with unit identifiers** versus those without unit identifiers. A number can be either an integer like 1 or 5, or a real (that is, decimal) number like `.3` or `2.5`. Ordinary numbers can be prefixed with either a - or a + to indicate their sign, while non-negative numbers cannot.[13]

A **unit identifier** denotes what sort of measurement the number is intended to represent. Unit identifiers reference different types of values, and certain unit identifiers can be used only in certain places. CSS can represent units of lengths, percentages, angles, time, and frequencies.

Lengths

Units that represent length are the most common category of unit identifier. A **length** in CSS refers to a horizontal or vertical measurement. Length units are used in values for properties like `width`, `height`, and the other CSS box model properties.

A length measurement can be one of two possible types: **relative lengths** or **absolute lengths**. Relative length units specify measurements based on the computed value of some other length, while absolute lengths reference exact dimensions of the output medium. As such, style sheets that use relative units can scale across different output mediums with more ease than can absolute units.

Relative length units

For all values in which you specify relative units, the user agent needs to arrive at an actual value before the properties they are used in can be rendered. To perform this calculation, the user agent takes the relative value and computes it against some reference value, typically either another element's computed length or some formula defined by the rendering engine itself.

In CSS2.1, there are three relative length units:

- The em unit denotes lengths in terms of the element's font size, or its parent's font size when an em is being used to compute the element's own `font-size` value. One **em** (1em) is a typographic unit[14] equal to a font's point size. In other words, the width of one em is identical to the width of an em dash (—) as drawn in whatever the current font and font size is.

- The ex unit denotes lengths in terms of the element's font's **x-height**, so termed because it is often equal to the height of a lowercase letter "x." One x-height (1ex) is more precisely equal to the distance between a typeface's baseline and its mean line. In many instances, this also approximates half of an em (`.5em`).

- The px unit denotes lengths in terms of pixels on the viewing device. Although web designers are accustomed to thinking of pixels as absolute units, they are actually defined relative to the

---

13. Actually, you *can* prefix a non-negative number with a + but this is completely redundant as the number's sign is already known. Obviously, you can't prefix a non-negative number with a -.

14. In some typographic texts, an em is more formally known as a quad-width. Interestingly, typographers also refer to a unit known as an en, which is defined as one-half of an em. However, CSS does not specify an en unit.

resolution of the device. In fact, the CSS specifications explicitly remark that user agents should rescale pixel values if the device's pixel density is dramatically different from typical monitor resolutions.

> *Pixels are interesting beasts. The word itself is an abbreviation for "picture element." Traditionally, pixels are understood to be colored dots on a device's display, called* **device pixels***. They are the physical mechanism by which the device creates an image using a collection of pixels.* **CSS pixels***, however, are not the same thing because different devices have different pixel-to-space ratios and, moreover, various display systems have variable screen resolutions.*
>
> *Large kiosk-style displays may have a very low pixel to space ratio, while some of the newer high-resolution mobile devices such as the iPhone have very tight pixel densities. This pixel density is measured in* **dots per inch** *(dpi). At some point, an assumption about what one CSS pixel is going to represent must be made, because trying to control device pixels directly is simply infeasible. Browsers and CSS parsers today all assume a resolution of 96dpi by default. In other words, whatever the browser renders as one inch across is the same as 96 pixels.*
>
> *Certain browsers (Internet Explorer, we're looking at you) incorrectly treat CSS pixel units as fixed, absolute values. They are not resizable using built-in features to change text sizes.*

Though still a W3C Working Draft, the CSS3 Values and Units module is slated to add support for six more:

- The gd unit denotes lengths in terms of a text layout grid, which is a common typographic layout technique used in East Asian languages. The unit's computed value depends on the value of the layout-grid property, but this property has yet to be fully formed. We don't anticipate gd units to be viable for quite some time.

- The rem unit functions similarly to the em unit, except that it always references the computed value of the root element's font-size property instead of the current element's font-size value. When used on the root element itself, one of these units (1rem) computes to the same value as the medium keyword. Using rem units would be useful when inheritance issues make sizing elements and text with em units difficult.

- The vw unit denotes lengths as hundredths of the viewport's width. One hundred vw units (100vw) are equal to the current width of the viewport. This will allow designers to easily scale lengths based on the width of the browser window.

- The vh unit denotes lengths as hundredths of the viewport's height. One hundred vh units (100vh) are equal to the current height of the viewport. Again, this provides a capability to scale lengths based on the browser window's current size.

- The vm unit denotes lengths as hundredths of the shortest viewport axis (either its height or its width, whichever is smaller). If the viewport is wider than it is high, then one hundred vm units (100vm) equal its height; otherwise they equal its width.

- The ch unit denotes lengths roughly in terms of the average width of the current typeface's characters. Like the gd unit, there are still unanswered questions that surround this unit, and its use is not expected to be viable for some time.

Absolute length units

There are five absolute length units (in both CSS2.1 and CSS3):

- The in unit denotes lengths in terms of **inches**.
- The cm unit denotes lengths in terms of **centimeters**.
- The mm unit denotes lengths in terms of **millimeters**.
- The pt unit denotes lengths in terms of **points**. One point (1pt) is exactly $1/72$ of an inch.
- The pc unit denotes lengths in terms of **picas**. One pica (1pc) is exactly 12 points (12pt).

Using absolute units makes a lot of sense when you are designing for physical media, most notably such as when you are using the print media type. On the other hand, if you're styling for screen output, then relative units will typically serve you better than absolute ones. Being able to reformat content for the specified output is a simple and powerful way to make your content more readable and accessible. Although many user agents are capable of translating relative units into absolute sizes, precision is more easily available to you when you use the native unit in the rendering media.

Percentages

Properties that allow percentage values always reference some other value, defined by the property itself. Percentages are defined by CSS as any number followed by a percent sign (%). They're especially useful when you want to denote values in a relative fashion without worrying about the specific measuring unit being used.

For example, an element's width property can take a length value using any of the units described earlier. Therefore, the following two CSS rules specify the same length:

```
#example { width: 2in;}
#example { width: 144pt; }
```

If we add a child <div> element to this example and we wish it to be three-fourths the width of its parent, we could use any of the following three CSS rules to accomplish that. Only the one that uses percentage values, however, won't have to be changed if the CSS rule that defines the width of the <div>'s parent does:

```
#example div { width: 1.75in;}
#example div { width: 108pt; }
#example div { width: 75%; }
```

Put another way, when you need to alter your design by changing the elements' widths, using the percentage value for the child <div> means you only have to change the parent's CSS rule. In complex designs, taking advantage of opportunities to reduce your edit-per-change ratio like this can be a significant factor in easing maintenance chores.

Time, frequencies, and angles

In aural media, there are some properties that accept units in terms of temporal lengths (time), frequencies, and angles. Both times and frequencies are (sensibly) non-negative numbers. Times can be denoted in either milliseconds, using the ms unit identifier, or full seconds, using the s unit identifier. Frequencies can be denoted either in hertz, using the hz unit identifier, or kilohertz, using the khz unit identifier.

Frequency units make it possible to write aural style sheets with bass and treble control for things such as the speaker's pitch. For instance, a declaration such as voice-pitch: 120hz *specifies the pitch for a typical human male voice (*200hz *is a bass sound, whereas* 6khz *is treble sound; typical female voices are around* 210hz*). Time units allow aural style sheets to influence the rhythm of speech[15] with properties such as* pause-before *or* pause-after*. For instance, a dramatic pause before beginning to quote a speech may be appropriate and could be specified in CSS with a rule such as* blockquote.speech { pause-before: 3s; }*.*

_____

15. In linguistics, the rhythm, stress, and intonation of speech are collectively known as prosody. CSS also provides many keyword values for properties that influence stress and intonation as well as rhythm of speech.

Angles are used in properties such as azimuth that define where the listener is in three-dimensional space. Angle values can be defined in terms of degrees using the deg unit identifier, grads ($1/400$ of a full circle, or $1/100$ of a right angle) using the grad unit identifier, radians using the rad unit identifier, and turns using the turn unit identifier. Negative angles are normalized to a 360° range such that, for example, -90deg is equivalent to 270deg.

Strings

A **string value** is an arbitrary run of characters denoted by single or double quotation marks. We've already seen string values inside of attribute selectors, but they are also used within property values. The content property, which produces CSS generated content, is one such example:

```
/* Double-quoted string value in attribute selector. */
blockquote[cite^="http://en.wikipeia.org/wiki/"]::before {
    /* Single-quoted string value in property value. */
    content: 'From Wikipedia: ';
}
```

We discuss string values and how to escape characters within them (using string escape sequences) in more detail Chapter 3.

Functional notation

In CSS, functional notation is used to specify values for a number of properties. If you have any experience with formal programming languages, you know that a function optionally takes arguments (parameters) and returns values. To use an example from PHP, a call to a function like date("Y-m-d") returns a string from the date function formatted using the argument Y-m-d, which (at the time of this writing) ultimately evaluates to 2009-02-05. PHP syntax is derived from the C programming language, as is the syntax for CSS values that use functional notation.

Values in functional notation look similar: a term (function name) is followed by a pair of matched parentheses, between which arguments may appear in a comma-separated list. The arguments themselves are dependent on the function being called.

URI references: the url() function

The url() function takes one argument, which is—predictably—a URI.[16] It is used in CSS rules such as background-image or @import to reference the URI of another resource like an image or different CSS file. The URI may be a relative, or absolute, path, or it may be a fully qualified URI. Relative URIs reference resources relative to the location of the CSS file itself, not the documents that they are linked to. The argument value may be surrounded by quotes or left unquoted. Here are some examples:

```
/* Unquoted, relative URI. */
div#violas { background-image: url(violas.png); }
/* Single-quoted fully qualified URI. */
@import url('http://natasha.example.com/main.css');
```

If a URI value contains whitespace, parentheses, single quotes, or double quotes, those characters should be appropriately escaped. This is done either by preceding them with a backslash (\) or by using the correct URI-escape sequence. For instance, the following two URIs are equivalent:

```
/* Whitespace is URI-escaped. */
#logo { background-image: url(Company%20Logo.jpg); }
/* Whitespace is backslash escaped. */
#logo { background-image: url(Company\ Logo.jpg); }
```

Color functions: rgb(), rgba(), hsl(), and hsla()

Representing color in CSS2.1 can only be accomplished by mixing values of red, green, and blue (RGB).[17] The current draft of CSS3 adds the ability to do so using a combination of hue, saturation, and lightness (HSL) as well. Both methods are widely understood by graphic designers and supported by computer graphics applications.

RGB color values are expressed as a list of three integers or percentages. Integers can range from 0 to 255, while percentages can be any decimal value from 0% to 100%,[18] so a numerical value of 255 is equivalent to a percentage value of 100%. Each value in the list represents the color channel for its position. A declaration such as color: rgb(85, 107, 47) specifies 85 as the red value, 107 as the green value, and 47 as the blue, resulting in a sort of olive color.

Any visual element can also be made partially transparent with the use of the opacity property. This property accepts a non-negative number in the range of 0 (completely transparent) to 1 (completely opaque). CSS3 introduces an rgba() function, where the "A" stands for the alpha (transparency) channel. This functions identically to rgb(), but accepts a fourth argument representing an opacity value. As such, the following two CSS rules are equivalent:

---

16. The url() function recognizes any valid IRI (that is, Internationalized Resource Identifier), not merely URLs. Despite this, for legacy reasons, the function's name is still url() and not iri().
17. This is true even for print media—color cannot be declared as a combination of cyan, magenta, yellow, and black (CMYK) inks. It is up to the user agent to perform an appropriate translation from RGB to CMYK colors, if necessary.
18. Technically, you can specify values outside of this range, but the user agent is expected clip them. In other words, a specified value of -50 is equivalent to 0, and a specified value of 110% is equivalent to 100%.

```
#example {
    color: rgb(85, 107, 47);
    opacity: .5;
}
#example { color: rgba(85, 107, 47, .5); }
```

Representing colors as RGB triples have certain limitations: they imply certain kinds of hardware (such as CRT monitors), and they aren't how humans natively perceive light. To address these concerns, the latest drafts of the CSS3 Color Module add HSL values, which are considered to be more intuitive than RGB values and easier to comprehend. Using the hsl() function, you can declare a color hue as an angle on the color wheel and that color's saturation and lightness as percentages.

A value of 0 or 360 in the first argument represents red, 120 represents green, and 240 represents blue. Full color saturation would be denoted as a value of 100% in the second argument, while a value of 0% would display a shade of gray. Finally, the third argument denotes the lightness (sometimes also called luminosity) value; 100% is white, 0% black, and 50% "normal." Here are a few examples of the hsl() function:

```
hsl(0, 100%, 50%) /* Red, equivalent to #F00 or rgb(255, 0, 0). */
hsl(0, 100%, 100%) /* White, or #FFF */
hsl(240, 0%, 100%) /* Also #FFF */
hsl(190, 25%, 50%) /* Blue-ish gray, specifically #5F949F */
```

There is also an hsla() function in the specification to allow for alpha transparency as a fourth argument identical to the rgba() function. Since the CSS3 specification is still in the works and only Gecko and WebKit currently support hsl() or hsla() values, you needn't concern yourself with these options too much. They are, however, something to keep an eye on and look forward to.

> The color property is also unique in accepting a special kind of notation to represent color values called hexadecimal notation.[19] Hexadecimal values use hexadecimal digits (0 through F, which is base 16) and look like #FFFFFF, called a **hex triple**. That value is equivalent to the white keyword and to rgb(100%,100%,100%).
>
> Hex values are really just RGB values in disguise: the first pair of numbers indicate the amount of red, the second pair indicate the amount of green, and the third the amount of blue. For any hex color where the R, G, and B values are doubled, such as #CC33FF, you can use a three-character shorthand: #C3F. Hex values are case insensitive, so #CC33FF is the same as #cc33ff (or #c3f for that matter).

---

19. Actually, the color property is unique for additional reasons than merely this one, but a full discussion of the color property is beyond the scope of this book. In CSS3, how colors are defined is the topic for an entire module called CSS Color, and it is currently making its way toward standardization as of this writing. The latest working draft of the CSS3 Color module is available online at http://www.w3.org/TR/css3-color/.

Generated content functions: attr() and counter()

The `attr()` and `counter()` functions work in tandem with the content property to return the value of an element's attribute or the counter named in its argument, respectively. In CSS2.1, both functions return a string, although in the current draft of CSS3 the `attr()` function will accept an optional second argument that specifies the type of value to return.

This can often be used to extract additional content from your markup and make it visible as rendered content. For example, given this HTML:

```
<a href="http://natasha.example.com/"
title"Natasha O&rsquo;Reilly, Baroque Cellist">My site!</a>
```

the following CSS declaration can render the value of the `href` attribute:

```
content: attr(href); /* Displays "http://natasha.example.com" */
```

Both the `attr()` and `counter()` functions are discussed at much greater length in Chapter 3.

Basic math for computing lengths: the calc() function

The `calc()`function is part of the CSS3 draft, but is not yet implemented by any of the mainstream browsers. Permitted anywhere length values are, it is intended to be a way to calculate length values dynamically using basic math operators like addition (+), subtraction (-), division (/), and multiplication (*). This would enable expressions that mix relative length units to be specified, but have the actual value of the expression substituted as the resulting value.

One situation where this capability would be useful is where elements have margins specified using relative units but need width values specified by taking into account some amount of fixed units. For instance, here's a CSS rule that would (theoretically) make an element's width exactly 25 pixels wider than half of its parent's width, and will also subtract the width of its margins, whatever that is at any given time:

```
#example {
    margin-left: 1em;
    margin-right: 1em;
    width: calc((100%/2 + 25px) - (1em*2));
}
```

Note that grouping parentheses are likely to be allowed in `calc()` expressions, and that the + and - operators have lower precedence than the / or * operators. Again, we stress that this function is not implemented in any mainstream browser. However, basic math like this has been a desirable feature for quite some time, and we're excited about the possibility of seeing it implemented one day.

Visual rendering and formatting concepts

When it comes to implementing visual designs in CSS, two intrinsic concepts are perhaps the most often overlooked. These two concepts are document flow and the CSS box model, and the two are very closely related. It's these two fundamental concepts that make using CSS radically different than using other tools. Therefore, these fundamentals of how CSS works deserve a closer look.

CSS boxes and document flow

When any element is rendered visually, it occupies a rectangular region of visual space. These rectangles are referred to as **CSS boxes**. For instance, every visible <p> element on a page creates an invisible rectangle on the screen inside of which the content of that paragraph is displayed, or *flows into*. All of a paragraph's content, typically text, also render as CSS boxes, albeit boxes of a different kind. The <p> elements create what are known as **block-level** boxes, whereas the strings of text within them create **inline-level** boxes. These two different kinds of CSS boxes flow onto the screen in very different ways.

How CSS boxes flow when they are rendered is not determined by chance, but by a precise system that a renderer (such as a web browser's rendering engine) uses called **document flow**. Being aware of how this system works—and how to manipulate it—is a core part of mastering CSS-based design. Every element on a web page, every headline, every list item, every paragraph, and even every line of text and each individual character within every line of text follows the rules of document flow to determine where they end up on the screen.

Fundamentally, the rules are simple: block-level boxes always flow *one on top of another*, like bricks in a vertical stack. In contrast, inline boxes flow one after the other horizontally, literally *in the same horizontal line* as any neighboring inline elements. A user agent's built-in style sheet determines what elements create what kinds of CSS boxes.

For example, paragraphs are initially declared to be block-level boxes, so each time you define a new <p> element (and thereby generate a new block-level CSS box), the browser places that paragraph underneath any block-level boxes that came before it in the document flow. This is why two sibling <p> elements always create two distinct chunks of text, one atop the other, by default. Other elements that create block-level boxes are headlines, <div> elements, and lists (not list items, but the list item's containing elements, <ul>, <ol>, and <dl>).

Runs of text, and indeed each individual character, or **glyph**, are rendered as inline boxes. If there's not enough horizontal space for an inline box to fit on one line, then the boxes get bumped down to the next line. This is why English text inside of a paragraph begins at the paragraph's top-left corner, flows horizontally across the width of the paragraph, and then ends at the bottom-right corner (known as left-to-right, or "LTR" text flow).

Such runs of text that are inside block-level elements create **anonymous inline boxes**. They are "anonymous" because a CSS selector can't explicitly target them (without the help of pseudo-elements). However, many elements that can be targeted create inline boxes by default, too. Some examples of such elements are images, links, and emphasized text (the <em> and <strong> elements, for instance).

These rules, where paragraphs are laid out vertically and runs of text start at a content area's top-left corner and flow to their destination at the bottom-right corner is, of course, the normal direction in which content flows when written in the English language. However, this is not the case for all languages. Hebrew is an example of a language that reverses the direction of flow so that it begins from the top-right corner and ends at the bottom-left corner (known as right-to-left, or "RTL" text flow). Arabic, Farsi, and Urdu are also written using right-to-left text flow. Chinese is an example of a language that can be represented by writing ideographs in either direction, so it is said to be bidirectional (or "BiDi" for short).

It's easy enough to see how document flow affects how certain glyphs are rendered. Based on the language specified in the web page's <html> element, the web browser simply places the first character at either the top-left or top-right corner of the paragraph and then places each successive character it sees to the right or left of the one before it. Recall that the root elements in our web pages in this chapter have begun like this:

```
<html xmlns="http://www.w3.org/1999/xhtml" xml:lang="en" lang="en">
```

Since you've defined that this web page is written in English by specifying the xml:lang="en" and lang=»en» attributes, the web browser will assume a normal flow for what is expected in English, specifically a direction of left-to-right text. If you're feeling experimental, go ahead and add the dir attribute with a value of rtl (short for right-to-left) to the <html> element, and you'll see that now every headline and paragraph is right-aligned (instead of how it was previously left-aligned) and the punctuation marks are all on the "wrong side" of the words.

CSS boxes interact with one another in particular ways. Inline boxes are always rendered inside a block-level box, known as their **containing block**. If a CSS box's containing block is sized at unchanging dimensions and the box is too large to fit within it, then it will **overflow** (become visible outside of) the container. However, this overflow doesn't typically affect the visual positioning of any other CSS boxes inside of *different* containing blocks, such as text in the next paragraph. The result, of course, is overlapping text. In such a case, each of the two paragraphs' individual inline boxes are said to be *in a different flow* from the other.

As a designer, you influence the layout of a page by manipulating CSS boxes so that they fall into the document flow the way you want them to, much like a game of Tetris. The value of an element's display property determines what kind of CSS box it will create. Here's an example of what the default CSS rules that web browsers use to make <p> elements block-level and <strong> elements inline-level might look like:

```
p { display: block; }
strong { display: inline; }
```

Of course, you can override these default styles and make any element generate any kind of box you want—something that was flat-out impossible before the advent of CSS. For example, you could add a CSS rule that makes <img> elements generate block-level boxes instead of inline-level boxes, as shown by the following CSS rule. Among other things, this obviates the need for explicit line breaks inside the markup of documents that are used for the same effect.

```
img { display: block; }
```

Block-level boxes that have no specific width declared extend as wide as they can while still fitting within their containing block. Inline-level boxes, however, grow only as wide as they need to be to make their content fit within them. Inline boxes are like shrink-wrap that surrounds whatever their content is.

The display property can also be given a plethora of other values, each of which relates to a specific formatting context. The two most common formatting contexts are the ones we've just discussed, block and inline, which provide the basis for the behaviors of the others. Another common kind of CSS box that you've no doubt encountered is a **list-item box**. Not surprisingly, <li> elements are defined with a default CSS rule such as li { display: list-item; }. We discuss list-item boxes in detail in Chapter 3.

A fourth formatting context is one for laying out tables. Of course, the <table> element uses this by default, perhaps initialized in a user agent's default style sheet with a CSS rule such as table { display: table; }. Tables themselves behave like block-level elements, but unlike block CSS boxes, the contents of table CSS boxes can behave like rows (using display: table-row) or columns (using display: table-column).

The point here is that a CSS box is to a CSS developer as a paintbrush is to a fine artist; choosing different brushes will create different effects on a canvas, and choosing which kind of CSS box to render will similarly create different effects in your visual design. Learning to use each of them for their intended purpose can dramatically improve your capabilities. If you "go with the flow," your CSS code will be more robust, less prone to browser bugs, and more optimized, all without any additional efforts.

CSS positioning schemes

In addition to the display property, other CSS properties also affect how a CSS box is rendered and how it interacts with the rules of document flow. Two of these are position (which accepts a value that's one of static, relative, absolute, or fixed), and float (which can have a value of either left or right.) Together, these two properties render an element using one of three different positioning schemes.

The first of these schemes is the **normal document flow** that we discussed in the previous section. Another is **absolute positioning**, in which the absolutely positioned element (and all its descendant elements) is removed from the normal document flow and put into its own context, as though it were the only element being rendered. This makes it possible to position any chunk of content independently from any other chunk, as each chunk is guaranteed not to influence the layout of the other—each chunk is in its own flow.

The third positioning scheme is **floated positioning**, a sort of middle point between the normal flow and absolute positioning. Floated boxes are "half removed" from the normal document flow, so that they flow somewhat independently of block-level boxes but still affect the flow of inline-level boxes. Let's take a quick look at each of these by examining the position and float properties and their possible values.

Static positioning

By default, all elements are positioned statically, and indeed static is the initial value of the position property. In other words, an element that is "statically positioned," or "not (specially) positioned," is simply in the normal document flow. Typically, you'll use the static value to restore a previously positioned element back to the normal document flow.

Using the previous example of two sibling paragraphs, you can say that each is statically positioned and therefore they flow as you would expect, one atop the other. Similarly, other block-level elements such as the <div>s in the following example are also statically positioned:

```
<div class="strings" id="violins">
</div>
<div class="strings" id="violas">
</div>
```

Since <div> elements are also block-level elements by default, these will also stack one atop the other as you would expect them to when a position declaration is not in effect. Therefore, lacking other CSS rules, every element is initially positioned statically. This is equivalent to a default style sheet's CSS rule like this:

```
* { position:static; }
```

Relative positioning

Using relative positioning, you can change where an element's CSS box is rendered without changing the document flow or influencing the layout of other elements. Therefore, elements that are relatively positioned are still in the "normal" document flow, and their neighbors behave as though they were positioned statically, even though they're not. An example will help to illustrate this, so let's build on our previous example and look at what relative positioning does.

In this document, you have three block-level <div> elements that demarcate the contents of sections of an orchestra. The violin section is first in the markup source, and so it is rendered at the top of the document. The next <div> is for the violas, and it renders underneath the violins, and the final <div> element for the cellos similarly follows suit. Each of the <div> elements is given width and height dimensions, a background-color, and a border to help them stand out for the sake of this illustration.

```
<!DOCTYPE html PUBLIC "-//W3C//DTD XHTML 1.0 Strict//EN"
    "http://www.w3.org/TR/xhtml1/DTD/xhtml1-strict.dtd">
<html xmlns="http://www.w3.org/1999/xhtml" xml:lang="en" lang="en">
<head>
<title>String Sections</title>
<style type="text/css" media="screen">
    div {
        width:200px;
        height:100px;
        background-color: #B3B3B3;
        border:2px dotted #4C4C4C;
            }
</style>
</head>
<body>
<div id="violins" class="strings">
    The violin section
</div>
<div id="violas" class="strings">
    The viola section
</div>
<div id="cellos" class="strings">
    The cello section
</div>
</body>
</html>
```

There are no surprises with all the elements statically positioned as they are here. Now let's position the middle <div> (the violas) relatively using the CSS rule shown here. You can see the results in Figure 2-8.

```
<style type="text/css" media="screen">
div {
    width:200px;
    height:100px;
    background-color: #B3B3B3;
    border:2px dotted #4C4C4C;
}
div#violas {
    position: relative;
    top: -20px;
    left: 25%;
}
</style>
```

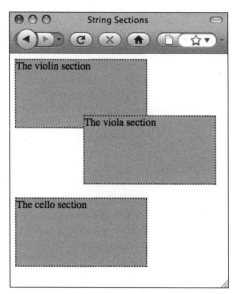

Figure 2-8. Positioning the viola <div> relatively moves the element's CSS box to a new location but doesn't affect the normal document flow.

As you can see, after you declare that the violas <div> will use relative positioning, you use any of the four **box offset properties** (top, right, bottom, and left) in conjunction with one another to move the CSS box to its new place. This example uses a *negative* value (-20px) on the top property to move the CSS box "up" by the specified amount, but a *positive* value on the bottom property (such as bottom: 20px;) would have achieved the same result. The example also uses the left property with a positive percentage value to move the CSS box to the right. Relative positioning can therefore be described as moving the display of a CSS box to a new location by a certain offset as calculated by where it *would have been* displayed if the element were statically positioned.

Two things are especially noteworthy here. First, notice that there are 20 extra pixels of blank space below the viola <div>. While the display of the relatively positioned <div> has moved, the space it occupies in the document flow has remained the same—the viola <div> is still in the normal document flow, but is relatively positioned within it. In other words, as far as this <div>'s siblings are concerned, *it hasn't been moved at all*, which is why its CSS box now overlaps the one that came before it and why there is extra "blank" space beneath it.

Second, notice that if you resize the browser window and make it bigger, the <div> will move farther right, while resizing the browser window so that it is smaller will move it farther to the left. What we have here is a situation where the browser automatically computes the appropriate left offset value by dividing the current viewport's width by 4 (that is, by 25%). If the browser viewport is exactly 400 pixels wide, then the left offset value will be computed as 100px.

Using relative units can lead to some interesting results, but when you use them it's very important to know what the unit is being calculated against. The reason 25% references "one fourth of the *viewport's* width" in this example is because there is no explicit **nearest positioned ancestor**, and in such a case the root element (that is, the browser viewport) is implicitly given that role. We can change that, however, by adding another element and giving it a position value other than static. Now our markup looks like this:

```
<div id="violins" class="strings">
    The violin section
</div>
<div id="viola-wrapper">
<div id="violas" class="strings">
        The viola section
</div>
</div>
<div id="cellos" class="strings">
    The cello section
</div>
```

And our CSS looks like this:

```
<style type="text/css" media="screen">
div {
    width:200px;
    height:100px;
    background-color: #B3B3B3;
    border: 2px dotted #4C4C4C;
}
div#viola-wrapper { position: relative; }
div#violas {
    position: relative;
    top: -20px;
    left: 25%;
}
```

Now, the 25% offset in the CSS rule targeting div#violas will always be calculated as 50px because the calculation is being performed against the width of div#viola-wrapper (earlier declared to always be 200px). By positioning the new wrapper <div>, it has become the nearest positioned ancestor for the violas <div>. You can optionally move the wrapper around by declaring offsets for it as well, but that's not necessary for establishing a positioned ancestor like this.

Absolute positioning

A single rendered document must have at least one normal flow, but you can define any number of additional ones by using the absolute positioning scheme. Doing so removes the absolutely positioned element from the first flow and places it into an entirely new flow of its own. The CSS box of the absolutely positioned element becomes the nearest positioned ancestor of that element's descendants, and the descendant elements' CSS boxes all assume a normal flow within their containing block.

All CSS boxes are drawn on a theoretically infinitely sized **canvas**. A web browser's viewport shows you only a portion of the canvas at any one time (that's why it's called a viewport in the first place), and provides you with scroll bars to position it over the area of the canvas you want to see. The size of the canvas is determined by examining the dimensions of CSS boxes and the current size of the viewport. If the viewport is taller than the height of the longest document flow, then the canvas extends to the bottom of the viewport and no farther. If a document flow is taller than the height of the viewport, then the canvas extends to the end of the tallest document flow.

The absolute positioning scheme takes effect when an element's position property is given either absolute or fixed as its value. Let's position the viola <div> again, but this time you'll use absolute positioning. The result of this change is shown in Figure 2-9.

```
<style type="text/css" media="screen">
div {
        width: 200px;
        height: 100px;
        background-color: #B3B3B3;
        border: 2px dotted #4C4C4C;
}
div#violas {
        position: absolute;
        top: -20px;
        left: 25%;
}
</style>
```

As you can see, this simple change has produced a dramatically different visual result. The viola <div> has shifted so far up the screen that it's being cropped at the top of the viewport. Moreover, there is no longer any blank space between the <div>s for the violins and cellos. Instead, they are touching one another, as though they were statically positioned sibling elements in the source code.

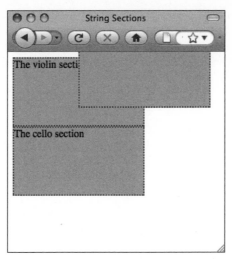

Figure 2-9. The viola `<div>` now uses absolute positioning with the same `top` and `left` offsets as before, but the visual result is markedly different than the result of using `relative` positioning.

By removing the viola `<div>` from the normal document flow with absolute positioning, the browser's rendering engine lays out the CSS boxes as though the viola section is a completely different visual layer. You now have two flows: one that exists inside the `<body>` element as normal, and one that exists only within the viola `<div>`, which no longer participates in the `<body>` element's flow. As happened before, since the viola `<div>` doesn't have a nearest positioned ancestor, its CSS box offsets are calculated against its new containing block, which in this context is known as the **initial containing block** (that is, the root CSS box).

It's trivial to determine when an absolutely positioned box, sometimes more succinctly referred to as an **AP box**, is being offset from the initial containing block. Using a CSS rule like the following will affix the top-left corner of the viola `<div>` to the top-left corner of the viewport:

```
div#violas {
    position: absolute;
    top: 0;
    left: 0;
}
```

This next CSS rule will affix the top-right corner of the violas `<div>` to the top-right corner of the viewport:

```
div#violas {
    position: absolute;
    top: 0;
    right: 0;
}
```

Ultimately, however, absolutely positioned elements are rendered based on their location in a particular flow of content, which is not necessarily relative to the viewport. As before, if we explicitly add a positioned ancestor element to our document, the CSS box of the nearest positioned ancestor element will be the one from which all box offsets for the absolutely positioned box are calculated. By appropriately structuring your document's markup in this way, you can move CSS boxes around to create arbitrarily complex visual layouts.

Fixed positioning

The other way to position an element with the absolute positioning scheme is to use fixed positioning. Fixed positioning works in the same way as absolute positioning does except that the CSS box offset is *always* calculated relative to the coordinates of the viewport, not the canvas. This subtle distinction means that the fixed element will remain motionless as the canvas for continuous media is moved underneath the viewport when you scroll. In paged media contexts where you have a page box instead of a viewport, fixed CSS boxes will be repeatedly rendered in the same place on every page.

In the following example, which includes numerous filler paragraphs in order to lengthen the normal document flow beyond the height of our canvas, the violas <div> is fixed in the center of the viewport, as though it were a watermark. As all offset properties and CSS box sizes are calculated relative to the viewport, we use percentage values to fill 50% of the viewport with the contents of the <div>'s CSS box and then center it by placing its top-left corner 25% away from the top-left corner of the viewport's 0,0 coordinate. Figure 2-10 shows the print preview result as rendered by Firefox 3.

```
div#violas {
        position: fixed;
        top: 25%;
        left: 25%;
        height: 50%;
        width: 50%;
        font-size: xx-large; /* merely for illustrative purposes */
}
```

Sadly, position: fixed is not supported at all in Internet Explorer 6 and earlier. Additionally, the WebKit rendering engine fails to treat each page box as individual viewport-like objects and instead seems to treat all of the page boxes together as though they were a single, extremely tall one. This results in fixed positioned elements not being repeated, but rather stretched and broken across page boxes. WebKit's print preview rendering of the same code is shown in Figure 2-11, and the print medium is discussed in further detail later in this book.

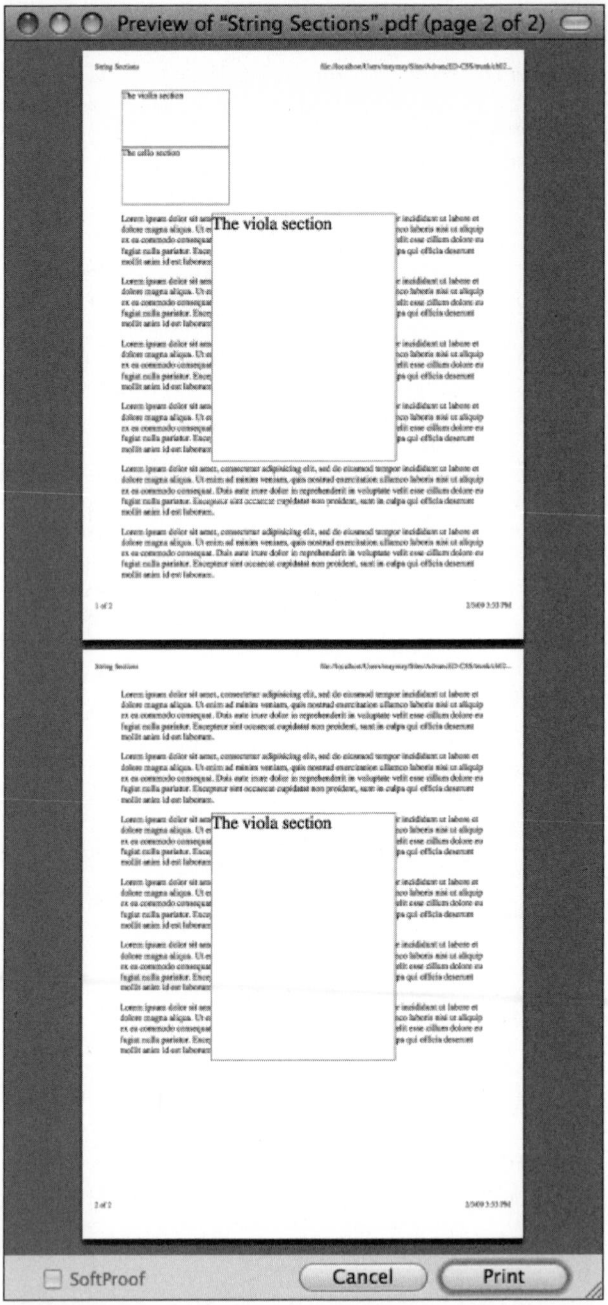

Figure 2-10. Firefox's Gecko rendering engine correctly repeats the `fixed` position `<div>` on each page of the printed output.

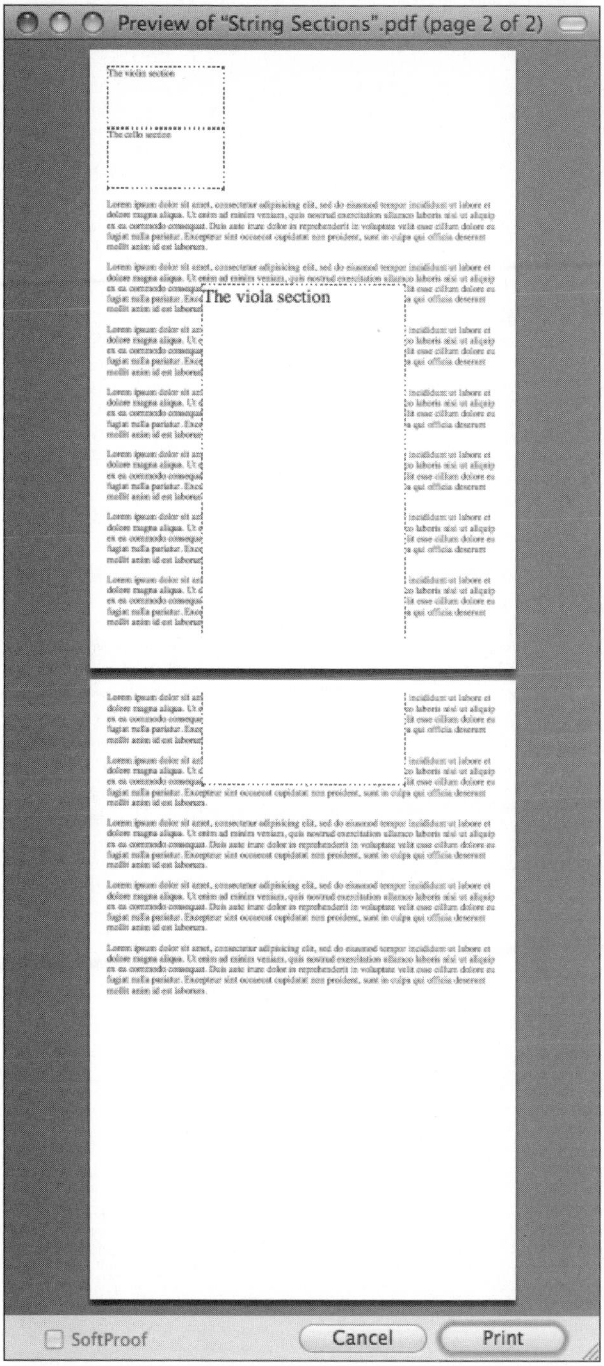

Figure 2-11. Safari's WebKit rendering engine incorrectly stretches the fixed position <div> across all pages of the printed output.

Floated CSS boxes

Any CSS box can be rendered using **floated positioning** by declaring the float property with a value other than none. Floated boxes are always implicitly transformed to block-level boxes, even if display: inline is specified on their elements. Despite this, because they are pulled out of the normal document flow, they size themselves similarly to inline boxes, shrinking their width and height to accommodate their contents unless explicit width or height dimensions are declared.

Floating a box moves it horizontally in the direction specified (either left or right) until its margin edge reaches the content edge of its containing block. Floated boxes are unique because they affect neighboring floated or inline CSS boxes, not other block-level boxes that aren't also floating. In fact, nonfloating block-level boxes behave as though the floated box doesn't even exist.

```
div#violas {
      float: left;
      width: auto;
      height: auto;
      border-color: yellow;
}
```

In this example, the violas <div> is floated to the left, its explicit width and height are removed, and it's given a different border-color for illustrative purposes. The result of these CSS rules is shown in Figure 2-12. As you can see, the dimensions of the floated violas <div> have shrunk to fit around its content, and moreover, the surrounding block-level <div> elements have shifted upward and are now touching one another. The only CSS box affected by the floated box is the inline box within the cellos <div>, which has been pushed aside.

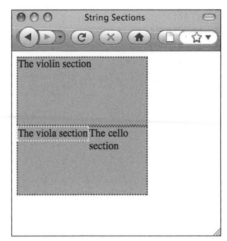

Figure 2-12. The floated violas <div> is removed from the normal document flow so block-level boxes ignore it, but inline boxes are still affected by its presence.

Stacking contexts

We're accustomed to thinking of web pages as a two-dimensional plane with an x- and a y-axis, but rendering engines lay out CSS boxes in three dimensions. The canvas can therefore be thought of as having an x-, y-, and z-axis. Depending on a web page's direction of flow, the top-left corner of the document flow (or the top-right corner in right-to-left flows) can be said to be at coordinate 0,0 on this imaginary graph of the canvas. The z-axis determines how near or far a particular CSS box is to the viewer's eyes. Each CSS box on a web page is positioned somewhere along the x-, y-, and z-axes on this imaginary graph.

In CSS, this z-axis is called the **stack level**. CSS boxes with higher z-axis values are considered "closer" to the viewer than CSS boxes with lower values so, for example, a box at coordinate 0,0,0 is said to be "behind" a box at coordinate 0,0,1. Figure 2-13 shows what such a graph might look like from a web browser's point of view.

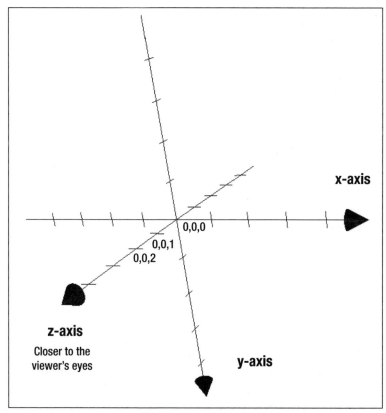

Figure 2-13. A three-dimensional graph has an x-, y-, and z-axis. CSS boxes are positioned somewhere along each of these three axes.

Each CSS box generated within the content area of another CSS box is actually being stacked on top of it, like a collage made with construction paper. As you continue nesting elements, you continue to stack CSS boxes one on top of another in an endless (and often invisible) tower. Among other things, it's for this reason why any background applied to the <body> element always appears to be behind any other element on the web page and why the most deeply nested elements always appear to be in front of all their parent elements.

Moreover, you can control where a CSS box is placed along this z-axis with CSS using the z-index property, which specifies a number that represents a point along this z-axis relative to the other CSS boxes in the same containing block. In other words, one CSS box with a z-index value of 5 is only in front of another CSS box with a z-index value of 1 if they are both rendered inside the same containing CSS box. If they are not, it is the relative z-index values of their containers that determine which element overlaps the other.

To illustrate this, let's first reposition our orchestra's three string <div>s absolutely such that they overlap one another. The results of the following CSS rules are shown in Figure 2-14.

```
div {
    width:200px;
    height:100px;
    background-color:#B3B3B3;
    border:2px dotted #4C4C4C;
    position: absolute;
}
div#violins {
    top:10px;
    left:30px;
}
div#violas {
    top:80px;
    left:90px;
}
div#cellos {
    top:50px;
    left:210px;
}
```

With no z-index properties declared explicitly, each element's z-index value is set to the initial (default) value of auto. The effect is the same as setting each element's z-index value to the same number since, when positioned absolutely like this, each box has the same containing block (the initial containing block, in this case). We can see that each box is layered according to its source order. That is, the cellos <div> is positioned "on top of" the previous <div> elements that came before it in the document markup.

Now, let's change the stacking order of these CSS boxes so that the cellos <div> is behind the others. This is achieved simply by giving it a negative z-index value. The effect of this additional declaration is shown in Figure 2-15.

```
div#cellos {
    top: 50px;
    left: 210px;
    z-index: -1;
}
```

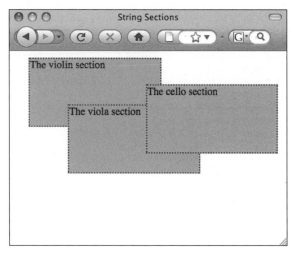

Figure 2-14. Each `<div>` element is now absolutely positioned so that they overlap one another in predictable ways.

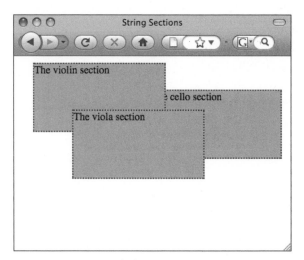

Figure 2-15. Adding `z-index` declarations changes the stacking order of CSS boxes within the same containing block relative to one another.

Another way to achieve this same effect could have been by giving positive z-index values to the other <div> elements. It also doesn't matter what these z-index values are, as long as they are higher than the one given to the other box. Here, we give the other <div> elements a z-index value of 5.

```
div#violins {
    top: 10px;
    left: 30px;
    z-index: 5;
}
div#violas {
    top: 80px;
    left: 90px;
    z-index: 2;
}
```

These CSS rules would position the div#violins element on top of both of the others, with the div#violas directly behind it. However, these values are relative to the others in the same containing block—they're not absolute coordinates. Therefore, if we once again added a wrapper <div> element to the violas <div> element and gave *it* a higher z-index value than the violins <div> element (say, 10), then the div#violas would once again overlap the div#violins, as before.

```
div#violins {
    top: 10px;
    left: 30px;
    z-index: 5;
}
div#viola-wrapper {
    position: relative;
    z-index: 10;
    /* Remove extraneous visuals for clarity. */
    background-color: transparent;
    border: none;
}
div#violas {
    top: 80px;
    left: 90px;
    z-index: 2;
}
```

As you can see, the z-index property therefore allows you to define a sort of layering behavior that mimics the common notion of layers prevalent in many computer graphics programs like Adobe Photoshop. Indeed, for a time, many CSS-capable integrated development environments (IDEs), such as earlier versions of Dreamweaver, referred to "layers" in their user interface.[20] What they referred to are typically absolutely positioned boxes with an explicit z-index declaration. Dreamweaver CS3 now refers to "AP Div" objects instead, and has menu options and controls that allow you rearrange them using the z-index property.

CSS box models: content-box model vs. border-box model

Design, and especially visual design, is all about relationships between different elements. A headline only stands out as such because it's bigger, or bolder, than the body text. The content sections in a site's sidebar are visually distinct because they have more whitespace around them than exists within them.

In CSS, each element creates a box of a certain display type and each box has four distinct **areas** that can be individually manipulated. From inner- to outermost areas, these are a **content area**, a **padding area**, a **border area**, and a **margin area**. Each of these areas has four **sides**, which themselves can be individually manipulated. You can use tools such as Firebug or the Web Developer Toolbar add-on for Firefox, or the Web Inspector's Metrics pane in Safari to see the dimensions of CSS boxes, as shown in Figure 2-16.

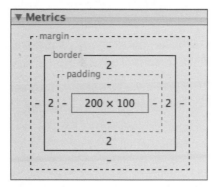

Figure 2-16. The properties of a CSS box, as shown in Safari's Web Inspector. Similar views are available from the Firebug add-on for Firefox.

---

20. The notion of *layers* in a web page originally came from Netscape, which supported the proprietary <layer> element.

Currently in CSS2.1, a box's dimensions are calculated by cumulatively adding the sizes of each side of each area. In the example box shown in Figure 2-16, we have a CSS box that is a total of 204 pixels high and 104 pixels wide. This is because the content area's width is 200 pixels wide and 100 pixels high, and the only other area sized with nonzero values is the border area, which is drawn with 2 pixels on all sides. These values might have been set in a CSS rule such as the following:

```
#example {
    width: 200px;
    height: 100px;
    border-width: 2px;
}
```

Therefore, the total width of the rendered CSS box is 200 pixels of content area, plus 2 pixels of left border area, plus 2 pixels of right border area, equaling 204 pixels of screen space. A similar calculation is performed to size the box's height. A box sized in this way is said be sized using the **content-box model** because of the way the content area's dimensions are explicitly specified in the width or height declarations.

In CSS3, a new box-sizing algorithm has been introduced called the **border-box model**. Using this algorithm, rather than adding to the rendered size of a CSS box when declaring non-content-area lengths (such as margin or padding), the length of those areas are *subtracted* from the content area's dimensions. If the box shown by Figure 2-16 was sized using the border-box model, then the code to achieve a width of the box at 204 pixels with the same border area as before, we'd have to use CSS code that looks like this:

```
#example {
    box-sizing: border-box;
    width: 204px;
    height: 104px;
    border-width: 2px;
}
```

Notice that our width and height declarations have been changed so that they declare the total rendered size of the box, instead of the size of the content area only. As the content-box model is the default box sizing method for all standards-compliant user agents, we also have to explicitly tell the renderer to use the border-box algorithm using the box-sizing property.

Although only experimentally implemented in many mainstream web browsers like Firefox 3 and Safari 3, the border-box model will be useful for elements that use relative units to size non-content areas. For example, using border-box sizing, you can create two equal-width columns within a single container, without additional markup that would otherwise be necessary.

```
.example-column {
    box-sizing: border-box;
    float: left;
    width: 50%;
    /* total width now includes 2em total border area, set below */
    border: 1em silver ridge;
}
```

The previous CSS could be applied to simple markup such as this:

```
<div id="container">
<div class="example-column">This will appear on the left.</div>
<div class="example-column">This will appear on the right.</div>
</div>
```

These two box models are entirely incompatible with each other, since different width or height values are required to achieve similar results. Nevertheless, for legacy reasons, all current versions of Internet Explorer use the border-box model instead of the standard content-box model to size all CSS boxes when the browser is rendering page in quirksmode. Therefore, it's important to ensure that your page is being rendered in a standards-compliant mode. To do this, always use a valid DOCTYPE at the top of your markup.

Summary

In this chapter, you've looked at a number of fundamental constructs for Cascading Style Sheets, including a user agent's initial styling, how to apply styles to elements, and how author and user style sheets interact. You also explored CSS selectors in detail as well as the many different units CSS makes available for your use. Finally, we discussed the intricacies of CSS's visual rendering models by exploring the critical aspects of document flow and CSS boxes, how the two interact with each other, and how you can manipulate them to achieve your layout objectives.

You learned how the document flow can be altered using a combination of the display, position, and float properties, and how combinations of CSS boxes in the three different positioning schemes interact. You learned that the canvas on which CSS displays content is actually a three-dimensional grid, and you saw how to use the z-index property to stack CSS boxes in a particular order one on top of the other. Finally, you saw how the two CSS box models, the traditional content-box model and the newer border-box model, differed from each other, and where one might be preferable to use over the other.

This is a comprehensive but not an exhaustive reference of the CSS specifications. It is instead a solid foundation in the concepts that you will need to be intimately familiar with in order to take your CSS skills to the next level. There is a lot to digest from this chapter, so rather than spending your time solely rereading it, we encourage you to keep these discussions in mind as you author your next style sheet.

Part 2

ADVANCED CSS IN PRACTICE

The conceptual frameworks introduced in the first part of this book are the foundations on which a thorough understanding of CSS is laid. Document flow, the various positioning schemes and formatting concepts, and stacking contexts are what make it possible for CSS rules to define the form of content so completely. Transforming a piece of content into multiple alternative presentations is at the core of most CSS development, even if you're ostensibly only working with a single design mock-up.

In this part of the book, we're going to move further into the practical aspects of working with CSS and what it can do. Each chapter focuses on a different cross section of CSS development that draws on numerous concepts from the previous part. Let's dive right in, beginning with exploring the specifics of CSS-generated content.

Chapter 3

CSS-GENERATED CONTENT

In addition to providing many means to present the content that already exists within a document, CSS provides a mechanism for rendering additional content. This content is called CSS-generated content, or pseudo-content, because it doesn't actually exist as part of the document structure. Instead, it exists in a sort of ghost state, rendered and painted on screen (or in whatever other way is being presented) but not "physically" there. In many instances, interaction with such content is therefore restricted so that it can't be selected by a cursor, accessed via scripting APIs, and so on.

In this chapter we'll explore CSS-generated content in more detail and showcase some of the ways it can be used to enhance presentation. It's important to remember that CSS-generated content, despite its name, is still a presentational effect. Therefore, we'll also supply some guidelines for using CSS-generated content in ways that adhere to development best practices such as progressive enhancement.

How generated content works

Whether or not you realize it, you've probably already used CSS-generated content in your day-to-day web development tasks. In CSS2.1, there are two mechanisms you can use to generate content with style sheets. The one you're already familiar with from previous chapters in this book is the markers, such as bullets and numbers, at the side of list items.

Thanks to their ubiquity, ordered (numbered) lists are a great example of where CSS-generated content is useful. In such lists, each item in the list is numbered according to its position relative to the other items. The first one therefore has the numeral 1 next to it, the second has the numeral 2, and so on. If we were marking up the notes in an ascending scale in such an HTML ordered list, the markup would look like this:

```
<ol>
    <li>A</li>
    <li>B</li>
    <li>C</li>
    <li>D</li>
    <li>E</li>
    <li>F</li>
</ol>
```

The actual rendering of this list would predictably look something like this:

1. A
2. B
3. C
4. ...

Interestingly, the numerals at the side of the notes are rendered as well. How is this happening, since nowhere in the HTML are these numerals specified as content? The answer has two distinct components.

First, CSS-generated content provides a means to render CSS boxes and *attach* them to CSS boxes created by "real" content. As shown earlier, one way to generate these pseudo-content CSS boxes is to create list items or—more precisely—to declare display: list-item on an element (indeed, any element). Elements with the list-item value to the display property automatically generate a **marker box**, one kind of CSS-generated content. We'll examine marker boxes in much more detail later in this chapter.

The other way to render CSS-generated content is to declare a value for the content property in a CSS rule that selects the :before or :after pseudo-elements. These pseudo-elements are abstracted hooks that allow you to attach CSS boxes to any arbitrary element and then flow whatever content you specified with the content property into that newly generated box. This mechanism of generating pseudo-content is discussed in the next section.

The second piece of the puzzle to an ordered list's automatic numbering is that CSS also provides a simple mechanism for counting the occurrences of a particular thing (in this case, <li> elements). The count of these occurrences is saved in a **counter**, which is somewhat analogous to a simple variable. Each time one of these counters is rendered using CSS, the counter value is retrieved and used to number each of the individual instances being rendered.

The capability to render additional content not in the document itself and to number instances of elements that are in the document tree provides authors with a number of conveniences beyond additional styling hooks. For instance, let's say we want to include sharp notes on our ordered list of the musical scale. In that case, we need to add new list items in between the ones we currently have. Our new markup will therefore look something like this:

```
<ol>
    <li>A</li>
    <li>A sharp</li>
    <li>B</li>
    <li>B sharp</li>
    <li>C</li>
    <li>C sharp</li>
    <li>D</li>
    <li>D sharp</li>
    <li>E</li>
    <li>E sharp</li>
    <li>F</li>
    <li>F sharp</li>
</ol>
```

Thankfully, we don't have to worry about renumbering any of the elements ourselves, since the original list was numbered with CSS in the first place. The new list is numbered correctly, too.

1. A
2. A sharp
3. B
4. B sharp
5. C
6. C sharp
7. ...

As you'd expect, you can manipulate both aspects of this behavior through CSS properties. Let's dive in by generating some pseudo-content first, and then take a closer look at how CSS counters work later in this chapter.

Generating content :before or :after any element

Pseudo-content is generated with CSS by taking advantage of the :before or :after pseudo-elements. These pseudo-elements, which can be applied to any element in a document, are effectively placehold-ers where you can inject other content. The content property determines what actual content gets injected.

The simplest value you can give the content property is a string. Unsurprisingly, the result of using a string value is that the generated content is a line of text inside an inline CSS box. For example, if you were feeling particularly poetic, you could prepend the phrase "Quoth the raven" in front of every quoted paragraph in your document like this:

```
blockquote p:before { content: "Quoth the raven, "; }
```

When you link this CSS with an HTML snippet such as this one:

```
<blockquote>
    <p>Nevermore.</p>
</blockquote>
```

the result is a CSS box tree that behaves as though the underlying HTML were changed to something like this:

```
<blockquote>
    <p><span>Quoth the raven, </span>Nevermore.</p>
</blockquote>
```

In particular, notice that the trailing space character in the content property results in a trailing space character in the generated content right before the (theoretical) </span> tag. This is important for inline CSS boxes when concatenating text strings. Also notice that the generated content results in a CSS box that lives "inside" the element to which it is attached. This way, the generated content can naturally inherit the CSS properties of its associated "real" content.

Conversely, using the :after pseudo-element as shown in the CSS that follows, the CSS box rendering would change accordingly but the "real" HTML content can't be altered.

```
/* CSS using :after instead of :before */
blockquote p:after { content: ", quoth the raven."; }
<!-- HTML might therefore look like this: -->
<blockquote>
    <p>Nevermore.<span>, quoth the raven.</span></p>
</blockquote>
```

To override a previous rule that renders CSS-generated content, you need to specify a value of none to the content property instead of to the display property. Technically, specifying display: none does prevent CSS-generated content from being displayed, but the content may still be generated and kept in the user agent's memory. Therefore, it is more explicit and possibly less resource-intensive to say content: none in the context of pseudo-content. You can also use content: normal, which does the same thing but takes slightly longer to type (and sounds somewhat strange).

In addition to the none value or simple strings, the content property can also accept a url() value. When a url() value is used, the user agent determines the appropriate rendering based on the MIME type[1] of the referenced URI. In other words, if the url() value references an image, then the image is rendered as though it were an <img> element placed in the normal document flow. If the url() value references an audio file, then screen readers will play the audio when they encounter the element to which the generated content is attached. Some user agents can also render other files such as SVG or PDF documents this way, inserting them directly in line with the rest of the flow of content.[2]

Here's an example like the one earlier but instead of inserting a string of text, we'll insert an image of a raven:

```
blockquote p:before { content: url(http://example.com/raven.jpg); }
```

Again, this has the basic effect of modifying the CSS box tree so that the resultant HTML would look like this:

```
<blockquote>
    <p><img src="http://example.com/raven.jpg" />Nevermore.</p>
</blockquote>
```

Using CSS-generated content functions most reliably on non-replaced elements (that is, elements that have intrinsic layout dimensions). None of the major browsers save for Opera will apply CSS-generated content to replaced elements such as images because the rendering engine needs to actively change the element's structure to do so. Additionally, as replaced elements reference external resources, they rarely have children. Generating content on an <img>, for example, forces the browser to render CSS boxes that can be represented in markup like this:

```
img:before { content: "Hello"; }
img:after { content: "world."; }

<img src="http://example.com/raven.jpg">
    <:before>Hello</:before>
    <:after>world.</:after>
</img>
```

Nevertheless, this works beautifully in Opera and isn't technically in violation of the CSS2.1 specification. However, the CSS specifications are unfortunately vague, offering little implementation guidance on how generated content should function with regard to replaced elements. As a result, some of the more compelling uses for generated content are still not cross-browser compatible, although it is hoped that the CSS3 Generated and Replaced Content module will address these concerns.

---

1. A MIME type is the term used to catalog different kinds of data in a standard, conventional way so that they can be attached to various forms of networked communications, originally email messages. For example, image/gif is the MIME type for GIF images.
2. Most notably, this includes WebKit-based browsers such as all versions of Safari. Sadly, as of this writing, the Mobile Safari derivative that runs on iPhones and iPod touch devices does not yet support SVG at all.

Exposing metadata through the CSS attr() function

The attr()function is similar to the url() function just shown, but instead of referring to another resource it refers to the value of an attribute of the element to which the CSS-generated content is attached. Using an attr() value with the content property can therefore expose some metadata about the content to the user, since such metadata is often encoded in an element's attributes. This can be used to enhance visitors' experience by providing contextual but possibly peripheral information about the content they are viewing.

In fact, many user agents already do this with built-in features. For example, when you provide an element with a title attribute, web browsers will often reveal the contents of that attribute as a tooltip whenever users hover their cursor over that element. Generating pseudo-content with the attr() function takes this idea one step further. Instead of relying on individual user agents to expose this multilayered interaction in limited ways, you can proactively feature it and style the information as you see fit.

Here's one example to do exactly that. Along with providing a meaningful semantic value to <img> elements in their alt attributes, you could use their title attributes to provide a caption.[3] We'll use Opera to do this, as it's the browser with the most support for CSS-generated content. If you had an <img> element such as the one shown next, you could use its title attribute to automatically generate its caption with no markup beyond the element's required attributes:

```
<img
src="http://upload.wikimedia.org/wikipedia/commons/2/27/➥
Edgar_Allan_Poe_2.jpg"
alt="" width="100"
title="This photograph of Edgar Allan Poe was taken in 1848 when he was
39, a year before his death." />
```

The title attribute in this <img> element provides everything you need for a caption, so to render it you could use the following CSS rule. The result is shown in Figure 3-1.

```
img[title]:before {
    content: attr(title);
    display: block;
}
```

You use the attr() function to the content property to extract the title attribute's contents. The display property is simply used to present the caption and the image their own lines, instead of in the same inline box. Alternatively, you could place the image on top of the caption instead of beneath it by injecting the generated content (the caption) :after the image instead of :before it.

---

3. Not only is providing both an alt attribute (itself required for validation) and a title attribute sort of handy, it's also a best practice accessibility guideline. See Joe Clark's book, *Building Accessible Websites* (New Riders Press, 2002), for a detailed explanation of the accessibility uses for the <img> element's alt and title attributes, and how they compare with each other.

The [title] attribute selector is used to ensure that only <img> elements with title attributes are selected by the rule. If the element you select doesn't have a title attribute, the result of the call to attr(title) will be the empty string (i.e., it will be the same as ''). Alone, this isn't problematic, but when combined with the display: block; declaration, even an empty string value creates a line break, which will result in some unintended vertical spacing.

Another interesting characteristic of the content property is that you can supply it with multiple values and each of them will get injected one after the other, in the order you prescribe. So, for example, using the image caption example earlier, you might want to not only provide the caption but also explicitly name the image's source in the caption itself. You could manually write out the source of the image in the title attribute, of course, but CSS offers this better way:

```
img[title]:before {
    content: attr(title) " Image retrieved from " attr(src);
    display: block;
}
```

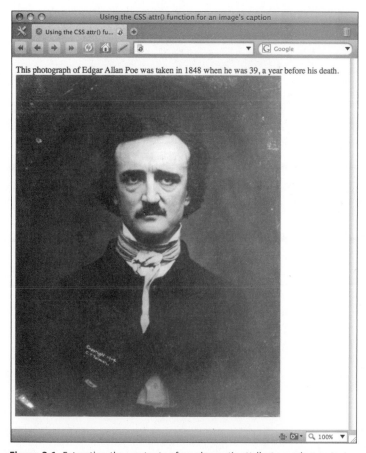

Figure 3-1. Extracting the contents of an element's attribute renders as text

This time, we provide three distinct values to the content property. Once again, note the leading and trailing single spaces within the quotation marks for the second (plain string) value. With this declaration, your image captions will show the contents of the <img> element's title attribute, followed by a space, followed by the words "Image retrieved from" and then another space, and finally ending with the address of the image file itself, as Figure 3-2 shows.

Figure 3-2. The attr() function can be used any number of times in the content property.

Another thing to note is that our selector hasn't changed. That's because the src attribute is required on <img> elements (for somewhat obvious reasons), so we can safely assume it's always going to be there.

You may also attach CSS-generated content both :before and :after any single element, which means that every real element in your markup has at least two (and sometimes up to three) styling hooks for generated content. (:before is one, :after is another, and if the element is display: list-item, that gives us a third.) So, for example, if you wanted the caption above the image and the image source below it, you could use the following CSS to do that:

```
img[title]:before, img[title]:after { display: block; }
img[title]:before { content: attr(title); }
img[title]:after { content: "Image retrieved from " attr(src); }
```

In this case, we use the [title] attribute selector in every rule, even in the rule that uses attr(src), since that's how we've determined that an image has a caption.

The key point is to realize that today you always have at least $N \times 3$ potential CSS boxes to style in any document, where N is the number of real elements in your markup (unless these are replaced elements, as noted earlier). Usually, thanks to the prevalence of lists, you actually have a little more than that (although see our cautions on avoiding "list-itis" later in this chapter). You can't attach CSS-generated content to CSS-generated content, however, so you don't get an infinite number of potential CSS boxes to work with, although this capability *is* included in the current working draft of the CSS3 Generated and Replaced Content module.[4] That means that while the following two rules are both valid CSS, the second one will never be used because it can't possibly apply to anything in CSS2:

```
p:before { content: "I'm a generated box."; }
p:before:before { content: "I'm not ever going to be rendered."; }
```

If you think you need to do something like this in a style sheet, you may not be making full use of the document's structure. Look at the markup around the element you want to style and see if there are any other styling hooks available to you, such as other nearby elements. If you still can't come up with a way to achieve what you want, you probably have poorly structured markup that you might need to rework.[5]

Additionally, though we hate to temper any sudden enthusiasm for the incredible potential of CSS-generated content, there are some important styling restrictions that such pseudo-content adheres to. Despite this, styling CSS-generated content can be an incredible boon to many, if not all, designs.

Replacing content with pseudo-content

A number of techniques are used in web development today that allow one element to be entirely replaced with another. Typically, this is a presentational effect that lets web designers use images or other media such as Flash movies in place of more limited options. Textual headings are frequent candidates for such media replacement.

Although not widely supported today, the current working draft of CSS3's Generated and Replaced Content module provides this capability directly by building on the functionality provided by previous levels of CSS-generated content. The familiar syntax merely uses the content property and applies it to a *real* element, that is, without the use of the :before or :after pseudo-classes.

```
/* Replace a textual headline with an appropriate image. */
h1#company-name { content: url(/company-name.png); }
```

---

4. It is proposed that nesting CSS-generated content function merely by chaining ::before or ::after pseudo-elements to each other, as described at http://www.w3.org/TR/css3-content/#nesting.
5. Speaking of reworking markup structure for better semantics and styling hooks, might we recommend Paul Haine's book, *HTML Mastery* (friends of ED, 2006).

Replacing content in this way can also be used for easily creating low-fidelity alternatives to hi-fi content, instead of the other way around, as we discuss further in Chapter 5. Sadly, as of this writing, the only mainstream browser that the previous CSS rules work in is Opera 9.6. However, we hope that since *replacing* content in addition to *generating* content is such a powerful mechanism for web development other browsers will implement this capability sooner rather than later.

Limitations on styling CSS-generated content

As we mentioned earlier, pseudo-content doesn't actually exist as part of the document structure. Once it is generated by a CSS rule, however, it behaves in the same way "real" content would—but only as far as CSS is concerned. This is an important caveat because it means that even after the content is rendered, it is still not accessible outside of CSS (such as by JavaScript) via the DOM. In other words, CSS-generated content is kept very strictly segregated in the presentation layer of your page.

That said, since CSS-generated content is rendered with real CSS boxes, the generated box obeys most of the rules you might expect. They inherit properties from the content to which they are attached as though that content were their parent elements, they have the same interactions with their neighboring CSS boxes according to the rules of document flow, and so on.

One notable difference, however, is that CSS-generated content always remains positioned statically. That is, CSS-generated content always has position: static and the various values of the position property do not affect generated content as they would "real" content. The same is also true for the float property. Sensibly, this is to ensure that CSS-generated content always renders near the content to which it is attached. Due to this restriction, all the following CSS rules are effectively identical to the image caption example in the previous section:

```
img[title]:before {
    content: attr(title) " Image retrieved from " attr(src);
    display: block;
    position: absolute; /* This does nothing to pseudo-content. */
    position: relative; /* Neither does this. */
    top: 50px; /* Naturally, this is also ignored. */
}
img[title]:before {
    content: attr(title) " Image retrieved from " attr(src);
    display: block;
    float: right; /* This also has no effect. */
}
```

Another limitation of the :before and :after pseudo-elements is that regardless of their contents, they can only generate a single CSS box. Practically, this means that there is no way to specify that, for instance, the attr(title) portion of the previous example's declaration should be a block-level box (with display: block) while the rest of the content property's values should be inline. In other words, any additional CSS properties you declare in a declaration block that targets CSS-generated content applies to all the content property's values.

Finally, as hinted at earlier, in all mainstream browsers except for Opera, CSS-generated content will not apply to any replaced elements (that is, elements whose layout dimensions are determined by external resources). Such elements include <img> elements, <object> elements, and a number of form controls. Even in Opera, only some elements work this way, and they function because the browser jumps through a number of rendering hoops. The CSS2.1 specification made no restrictions regarding where generated content could be applied, but implementation proved difficult. As the CSS3 specification is still not complete, browser makers are unlikely to enable CSS-generated content on replaced elements in the near future.[6]

In most situations these limitations are not an issue because generated content should be kept succinct. If you're trying to fit too much into pseudo-content, you might consider reevaluating whether the pseudo-content you're presenting is actually real content. If it is, you should provide the content as part of the underlying document itself instead of declaring it in a style sheet.

Although using strings in the content property is relatively simple and somewhat limited, there are nevertheless some remarkably useful things you can do with them. For example, you can force text into multiple lines much like you might have done with an HTML <br /> element. Since we're inside of CSS and not HTML, though, using an HTML line break won't work. To understand why that is, let's examine CSS string values and escape sequences in detail.

Understanding escape sequences in CSS strings

Regardless of where they appear, string values in CSS behave in a similar way. The most important thing to remember about them is that they are not HTML. This means, for instance, that inserting literal angle brackets without escaping them as HTML entity references (< and >) is perfectly legal. In other words, the rule

        #example:before { content: "3 < 5"; }

would result in a pseudo-element whose contents are the five characters (including spaces) 3 < 5 and *not* a broken HTML start tag. Similarly, this rule

        #example:before { content: "<"; }

results in a pseudo-element whose contents are the four characters < and *not* an HTML-escaped less-than glyph. This tells us that the < and & characters are not treated specially by CSS string parsers, even though they are characters with special meaning in SGML-derived languages like HTML and XML.

Within CSS strings, the only character with any special meaning is the backslash (\). This character delimits the beginning of an *escape sequence*, a sequence of characters used to collectively represent a different character, in much the same way as the ampersand (&) does in HTML code.

Escape sequences are useful because they allow style sheet authors to represent characters that would normally be ignored or interpreted differently by traditional CSS parsing rules. The most obvious example of this is representing a literal backslash in a CSS string. At first, you might think that the following CSS rule would produce a backslash at the start of every paragraph, but you'd be mistaken.

        p:before { content: "\"; }

---

6. The issue with CSS-generated content with regard to replaced elements is in the difficulty of determining its dimensions correctly when the element's initial rendering depends on an external resource to begin with. A Mozilla Firefox bug discusses this issue specifically and may prove interesting. It can be found at https://bugzilla.mozilla.org/show_bug.cgi?id=169334.

When a CSS parser reads the declaration in this rule, it thinks that the backslash is the start of an escape sequence, and so it ignores it. Next, it encounters a straightened double quote and, since this character is not a legal component in an escape sequence, it recognizes it as the end of the string value and returns. The result is an empty string, sans backslash: "".

To get the backslash to appear, we therefore need to *escape* it, or "undo" its special meaning. This is simple enough. We merely prepend the backslash with another one, like this:

```
p:before { content: "\\"; }
```

This time when a CSS parser reads the declaration in the rule, it finds the first backslash, switches into its "escape sequence mode," finds a literal backslash character as part of the string value it is parsing, and then finds the end-of-value straightened quotation mark. The result is what we were originally after, and the value that the CSS parser returns to the renderer is a single backslash: "\". Note that CSS makes no distinction between single-quoted or double-quoted strings, so in either case two back-slashes are needed in code to output one.

A similar situation exists if you wish to produce a literal double-quote within a double-quoted string. Instead of writing content: """; you would write content: "\""; to tell the CSS parser to treat the second quote as part of a value instead of the end-of-value delimiter. Alternatively, you could use single quotes as the string delimiter (content: '"';).

After the starting backslash, only hexadecimal digits (the numerals 0 through 9 and the English letters A through F) are allowed to appear within an escape sequence. In such escape sequences, these digits always reference Unicode code points[7] regardless of the character set used in the style sheet itself. As a result, it's possible to uniformly represent characters in a style sheet that are not possible to embed directly inside the style sheet itself. Accented characters (like the "é" in résumé or café) is an example of one class of characters that would need to be escaped in a CSS string if the style sheet were encoded in plain ASCII instead of, say, UTF-8.

One useful application for this is to embed line breaks into generated content. The Unicode code point for the newline character is U+00000A. In a CSS string, this can be written as \00000A. In a way similar to the way a hex triplet for color values can be shortened, escape sequences can also be shortened by dropping any leading zeros from the code point, so another way to write a newline is \A. Here's a CSS rule that separates the two words "Hello" and "world" with a newline, placing each on their own line.

```
#example:before { content: "Hello\Aworld."; }
```

Something to be careful of when using escape sequences in CSS strings is ending the escape sequence where you intend to. Observe what happens if our "Hello world" text changed to "Hello boy."

```
#example:before { content: "Hello\Aboy."; }
```

Now, instead of a newline (code point \A), our escape sequence is a left-pointing double angle quotation mark, or « (code point \AB). Our generated content now reads "Hello«oy." This happens because the "B" in "boy" is interpreted as a hexadecimal digit. The escape sequence terminates at the next character, the "O," because that letter isn't also such a digit.

---

7. Actually, all CSS string escape sequences are really references to Universal Character Set (ISO-10646) encoded characters. However, for nearly all intents and purposes, these values are equivalent to Unicode code points.

You can explicitly conclude an escape sequence in one of two ways. First, you can specify the sequence in full using all six hexadecimal digits (including leading zeros, if there are any). Second, you can append a space. The following two CSS rules are therefore equivalent:

```
#example:before { content: "Hello\00000Aboy."; }
#example:before { content: "Hello\A boy."; }
```

Knowing this, we can now split our earlier image caption example across two lines just where we want to. Pay close attention to the addition of the `white-space: pre;` declaration. Since we're generating whitespace characters and in most situations all whitespace in HTML gets collapsed to a single space, the `white-space` declaration is needed to interpret the newline literally (as though all the generated content were inside a <pre> element).

```
img[title]:before {
    content: attr(title) "\AImage retrieved from " attr(src);
    white-space: pre;
    display: block;
}
```

> If you wish to be explicit about it, you can declare an @charset rule at the very start of your style sheet to give user agents a hint of what the character encoding of your style sheet is. For instance, to declare UTF-8, use @charset "UTF-8";. If you do include an @charset rule, it must be the very first thing in your style sheet, before any preamble—even before comments or whitespace. If it's not, the rule simply gets ignored. Being explicit like this is often helpful when working with larger teams, but you should be wary of relying on the @charset mechanism too heavily. Like HTML <meta> elements, some user agents ignore @charset rules in style sheets in favor of the HTTP Content-Type headers set by the server.[8]

Advanced list styling: marker boxes and numbering

The HTML language gives us three different basic structures to encode lists. These are an ordered list, an unordered list, and a definition list (<ol>, <ul>, and <dl>, respectively). Of the three, the definition list is the oddball; the children of both ordered and unordered lists must be the somewhat nondescript list item (<li>) element. The <li> element, however, must *not* be the child of a definition list and instead only definition terms (<dt>) and definition descriptions (<dd>) are permitted.

Each kind of HTML list element comes with some interesting default styles. Both <dt> and <dd> elements in definition lists create block-level CSS boxes. However, <li> elements in ordered and unordered lists typically create list-item CSS boxes. As briefly mentioned at the start of this chapter, these list-item

---

8. The CSS specifications actually specify that a server's HTTP headers have precedence over any @charset declarations in the style sheet itself. Additionally, they demand that a user agent that doesn't recognize the character encoding of a CSS style sheet ignore the entire file. Though rare, some combinations of user agents and server or style sheet (mis)configurations can therefore cause confusing bugs during development that appear to drop CSS rules. At the very least, it behooves front-end web developers to pay attention to how the server is delivering style sheets to the end user's device.

boxes are special because as well as having the characteristics of a block-level CSS box, they have an *additional* CSS box, known as a *marker box*, that is "attached" to one of its sides. Predictably, the marker box is attached to the left side of the list-item box in an element with left-to-right document flow and is attached to the right side in a right-to-left document flow.

Marker boxes have some unusual characteristics. First, because they are not physical structures—indeed, they are a form of CSS-generated content—they can be used to great effect for stylistic purposes. Second, because they are automatically generated, they provide a certain amount of automation for convenience's sake. Take a simple ordered list, for example:

```
<ol>
    <li>I'm the first item.</li>
    <li>I'm the second item.</li>
</ol>
```

When rendered with a CSS-capable user agent, the first list item will probably have the number "1" next to it and the second will have the number "2" next to it, perhaps like this:

1. I'm the first item.

2. I'm the second item.

Those numbers are nowhere to be found in the HTML source code, yet they appear in the correct order anyway. Indeed, if we add a third item to the end of the list, we'll likely see a "3." Even better, if we insert a new item *before* the end of the list, all the list items will automatically renumber themselves based on their new position relative to the other list items.

This turns out to be extremely useful, and we can do a number of things (no pun intended) to control the way these lists get numbered. We'll take a closer look at numbers in the next section on CSS-generated counters. In the meantime, however, let's take a closer look at those marker boxes that these numbers are living in and explore what else we can do with them.

Using built-in marker box styles

Several default styles are available for marker boxes. To pick one, you use the list-style-type property. CSS2.1 defines 14 built-in list marker styles. These are all keyword values that fall into one of three types: glyphs, numbering systems, or alphabetic systems.

The disc, circle, and square values are the three types of glyph values, and using them gives you discs (bullet points such as •), circles (white bullets such as ◦), or squares (black square bullets such as ■) as your marker box contents. For the most part, web browsers initialize an unordered list with list-style-type: disc. Nesting one unordered list inside another is less consistent. In all cases, though, unordered lists nested within other lists use either the circle or the square value to the list-style-type property.

Using one of the glyph marker styles, all the list items in a list will use that glyph. Both the numbering and alphabetic marker styles that CSS2.1 specifies behave differently. With these, the specific glyph used depends on the position of the individual list item relative to all the others. In other words, the specific glyph increments with each new list item element added to the list.

Of course, this is pretty intuitive since both numbering systems and alphabetic systems have a well-known sequence. Three comes after two, which comes after one, and so on. The numbering systems available in the CSS2.1 spec are decimal, decimal-leading-zero, lower-roman, upper-roman, georgian, and armenian. Sensibly, decimal is often used as a default for ordered lists.

In addition to sequential numbering, you can also specify the following alphabetic systems: lower-latin (or its synonym, lower-alpha), upper-latin (or its synonym, upper-alpha), or lower-greek. In some of the world's languages, alphabetic systems also double as numbering systems. A prime example is Hebrew, which uses the first letter of its alphabet (א) as both a letter and the symbol for the numeral one. CSS3 is expected to add support for additional alphabetic systems, including hebrew as well as the Japanese hiragana and katakana syllabary.[9]

For lists of any significant length, the numbering system styles are preferred over the alphabetic ones because CSS doesn't define what happens to markers for which no subsequent letter is available. For example, lists of 27 or more items using the lower-latin alphabetic system might only display markers for the first 26 elements, since the English alphabetic only contains 26 distinct glyphs. In the majority of instances, lists that are longer than the alphabetic system used in their markers will revert to the decimal style at that point.

Naturally, any markup structure can be made to render as a list-item CSS box and thus can accept any of the list styling properties. This becomes useful when you have a design that needs lots of background images but are running out of elements that you can attach those background images to. In such tight situations, you can sometimes get away with transforming one or more block-level elements to list-item elements and then replacing the built-in marker box style with one of your own, which is discussed in the next section.

Here's a trivial example that makes a series of paragraphs look like an unordered list:

```
p {
    display: list-item;
    list-style-type: disc;
    margin-left: 2em;
}
```

Now each paragraph generates a block-level box as well as a marker box. It's generally only useful to do this when you intend to provide your own custom imagery to fill the marker box with using the list-style-image property, since the counters in either the numbering or alphabetic systems will not actually increment as they would with a real <ol> or <ul> element using the above CSS rule.

Replacing marker boxes with custom images

The list-style-image property lets you choose your own image in place of the built-in marker box styles using a url() value. Any valid URI is acceptable here. When this property is used and is not declared to be none, the value of list-style-type is ignored.

---

9. Some of these systems were already present in earlier CSS specifications, but due to a dearth of real-world implementation support, they were removed in CSS2.1 to make the specification leaner. Recently, with additional focus on the W3C's internationalization efforts, these requirements are finding their way back into the proposals for future CSS specifications. Nevertheless, some mainstream browsers do currently support marker styles such as hebrew.

Traditionally, this is used to provide custom bullet images for lists in a gracefully degrading way. If the custom image can't be fetched, the value of list-style-type (whether inherited or explicitly declared) is used instead. Such CSS could look like this:

```
ul li {
    list-style-image: url(http: //example.com/fancy-bullet.gif);
    /* degrade to normal bullets if the fancy ones are unavailable */
    list-style-type: disc;
}
```

Another interesting use for custom marker boxes is as limited background images, as mentioned in the previous section. Since marker boxes grow the size of their associated list-item CSS box, you can use them to provide an additional styling hook for one side of a complex visual element's background image. Specifically, a marker box's height is either the height of its associated list-item CSS box or the height of its own content, whichever is greater.

Manipulating the marker box's position

Like other CSS-generated content, markers are not quite as flexible as "real" elements. Sadly, the original CSS2 specification actually provided more control over the styling of marker boxes than the later CSS2.1 revision. Nevertheless, you can still influence where a marker box is rendered using a couple different techniques.

Positioning marker boxes outside or inside normal document flow

A list-item's marker box is unique among CSS-generated content because, by default, it renders *outside* of the CSS box it is attached to as opposed to inside it. This behavior has its heritage in traditional typography, where (believe it or not) the bullets of lists were actually *intended* to sit in the margins of pages and protrude out from the main body text.[10] Nevertheless, if you'd like to present lists in your page with the more contemporary typographic alignment, you can change this behavior using the list-style-position property.

Using the list-style-position property, you can control whether a list-item CSS box's marker box is rendered outside or inside the list-item CSS box itself. Specifying a value of inside (instead of the default, outside) on list-style-position tells marker boxes to mimic the behavior of other CSS-generated content. More precisely, when the marker box is positioned inside the list item, the marker box's contents become part of the inline CSS box created by the list item's contents themselves.

In code, you can see this by observing that the following two rules create an equivalent effect as one another, but the first does so with list-item marker boxes while the second does so with pseudo-content generated using the :before pseudo-element:

```
ul li {
    list-style-type: disc;
    list-style-position: inside;
}
```

---

10. For an absolutely fascinating history of typography as well as an infinitely practical reference to it, we highly encourage you to read *The Elements of Typographic Style* by Robert Bringhurst (Hartley & Marks Publishers, 2002). Also see http://WebTypography.net for ways in which you can apply Bringhurst's lessons to the Web.

```
ul li:before {
    content: "\2022  "; /* Unicode for a bullet */
}
```

Once the marker is positioned inside the list-item CSS box, it becomes part of the inline box in the normal document flow. Interestingly, however, the :first-letter pseudo-element still refers to the first letter of the list-item's contents and not the marker box, which means you can use it to precisely position the marker at a horizontal offset from the start of the text. Here's how you can position a bullet exactly 10 pixels away from the beginning of a list item's text in all conforming browsers:

```
ul li { list-style-position: inside; }
ul li:first-letter { margin-left: 10px; }
```

Marker offsets and marker pseudo-elements

Interestingly, CSS2 defined a marker-offset property whose intent was to provide a more flexible mechanism for specifying how far aside a marker box should be rendered relative from its list-item CSS box, but this was later removed in CSS2.1 and as of this writing marker-offset is slated for obsolescence in CSS3.

In the future, marker boxes will hopefully become more generically useful as CSS3 attempts to bring some capabilities lost in CSS2.1 back. In the CSS3 List module, markers are subject to the traditional CSS box model so they can be manipulated using margins and the like. Further, you can target them wherever they appear using the ::marker pseudo-element. Recall that all CSS3 pseudo-elements (such as ::marker and ::selection) are prepended with a double semicolon, while CSS2.1's syntax uses single semicolons. Sadly, as of this writing, support for the ::marker pseudo-element (and many other CSS3 pseudo-elements) is negligible.

Automatic numbering using CSS-generated counters

Since CSS2, the automatic numbering mechanism used to display sequential markers for list items has been available for use by style sheet authors directly. One of the major advantages of exposing this mechanism is that it gives developers the capability to automatically number any element or set of elements that appear within their document markup, so we're not limited to list items inside of lists. Moreover, because the numbering system builds on all the fundamentals of CSS-generated content we explored earlier in this chapter, designers have far greater stylistic control over the appearance of these numbers.

A *counter* is merely a named reference to a set of elements to count. If you're familiar with programming, you can think of it like a kind of limited variable. Automatic numbering in CSS works by setting various counter-related properties on different elements. The following three CSS rules, for example, is one way to replace an ordered list's default marker box numbering with your own implementation to achieve an equivalent (although not identical) visual appearance.

```
ol {
    list-style-type: none; /* turns off the built-in marker boxes */
    counter-reset: mylist; /* create the named counter */
}
ol li { counter-increment: mylist; } /* increment the counter at each list item
*/
ol li:before { content: counter(mylist) ". "; } /* display the counter's value */
```

There's nothing magical in these rules. There are only two new properties and one new value: counter-reset, counter-increment, and counter(), respectively. Together, these three pieces form the building blocks of CSS counters.

All CSS counters follow the same basic pattern: reset, increment, and render, in that order. The counter-reset property initializes a new counter whose name is the value you specify. It also creates a *counter scope*, which is simply the hierarchical context of the markup tree that this particular counter operates within (in this case, that's <ol> elements). A counter's scope is discussed later in the section "Counter scope: exposing structure with nested counters." The counter-increment property defines when and by how much the counter should increment (or decrement). Finally, the counter() function is used to display the counter in the normal way all CSS-generated content is displayed.

In the previous example, we've initialized a new counter called mylist, so that's the identifier we'll use to reference the same counter in subsequent declarations. By default, counter-reset initializes counters to 0, but you can specify an integer for initialization by declaring it after the counter's name. The previous declaration is therefore really shorthand for counter-reset: mylist 0;.

After resetting the counter on <ol> elements, we select <li> elements and apply the counter-increment property to them. In English, these two rules read, "Number list items for each ordered list." Similar to counter-reset, the counter-increment property can also take an integer value after the counter name to specify by how much the counter should be incremented, which defaults to 1. Again, this means the declaration in the example is really shorthand for counter-increment: mylist 1.

Finally, we can then display the value of the counter by generating pseudo-content :before the list item and accessing the current value of the counter by passing its name to the counter() function. By default, a counter's value is rendered as a decimal number, but again, this can be changed by providing a second parameter to the counter() function. This second parameter takes any of the supported values you can give the list-style-type property. Therefore, the above declaration is really shorthand for content: counter(mylist, decimal);.

Atypical numbering: counting backward, skipping numbers, counting with letters, and more

By using different starting and increment values with the counter-reset and counter-increment properties, you can do some interesting things. These are quite illustrative, so here are some examples.

Initializing a counter to 0 means that the first number displayed is a 1 because counters are incremented *before* they are rendered. Here's how to start numbering list items at the number 5:

```
ol {
    list-style-type: none;
    counter-reset: mylist 4; /* start counting at number 5 */
}
ol li { counter-increment: mylist; }
ol li:before { content: counter(mylist) ". "; }
```

If your document is marked up in HTML4.01 Strict or XHTML, these CSS rules are the only way to start an ordered list at an arbitrary value because the start attribute for <ol> elements is deprecated.[11]

You can use the counter-increment property to count in even (or odd) numbers only. For example, to count using only positive even integers, you can use these CSS rules:

```
ol {
    list-style-type: none;
    counter-reset: mylist;
}
ol li { counter-increment: mylist 2; } /* increment by two each time */
ol li:before { content: counter(mylist) ". "; }
```

To do the same thing but starting with 1 and only counting odd numbers, use the following somewhat counterintuitive values:

```
ol {
    list-style-type: none;
    counter-reset: mylist -1; /* initialize to a negative value */
}
ol li { counter-increment: mylist 2; }
ol li:before { content: counter(mylist) ". "; }
```

This works because the counter begins at negative one (-1) and is then incremented by 2 to produce a value of positive one (1). Further additions of 2 at each list item produce odd numbers only.

Given ten items, here's how to count backward from 10 to 1, perhaps for a "top-ten" list:

```
ol {
    list-style-type: none;
    counter-reset: mylist 11;
}
/* decrement by 1 instead of incrementing */
ol li { counter-increment: mylist -1; }
ol li:before { content: counter(mylist) ". "; }
```

And, given 26 items, here's a CSS counter that displays all the letters of the English alphabet backward:

```
ol {
    list-style-type: none;
    counter-reset: mylist 27;
}
ol li { counter-increment: mylist -1; }
/* count with Latin letters instead of numbers */
ol li:before { content: counter(mylist, lower-latin) ". "; }
```

---

11. There is some disagreement over whether the start attribute is presentational, and as a result this deprecated attribute, along with its relative (the value attribute), may both be revived in the forthcoming HTML5 specification.

Since CSS counters are completely decoupled from their display, we can count occurrences of one kind of element and display the count somewhere else entirely. For example, these CSS rules will display the total number of quotations in an HTML document at the very bottom of the page:

```
body {counter-reset: number-of-quotations; }
q, blockquote { counter-increment: number-of-quotations; }
body:after {
    content: "Total number of quotations on this page: "➥
        counter(number-of-quotations);
}
```

Given the following example HTML page, the above CSS will count three quotations:

```
<body>
    <h1>A CSS counters example</h1>
    <p>The quick brown fox said, <q>jump over the moon!</q>.</p>
    <p>
        <q>No, no, no!</q> the cow retorted, and continued to recite the➥
        lullaby improperly itself:
    </p>
    <blockquote>
        <p>There once was a muffin maid named Jim.</p>
    </blockquote>
</body>
```

However, if we change the CSS so that the number-of-quotations counter is displayed :before the <body> instead of :after it, we'll get a different result. Specifically, the counter will report that there are 0 quotations on the page. This happens because at the start of the document the counter has not encountered a <q> or a <blockquote> element yet, so it has not been incremented beyond its initial value of 0.

Using multiple counters

There is no limit to the number of counters you can use in a single page, or even in a single scope. Using multiple counters is mostly a matter of referring to additional counters in the appropriate places. However, due to CSS's declarative nature, the syntax used for multiple counters may feel strange at first blush.

To reset (initialize) multiple counters at the same time, do so in a single counter-reset declaration. The following example resets both counter1 and counter2:

```
#example { counter-reset: counter1 counter2; }
```

In contrast, this next example only resets counter2 while leaving counter1 untouched, which is almost certainly not what was intended by the style sheet author. This is because the second counter-reset property overrides the first, as per normal CSS cascading rules:

```
#example {
    counter-reset: counter1;
    counter-reset: counter2;
}
```

Numbering groups of elements and their siblings

Another way to think of CSS counters is that they let you expose information about an element's source order and its hierarchal context in a flexible way. You can reset and increment any number of counters on the same elements, which lets you automatically number not only groups of elements but also their sibling and child elements.

For instance, let's assume you were given the script to a three-act play where the title of each act was marked up in an <h1> element, each scene in <h2> elements, and each line in <p> elements. Using CSS counters, you can number each actor's lines so that you can all refer to them easily. The CSS rules for doing this might look like the following:

```
/* Initialize and increment act, scene, and line counters. */
body { counter-reset: act; }
h1 {
    counter-increment: act;
    counter-reset: scene;
}
h2 {
    counter-increment: scene;
    counter-reset: line;
}
p { counter-increment: line; }

/* Display act, scene, and line counts appropriately. */
h1:before { content: "Act " counter(act, upper-roman) ": "; }
h2:before { content: "Act" counter(act, upper-roman) ",➡
            Scene " counter(scene) ": "; }
p:before { "[" content: counter(act) "-" counter(scene) "-" ➡
            counter(line) "] "; }
```

With this styling, the three act titles (<h1> elements) will be labeled "Act I," "Act II", or "Act III." Each scene (<h2> elements) will also be labeled appropriately; the first act in the first scene will be labeled "Act I, Scene 1." while the sixth scene in the third act will be labeled "Act III, Scene 6." Finally, each of the actors' lines (<p> elements) will have a three-digit reference number prepended to them so that the line that begins with "[3-1-7]" will be the seventh line in the first scene of the third act.

It's worth noting that, just like lists, since all of these numbers are automatically generated with CSS, shuffling an actor's lines around while editing the script will not require you to renumber anything *even though there isn't a single list structure used in the markup.* Moreover, the script is hierarchically flat; all the elements it contains are siblings of one another. Using counters this way is therefore also a powerful technique to avoid symptoms of "list-itis" that sometimes plague badly structured markup.

"List-itis" is a term used to describe poorly structured markup that overuses lists to various ill effect. One common cause of list-itis is an attempt to give large portions of a document numbered labels without CSS counters. For example, the play script example just discussed could theoretically also be marked up in a nested list like this:

```
<ol>
    <li>
        <h1>Act I: Title Here</h1>
        <ol>
            <li>
                <h2>Act I, Scene 1: Title Here</h2>
                <ol>
                    <li>
                        <p>1-1-1: Actor's line here.</p>
                    </li>
                </ol>
            </li>
        </ol>
    </li>
</ol>
```

Of course, this works, but it's obviously an enormous amount of additional markup when compared with the lean markup that doesn't use the nested lists. Moreover, it's not quite as stylistically flexible as compared to the CSS counters example. On the other hand, the script for a play might philosophically be an ordered list, since you have a set sequence of acts, scenes, and lines, right?

Well, the answer—as you might expect—is "it depends." Theoretically, every piece of textual content is indeed sequential by virtue of the linearity of the medium. You read one sentence or paragraph, then the next, and so on. Despite this, it still seems ridiculous to nest all paragraphs on your pages inside of an ordered list even though it might be technically appropriate.

There is a balance to be struck here. Taking this too far down the road of creating lists results in "list-itis." I've seen some web designers get so excited about lists that every single element in their pages become one list nested within others. Unfortunately, lists that span from the opening <body> tag to the closing </body> tag are not actually that useful, and carry some of the same problems that <table>-based layouts did.

It's important to be aware that the structural flow of "one to the next" is already implicitly defined by the content's source order, so using a list to make this implicit linearity explicit is wasted effort. Second, and probably more important, forcing unnecessarily rigid structure like this makes it difficult to reuse the same HTML code later. Rather than working with the content naturally, you now have to fight against all the opposing style rules that you've defined for lists elsewhere in your CSS.

All that said, avoiding list-itis is very much a judgment call. Our example is extreme, but is actually based on a real HTML mockup we received. Be mindful of the semantics of your content, and you should easily be able to discern where one list should end and another one should begin.

Displaying total counts

Since you can have multiple counters, and since anything that can be targeted with a CSS selector can be counted with them, you can use CSS counters to supplement or, in some cases, completely replace JavaScript-generated statistics. Here are a few CSS rules that count the total number of headings, paragraphs, links, and quotations, in a blog post. Of the total number of links, the number of them that are rel-tag microformats and the number that refer to other blog posts on the same site (assuming the site uses a URI path that begins with /blog/ for blog posts) are shown distinctly.

```
.hentry {
    /* Initialize all counters. */
    counter-reset:
        num-headings
        num-paras
        num-links
        num-links-tag        /* rel-tag microformats */
        num-links-internal
        num-quotations
    ;
}

/* Count paragraphs. */
.hentry p { counter-increment: num-paras; }

/* Count entry headings. */
.hentry h1,
.hentry h2,
.hentry h3,
.hentry h4,
.hentry h5,
.hentry h6 { counter-increment: num-headings; }

/* Count link totals. */
.hentry :link { counter-increment: num-links; }
.hentry :link[rel="tag"] {➥
    counter-increment: num-links num-links-tag;➥
}
.hentry :link[href^="/blog/"] {➥
    counter-increment: num-links num-links-internal;➥
}

.hentry q, .hentry blockquote { counter-increment: num-quotations; }

.hentry:after {
    content:
        "This entry has a total of " counter(num-headings) " headings, "
        counter(num-paras) " paragraphs, " counter(num-links) " links "
        "(of which " counter(num-links-internal) " point to other blog "
        "posts on this site and " counter(num-links-tag) " are tags),➥
```

```
        and "
        counter(num-quotations) " quotations."
    ;
}
```

Of special note in the previous code listing are the counters for the links: num-links and num-links-tag or num-links-internal. For the first link counter using the selector .hentry : link, we only need to increment num-links. However, for both subsequent link counters, we increment both the num-links counter *and* the second, more-specific counter.

If we fail to increment the num-links counter at this more specific selector, then at the time the user agent is ready to display the results, we'll have an incorrect total for the num-links counter because our capability to increment the counters is directly tied to the markup. Further, due to this same limitation, we can only display totals like this :after the content we've counted, not :before it. In other words, CSS counters can only increment as the markup of a document is parsed.

Counter scope: exposing structure with nested counters

As mentioned earlier, when you initialize a counter with counter-reset you also create a *counter scope* of the same name. Setting counter-reset on an <ol> element, for instance, means that an *additional* instance of the counter you initialized is also initialized at every child <ol> element of the first <ol> element. This facility makes it possible for CSS authors to create counters that can refer to elements nested at any arbitrary depth without needing to know how deeply nested the document markup will be ahead of time.

The counters() function concatenates all counters in the named scope provided as the first parameter with a string provided as the second. An optional third parameter defines what numbering or alphabetic system to use to style the counter with (again defaulting to decimal). In this way, a single counter can be used to expose an element's hierarchical context.

A common use for the counters() function is in creating outlines out of nested ordered lists. Only two CSS rules using one counter, such as those that follow, are necessary to do this:

```
ol {
    list-style-type: none; /* turn off built-in counting*/
    counter-reset: item; /* set up an "item" counter */
}
ol li {
    counter-increment: item; /* increment only the current instance */
    /* but display all of the instances together */
    content: "[" counters(item, ".") "] ";
}
```

When this CSS is combined with the HTML that follows, the result is the rendering shown in Figure 3-3:

```
<body>
    <ol>
        <li>Lorem</li>
        <li>ipsum
```

```
<ol>
    <li>dolor</li>
    <li>sit</li>
    <li>amet
        <ol>
            <li>consectetuer</li>
            <li>adipiscing</li>
        </ol>
    </li>
</ol>
    </li>
    <li>elit,</li>
</ol>

<ol>
    <li>eiusmod</li>
    <li>tempor</li>
</ol>

</body>
```

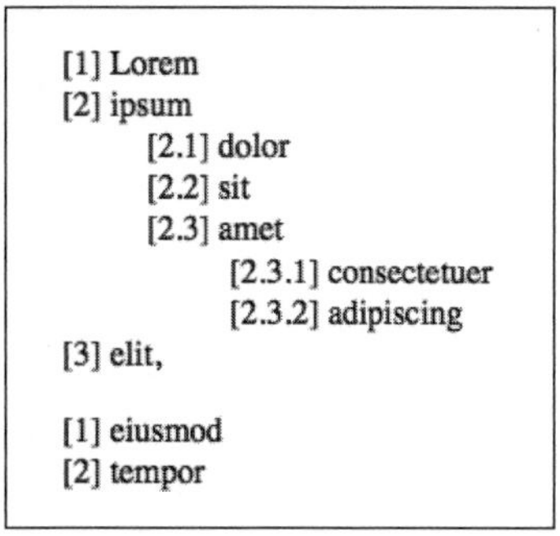

```
[1] Lorem
[2] ipsum
        [2.1] dolor
        [2.2] sit
        [2.3] amet
                [2.3.1] consectetuer
                [2.3.2] adipiscing
[3] elit,

[1] eiusmod
[2] tempor
```

Figure 3-3. The counters() function uses the markup's hierarchical structure to determine when and how to increment each individual scope's counter.

Summary

Using generated content gives CSS the capability to not only style content, but to actually use that content as the basis for additional, supplementary content that can be similarly styled. As we discussed, generated content turns out to be something relatively low-level, as it is used by default in the marker boxes of lists. Despite a frustrating lack of support in some areas, creative use of these low-level capabilities makes using CSS-generated content a compelling addition to your CSS development toolset.

Each element in your markup gives you at least an additional two CSS hooks that you can style by taking advantage of the :before and :after pseudo-elements. For any element that you declare display: list-item on, you gain an additional, if more limited, styling hook in the form of the marker box. These three generated content CSS boxes can be filled with almost anything you like by using the various values to the content or list-style-image properties.

The counter() and counters() functions, along with their various CSS properties, are a mechanism for automatically numbering the occurrences of anything you can target with a CSS selector and then displaying the results. You have a great deal of flexibility using counters, as you can use any of the list-style-type property's numbering or alphabetic systems to display the counter's number. The trickiest thing about counters is making sure you set counter-reset on the appropriate element, but this becomes easier with experience.

Using CSS-generated content to expose metadata such as element attribute values, source order, or hierarchical context are techniques to provide visitors with valuable supplementary information in line with the development principles of progressive enhancement. However, as we all know, with power comes responsibility, so be certain to use CSS-generated content thoughtfully and in moderation or for accentuating other facets of your desired presentation. A lot of what could be generated content could also be actually in the markup, particularly if your project uses a decent content management system and makes effective use of server-side template tools.

CSS-generated content can also be useful in a variety of arenas beyond traditional browser- and screen-based environments. One notable area where such pseudo-content makes a lot of sense is in the headers and footers of printed pages, for page numbering or for displaying metadata about a printed page originally published online. Indeed, many capabilities that exist in CSS-generated content originated from printed forms of publications (such as marker boxes), so you'll next examine the impressive capabilities that CSS gives you for styling printed media.

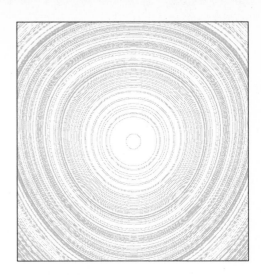

Chapter 4

OPTIMIZING FOR PRINT

As CSS developers, we spend most of our time writing styles for screen or *continuous* media platforms. This is no surprise since the vast majority of content on the Web is consumed via computer screens. *Paged* media, the kind of media where output is articulated into specific distinct pages (such as printing to paper) doesn't get nearly as much love as its continuous media counterparts, but paged media is still quite important for web developers to consider.

People print web pages less frequently than they browse sites on-screen, but when they do take the action to print, it is usually for a specific reason where screen output falls short. Perhaps some user is headed off to a meeting and wants to print out and distribute a few copies of the latest press release from a competitor. Some individuals have a habit of putting together some reading material for the evening commute or for that long wait at the dentist. It could be an intended need, such as printing a form that needs to be signed on paper and handed in. For whatever the reason users choose to print pages, without the developer's consideration for this media, the result is usually inadequate at best, or completely overlooked at worst.

When printing to paper, users typically are interested in accessing the content of the specific page in question. They aren't likely interested in the navigation tools and unrelated sidebar content, and they tend to get put off when articles print in a narrow column in the center of a dozen sheets of what used to be a majestic, carbon-sequestering tree. Now imagine that when your content-rich site becomes wildly popular, articles are going to be printed from tens, hundreds, and possibly thousands of users worldwide on a regular basis. By reducing the amount of paper your content prints on and maximizing the efficiency of the space used in your paper-based layout, you can help protect the environment!

Sadly, through much trial and experience, you will find the average web browser's print media to be less rich and less precise than other methods of producing printed material. PDF files, for example, provide a much more exacting method of delivering print output. When printing web pages, we will find many limitations when it comes to things like color, layout precision, and line dimensions. There is no way for the designer to predict what color or size sheet of paper their dear users have chosen to insert into their printer's paper feeder, although it is typically safe to assume white US Letter or A4.

When styling for print, it is important to remember what your users will experience and what special constraints CSS developers are faced with. People can't click on links printed to the physical page. Printing to paper means a fixed page size that is opaque and easy to read, carry, and fold. Only so many characters and images can fit on the printed page. In this chapter, we will examine the reasoning for optimizing for print output using Cascading Style Sheets (CSS). We will look at some of the basic constructs in CSS that work in today's browsers. Following that, we will examine considerations that will arise when styling for print, cover a few of the advanced page selectors, and wrap up with a working example to see how some of these techniques might be applied to a web page as it goes to the printer.

Targeting a print style sheet

Historically, the solution to achieving printer harmony was to provide a button or link labeled something along the lines of "Print this article," which redirected the user to a completely separate web page formatted in a way that allowed the user to have a nicer print output than what the previous page was able to provide. But this alternate version of the content is largely unnecessary. Every web browser already has a print command that virtually all computer users are very comfortable with—File ➤ Print. This menu command is consistent across all platforms, and even comes with its own native keyboard shortcut: ⌘+P on the Mac, Ctrl+P on Windows and Linux.

CSS has a wonderful built-in construct to handle this sort of output media automatically, which will take care of your reformatting needs. Therefore, asking users to learn your own custom way to print a page effectively, rather than taking advantage of the established convention on their platform, is not the best idea from either a usability or a technical perspective. Using CSS's innate ability to target print media will save you time and money, so put away the idea that you have to direct your users to a separate version of your content for printing.

There are three methods we can use to target styles for print media. We can use the media="print" property for the <link> HTML tag, and we can use the @import or @media at-rules within a style sheet with the print media type specified. Let's take a look at an example for each.

At The Guardian (http://www.guardian.co.uk/), a hybrid approach is used to solve the problem of printing articles that speaks to a wide range of users. A print icon appears next to the content, which takes the user to a print version of the page with a separate URL. All this actually is, though, is the same piece of content with the print style sheet swapped out to the screen media. This helps people see an approximation of what they're about to print without having to run it through the browser or system's print preview function. As an added benefit, many people prefer reading a print version of such articles on screen, which presents far less distracting clutter around the content of prime interest. Implementing both solutions is an effective strategy for making your site content more accessible and user friendly from the print perspective.

Linking to print styles in HTML

To target a style sheet specifically for print, indicate the print media type: `<link rel="stylesheet" type="text/css" media="print" href="print.css" />`. We might choose this method of linking if we have flexibility in how the HTML is constructed, and using this method is easy to keep track of from a developer's perspective.

It is easy to use the HTML `<link>` element for adding style sheets, especially in the case of adding multiple style sheets. However, each byte you add linking style sheets is a byte that won't be cached as a shared asset when your pages load, and extra bandwidth will be incurred. When using multiple style sheets, it might be better from a bandwidth perspective to use the `@media` and `@import` rules, which are discussed next. At any rate, using the `<link>` method is the only method we can use to target specific style sheets using the conditional comments feature in the Internet Explorer line of web browsers.

Targeting print styles using @media

Using `@media` constructions can be quite handy when you have a limited number of style sheets that you can work with and can't add more via the `<link>` element, or when you otherwise might want to have a single self-contained CSS file that has all the media types handled in one file. All `@media` rules appear within an existing style sheet, and are followed by a set of curly braces (`{}`), which are used to contain our print rules. For example:

```
<style type="text/css">
    @media print {
        body { font-family: Georgia, serif; }
        a {
            text-decoration: none;
            border-bottom: thin solid #ccc;
            color: #000;
        }
    }
</style>
```

In this brief example we have specified within the @media print block that the body element will use a serif font family, which tends to be more readable on paper than the sans-serif font varieties. And since hyperlinks no longer are clickable elements in the print media, it really no longer makes much sense to have them visually separated from the content in any extreme way. So with that in mind, we've removed the default underline and instead replaced it with a thin gray underline to hint at the existence of a link back in the online version without creating a major distraction for the reader.

Targeting print styles using @import

Targeting print styles using @import is very similar to the prior example of using @media rules. The difference is that instead of embedding a particular set of media styles in a style sheet, you are linking to a separate file. There are two ways to write the @import rule:

```
<style type="text/css">
    /* uses the url() construct to contain the path to the file
       quote marks are optional */
    @import url("/styles/print_example1.css") print;
    /* loses the url() construct, quoting becomes compulsory */
    @import "/styles/print_example2.css" print;
</style>
```

The url() wrapper is not necessary, but this can be very helpful to define things, especially when searching around for file paths that need to be changed. The quotes should be used for valid XHTML in an embedded style sheet, even though modern browsers seem not to care.

One of the wonderful things about using @import within CSS is that you can create a rich network of CSS style sheets that are all linked from a master CSS file. This is particularly advantageous when dealing with templating systems that are part of a locked-down content management system, where you might only have access to a single style sheet to start with and no rights to edit the HTML. Or perhaps the developer has a preference for keeping the HTML as lean as possible, and linking to only one style sheet in the HTML can cut down several bytes' worth of precious file size. Since CSS files are usually cached as assets in the browser, placing as much of your code into cacheable resources outside the HTML—which has to be downloaded each time as the user moves to each unvisited page—can help speed things up a bit. This is useful in mobile and resource-constrained settings. In high-traffic web sites where there might be a large cluster of servers and high-bandwidth dedicated network connections, a simple thing like reducing a couple of lines of the HTML template might add up to several thousand dollars' worth of savings in hardware and bandwidth requirements annually.

As with using multiple <link> elements to bring in external style sheet assets, using multiple @import rules can incur some overhead. This becomes especially apparent during the initial page loads for new visitors, or in cases where caching has been disabled by the site authors or on the client side. For higher-traffic web sites where bandwidth is a concern, it may be advisable to merge all linked and imported style sheets into one file as part of a build system, and have the media types separated in @media rules.

The only web browser with remaining significant market share that has problems with @import as of this writing is Internet Explorer 6. Versions of IE6 and lower ignore @import rules for which a media type is specified. Thankfully, those numbers are falling in favor of better browsers such as IE7 and Firefox, and given that IE8 is in beta also as of this writing and will likely be released by the time you read this, IE6 is looking like less and less of a concern.

The @import rule construction was largely unsupported until the version 4 generation of web browsers, and transitional browser generations between then and now have had varying degrees of support. These variances have resulted in a number of interesting CSS filters and hacks used to show or hide certain styles. While frustrating on many levels, such variances were the basis of techniques that worked to solve additional deficiencies.

Now that we've looked at some of the basics with creating a print style sheet, let's examine some of the practical issues that we must consider when developing printer-friendly output. Issues such as dealing with layout, page size, color, measurement units, and image resolution all have different behaviors in print than what you might be used to with screen-based output.

Printer style considerations

Most of the time when composing a print style sheet, you're going to reformat a page that exists on screen such that it will print nicely on a white sheet of standard US Letter or A4 paper coming out of someone's inkjet or laser printer. Typically the first goal is to reduce wasted white space on the page by removing unnecessary elements such as banners, advertising, and navigation, and widening the content to the maximum printable width of the paper. The next design considerations might strive for improving readability. Serif fonts are typically considered to be easier to read on paper, so you might choose a good serif font family that is well suited for that purpose. Be sure to include a few similar serif varieties in your preferred order, such as

```
#content { font-family: Garamond, Georgia, Times, sans-serif;}
```

Garamond looks great in print, but not everyone has that font installed on their system. In its absence, the Georgia font is a common option included on Windows and Macintosh systems. Georgia is designed especially to be a readable serif-based web font for screen output, but it looks good and is comfortable to read in print as well.

In this section, let's look at the issues of color, units, and image resolution. As you will see, color handling can be problematic, especially when dealing with typography. Units have different meanings in the print media than in the screen media that you're probably used to. And images can look grainy and pixelated in print where they look fine on screen. We will present some strategies for helping ease the burden of these issues.

Printing in color

Another critical point to consider is font color. Remember that you can't be 100 percent sure what type of paper your end users have stocked in their printers, but it is reasonable to assume that the paper is going to be white letter or A4 the vast majority of the time. Also consider the fact that most browsers by default are set to *not* print background images or colors. Think about that: this would be an enormous use of expensive ink or toner, and can make for some soggy pages. Now if your web page is on a dark background on screen and you have light-colored text, this is going to fail in print. White text will be completely invisible, and pale colors applied to text will not be fun to read. Furthermore, a large percentage of printers are going to be black and white only, and if colors are important for contrasting shapes in print, then these items will likely appear washed out or indistinguishable in print.

Color printers usually deliver their output in the CMYK color model. CMYK stands for Cyan, Magenta, Yellow, Black, which refers to the four inks used in the standard printing process. Compare this with RGB (Red, Green, Blue), which is the typical color space for computer screens. The color range for CMYK is not as rich and vibrant as what you see on a good PC monitor, and often colors will vary considerably from what you would have expected looking at the screen version. Going from screen to print will typically mean all those RGB colors that are "out of gamut" will be matched to their closest CMYK equivalents, which can yield some unexpected results. Savvy design programs such as Adobe Photoshop have built-in features to distinguish the expected color output differences between RGB and CMYK, which can help deal with these issues up front. To elaborate more on the Photoshop example, you can force an image to be in the CMYK color space by choosing Image ➤ Mode ➤ CMYK Color. This is a lossy process, meaning your RGB colors will be discarded in the conversion, and this may not be what you want. Fortunately, there is a way to preview color conversion in Photoshop without actually having to switch the color space. Choose View ➤ Proof Setup ➤ Working CMYK to establish that we're in CMYK proofing mode, and then use View ➤ Proof Colors (⌘+Y on the Mac, Ctrl+Y on Windows) to see the difference. Run the Proof Colors command again to toggle back to the normal view. Usually differences won't be too significant, but you will likely notice an overall loss of saturation, and green hues tend to be affected more than the others.

The tragedy of font color

If you thought you had a reasonable amount of control over the color of your typography using CSS, you thought wrong. One of the absolute flakiest, inconsistent issues you will ever encounter in CSS is trying to get accurate color applied to your fonts. In all major browsers, certain color values are modified if the browser deems them to be "too light for print," and it will render a color that it thinks will be better suited for your output on a printed page.

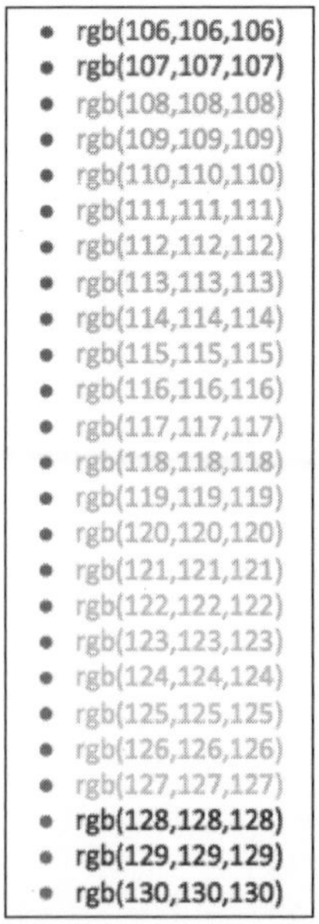

Now the reason why the browser vendors have made this assumption is fairly obvious: printing light text on what is almost always white paper is largely unreadable, and it is sadly very rare that web authors will take the time to style their pages for print using an alternate print style sheet (if they ever style it for print at all). Furthermore, printing in pure black, devoid of any complex color mixing, can make printing much faster, because the printer doesn't have to mix in any red, green, or blue ink and can focus on getting the task done. But what is maddening to the designer trying to achieve accurate color representation in print from their web pages is that all of the major browsers assume that they are smarter than you, and recolor the text based on their own inconsistent algorithms. If you wanted a string of text to appear very light gray in Firefox, too bad. You are getting black whether you like it or not. Let's look at some of the problems you might encounter.

In Safari 3 (see Figure 4-1), gray colors print fine up until rgb(107,107,107). After that point there will be a strange conversion to a light gray shade, arguably the lightest gray you can get in text on Safari, between rgb(108,108,108) and rgb(127,127,127). At rgb(128,128,128), the text color then jumps to black and as you ascend the values toward an expected white color, Safari yields a progressive amount of additional lightness to the text until it finally winds up at around rgb(171,171,171), where it should

- rgb(106,106,106)
- **rgb(107,107,107)**
- rgb(108,108,108)
- rgb(109,109,109)
- rgb(110,110,110)
- rgb(111,111,111)
- rgb(112,112,112)
- rgb(113,113,113)
- rgb(114,114,114)
- rgb(115,115,115)
- rgb(116,116,116)
- rgb(117,117,117)
- rgb(118,118,118)
- rgb(119,119,119)
- rgb(120,120,120)
- rgb(121,121,121)
- rgb(122,122,122)
- rgb(123,123,123)
- rgb(124,124,124)
- rgb(125,125,125)
- rgb(126,126,126)
- rgb(127,127,127)
- **rgb(128,128,128)**
- **rgb(129,129,129)**
- **rgb(130,130,130)**

Figure 4-1. Clip from a print test showing where the break is between rgb(107,107,107) and rgb(128,128,128)

be 255 for all values. This problem also occurs in the red, green, and blue colorspaces. If we fix red at 127, about halfway between the minimum value of 0 and the maximum value of 255, we get a dead zone between rgb(127,100,100) and rgb(127,127,127). The same ratios happen starting at rgb(100,127,100) and at rgb(100,100,127). Finally, Safari renders rgb(0,255,255), rgb(255,0,255), and rgb(255,255,0) inconsistently from their adjacent color values.

Gecko browsers such as Firefox (before version 3), Camino, and Flock print the entire gray space in black. You cannot specify a light gray such as rgb(127,127,127) or anything else. It will always default to pure black whether you like it or not. If you fix a color bucket at 0, you will get semi-accurate color for the rest of the gamut, but the other color combinations will trend toward black text the lighter it gets. The exception here is Firefox 3, which will print your color exactly as specified. As of this writing, Firefox 3 is the only browser we've tested that gets the color matching between screen and print relatively correct.

Interestingly, the marker (the little bullet to the left of each list item) will display the correct color value in print for Firefox and Safari, even though the text itself won't match! So at least here you can use the markers to see what the color was supposed to be...

In Opera 9, gray shades render accurately up until rgb(185,185,185), and then higher values default to black. In the points tested, the same conversion to black happens in various other colorspaces at different points. For instance, color values higher than rgb(127,211,211), rgb(255,156,156), rgb(87,255,255), rgb(209,209,0), rgb(193,193,127), and rgb(177,177,255) will stop rendering their expected colors and just print black instead, thank you very much.

IE7 never gets any lighter than rgb(108,104,102) for grayscale, and the rest of the color spaces don't seem to allow anything lighter than a midrange hue equivalent in any given color range.

Since all the major browsers have made the assumption that you've neglected to pay appropriate attention to your print output with regard to color and contrast, you have to live with that and deal with some fairly tricky constraints. One argument is to give in and just go for all black text on all white paper, and certainly there's an argument for that in terms of readability and performance. But for that argument we should all be designing white web pages with black text too and just toss out all our assumptions about color theory, design, and inspiration. We know clearly that the primary function and goal for printing a page is for reading purposes, but what if you wanted to do something else. Something more artistic, perhaps? For truly accurate printing from the Web, you may want to stick with PDF or similar output. But there's still plenty we can do with print using plain-old HTML and CSS, and it can be an interesting academic exercise to try to design within these constraints. Think of it as a challenge that will make your professional world that much more interesting!

Units

As we mentioned earlier, certain CSS properties and units are more appropriate for print, or are even only going to work in the print media alone. The units mentioned earlier include inches (in), centimeters (cm), millimeters (mm), points (pt), and picas (pc). Twelve-point type is fairly readable in most typefaces and is a good choice for your standard body text, although you can often go to 11-point or 10-point for many situations. Points are a common unit of measurement, although if you're using 12-point then why not just use 1 pica instead? One pica is equal to 12 points, and you get to shave a byte off of your total file size. But for whatever size you go with, just remember that the more youthful eyes that you may have may be quite a bit keener than an older counterpart—do the world a favor and test your print output on your vision-challenged friends and colleagues.

Images

Images in web pages typically look poor when printed. This is because of the low default resolution of 72 dpi, and printers like things to be a bit more in the 300 dpi range and higher. Your photos may not look as sharp in print as they do in the browser, so either we learn to accept this degradation or we find ways to compensate.

To get around this issue, there is a simple solution. You can use a large image that is at, say, 72 dpi and use CSS to shrink it down to a ratio that would result in a 300 dpi image in print. For instance, take an image that is 180×240 pixels wide and looks good on screen in the placement you want for the printed page. For this to work as a 300 dpi image, you would need your source image to be at 750×1000 pixels.

The obvious drawback here is bandwidth. An image at 750×1000 pixels is excessive, especially when considering how fast your pages should load. It is probably a good idea to use such a technique conservatively and set expectations when doing so.

Advanced page selectors

When you design for paged media, such as designing for print, you have a number of additional CSS constructs to help you out.

When working with printed media, your canvas changes from a browser viewport to something known as a page box. The page box is more informally known as the "printable area" of a sheet of paper. It's here that printers will put ink, and therefore it's here—and only here—that you can put and style content.

Unlike the browser viewport, however, you can control certain elements of the page box using CSS. To do so, you need to use a special at-rule selector to target the page box itself. This rule is the @page rule.

What properties can you specify on the @page rule? For one, you can set page margins. These margin values are applied to all pages as they are printed and are applied *before* any other styles are applied to the normal styling of the page content. This example will set four centimeters of margin to the top, left, right, and bottom aspects of all pages:

```
@page {
    margin: 4cm;
}
```

In the context of book printing, there exists the concept of having a left page and a right page that face each other, together constituting a spread. This is commonly handled in word processors and desktop publishing programs, and CSS includes constructs for handling these conditions as well. Using the :left and :right pseudo-classes, you can specify different rules for pages that face each other:

```
@page :left {
    margin-left: 6cm;
}
@page :right {
```

```
        margin-right: 6cm;
    }
    @page :first {
        margin-top: 8cm;
    }
```

Unfortunately, @page selectors are not very well supported at this time. The Opera web browser handles @page selectors nicely, but as of this writing this feature of CSS is unsupported in all shipping versions of Internet Explorer, Firefox (and related Gecko-based browsers), and Safari.

Inserting and avoiding page breaks

Another area where paged media differs from continuous media is in the fact that content must be split across multiple items. With CSS, you can influence where these splits occur by making use of the page-break properties.

For example, you typically don't want to print headlines at the end of pages. Specify this in your print style sheet like so:

```
    h1, h2, h3, h4, h5, h6 {
        page-break-after: avoid;
    }
```

The page break properties in the CSS 2.1 specification are page-break-before, page-break-after, and page-break-inside. Setting the value to avoid in all cases will instruct the user agent to not allow a page break before, after, or within a given element, respectively.

Again here browser support is incomplete, although considerably better than the @page rules. Safari, Opera, and Firefox and related Gecko browsers support the page-break-before and page-break-after rules. Opera supports all of the page break rules fully. Internet Explorer supports page-break-before and page-break-after for versions 5.5 and 6, but in IE7 this implementation has regressed and is flawed. The Microsoft-recommended solution is to insert a conditional comment with a break tag immediately after the element that is assigned page-break-before:

```
    <!--[if IE 7]><br style="height:0; line-height:0" /><![endif]-->
```

This is a less-than-optimal hack that involves insertion of meaningless markup into your document. However, it may prove handy in cases such as with enterprise deployments, where you must have to resolve printing issues on corporate applications where IE7 is a dependency.

Orphans and widows

The concept of orphans and widows is based on the idea of having page breaks occur at the beginning or end of a block. It is considered more readable and visually balanced if a page break occurs toward the middle of a text block, and the idea here with defining page breaks using orphans and widows is to avoid having one or two lines appear at the top or bottom of a page.

The orphans property is used to define the number of lines on a page that are allowed to display before a page break is inserted. For example, p { orphans: 4; } would mean that if a paragraph at the end of a page were to show four or fewer lines before breaking to the next page, that paragraph should instead start at the beginning of the following page. In contrast, the widows property is used to define the number of lines on the following page that would be allowed. The rule p { widows: 4; } would select any paragraph where four lines would appear on the following page, and then move that paragraph unbroken to the top of said following page.

Support for orphans and widows is weak at this time. At the time of this writing, only the Opera browser handles these properties, and Firefox, Safari, and Internet Explorer 7 and lower will ignore these rules. Internet Explorer 8 is expected to have support for orphans and widows, and the implementation exists in the current release candidate.

Establishing a page size with @page

Page sizes and orientation may be set using at-page rules. Page sizes are set using print units such as centimeters or inches for the width and height dimensions, or a page size keyword may be used such as A4 or letter. This feature is supported in Opera and will be supported in IE8, but is not currently handled in Safari or Firefox. To set a page size and orientation, use the size property:

```
@page {
  size: legal landscape;
}
```

This rule will print to a legal sheet of paper (8.5×14 inches) and it will print in landscape mode, a combination of properties that might be a good setting for printing data tables. To change this to specific units instead of the page size keyword, we could write size 8.5in 11in landscape;.

The landscape keyword means that the widest edge will be in the left-right aspect, while portrait means that the widest edge is presented top to bottom. These keywords are

- A3: 297mm×420mm
- A4: 210mm×297mm
- A5: 148mm×210mm
- B4: 250mm×353mm
- B5: 176mm×250mm
- ledger: 11in×17in
- legal: 8.5in×14in
- letter: 8.5in×11in

Setting @page margins with :left, :right, and :first pseudo-classes

With the :left and :right pseudo-classes, you can assign different values to page margins on either side of your printed pages. This can be especially useful in dealing with facing and double-sided pages, where you might need extra margin for the signature. For these constructs, @page :left means the page on the left, and @page :right means the page on the right.

```
@page :left {
  margin-right: 3in;
}

@page :right {
  margin-left: 3in;
}
```

Additionally, you can use the :first pseudo-class to have a different first page—a title page for instance:

```
@page :first {
  margin-top: 4in;
}
```

These rules will work together to figure out automatically how your margins should work based on which one is on the left, which one is on the right, and which one comes first. Support for the @page pseudo-class exists in Opera and IE8, and has not been implemented with IE7 and earlier, Firefox, or Safari as of this writing.

Using margin at-rules

With the margin at-rules, you can specify content, including autogenerated content, that will appear in the respective margin corners. The specification for such rules is still a working draft as of this writing and these features haven't made their way into any browsers, but this is an often-requested feature and the prospect of being able to use it is exciting. The draft of the specification may be found at http://www.w3.org/TR/css3-page/ if you'd like to keep track.

The at-rules for margins are as follows:

- top-left-corner
- top-left
- top-center
- top-right
- top-right-corner
- right-top
- right-middle
- right-bottom
- left-top
- left-middle
- left-bottom
- bottom-left-corner
- bottom-left
- bottom-center
- bottom-right
- bottom-right-corner

The top, right, left, and bottom boxes are distinct from their top-left-corner, top-right-corner, bottom-left-corner, and bottom-right-corner counterparts. The corner boxes are reserved for the boxes that have no adjacent content, while the top and bottom boxes would have content above or below. So any rule such as top-left or right-top is really indicating which side of the top or right box that content should appear—not the content of the corner boxes. Confused? Not surprised—Figure 4-2 should make it clearer.

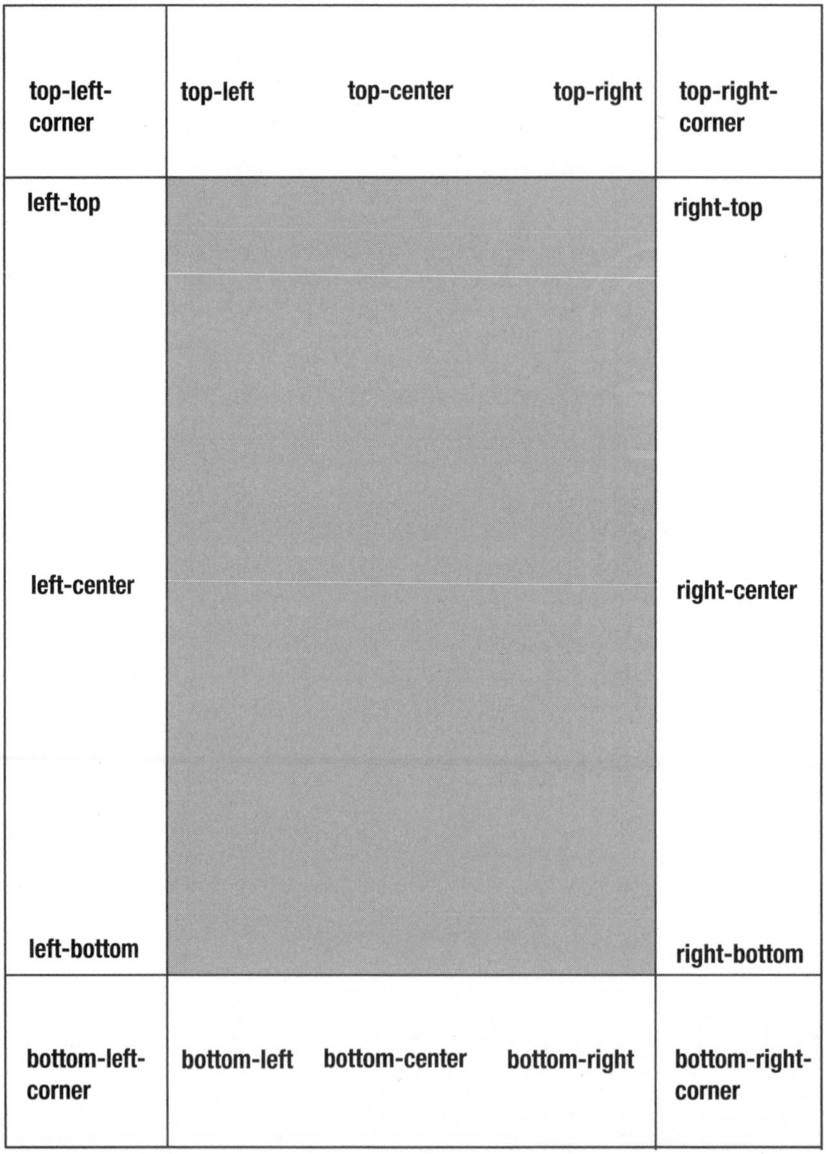

top-left-corner	top-left	top-center	top-right	top-right-corner
left-top				right-top
left-center				right-center
left-bottom				right-bottom
bottom-left-corner	bottom-left	bottom-center	bottom-right	bottom-right-corner

Figure 4-2. Location of margin box keywords. The white areas are margins; the gray area is content and padding. Each keyword illustrates its default orientation with the text-align and vertical-align properties.

With margin at-rules, it would be simple to add features such as author names, messages such as "draft" or "classified," a company logo, or generated content such as automatic page numbers across all of the pages in a print job. How convenient would it be to be able to instruct your print jobs to do something like the following?

```
@page {
    @top-left {
        content: url(DoD_logo.png);
    }
    @top-left {
        font-weight: bold;
        font-color: red;
        content: "Classified";
    }
    @bottom-left {
        content: "2009 Report on UFO Sightings"
    }
    @bottom-right {
        content: "Page " counter(page);
    }
}
```

In this example, we print a DoD logo in the upper-right corner; in the upper left, we have some nice red bold text saying "Classified"; in the lower-right corner we have the document title; and in the lower-right corner, we print the page number. This would certainly simplify printing things like official government reports, corporate marketing documents, or lengthy research papers.

Future of CSS print style sheets

As of this writing, the future of CSS for print designs is extremely promising. In addition to many more page box margin areas (four across the top and bottom and three across the left- and right-hand sides), we will also see a plethora of new generated content. For example, we will be able to easily generate dotted (.), solid (_), and spaced leaders; we will be given the ability to refer to named strings; and more.

Like many other features of CSS, many print-related features that were originally present in the CSS2 specification were removed in the CSS2.1 revision for one reason or another. Some of these features, such as named pages, may make it back into an official CSS Recommendation when CSS level 3 is finalized.

Example: styling a résumé

To learn these and other techniques for creating print styles, let's work through a live example. We'll use an example of a résumé for a classical cellist. We'll start with a page that already looks great on screen, and we're going to make this one look spectacular in print as well. First, let's take a look at the full HTML representation of this page. It is a rather long example, but that is intentional since we're going to deal with various concepts that require us to fill more than a single printed page of content:

```
<!DOCTYPE html PUBLIC "-//W3C//DTD XHTML 1.0 Strict//EN"
    "http://www.w3.org/TR/xhtml1/DTD/xhtml1-strict.dtd">
<html lang="en-us" xmlns="http://www.w3.org/1999/xhtml"
    xml:lang="en-us">
<head>
<title>Natasha O'Reilly, Baroque Cellist</title>
<meta http-equiv="Content-type" content="text/html; charset=utf-8" />
<link rel="stylesheet" href="screen.css" type="text/css" media="all" />
</head>
<body>
<div class="hresume layout" id="natasha-oreilly-orchestra-resume">
    <div id="sitenav">
        <ul>
            <li><a href="http://natasha.example.com/">Home</a></li>
            <li><a href="http://natasha.example.com/about/">
                About</a></li>
            <li><a href="http://natasha.example.com/cv/">
                Résumé</a></li>
            <li><a href="http://natasha.example.com/cal/">
                Upcoming Events</a></li>
            <li><a href="http://natasha.example.com/av/">
                Audio and Video</a></li>
        </ul>
    </div>
<div id="natashaoreilly" class="vcard">
  <h1 id="bw-name" class="fn n"> <span class="given-name">
    Natasha</span> <span class="family-name">O'Reilly</span>
  </h1>
  <ul class="summary">
    <li>Expert in Baroque performance and period instruments.</li>
    <li>Seeking positions with major ensembles that are focused on
        historical performance.</li>
  </ul>
  <dl>
    <dt>Photo</dt>
    <dd><img src="headshot.jpg" class="photo"
        alt="Photo of Natasha O'Reilly, cellist." /></dd>
    <dt>Telephone</dt>
    <dd class="tel">(415) 555-1212</dd>
    <dt>Email</dt>
    <dd><a class="email" href="mailto:natasha@example.com">
        natasha@example.com</a></dd>
    <dt>Web</dt>
    <dd><a class="url" href="http://natasha.example.com"
        rel="me">http://natasha.example.com</a></dd>
  </dl>
</div>
<div class="vcalendar" id="experience">
  <h1>Experience</h1>
```

```
<div id="exp-farallones" class="experience vevent">
  <h2 class="summary">Principal Cello, <a class="url fn org"
      href="http://fso.example.org">Farallones Symphony
      Orchestra</a></h2>
  <p><abbr class="dtstart" title="2007-09-01">September 2007
      </abbr>-Present</p>
  <div class="description">
    <p>Principal <a rel="tag" class="skill"
    href="http://en.wikipedia.org/wiki/Violoncello">cellist</a>
    for the Farallones Symphony Orchestra, a small rocky islet
    off the coast of San Francisco, which is a very lonely spot
    considering it's just me and the seagulls out here. On the
    upside, lots of solo opportunities! Building a baroque cello
    based on 17th Century Cremonese style out of found
    driftwood and old planks from an abandoned lifeboat.</p>
  </div>
</div>
<div class="experience vevent" id="exp-rockcity">
  <h2 class="summary">Section Cello, <a class="url fn org"
      href="http://rockcitychamber.example.org">Rock City
      Symphony Orchestra</a></h2>
  <p><abbr class="dtstart" title="2001-01-01">2003</abbr>-present</p>
  <div class="description">
    <p> Section <a rel="tag" class="skill"
      href="http://en.wikipedia.org/wiki/Violoncello">cellist
      </a> for the Rock City Chamber Orchestra, with
      performances from Western Mt. Diablo to as far east as
      Lodi. Performances of major composers including Grieg,
      Dvorák, Beethoven, Bach, and others.</p>
  </div>
</div>
</div>
<div class="vcalendar" id="education">
  <h1> Education </h1>
  <div class="education vevent">
    <h2 class="summary">Doctor of Musical Arts, <a class="url
location" href="http://www.newenglandconservatory.edu/">New
England Conservatory of Music</a></h2>
    <p><abbr class="dtstart"
title="2003-09-01">2003</abbr>-<abbr class="dtend"
title="2006-06-06">2006</abbr></p>
    <div class="description">
      <p>Performed research in baroque cello performance with an
emphasis on authentic reproduction of the solo violoncello
suites of J.S. Bach. Held a series of lecture-performances on
these works in Boston (NEC), New York City (NYU), and Los
Angeles (UCLA).</p>
    </div>
  </div>
```

```
<div class="education vevent">
    <h2 class="summary">Master of Music, <a class="url location"
href="http://www.sfcm.edu/">San Francisco Conservatory of
Music</a></h2>
    <p><abbr class="dtstart"
title="2001-09-01">2001</abbr>-<abbr class="dtend"
title="2003-06-06">2003</abbr></p>
    <div class="description">
      <p>Focus in orchestral performance, baroque performance,
and chamber music.</p>
    </div>
  </div>
  <div class="education vevent">
    <h2 class="summary">Bachelor of Music, <a class="url
location" href="http://www.oberlin.edu/">Oberlin College
Conservatory of Music</a></h2>
    <p><abbr class="dtstart"
title="1997-09-01">1997</abbr>-<abbr class="dtend"
title="2001-06-06">2001</abbr></p>
    <div class="description">
      <p>Focus in orchestral performance, baroque performance,
and chamber music.</p>
    </div>
  </div>
</div>
<div id="interests">
  <h1>Interests</h1>
  <ul>
      <li><a rel="tag"
href="http://en.wikipedia.org/wiki/Chamber_music">chamber
music</a></li>
      <li><a rel="tag"
href="http://en.wikipedia.org/wiki/Wine">wine</a></li>
      <li><a rel="tag"
href="http://en.wikipedia.org/wiki/Astrophysics">astrophysics</a>
      </li>
      <li><a rel="tag"
href="http://en.wikipedia.org/wiki/Baroque">the Baroque period</a></li>
      <li><a rel="tag"
href="http://en.wikipedia.org/wiki/Viola_jokes">viola jokes</a></li>
      <li><a rel="tag" href="http://www.w3.org/Style/CSS/">CSS</a></li>
  </ul>
</div>
<p>References available upon request.</p>
</div>
</body>
</html>
```

An experienced HTML coder might take a look at this example and notice that there appears to be a large number of classes assigned—perhaps more classes than they were used to. This is intentional—the classes represent embedded "microformats," and in particular this markup follows the hResume microformat design, which includes embedded instances of hCard and hCalendar. Don't worry too much about all those details now—we'll learn more about that in a later chapter when we discuss the Semantic Web in detail. For now, just appreciate that we have a rich Semantic Web structure to work from, with plenty of hooks in the form of class attributes for us to build our styles from. We've predesigned a screen layout, and the page looks like Figure 4-3 in your typical modern, standards-compliant web browser.

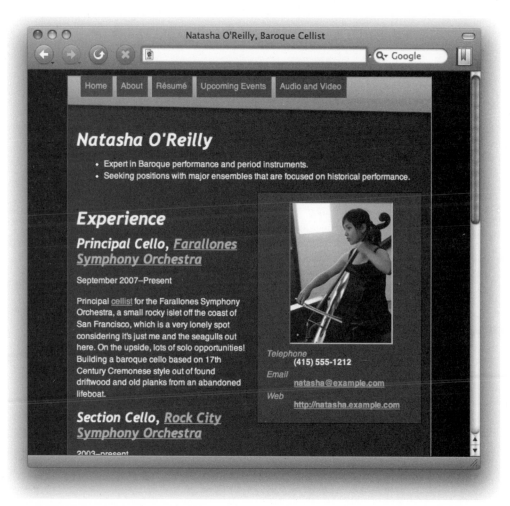

Figure 4-3. Our page as viewed in a browser

If you examine our source code, you'll see that the styles that rendered this page were brought in via a link tag using a media type set to `all`. That means that the styles we've applied here to screen will apply to print as well. As is, printing this document will give you a somewhat less-than-optimal page rendering, as shown in Figure 4-4.

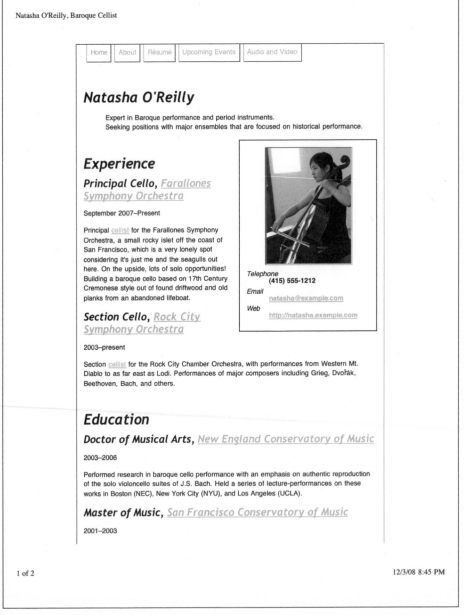

Figure 4-4. Our page, printed as is

OK, we've seen worse. But there are definitely some opportunities for improvement here. For one, the center column of content has extra-wide margins. In fact, the width of this center content is set to be 60 percent, so that means we might have an opportunity to improve the efficiency of our page real estate use by up to 40 percent. Also remember in our screen design that the font color was white, but somehow the color of the printed text here became black in our Gecko-based browser. This is good considering the fact that the vast majority of standard printer paper is white, but we certainly didn't specify that. In Safari and Internet Explorer, the font color is set to gray, giving us a readable level of contrast on the expected white background, while still paying homage to the fact that our font color was white on screen. Most modern browsers will gauge the level of darkness on a font and make an assumption as to how much darker the font needs to be to render in a readable contrast on white paper. Nevertheless, our hyperlinks are still yellow and that doesn't look so good on white.

Speaking of contrast—the background colors are not printed by default in most browsers, and the same goes for background images. Some browsers allow for the preference to turn on background printing, but it is not on by default and you should never assume it to be enabled. We've already seen that the black background colors have been largely ignored along with our font color preference, and the same level of disregard for our color specifications has been applied to the top banner background image as well.

Another annoyance is where the page breaks. In most browsers at the default setting, the break is somewhere after the heading "Section Cello, Rock City Symphony" and the heading's descriptive text. It would be better to get the break in a spot where this content isn't separated by a page. And while we're being nit-picky, those underlines on the hyperlinks are fairly useless in the print medium, as is the entire existence of the primary navigation. We'd like to see better typography overall, and we notice that IE renders our borders poorly. Is that enough complaining? Good. OK, then, let's see if we can doll this thing up a bit.

First of all, let's separate our screen styles from our print styles. This can be done easily enough—here we'll simply change the media type of our style sheet to screen:

```
<link rel="stylesheet" href="screen.css" type="text/css"
    media="screen" />
```

This means that only the devices identified by the user agent as screen devices will display styles from this style sheet. Other style sheets will render the default styles as shown in Figure 4-5.

This is already a step in the right direction. We've already gotten rid of those extra-wide margins, and the default serif font used in this browser is appropriate for printing. It already looks more like a typical printed page from a word processor, and we haven't done a thing to it really. However, we now notice that the portrait seems to be much larger than before, and we know we can do so much more with the typography and layout. To get things moving, let's embed a print style sheet into our markup and build some print-specific styles. On line 8 of the markup, insert the following code:

```
<style type="text/css" media="print">
    body {
        font-family: Garamond, "Times New Roman", Times, serif;
        font-size: 0.8em;
        line-height: 1.5;
        color: #191919;
    }
</style>
```

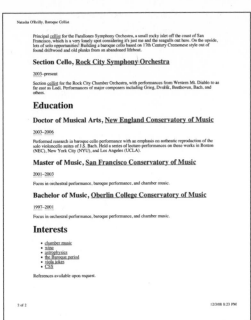

Figure 4-5. Our page as viewed in print without styles

Here we've embedded a print style sheet and established a rule to make all the text default to a nice-looking serif font family. We know that serif fonts are regarded for their superior readability in print, but we want to go with a font that was a little more attractive than the usual default Times New Roman that most browsers default to. Garamond is a popular font that is not quite as popular or as ubiquitous, but it can offer us that added element of style to our typography and it's worth offering it up to our users who have it. In the font-family declaration, fonts are listed left to right in order of preference. The leftmost item gets highest precedence, and the user agent will search this list of fonts from left to right until a match for an installed font is found on the system. So in our font-family declaration, we specify Garamond first. If that isn't available, we still like Times New Roman and Times as backups. In case none of those are available, we defer to the browser's serif font preference.

Figure 4-6 also shows that we have tightened up the font size a bit by reducing the default font size to 10 points, and added a line height value of 1.5 to make our text more readable on paper. Ten-point text is a good standard for most computer-printed documents, although you could easily justify anywhere between 9 point and 12 point for document copy. Wider line heights can help with legibility in paragraph text, and also might add a touch of style to a document layout. The value of 1.5 can be read as "one and a half lines." The default line height is 1, so we're increasing that default by 50 percent. To finish it off, we assign an explicit color of #191919, which will be applied to all text in our document. It's a nice dark shade of gray, almost black, that will be very readable on white paper. We know ahead of time that Firefox and other Gecko-based browsers will probably render this text black anyway, but that's fine since we've chosen a fairly dark color. Now that we have our print style sheet started, let's get rid of some artifacts in our print output that we don't need, starting with the hyperlinks and site navigation:

```
<style type="text/css" media="print">
    .layout {
        font-family: Garamond, "Times New Roman", Times, serif;
```

```
        font-size: 10pt;
        line-height: 1.5;
        color: #191919;
    }
    a {
        text-decoration: none;
        color: #333;
        border-bottom: 1pt solid #CCC;
    }
    #sitenav {
        display: none;
    }
</style>
```

Figure 4-6. Our page with the site navigation removed and hyperlinks toned down

The default underlines that most browsers give to hyperlinks are fairly useless in print—they detract from the readability of our document by creating unnecessary visual cruft and distract our eyes with something that we can't really act on in paper. To remove the default underlines from our document, we use text-decoration:none. But at the same time we've decided to retain a bit of this information—after all, it may be useful for the reader to know that there *is* a hyperlink there for reference purposes, even if they cannot click on it on the printed page. So we are going to provide a lightening of the color of the text to #333. Since we know that Gecko browsers will fail to render the lighter gray text color, we also add back in a border at the bottom by using border-bottom:1pt solid #CCC. Why on earth would we readd the underline this way, you ask? Simple: the reason is that browsers will honor the light gray #CCC underline specification, creating a subtle and less obtrusive visual differentiation between it and the text above. If we left this up to the default text-decoration:underline property, then we'd have uniform color between the text and the underline, which again would be ignored by Gecko browsers.

Since we have preserved the idea of a hyperlink in our print-based styling, we could consider taking this one step further. Using the CSS content property and attribute accessors, we can print the URL that lies embedded within our hyperlinks and bring them out into the open. It makes most sense to have such links appear in the content area and not bother with exposing the navigation element URLs or URLs found elsewhere in the page layout, so let's use descendant selectors to target just a couple of areas where these URLs might be more informative:

```
#experience a:after, #education a:after {
    content: " [URL: " attr(href) "]";
    color:#555;
    }
```

An article by Eric Meyer that demonstrated this technique and several other similar print-specific topics appeared in A List Apart back in back in 2002. Titled "CSS Design: Going to Print" (http://www.alistapart.com/articles/goingtoprint/), the article is perhaps even more useful today now that many more user agents have implemented better support for the CSS2 specification.

Some might argue that embedding the URL in printed media detracts from the readability of the content of the document, while others will argue that having this information available makes it possible for the reader to use the URL in other contexts away from the printed page. Consider these issues and use whichever method makes the most sense for your project goals.

It's useless for your design purposes here to deliver site navigation on this page; it takes away from the intended purpose of this content, and is a waste of space and paper. You can therefore remove the site navigation from the print output by applying the display:none declaration to the #sitenav block. The <div id="sitenav"> element and all of the contained children elements are completely removed from the page output and document flow, allowing the more useful content to filter up toward the top of the page.

It is important to note something about our border-bottom:1pt solid #CCC line specification that we used earlier. In particular, please direct your attention to the 1pt part. If you look at the line settings for many word processors, graphic design tools, and desktop publishing programs, you will notice that lines can be much thinner than 1 point. They are often set at values such as 0.75 point, 0.5 point, or even thinner. This produces a nice, crisp line that can look more attractive in print. Unfortunately in modern browsers, you really can't get any thinner than 1 point for the border property. Any value less than 1 will be rounded up to 1 point. We can hope that this function will one day become more powerful in browser implementations, but for now you should assume that 1 point or 1 pixel is going to be as thin as you can get in print for lines. You can, however, use border-bottom:**thin** solid #CCC; instead. The thin keyword, while not very specific, will usually display a crisp, thin line in most of the modern browsers.

Our next goal is to fix the display of the information box—the box that contains the photo, telephone number, email address, and URL for our featured cellist. In print we can see that the photo appears much larger compared to the screen version, and we've lost our floating to the right. Let's keep the float and reduce the size of the image to be more appropriate for the printed view, and apply a few more stylistic enhancements to our printed résumé, the results of which are shown in Figure 4-7:

```
<style type="text/css" media="print">
    a {
        text-decoration: none;
        color: #333;
        border-bottom: 1pt solid #DDD;
    }
    dl {
        width: 8cm;
        float: right;
        text-align: center;
        margin: 5em 0;
    }
    dt {
        font-style: italic;
        margin: 0;
        padding: 0;
    }
    dl > dt:first-child {
        display: none;
    }
    dd {
        font-weight: bold;
        margin: 0;
        padding: 0;
    }
    .photo {
        width: 3cm;
        height: 4cm;
    }
    .layout {
        font-family: Garamond, "Times New Roman", Times, serif;
        font-size: 10pt;
        line-height: 1.5;
        color: #191919;
    }
```

```
        #sitenav {
            display: none;
        }
    </style>
```

Experience

Principal Cello, Farallones Symphony Orchestra

September 2007–Present

Principal cellist for the Farallones Symphony Orchestra, a small rocky islet off the coast of San Francisco, which is a very lonely spot considering it's just me and the seagulls out here. On the upside, lots of solo opportunities! Building a baroque cello based on 17th Century Cremonese style out of found driftwood and old planks from an abandoned lifeboat.

Section Cello, Rock City Symphony Orchestra

2003–present

Section cellist for the Rock City Chamber Orchestra, with performances from Western Mt. Diablo to as far east as Lodi. Performances of major composers including Grieg, Dvořák, Beethoven, Bach, and others.

Telephone
(415) 555-1212
Email
natasha@example.com
Web
http://natasha.example.com

Figure 4-7. *Floating the information box to the right and applying some style*

The first thing to point out is that, now that our style sheet is getting longer, we've decided to slightly rearrange our CSS rules in a more logical order. We've chosen to adhere to a general order of specificity, with least specific rules toward the top and most specific rules toward the bottom. Placing more specific rules toward the bottom of our style sheet pairs well with the concept that rules appearing early in the cascade order might be overridden by later-appearing rules that have conflicts, and this is considered in many circles a best practice to follow. The only exception to this practice for this case is our dl > dt:first-child rule. This rule has a much higher specificity than the following dd rule, but since it applies a special modification to the preceding dl and dt rules, we've chosen to keep it here for readability's sake.

The image in print is too large for the printed page. In fact, we notice that this portrait has been reduced on screen as well, and that the source image weighs in at a native 300 pixels wide by 400 pixels tall. Since we know that this résumé will likely be printed on a sheet of US Letter or A4 paper, we can be reasonably sure about what image dimensions we want to have. Here we've specified width:3cm and height:4cm to our .photo class, which is a good proportional value to the native pixel dimensions of the photo.

To move our information box over to the right, we have applied a width of 3 inches to the dl element and floated it to the right. Making this element 8 centimeters wide and centering the content within using text-align:center provides plenty of white space to differentiate it from the main part of the document, and the 5 ems of margin on either side ensures that any text that might approach the edge of the dl container provides a final amount of buffer.

To give our information box some typographic style, we set our definition terms (dt) to display in italics and our definitions themselves (dd) to display in bold. Removing all of the margin and padding from these elements ensures that we won't run into any surprises with differences in the way various browsers style these by default, and it will allow our centered content in the info box to have a proper display without any unexpected indentations. We've also decided that the definition term "Photo" isn't needed since the definition for that item is fairly obvious, so we've removed it by using the first-child pseudo selector: dl > dt:first-child. This selects the first dt element that is a child element of dl, and then all we need to do is set display:none to remove it from the output.

What we have now is a fairly decent-looking printed page. This is much better than our original, and our users (in this case potential employers for Ms. O'Reilly) will appreciate having the higher-quality printed output. This would be fine as is, but there's actually much more we can do. So let's keep playing around with this résumé to see what we can come up with. We'll begin by styling those headings.

The headings currently print in the default serif font defined by our font-family rule applied earlier in the .layout rule. But this cellist wants something a little more stylish for her résumé and would like to see the headings in a more elegant typeface. But we know as CSS developers that finding a cursive font that is cross platform is difficult to do. Our customer Ms. O'Reilly has agreed that some flexibility with the headings is fine as long as it somehow looks pretty, so that frees us up to be a little creative with our font family designation. With that in mind, let's build a font family for the headings that will be almost guaranteed to look different between various browsers, but will look stylish and interesting either way. Let's explore our options.

A font that is more common on Windows but not unknown on the Mac platform is Edwardian Script ITC. This font is quite florid and full of loops and variations that make Edwardian Script ITC an excellent choice for a stylish-looking heading. Monotype Corsiva is a more popular font found frequently on Windows and occasionally on Mac, but it is not nearly as stylish as the previously mentioned selections. And if all else fails, we always have the cursive keyword in CSS. Edwardian Script ITC seems like a good choice for our primary font, so let's start there. Our backup is going to be Monotype Corsiva, and then we finish up with a cursive keyword to ensure something stylish gets picked. Edwardian Script can appear small, so we have bumped up the font sizes for h1 and h2 elements to 32 points and 18 points, respectively, and removed any underlines from <a> elements that happen to be a part of any <h2> elements—it looks terrible in print.

We'd really like to write .experience { page-break-inside:avoid; } in our style sheet to keep our experience blocks from printing on separate pages, but unfortunately this property is largely unsupported in modern browsers aside from Opera. Let's write it anyway and enjoy this behavior in at least the one browser that supports it. Perhaps soon the other browsers will catch up. Here's what we have added so far, the results of which are shown in Figure 4-8:

```
<style type="text/css" media="print">
a {
    text-decoration: none;
    color: #333;
    border-bottom: 1pt solid #DDD;
}
h1, h2 {
```

```
        font-family: "Edwardian Script ITC", "Monotype Corsiva", cursive;
        font-weight: normal;
        margin-bottom: 0;
        page-break-after: avoid;
    }
    h1 {
        font-size: 32pt;
    }
    h2 {
        font-size: 18pt;
    }
    h2 a {
        border: 0;
    }
    dl {
        width: 8cm;
        float: right;
        text-align: center;
        margin: 5em 0;
    }
    dt {
        font-style: italic;
        margin: 0;
        padding: 0;
    }
    dl > dt:first-child {
        display: none;
    }
    dd {
        font-weight: bold;
        margin: 0;
        padding: 0;
    }
    .photo {
        width: 3cm;
        height: 4cm;
    }
    .layout {
        font-family: Garamond, "Times New Roman", Times, serif;
        font-size: 10pt;
        line-height: 1.5;
        color: #191919;
    }
    .experience {
        page-break-inside: avoid;
    }
    #sitenav {
        display: none;
    }
</style>
```

Natasha O'Reilly

- Expert in Baroque performance and period instruments.
- Seeking positions with major ensembles that are focused on historical performance.

Experience

Principal Cello, Farallones Symphony Orchestra

September 2007–Present

Principal cellist for the Farallones Symphony Orchestra, a small rocky islet off the coast of San Francisco, which is a very lonely spot considering it's just me and the seagulls out here. On the upside, lots of solo opportunities! Building a baroque cello based on 17th Century Cremonese style out of found driftwood and old planks from an abandoned lifeboat.

Telephone
(415) 555-1212
Email
natasha@example.com
Web
http://natasha.example.com

Section Cello, Rock City Symphony Orchestra

2003–present

Section cellist for the Rock City Chamber Orchestra, with performances from Western Mt. Diablo to as far east as Lodi. Performances of major composers including Grieg, Dvořák, Beethoven, Bach, and others. Lorem ipsum dolor sit amet, consectetur adipisicing elit, sed do eiusmod tempor incididunt ut labore et dolore magna aliqua. Ut enim ad minim veniam, quis nostrud exercitation ullamco laboris nisi ut aliquip ex ea commodo consequat. Duis aute irure dolor in reprehenderit in voluptate velit esse cillum dolore eu fugiat nulla pariatur. Excepteur sint occaecat cupidatat non proident, sunt in culpa qui officia deserunt mollit anim id est laborum.

Figure 4-8. Cursive font family treatment for headings

It is too bad about `page-break-inside` not being as well supported as we'd like. But if we take a look at our page, we can see that there might be an opportunity to insert a more manually placed page break that *should* work in most settings. It looks weird to have the Education heading sitting there at the bottom of the page and then the remaining content falling onto the next page. We can apply `page-break-before:always` to the #education block, since we can see that in all our browsers tested this block begins toward the end of page one, and try to get a better placement of our content onto the two pages:

```
#education {
    page-break-before:always;
}
```

A word of caution on this: there is a fair amount of fudge factor here and we are giving up some control on how this will print by inserting a manual page break in this specific spot, because we don't know if our user has resized their fonts on the other end. This is something to be careful with and deserves some testing and thoughtful consideration before implementing.

We're almost done. Let's add a little style to the summary points at the top, and see if we can fill out the overall layout somehow. For the summary points we can simply italicize the font, which should give us a nice bit of emphasis for this section. The targeted content has been assigned a class of summary already, but there's a problem: the summary class is repeated elsewhere in the document, but we only want to target this one instance of the summary class. That means we're going to have to be more specific. And we're in luck: the instance of the summary class that we want is contained within the vcard class, so we can conveniently use a descendant selector to style the item we want:

```
.vcard .summary {
    font-style:italic;
}
```

After looking at that for a minute, we can see that the text appears a bit too tightly packed in an italic typeface for such a prominent part of the page. Let's space it out a bit by using the letter-spacing property:

```
.vcard .summary {
    font-style:italic;
    letter-spacing: 0.1em;
}
```

Now we have a decent-looking summary at the top; our last step is to fill out the pages a bit. It looks like there is enough room on our pages to increase the line height of our paragraph text a bit, which might help with readability while we're at it ,and provide an added touch of style to the output. So let's try using the line-height property:

```
p {
    line-height:2;
}
```

You can see the results in Figure 4-9.

This might be a good place to stop. We have clean, tidy-looking print output that is free of unnecessary junk from our screen view of the page, and we've applied some neat typography to make the printed résumé look more elegant. Our client is happy and can start using her online résumé to market her cello performance skills! The last step is to extract our style sheet from the HTML and place it into an external file. Create a new file called print.css in the same directory as our HTML file, copy and paste our CSS code (everything in-between the <style> element), and then replace the <style> element block with

```
<link rel="stylesheet" href="print.css" type="text/css"
    media="print" />
```

Our final style sheet in print.css is as follows:

```
a {
    text-decoration:none;
    color:#333;
    border-bottom:1pt solid #DDD;
}
h1, h2 {
```

```
        font-family:"Edwardian Script ITC", "Monotype Corsiva", cursive;
        font-weight:normal;
        margin-bottom:0;
        page-break-after:avoid;
    }
    h1 {
        font-size:32pt;
    }
    h2 {
        font-size:18pt;
    }
    h2 a {
        border:0;
    }
    p {
        line-height:2;
    }
    dl {
        width:8cm;
        float:right;
        text-align:center;
        margin:5em 0;
    }
    dt {
        font-style:italic;
        margin:0; padding:0;
    }
    dl > dt:first-child {
        display:none;
    }
    dd {
        font-weight:bold;
        margin:0; padding:0;
    }
    .photo {
        width:3cm;
        height:4cm;
    }
    .layout {
        font-family: Garamond, "Times New Roman", Times, serif;
        font-size:10pt;
        line-height:1.5;
        color:#191919;
    }
    .experience {
        page-break-inside:avoid;
    }
    .vcard .summary {
        font-style:italic;
```

```
    letter-spacing: 0.1em;
}
#sitenav {
    display:none;
}
#education {
    page-break-before:always;
}
```

Natasha O'Reilly

- *Expert in Baroque performance and period instruments.*
- *Seeking positions with major ensembles that are focused on historical performance.*

Experience

Principal Cello, Farallones Symphony Orchestra

September 2007–Present

Principal cellist for the Farallones Symphony Orchestra, a small rocky islet off the coast of San Francisco, which is a very lonely spot considering it's just me and the seagulls out here. On the upside, lots of solo opportunities! Building a baroque cello based on 17th Century Cremonese style out of found driftwood and old planks from an abandoned lifeboat.

Telephone
(415) 555-1212
Email
natasha@example.com
Web
http://natasha.example.com

Section Cello, Rock City Symphony Orchestra

2003–present

Section cellist for the Rock City Chamber Orchestra, with performances from Western Mt. Diablo to as far east as Lodi. Performances of major composers including Grieg, Dvořák, Beethoven, Bach, and others. Lorem ipsum dolor sit amet, consectetur adipisicing elit, sed do eiusmod tempor incididunt ut labore et dolore magna aliqua. Ut enim ad minim veniam, quis nostrud exercitation ullamco laboris nisi ut aliquip ex ea commodo consequat. Duis aute irure dolor in reprehenderit in voluptate velit esse cillum dolore eu fugiat nulla pariatur. Excepteur sint occaecat cupidatat non proident, sunt in culpa qui officia deserunt mollit anim id est laborum.

Figure 4-9. Page one of our final print design

Summary

Making print style sheets takes advantage of CSS's innate ability to provide alternative presentations of the same content, a concept whose benefits you should be familiar with from previous chapters. In this chapter, you applied this knowledge to the print media by reformatting an existing design for the screen so that it could be reproduced appropriately on paper. In addition, you learned how providing a print style sheet gives your dear website visitors a better experience when they take your content off-screen.

In composing your print style sheet, you first looked at the more common motivations and goals users have for printing physical pages from web pages. Next, you analyzed particular areas of concern to aid in your reformatting efforts, such as the content's typography, the dimensions and properties of the printing paper, and the existing content itself. By removing interactive navigation elements irrelevant to the print medium such as hyperlinks, repositioning or completely removing tangential information from sidebars, and changing the layout of the primary content area, you successfully leveraged the existing screen styles for your new print ones.

However, you can do a lot more than merely create a "printer-friendly" version of your page. From there, further optimizations can be employed, such as using a serif font for your written copy and identifying where background images, font colors, and page breaks might cause issues for your design. You can then deal with these problems so that the content they present is enhanced rather than dulled-down.

You also learned how CSS deals with different sizes of paper by defining page boxes, analogous to the browser's window (or viewport). However, since most users will probably be printing on white A4 or US Letter paper, many of CSS's intricate page sizing and selection features are still struggling to find support in modern web browsers. Further, you saw that many historical artifacts used for signaling printable pages, such as custom-built "Print this page" buttons, are still in use today for slightly different purposes.

Regardless of the content you have, it almost always makes sense to create a print style sheet for your content. Having one available makes a big difference to your users, and the effort required to provide an adequate baseline is so minimal you'd be remiss not to do so. Now, with significant experience using CSS that targets multiple media types for a single chunk of content, let's next turn our attention to yet another popular form factor for web sites: mobile, ultra-portable handheld devices.

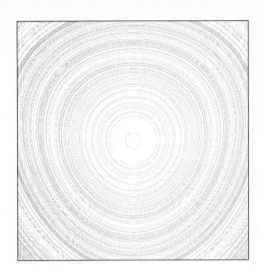

Chapter 5

DEVELOPING FOR SMALL SCREENS AND THE MOBILE WEB

As we've discussed earlier, the evolution of the World Wide Web has been extremely chaotic when compared to other technologies. This Darwinian model has arguably had both positive and negative effects. Developing for the desktop web browsing experience was tumultuous at best for a long time, with user agent capabilities varying wildly. However, if you thought that was wild, then you'd better buckle your seat belt because we're about to take you on the rollercoaster ride that is *mobile* web development, which has been described by experts as "the most hostile programming environment ever devised."[1]

Despite the countless limitations and challenges of mobile web development, we remain excited and even optimistic about the possibilities. The best news of all is that, thanks to the web standards we'll discuss in this chapter, it's possible to achieve a decent baseline of functionality and appearance for your site on the vast majority of current and future mobile devices. Moreover, if you embrace the same best practices we advocate throughout this book for the desktop's platforms, your view of the mobile market space will look like "one extra mile" rather than another marathon effort.

---

1. This is a famous statement by Douglas Crockford, a world-renowned JavaScript expert and senior front-end web development specialist at Yahoo!. He used to be well known for stating that the *desktop* web browser was the most hostile programming environment on the planet—that is, until the *mobile* browser was conceived.

In this chapter we'll explore styling CSS for the rapidly growing mobile web medium. We'll study some of the possibilities and advantages of mobile web design, such as the growth opportunity and ubiquity of the mobile web platform. You'll learn about the limitations that you'll be confronted with when targeting mobile devices, such as issues with screen size, bandwidth, usability, and limited capabilities. We'll then look at how to build mobile style sheets, and we'll get into some specifics with styling for the highly popular Opera browser and WebKit-based browsers such as Safari for the iPhone.

The arrival of the mobile Web

Mobile devices are becoming more and more prevalent in the hands of consumers, and the capability and usability of the mobile browser platform is making handheld web surfing increasingly commonplace. Leveraging the use of an embedded browser in stand-alone software and appliances is also becoming a common practice among traditional application developers. In other words, your web page might not be viewed from a classic web browser at all, but from any number of programs that *wrap themselves around* a web browser, even—perhaps especially—a mobile one. Quite simply, all web development does not exist for the desktop computer screen alone.

Despite being practiced for many years, support for mobile web browsing has arguably been little more than a line item on the feature sets of many mobile handset vendors and content providers. There really wasn't significant attention paid to the overall user experience of browsing traditional web content on the move from either content producers or hardware vendors. Naturally, lacking a good user experience limited user adoption, and without customer demand, why bother improving the situation?

All of this began to change with the development of more capable and usable web browsers specifically designed for mobile use, which was rightfully seen as a huge market opportunity. Two early examples are Opera Mobile and the Blazer browser, commonly found on Handspring (now Palm) Treo devices to this day. These browsers were the first to offer a more usable and functional experience, but were still bound by limitations in the hardware they were installed on and therefore rely on relatively painful workarounds to transform content originally intended for desktop viewing to a mobile aspect.

It was unmistakably the release of Apple's iPhone in summer 2007, with its innovative and refined touch screen interface and its Mobile Safari browser, that proved to be the game-changing event. Rather than invasively transform content to a mobile aspect, Mobile Safari offers an intuitive zoom-able interface to provide a full implementation of the web browsing experience on a handheld device. This new interface greatly reduced the barriers for mobile web use and access on Apple's product.

In February 2008 Google reported to the *Financial Times* that they were seeing *50 times more search queries coming from iPhone than from any other mobile handset* at that time. While this snapshot statistic is not necessarily representative of the entire mobile Web, it is an auspicious metric considering the iPhone had been out for only seven or eight months and constituted a tiny fraction of the mobile handset hardware market at the time. Nevertheless, despite its limited market share, the iPhone's Mobile Safari browser was clearly already on its way to becoming the dominant player in the mobile web market space.

What was the key to the mobile Web's adoption on the iPhone? The answer is usability. So much attention to detail was placed on the iPhone and its Mobile Safari web browser that users and developers alike were suddenly able to create and consume traditional web content with very little additional effort.

While this groundbreaking advancement is undoubtedly the direction mobile web browsing will take, developers are still required to take some special measures to ensure their sites function and appear appropriately on a mobile device. With the iPhone, Apple proved that a focus on optimizing for usability in a mobile context was the critical factor in successfully bringing the mobile web to mainstream adoption. Now it's up to you, the web developer, to optimize your sites for that same mobile context if you want to succeed in the mobile space.

The limitations and challenges of mobile web development

Constraints can be seen as a limitation and a barrier, or they may be viewed as challenges and even opportunities. Sometimes working within strict restrictions can inspire us to more creative, more effective, and more efficient solutions than we would have otherwise settled for. Often, the major challenge of mobile web development is related to the reduction in available screen real estate. You have to creatively pack a lot of information into a tiny space, but there are also many other variables you must consider and challenges you must overcome.

The reduced screen size on handheld devices has immense usability implications as well. The heterogeneous ecosystem of mobile hardware and software also implies varying levels of support for various different technologies. You can no longer rely on the same assumptions you might have for desktop web development. Even the very human-computer interaction models we are used to developing for are sometimes completely different, since users rarely have access to input devices such as mice and keyboards while on the go.

Therefore, let's begin our exploration of the practicalities of mobile web development by acquainting ourselves with the various aspects of the medium, and their similarities and differences to web development on the desktop. Get ready to throw all your ideas about "minimum screen sizes" out the window right now, because they're about to get a whole lot smaller.

Reduced and unpredictable screen sizes

The most obvious thing we must consider in developing CSS for mobile devices is that their screen sizes are not only going to be much smaller than their desktop counterparts but will also vary wildly. The resolutions available to you will probably be anywhere from less than 100 pixels square on some mobile phones, to the 480×320 pixel resolution on an Apple iPhone or iPod touch, to an ASUS Eee PC 700 with an 800×480 display and beyond. Only one thing is certain: all of these are going to be significantly smaller than what is often considered common computer screen resolutions.

When dealing with these constraints at either end of the spectrum, you have to be very creative and very concise in displaying information. This means you not only have to be choosy with regard to how you display something, but also to what you display in the first place. In many cases, choosing to display one thing may mean that you no longer have space for something else without requiring some kind of user interaction to switch between the two.

Since there's so much less space "above the fold," displaying the most important content first is critical. Some browsers will actively transform your content, so your markup's source order may take even more precedence than your style sheets. Moreover, since bandwidth and CPU speed is also often severely limited, this could mean that "above the fold" might simply be "the HTML that gets downloaded first."

Also due to the relative lack of screen real estate as compared with our large screen or even print mediums, images and text will have different proportional considerations to the viewport and to each other. You need to ensure that these elements remain accessible, legible, and attractive. In some cases, elements will literally be cropped or resized in undesirable ways unless you explicitly give them an altered appearance. Stretching and warping is not uncommon, nor is inaccurate zooming that forces users to scroll back and forth horizontally to read paragraphs.

These guidelines also apply to entire layouts, not just individual elements. Since you may not be able to accurately determine user agent capabilities ahead of time, it's even more important to adopt defensive programming techniques in a mobile project than a desktop one. Although we'll examine these specifics in more detail later, briefly this means you should be relying on capability detection mechanisms like CSS3 media queries, flexibly specified dimensions such as liquid layouts, and other similar dynamically adjustable techniques as much as possible.

Varied interaction paradigms and usability implications

Another major consideration for mobile web development is the hardware itself and the human-computer interaction paradigms that it enables (or disables, as the case may be). When using desktop web browsers, we can be fairly confident that most users will have a mouse and a keyboard, and so our web sites and web applications make use of the continuous input provided by a cursor for things like :hover (rollover) effects. However, the same may not be true of mobile devices, since a finger or stylus can often only send incremental inputs that emulate "clicks," causing some elements like navigation menus to fail to expand. These can be absolutely critical usability or accessibility problems!

In many ways, mobile device usability for the Web is still uncharted territory. Users may be navigating selections with a trackwheel, trackball, joystick, arrow keys, or a toggle. They may be using a stylus as is found on many Palm- and Windows-based devices. Alternatively, they may be using their finger (or *fingers*) such as when using gestures on the iPhone and iPod touch. They may have a physical keyboard, a virtual on-screen keyboard, or simply a numeric keypad.

Whatever they have on the device, that's what they are stuck with. You must take into account the size, position, and order of page controls to allow the widest range of users effective access to the page, since many of these interaction paradigms are extremely limited or even completely linear (i.e., serial). You must also consider that for some devices part of the control apparatus, be it a stylus or a user's finger, may be obscuring part of the screen or require a different-sized parcel of screen real estate to be useful, and again you must balance that requirement with the limited screen size you have available in the first place.

Similar challenges exist for kiosks and embedded browser interfaces as well. Remember our fictional Frigerator2000 example from Chapter 1: do you know whether it will have a virtual keyboard or even come equipped with a touch screen? It might have these things, but low-end models may only have arrow keys or a track ball to navigate with. Again, merely the unpredictability proves to be one of the major challenges.

Kiosks are typically in public areas where the user has no interest in spending a significant amount of time standing in front of the unit. In fact, simply standing can be a difficult ergonomic position to deal with for some users, so anything you can do to make the experience less painful will be appreciated. Buttons and text will need to be larger, higher contrast, and the user interface must be all that much more intuitive to operate since you'll be lucky to get someone's attention for more than a minute in the best of circumstances.

Reduced technology options and limited technical capabilities

Since mobile devices are by definition smaller and more portable than stationary ones, it's more difficult for manufacturers to build comparably powerful hardware. Not only are the CPUs inside mobile devices slower (and cooler), but entire technologies may simply be unsupported for any number of reasons. For you as a web developer, this means that, for example, you can kiss all your Flash content goodbye if you're developing for Mobile Safari, since the Flash Player can't be installed on the iPhone OS.

However, as we know, not all devices are created equal, so Flash Lite can be found on some devices. A similarly mixed story can be told of Java. Sun's J2ME runs on some systems but not on others. Several mobile web browsers give you rich JavaScript support, but JavaScript implementations also vary between mobile browsers and have different levels of support for the ECMAScript standards.[2]

Even beyond all of that is the fact that scripts running reasonably well on a desktop computer might grind to a halt when confronted by the limited CPU or memory resources on a mobile browser. Optimizing the performance of your code therefore also becomes increasingly important in order to deliver the same speedy experience to mobile users as you want desktop users to have. Many of the performance optimizations you can get away with ignoring for desktop browsers are critical aspects of mobile web development. This is doubly true for front-end performance optimizations, including CSS.

Ultimately, when developing web pages to work on the widest variety of mobile devices, you really need to think in terms of the basics and use a progressive enhancement approach. You'll have the most success if you stick with standard XHTML, CSS, the fundamentals of the HTTP protocol (that is, basic GET and POST form behaviors), and images—and that's it. Things like Flash, Java, and to a large extent even JavaScript should be considered extras, nice-to-haves, and if you intend to insert such things into your pages you should plan for a graceful failover mechanism where the content or functionality remains accessible.

Again, the good news here is that you can take just about the entire arsenal of desktop web development best practices and apply them to a mobile context with few modifications to dramatically improve your results. To put it another way, if you develop a good standards-based *desktop* web site, then you'll already have the foundations of a good *mobile* web site for free. That way, all you'll need to do is build on that solid foundation with an eye on handheld devices.

Limited bandwidth and higher latency

Another challenge of mobile web development is worthy of a mention even though it doesn't relate to web development specifically: limited network bandwidth and higher latency.[3] While high-speed wireless network availability continues to grow across the globe, it's still far from ubiquitous worldwide. The more advanced 3G cellular networks are normally found in more densely populated urban

---

2. JavaScript is more formally known as ECMAScript, and the different versions of JavaScript actually correspond (more or less) to different levels of the ECMAScript standards, which is not unlike the situation with CSS. JavaScript is just one implementation of ECMAScript, as is ActionScript (the scripting language used within Flash movies).
3. Latency refers to the amount of time it takes a single network packet to travel across a single hop. On some cellular networks, typical latency can be as bad as 5 seconds and a bloated web page can contain hundreds of packets, if not more. We'll let you do the math.

areas and along the major traffic corridors that connect them, but slower networks fill up the rest of the globe and they deliver data at speeds that are comparable to a mediocre dial-up connection.

To put it bluntly, it would be entirely appropriate for you to treat all of your mobile sites as though every single visitor is stuck with a dial-up connection. Couple that with the limited technical capabilities such as less CPU power and memory that we just discussed, and you can clearly see why mobile web pages should be lean and free of complex markup or bloated images. This holds true even though there is an ever-increasing number of mobile requests being made by handheld devices from Wi-Fi networks, since for some kinds of content on some devices the limiting factor for performance may not be network speeds.

With that said, in the majority of contexts, bandwidth may be one of your top considerations—perhaps even *the* top consideration. Ruthless compression of your content is warranted: crunch your graphics to the smallest size you can live with; code the leanest, presentation-free markup you can muster; and optimize your front-end code by reducing the amount of extra line breaks and blank spaces it has to further reduce download costs. We'll also discuss numerous additional optimization techniques in later chapters of this book.

Competing, overlapping, and incompatible technologies

One additional challenge that compounds the difficulty in dealing with having reduced technology options is the fact that there are overlapping and incompatible technologies in use today. As the so-called mobile Web is still in its infancy, both the technologies that it uses as well as the standards that define these technologies are still undergoing major development efforts. Different makes and models of smartphones, PDAs, and other handheld devices may support one underlying technology but not another, or they may support multiple technologies to varying degrees.

Of course, there's only so much you as a web developer can do about this. Nevertheless, it's still useful to understand what the overlaps and incompatibilities are, if only to limit the scope of your efforts to the ones that make the most sense for you and your user base. To that end, we'll take the opportunity to briefly familiarize you with the thick and hearty soup of three-, four-, and five-letter (or more!) acronyms that exist in the mobile browser market space that each compete for the attention of web developers in the next section.

A brief history of mobile web technology

Recall that one of the challenges in developing for the mobile web is the overlapping and sometimes incompatible technology in use. To a large extent, the disjunct nature of the mobile web technologies up until this point has been due to the fact that mobile web browsing was often limited to the proprietary walled gardens controlled by a subscriber's mobile service provider. The user experience was decent if you stuck with the default set of bookmarks shipped with your particular phone, but quickly turned very poor if you ventured any further out into the Web. Therefore, most users were almost guaranteed to be making minimal use of their mobile device's web browser, there wasn't a strong community of independent web developers or content producers, and ultimately there weren't accessible or standardized technologies.

For a long time, the only feasible way to access web content on a mobile device required either browser makers or content producers to do all the heavy lifting. Either web browsers had to make invasive changes to desktop-oriented content (as some browsers such as Opera Software's mobile offerings still do), or content producers had to set up alternate, heavyweight, mobile-specific delivery methods for their content. To date, neither of these solutions has proved widely successful.

In the late 1990s, the mobile phone industry formed a standards organization called the WAP Forum and introduced the Wireless Application Protocol (WAP) standards, which included a full technology stack. It was hyped as a web-like application protocol designed specifically for handheld devices. Unfortunately, the nature of this technology severely limited access to the World Wide Web's native HTML content, requiring "the real Web" to be passed to the device via a sort of proxy server, known as a WAP gateway. Instead of creating Web "pages," developers wrote "card decks" in a distinct XML dialect, the Wireless Markup Language (WML).

Around the same time, in 1998, the W3C published a note[4] that described a subset of HTML for use in "small information appliances" called Compact HTML (cHTML). Since cHTML's primary developer, NTT DOCOMO, was a Japanese handset manufacturer and service provider, its implementations also borrowed some of WML's internationalization features. Thanks to its compatibility with HTML, cHTML was easier for developers to author but saw limited adoption in comparison with the WAP technologies because mobile web browser software had not matured at that point.

However, in 2000, Opera Software released Opera Mobile, a variant of their desktop web browser that originally ran on the Psion Series 7 and the NetBook "mini-laptops," and whose superior technology support later helped it become the dominant mobile web browser to this day. In 2003, Opera Mobile was ported to the Windows Mobile platform, and following that, the browser saw major advancement very quickly. By November 2005 Opera Mobile was already at version 8.5 and supported additional platforms, including the Symbian OS, as well as more features such as JavaScript and even the WAP standards, with SVG support coming only six months later in April 2006.

Meanwhile, the W3C had recast HTML as XHTML, and in much the same way as cHTML had been intended, they defined XHTML Basic as a subset of XHTML intended for resource-constrained web browsers. Advances in mobile hardware had also been occurring and now many more mobile phones had graphical displays. When the creators of cHTML and the WAP Forum wanted to build the next generation of their mobile platforms, they were attracted to XHTML Basic because its implementation also gave them CSS "for free."

In June 2002, NTT DOCOMO (cHTML's pioneer) and the WAP Forum led by Nokia merged and became the Open Mobile Alliance. Together, they decided to build on XHTML Basic to improve interoperability and resolve some of the criticisms of WAP and WML, which included frustrations with rendering inconsistencies. They added some of the features that were available in cHTML and WML but were lacking in XHTML Basic. The result was a new language that is a superset of XHTML Basic but a subset of XHTML called XHTML-MP, or the XHTML Mobile Profile.

With the creation of XHTML-MP, the Open Mobile Alliance declared that WML was to be intended for backward compatibility only. They deprecated WML 1.x and created a new XML namespace called WML 2.0, which merely combines XHTML-MP with WML 1.x. Thankfully, this chaotic state of affairs is finally set to transform into a more standardized model as the usability and popularity of mobile

---

4. The W3C note, titled "Compact HTML for Small Information Appliances," is available online at http://wwww3.org/TR/1998/NOTE-compactHTML-19980209/.

devices increases while the capabilities of mobile browsers advance simultaneously. In the end, the successful arrival of the mobile Web is a result of its "all of it, all together, all at once"[5] convergence toward web standards.

A brief overview of mobile browsers

There is a large cast of players in the mobile web browsing market. Versions of Opera are by far the most commonly installed browser on mobile devices as of this writing, but it's the WebKit engine that's getting the most press recently for setting the industry's technology trends. Together, these two players paint an overview of what mobile user agents look like, but there are plenty of additional ones in this space that a developer should consider. Moreover, the distribution of market share is wildly different in the mobile space than it is in the desktop world.

Opera Mobile and Opera Mini (Presto)

Opera Software, Inc., the company named after its suite of Opera web browsers and signature products, produced one of the earliest mobile web browsers still used today, Opera Mobile, released in the first half 2000. Opera browsers are based on a proprietary rendering engine called Presto, which solidly dominates the mobile browser market. Its two handheld variants, Opera Mobile and Opera Mini, are collectively installed on millions of smartphones and PDAs worldwide, and one of these is likely to be the default web browser on most popular devices sold today.

There is an important distinction for developers between Opera's two handheld versions, Opera Mobile and Opera Mini. Opera Mobile is a more fully featured browser suited for more capable smartphones often running Windows Mobile or Symbian. It delivers richer web content than the Mini version in an attempt to be more comparable to its desktop-based cousin in a stand-alone product.

Opera Mini, on the other hand, compresses data from requested sites by passing them through Opera's servers before downloading onto the phone.[6] Additionally, one of Opera Mini's two rendering modes actively reformats CSS page layouts so that they fit into a single column. This is called CSSR (Color Small Screen Rendering) and is always in effect, *unless* you specify a style sheet that applies to the handheld media type (so we recommend that you do).

> *Opera on the desktop has one of the best levels of CSS support among all the mainstream web browsers, and it includes excellent web development tools, such as the Small Screen feature that we'll look at in just a second. Versions of Opera are compatible with Mac, Windows, Linux, FreeBSD, and a number of other operating systems as well. Somewhat ironically, this makes Opera on the desktop a great choice for getting started with mobile web design on a wide variety of platforms.*

---

5. "All of it, all together, all at once" is a well-known quote by Mike Cohn, a recognized expert in agile software development methodologies. This description, as well as its context, happens to suit the state of the mobile Web very nicely.
6. It should perhaps be noted that this is true for SSL/TLS-secured pages as well as unencrypted pages. Therefore, Opera Mini is considered an insecure user agent from the vantage point of many privacy- and security-conscious users, who strongly prefer to install an alternative browser for the majority of their web surfing activities.

The Opera Mini web site provides a free and very handy simulator of the browser that you can use to test your web sites, shown in Figure 5-1. Browse to http://www.opera.com/mini/demo/ with your desktop browser to load and run the simulator. It is delivered as a Java applet, so be certain you have enabled Java in your browser when you use it.

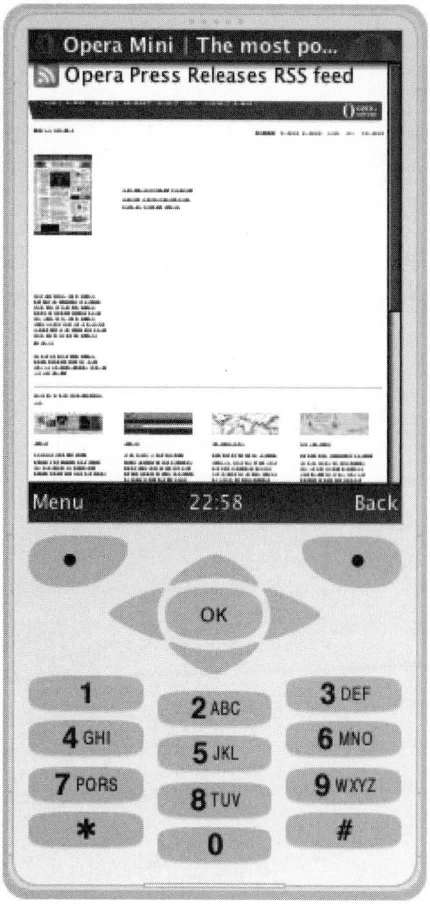

Internet Explorer Mobile

The mobile version of Internet Explorer Mobile, originally called Pocket Internet Explorer (or PIE), is Microsoft's mobile equivalent of their Internet Explorer browser, which actually was written from the ground up and is not based on the Trident code base like its desktop version. Unsurprisingly, Internet Explorer Mobile is found exclusively on Microsoft's mobile operating systems, Windows Mobile and Windows CE. All of these devices will have IE Mobile installed by default, although many vendors will install a mobile version of Opera as well.

Like Opera Mini, IE Mobile will actively reformat most web content so that it renders more linearly. Version 6 of IE Mobile includes a feature that allows users to toggle viewing sites as a mobile user or as a desktop user. The latter option displays web pages as if a mobile style sheet were not detected. IE Mobile is surprisingly versatile and even supports user style sheets, which you install via the Windows Registry.[7]

Blazer (NetFront)

On many PDAs such as the Palm Treo family, the Sony PlayStation Portable, and the Amazon Kindle to name a few, you're likely to find embedded browsers based on the NetFront engine. Blazer, the default browser on PalmOS devices, is one of the most well-known NetFront-based browsers. NetFront is technically an exceptionally capable engine that supports WAP and WML, cHTML, and XHTML Mobile, as well as SVG and JavaScript.

Figure 5-1. The Opera Mini simulator displaying the Opera Mini home page with default settings

Far from going extinct, newer versions of NetFront-based browsers are finding homes in networked appliances and consumer electronics devices of many shapes and sizes. Recent releases of NetFront have added support for RSS viewing and Ajax, among other features. It is especially popular in Japan, where NTT DOCOMO uses it on smartphones sold as part of their i-mode service.

---

7. The IE Mobile blog is possibly the best place to get information about Internet Explorer Mobile. Their entry on "Customizing IE Mobile with User Stylesheets" can be found at http://blogs.msdn.com/iemobile/archive/2006/03/15/552029.aspx.

Openwave Mobile Browser

Although much less pervasive today, the Openwave Mobile Browser once claimed over 60 percent of the mobile web browser market share. It is also significant from a historical perspective because Openwave, Inc., the company that created this browser, was heavily involved in the earliest mobile web browsing initiatives. Among other things, the company was a founding member of the WAP Forum, and was instrumental in pioneering both the Wireless Markup Language (WML) and its precursor, the Handheld Device Markup Language (HDML).

Modern versions of the Openwave Mobile Browser support XHTML-MP, CSS, and cHTML in addition to WML. You can get a full simulation environment for Windows that emulates the browser running on a smartphone at http://developer.openwave.com/dvl/tools_and_sdk/phone_simulator/.

Fennec (Gecko)

Gecko, the rendering engine underlying all variants of Mozilla's web browser (including Firefox), has the distinction of being the second most widely deployed desktop rendering engine behind Internet Explorer's Trident. Nevertheless, there is no competitive equivalent for mobile devices. To address this, in 2008 the Mozilla Foundation launched Fennec,[8] a project to port Firefox to a mobile aspect.

There are desktop versions of Fennec available for development and testing for Windows, Linux, and Mac OS X systems.[9] The UI of the browser is notably Spartan, as the screenshot of an alpha build for Mac OS X shows in Figure 5-2. As of this writing, Fennec only ships on the Nokia N800 and N810, devices that run Maemo, a Linux distribution purpose-built for Internet Tablets.[10]

Figure 5-2. Upon first launching Fennec, its welcome screen indicates that most controls are to the left or right of the viewport. Also noteworthy is that the address bar serves double duty, displaying the page's title.

---

8. You can get more details from the Fennec project page at https://wiki.mozilla.org/Fennec.
9. Fennec is in the very early Alpha stages of development as of this writing. Nevertheless, if you're curious, we encourage you to download a copy for your platform at http://ftp.mozilla.org/pub/mozilla.org/mobile/.
10. Internet Tablets are devices that can be described as halfway between an iPhone and a laptop. Nokia backs the Maemo project itself and information about the project can be found at http://maemo.org.

Firefox add-ons such as the Web Developer Toolbar by Chris Pederick can provide you with useful mobile web development tools. Using Chris's extension, you can select CSS ➤ Display CSS by Media Type ➤ Handheld to view a site as styled with handheld CSS rules, and you can use the Resize menu to preset many popular mobile display widths. You can also access these commands after installing the extension from Firefox's Tools ➤ Web Developer menu.

Mobile Safari and Android (WebKit)

Although Opera dominates the mobile web browsing space in terms of raw install base, Mobile Safari, the web browser found on iPhone and iPod touch devices, is the mobile user agent that most web sites are seeing the greatest amount of traffic from. The core of the Mobile Safari browser is WebKit, which has been garnering a growing amount of press and developer attention for some years now. WebKit originated as a fork of KHTML, an HTML rendering library intended for use in Linux's K Desktop Environment (KDE), and which was used for some time in its Konquerer browser.

Among WebKit's key benefits are its relatively small footprint and the ease with which it can be embedded in other applications. This makes it easy to customize, and—as an open source project[12]—its license is relatively unencumbered. WebKit is used in the default web browser on Nokia's S60 as well as Google's Android mobile platforms.

WebKit is also finding its way into an increasing number of desktop browsers, which can provide approximations of the WebKit experience for development purposes. Among these are Safari for Mac OS X and Windows,[13] Google Chrome,[14] and Konqueror.[15] However, desktop browsers can't always provide an adequate emulation of a mobile device, so for a more exacting experience, Mac OS X users are encouraged to download the full iPhone SDK,[16] which includes an iPhone Simulator, and the Android SDK,[17] which similarly provides an emulator, shown in Figure 5-3.

Figure 5-3. A screenshot of the Google Android emulator displaying the Google Android homepage

---

11. The Web Developer Toolbar by Chris Pederick can be downloaded from Chris's web site at http://chrispederick.com/work/web-developer/.

12. You can get daily builds of the latest development versions that the WebKit community produces by downloading nightly builds at http://nightly.webkit.org.

13. If you don't already have Safari on your machine, you can download it at http://www.apple.com/safari/.

14. As of this writing, Google Chrome only runs on Windows. It is also available for free at http://www.google.com/chrome.

15. The Konquerer home page is at http://www.konqueror.org/.

16. The iPhone SDK can be downloaded from http://developer.apple.com/iphone/.

17. The Android SDK can be downloaded from http://code.google.com/android/download.html.

Developers and analysts alike are describing Mobile Safari as the future of the mobile Web, so it and its engine are both software to pay close attention to. It's very likely that WebKit-based mobile browsers will continue to enjoy increases in market share over the coming months and years. Later in this chapter, we'll discuss Mobile Safari and some of its WebKit-specific features in greater detail.

Comparing browsers and displays

A mobile web browsing experience is affected by both hardware and software components. Although what software will ship with what hardware is often well known, in many cases users have the ability to install different browsers after making their purchase, or service providers selling these devices may choose to install a different web browser themselves, creating many additional possible combinations of user agents and devices. In Table 5-1, we compare screen resolutions and default browsers across a sampling of mobile devices.

Table 5-1. Screen Resolutions and Default Browsers

Make	Model	Resolution	Default Browser Engine
Amazon	Kindle	600×800	NetFront
Apple	iPhone	480×320	WebKit
Apple	iPod Touch	480×320	WebKit
BenQ	M315	128×128	Opera
HTC	G1	320×480	WebKit
Kyocera	Mako S4000	128×160	Openwave
Motorola	Hint QA30	320×240	Openwave
Motorola	Krave ZN4	240×400	Openwave
Motorola	KRZR K1	176×220	Opera
Motorola	RAZR V3	176×220	Opera
Motorola	ROKR E2	240×320	Opera
Motorola	SLVR L7	176×220	Opera
Motorola	V980	176×220	Opera
Motorola	VE240	128×128	Openwave
Motorola	ZINE ZN5	240×320	WebKit
Nokia	6300	240×320	Opera
Nokia	2605 Mirage	128×160	Openwave
Nokia	N81	240×320	WebKit
Nokia	N810	800×480	Gecko
Nokia	N82	240×320	WebKit
Nokia	N95	240×320	WebKit
Nokia	N96	240×320	WebKit

Make	Model	Resolution	Default Browser Engine
Palm	Centro	320×320	NetFront
Palm	Treo 680	320×320	NetFront
Palm	Treo 750	240×240	Internet Explorer
Palm	Treo 755p	320×320	NetFront
Palm	Treo 800w	320×320	Internet Explorer
Palm	Treo Pro	320×320	Internet Explorer
Palm	Pre	320×480	WebKit
RIM	BlackBerry Bold	480×360	BlackBerry Browser
RIM	BlackBerry Pearl	240×320	BlackBerry Browser
RIM	BlackBerry Storm	480×360	BlackBerry Browser
Samsung	Behold T919	240×400	NetFront
Samsung	BlackJack SGH-i607	240×320	Internet Explorer
Samsung	Epix i907	320×320	Internet Explorer
Samsung	Eternity SGH-A867	240×400	Openwave
Samsung	Highnote M630	176×220	Polaris
Samsung	Omina i910	240×400	Internet Explorer and Opera
Samsung	Rant M540	176×220	Polaris
Samsung	Rugby A837	176×220	NetFront
Samsung	Saga i770	320×320	Internet Explorer and Opera
Samsung	SPH-Z400	176×220	Obigo
Siemens	SX66	240×320	Internet Explorer
Sonim	XP3	128×160	Opera
Sony Ericsson	C702a	240×320	NetFront
Sony Ericsson	C905a	240×320	NetFront
Sony Ericsson	TM506	240×320	NetFront
Sony Ericsson	W595a	240×320	NetFront
Sony Ericsson	W760	240×320	NetFront
Sony Ericsson	X1	800×480	Internet Explorer and Opera

As you can see from the sampling in Table 5-1, screen sizes for mobile devices range from as small as 128 pixels square to as high as 600×800 pixels, with a great variety in between. Even if you consider that most users rarely (if ever) upgrade their default web browser or install a new one after they've acquired their device, this showcases relatively rough terrain for a developer to navigate. Nevertheless, as we'll discuss next, it can be done.

Delivering mobile style

Earlier in this chapter we touched on the constraints we are faced with when developing for mobile devices. These issues can make or break a mobile design, so be sure you've considered and tested for them in your designs.

Bandwidth and processing capability is probably going to be an issue for mobile devices, so be sure your code is as lean as possible. Use good markup practices: remove any presentational data from your HTML, use descendant selectors and classes in the broadest terms, optimize your code, and be ruthless about avoiding redundant rules and keeping your style sheets as succinct as possible.

Images may not always be available. When they are, they may be a huge bandwidth drain as well. Keep them small and optimized, and use scalable methods (such as percentage widths) to insert your graphics. Setting height and width values will help pre-arrange your slow-loading layout before all the images have been downloaded as well. An image that is too wide will push your content out and create those unsightly horizontal scroll bars. Be absolutely sure that your images have alt attributes with concise and meaningful text in case the client does not support images, or use display: none for images that you'd like to hide from the mobile browsers. (Note: Even though we have set the image to display: none, the browser may still download the image a linked asset, incurring a bandwidth hit. If you're ruthlessly optimizing pages, you may wish to consider alternate schemes, such as programmatic style sheet switching or sending mobile users to a separate URL. But for lightweight page designs with well-crafted code and optimized images, this may not be as much of a concern.) You might even intentionally decide to show alt attribute text instead of the image itself using CSS3's capability to replace real content with pseudo-content:

```
img { content: attr(alt); }
```

Things like frames and pop-up windows will not always work well on mobile. Avoid these constructs if you can. JavaScript may not work as well, so be sure you have a graceful failover mechanism installed for those fancy Ajax calls that you had baked into your site.

Color is likely to be less rich on the low-end and midrange phone devices, and the same is likely true for older smartphones. Early smartphones such as the Handspring Treo 180 and the BlackBerry 6750 had monochrome screens. Be sure that you plan on high-contrast color choices to ensure readability on the widest range of devices.

If designing specifically for handhelds, you will undoubtedly want to go for a single-column layout. Most of the time the user is going to have the wider part of the screen in a vertical aspect when holding a mobile device, and of course the screen width is far narrower than what you'd encounter on the desktop.

Forms are always going to be a bit tricky to handle on the user end. Entering text is more of a challenge on mobile devices than on desktop systems due to the limited text input and navigation capability, so do your form users a favor and make your forms simple. Use as few form fields as you can. Preload data into select menus, check boxes, or radio buttons whenever possible. Make the form elements fit the mobile interface, usually by increasing the height a bit and making text fields fit the width of the device screen. Also, textarea elements need to be conscious of height as well; too large and it may be difficult to enter text into the interface if the page scrolls above or below the element.

Finally, readability is the main thing your users are after in most cases. Make sure your fonts are set to be at a readable size and style for smaller screens. Many mobile browsers lack a lot of font resizing options, so don't make your type too small.

The handheld media type

The handheld media type is the simplest way to target a style sheet for mobile (i.e., "handheld") devices. This can be done either via a `<link>` element or via an `@media` rule. Recently Opera and WebKit have led the charge for mobile browsers to default to screen instead of handheld style sheets, with Opera providing an option to choose handheld for the media type over screen and WebKit going so far as to ignore support for handheld completely. But using the handheld media type is still great for targeting many of those other browsers out there and this will be our first working example for this chapter. Here are some examples of the various ways to invoke the handheld media type:

The link method:

```
<link rel="stylesheet" href="mobile.css" type="text/css" ➡
    media="handheld">
```

Applying handheld to an embedded style sheet:

```
<style type="text/css" media="handheld">
    div.foo { color: red; }
</style>
```

Using @media handheld to target handheld styles:

```
<style type="text/css">
    @media handheld {
        div.foo { color: red; }
    }
</style>
```

Using @media handheld to import a mobile style sheet:

```
<style type="text/css">
  @import url(mobile.css) handheld;
</style>
```

Of these various methods, the handheld media type applied to the link element or to an embedded style sheet tends to have the widest support.

Formatting a page for handheld media

To practice some of these concepts, let's work with our résumé example from the previous chapter. As a reminder, Figure 5-4 shows what the page looks like on a desktop browser:

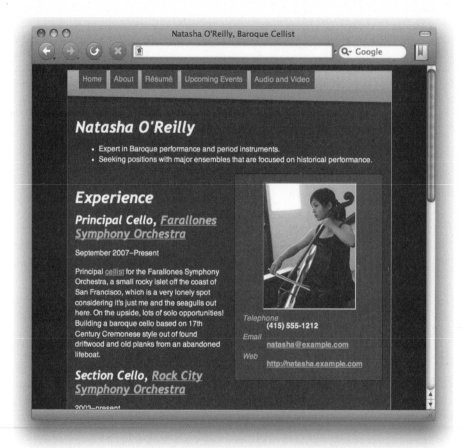

Figure 5-4. Our résumé page in its original state as shown in a desktop web browser

Our goal is to reformat the résumé so that it looks reminiscent of our desktop design on mobile screens, and so that the content is clear and accessible.

Let's pick up from where we left off in the last chapter by adding an embedded style sheet, this time with a media type of handheld:

```
<!DOCTYPE html PUBLIC "-//W3C//DTD XHTML 1.0 Strict//EN"
    "http://www.w3.org/TR/xhtml1/DTD/xhtml1-strict.dtd">
<html lang="en-us" xmlns="http://www.w3.org/1999/xhtml"
    xml:lang="en-us">
<head>
<title>Natasha O'Reilly, Baroque Cellist</title>
```

```
<meta http-equiv="Content-type" content="text/html; charset=utf-8" />
<link rel="stylesheet" href="screen.css" type="text/css"
    media="screen" />
<link rel="stylesheet" href="print.css" type="text/css"
    media="print" />
<style type="text/css" media="handheld">
    /* Our mobile CSS rules will, for the most part, go here. */
</style>
</head>
<body>
<div class="hresume layout" id="natasha-oreilly-orchestra-resume">
    [...]
</div>
</body>
</html>
```

For our initial testing purposes, we'll use the Opera desktop browser. This will allow us to write code and quickly preview our mobile styles from our computer, and it should work mostly the same on the operating system you are likely using. Before adding a handheld-specific style sheet, Opera will attempt to do something interesting to a website: it will attempt to reformat the page into a single-column and with a narrower aspect. Adding a blank handheld media style sheet will disable that feature in Opera and instead render an unstyled HTML document. In desktop version of Opera set to Small Screen mode, this would appear as shown in Figure 5-5.

Admittedly, not a huge improvement, but it's a start. The first thing we notice is that our image is too large, so let's fix that right away:

```
<style type="text/css" media="handheld">
    img {
        max-width: 100%;
    }
    dt {
        font-style: italic;
    }
    dd {
        margin: 0;
        padding: 0;
        font-weight: bold;
    }
</style>
```

With this set of rules, we've made sure that our image fits within the space of our device's window by using the max-width property set to 100%. This attempts to keep our image within the space of the viewport, but there's a problem. The <dd> element is pushing it out to the right, clipping our image and generating a vertical scroll bar. This is easily resolved by setting the margin and padding of the <dd> element to zero, and we set

Figure 5-5. Initial rendering of our (empty) handheld style sheet

165

it to both the margin and the padding to be on the safe side because we're really not sure how various user agents will handle this. Finally, we added a little italic style to the <dt> and bold to the <dd> to give them definition. And now we can say that this layout adequately fits our screen and should work in a variety of mobile browsers as is, and we can proceed with adding more cosmetic and functional elements to our style sheet. Figure 5-6 shows how it looks now in Opera's Small Screen mode.

Right here it is important to note a concern about the image in our web page. The image weighs in at 26 kilobytes, which may be considered kind of large by wireless network standards, and the native size of the image is 300×400 pixels, which is definitely overkill for all but the top end smartphones. Images should be reduced to a realistic size on dedicated mobile web sites and compressed as far as makes sense for your design requirements. Since we are going to only repurpose our page for mobile through CSS, let's not worry about this now.

Establishing color and typography

Now that we have our boxes established, let's fill in a few stylish items on our page and start to make it look somewhat reminiscent of our desktop browser version. First, the basics: we will apply some background and font colors and see the result in Figure 5-7:

```
<style type="text/css" media="handheld">
    body {
        background-color:#333;
        color:#FFFED1;
        font-family: Helvetica, Arial, sans-serif;
        margin:0;
        padding:0;
    }
    div.layout {
        padding:0 0.5em 1em 0.5em;
    }
    img {
        max-width:100%;
    }
    dt {
        font-style:italic;
    }
    dd {
        margin:0;
        padding:0;
        font-weight:bold;
    }
</style>
```

Figure 5-6. A preview of our initial mobile styles, with an image that fits and some styling on the definition list

Now we're getting somewhere. With these few additions, this mobile view is recognizable as being related to our desktop design. The background and font colors have been set to match the desktop version using `background-color:#333;` and `color:#FFFED1;` A little padding has been applied to our existing `<div id="layout">` element—this single column layout doesn't have much need for a layout `<div>` container on the surface, but it does give us a consistent place to apply padding. The next obvious things that need fixing are the hyperlinks to match the desktop view, which is easily done with a few anchor rules:

```
a:link {
    color:#FFC300;
}
a:visited {
    color:#FC6;
}
a:hover, a:active {
    color:#F00;
}
```

Now that the links are taken care of, we need to work on the navigation toolbar. For this, we're going to go for a similar effect to our desktop style sheet but make it work for mobile as best we can. To start with, zero out any margin or padding that might be applied to the `<ul>` and `<li>` elements, and set the `list-style-type` to none:

```
#sitenav ul {
    list-style-type:none;
    margin:0;
    padding:0;
}
#sitenav li {
    margin:0;
    padding:0;
}
```

Then we'll work on the #sitenav a rules to make nav buttons:

```
#sitenav a {
    display:block;
    float:left;
    padding:0.3em 0.4em 0.1em 0.4em;
    margin-bottom:0.2em;
    margin-right:0.2em;
    border:1px outset #999;
    border-top:0;
    background-color:#555;
    text-decoration:none;
}
```

Figure 5-7. Initial color styles

Here we've set the anchor element display to block and floated the buttons to the left. The margin and padding values are set to make the buttons appear proportional to the screen view, with the same border and background styles and of course the removal of the default anchor underline by using text-decoration:none.

If you preview our page now, you'll see that the nav bar elements that are floated now wrap to the left of the heading that represents the name of the musician. This is an easy remedy:

```
.vcard {
    clear:both;
}
```

The result of clearing the .vcard is shown in Figure 5-8.

Figure 5-8. Establishing the mobile nav buttons

The nav button text causes the last two buttons to definitely appear a bit wide, and it would be nice if we could use "CV" instead of "Résumé" as a conveniently short abbreviation. We can fix that by using some replaced content techniques (see the results in Figure 5-9):

```
#sitenav a[href="http://natasha.example.com/cv/"] {
    content: "CV";
}
#sitenav a[href="http://natasha.example.com/cal/"] {
    content: "Events";
}
#sitenav a[href="http://natasha.example.com/av/"] {
    content: "A/V";
}
```

Figure 5-9. Condensed buttons using content replacement

Not bad—we have the buttons fitting all on one line now in our arbitrarily sized window (230 pixels in this screen capture). The next step is to add the banner background graphic. Let's add it to the <body> element since we have some background color already applied there; Figure 5-10 shows the results:

```
body {
    background: #333 url(bak.tif) 0 -13px no-repeat;
    color:#FFFED1;
    font-family: Helvetica, Arial, sans-serif;
    margin:0;
    padding:0;
}
```

Figure 5-10. Background applied to the nav bar

Here we've replaced background-color with the background shorthand rule, applied the bak.tif image to give us that nice and warm-colored background, and moved the image up by using a value of -13 pixels, which serves to make the bottom edge of the buttons line up with the background image's gradient effect.

169

Since we are for the most part limited to designing single-column layouts for mobile web sites, we can add some separation of the sections by implementing a border:

```
.vcard, .vevent {
    border-bottom:1px dotted orange;
}
```

Here we've conveniently used the microformat classes for two existing semantic constructs, hCard (vcard) and hCalendar (vevent), and placed an orange dotted border beneath them. It is nice that we can target these specific classes, which give us good placement for the borders rather than trying to find the right combination of descendant selectors to get a similar effect. Leveraging the microformats structure can be useful to CSS authors due to the added number of semantic hooks that exist in the markup.

Now the rest is just nudging and tweaking things for polish. The headings can be styled to be slightly more fancy. Since we don't know what browsers will have in terms of fonts—it can be a complete free-for-all—let's just go with a keyword on the font family for <h1> elements, italicize <h2>, and make sure that first <h1> (with the #bw-name ID) isn't too close to the nav bar:

```
h1 {
    font-family:cursive;
}
h2 {
    font-style:italic;
}
h1#bw-name {
    margin-top:1.2em;
}
```

This gets us almost to the finish line. Now let's complete our design by styling the two summary list items, and add a little increase in the line height for some of the text to make it more readable. First, the summary, which is indented a little too far on the left side, and which looks too pronounced in normal font style:

```
ul.summary {
    padding-left:1.5em;
    font-style:italic;
}
```

Better. And finally, some line height for readability:

```
p, dd, .summary li, [rel="tag"] {
    line-height:1.4;
}
```

This could also be applied to the <h2> since those look a little tight:

```
h2 {
    font-style:italic;
    line-height:1.2;
}
```

And for the final touch, you will notice the default dotted underlines that Opera places on our <abbr> elements. Let's get rid of that—it is not much help in this example (the help text is a machine-formatted date):

```css
abbr {
    border:0;
}
```

And that does it. Here's our final style sheet and a view of our page in Opera in Small Screen mode (see Figure 5-11 for the results):

```css
<style type="text/css" media="handheld">
    body {
        background: #333 url(bak.tif) 0 -13px no-repeat;
        color:#FFFED1;
        font-family: Helvetica, Arial, sans-serif;
        margin:0;
        padding:0;
    }
    div.layout {
        padding:0 0.5em 1em 0.5em;
    }
    h1 {
        font-family:cursive;
    }
    h2 {
        font-style:italic;
        line-height:1.2;
    }
    h1#bw-name {
        margin-top:1.2em;
    }
    p, dd, .summary li, [rel="tag"] {
        line-height:1.4;
    }
    abbr {
        border:0;
    }
    a:link {
        color:#FFC300;
    }
    a:visited {
        color:#FC6;
    }
    a:hover, a:active {
        color:#F00;
    }
    img {
        max-width:100%;
    }
```

Figure 5-11. Final handheld styles

```
      dt {
          font-style:italic;
      }
      dd {
          margin:0;
          padding:0;
          font-weight:bold;
      }
      #sitenav ul {
          list-style-type:none;
          margin:0;
          padding:0;
      }
      #sitenav li {
          margin:0;
          padding:0;
      }
      #sitenav a {
          display:block;
          float:left;
          padding:0.3em 0.4em 0.1em 0.4em;
          margin-bottom:0.2em;
          margin-right:0.2em;
          border:1px outset #999;
          border-top:0;
          background-color:#555;
          text-decoration:none;
      }
      #sitenav a[href="http://natasha.example.com/cv/"] {
          content: "CV";
      }
      #sitenav a[href="http://natasha.example.com/cal/"] {
          content: "Events";
      }
      #sitenav a[href="http://natasha.example.com/av/"] {
          content: "A/V";
      }
      .vcard {
          clear:both;
      }
      .vcard, .vevent {
          border-bottom:1px dotted orange;
      }
      ul.summary {
          padding-left:1.5em;
          font-style:italic;
      }
  </style>
```

To finish our operation, we need to extract our style sheet into an external file. Copy all the CSS code in-between the `<style>` elements to an external file named handheld.css, delete the old `<style>` element and its content, and link to the new external style sheet:

```
<link rel="stylesheet" href="handheld.css" type="text/css" ➥
media="handheld" />
```

> There was a time in the past when detecting the user agent at the onset of a page request and redirecting things as appropriate was considered a good idea (if it was considered at all). This technique fell out of fashion with the onset of the web standards movement, and developers began to insist on serving one page to all devices. However, with the diversification of so many devices, capabilities, and sizes in the handset market, user agent detection may be a solution for certain situations.
>
> Such a situation might be where you want to deliver truly optimized content to a specific handset category. It is a fact that when any browser hits a web page, they are going to have to download all of the linked assets on that page whether or not they are set to display, and this can be a drag on bandwidth. Additionally, you may want to deliver custom content to a specific type of handset, such as touch-screen controls to an iPhone or BlackBerry Storm, which might not be necessary on other devices that use keypad controls or a stylus pointer.
>
> While this technique is useful for redirecting traffic to an optimized version of the site, there is a major drawback. User agent detection is tricky. The user agent strings have little consistency between them and tend to change over time, meaning a developer will continually have to return to the script to ensure that something isn't getting left out as the browsers and user agent strings evolve over time.

Designing for Mobile WebKit

WebKit is the basic rendering engine for a number of excellent web browser implementations in the smartphone market, the most prominent of which is the Safari browser on iPhone and iPod Touch. Google's Android platform is another prominent WebKit browser implementation, and Nokia's S60 browser also uses WebKit port for the Symbian platform on their handsets.

Why optimize for WebKit?

WebKit-enabled handsets do constitute a fraction of the current total mobile browser market share, but this market share growth is outpacing the rest of the industry. According to AdMob's Mobile Metrics Report for November 2008, Apple's iPhone had both the highest percentage of requests for any single handset as well as the highest percentage of increased worldwide market share. The second-fastest growing device was the iPod Touch, and the just-launched HTC G1, which runs Google's Android platform and a WebKit-based browser, has already garnered 7 percent of T-Mobile's web traffic and 2 percent of the global web traffic market. This is only the first phone to market on the Android platform. Android is the OS component of the Open Handset Alliance, a consortium of industry heavyweights banded together to pool their resources and create a next-generation open mobile handset platform. These industry heavyweights include such companies as China Mobile, NTT

DOCOMO, Sprint, T-Mobile, Vodaphone, Motorola, Samsung, Sony Ericsson, HTC, Toshiba, and of course Google, just to name a few. These are no minor players—these are some of the biggest names in the mobile market. Expect more and more providers and manufacturers over the coming years to be producing Android-based phones, equipped with the accompanying WebKit-enabled browser.

In many respects, you could simply choose to ignore WebKit-enabled handsets. WebKit intentionally is set to ignore the handheld media type and deliver the screen media type by default. The idea behind this is that WebKit is delivering "the whole, unfiltered Web," without any compromises to the layout, and that you would be able to leverage the zooming capabilities of their web browser to view columns of text and images up close, and then zoom back out when they need to navigate to other parts of the page. It is an ingenious little feat of usability in the way Safari works on the iPhone—you simply need to double-tap on a block-level element to zoom in on exactly that element, or you can use the two-finger pinch maneuver to zoom in and out of pages as desired. While other implementations of WebKit may vary, this basic principle of being able to zoom in and out of content quickly is what makes WebKit so useful for viewing full-scale web layouts.

But for the purposes of this discussion, let's assume that your project requires an optimized view for the iPhone and related WebKit-enabled handsets. You want your content to be readable and accessible, and are willing to trade off a few features normally found on the full-scale version of your web site.

Previewing WebKit pages

When testing on mobile devices, nothing beats having the real device in your hands to test things with. However, owning one of each of the multitude of WebKit-enabled devices is not fiscally practical, save for the most high-end production teams doing sophisticated web application development. For the rest of us, some simulation of the mobile WebKit environment is going to be just fine.

To get started, the simplest way to preview your work may be to simply use the desktop version of Safari. Safari is available for the Mac OS X and Windows operating systems, and checking your code here will give you a decent approximation of how your site design will appear in the mobile version of the browser. What is even better is that Safari has a built-in developer feature. In Safari preferences, click the Advanced tab and select the Show Develop Menu in Menu Bar check box, as shown in Figure 5-12.

However, Safari isn't going to be much help if you are going to be doing any kind of specialized mobile style sheet delivery, and we will certainly be using media queries to accomplish this goal in this example. To use Safari for previewing your work, you must set the style sheet you are working on to use a media type of screen or all, and then reduce the width of your browser accordingly as you preview pages.

There are some iPhone simulators out there that will allow you to see what dedicated WebKit-optimized sites will look like. However, as of this writing none of them are capable of either detecting user agent strings or handling media queries, the latter of which will be required for our examples later on. They won't be much better than just using Safari itself, outside of the fact that at least they'll represent the screen size correctly.

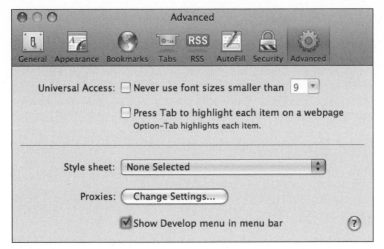

Figure 5-12. Check the Show Develop Menu in Menu Bar option to enable developer features in Safari.

A better way is to install a software developer kit that contains a desktop device simulator. If you're running Mac OS X, the recommended one to start with is the iPhone Developer SDK. This is going to be a large download, which includes the entire Xcode Developer Tools suite plus all the iPhone utilities, but the tools that are included with the SDK are quite useful. What is particularly useful is the iPhone Simulator application, which includes a full version of Mobile Safari. This is the closest you are going to get to running an iPhone without actually having one. There are more goodies in the iPhone SDK for mobile web development, but the iPhone Simulator will be a great place to start. After installing the iPhone SDK on your Mac, look in /Developer/Platforms/iPhoneSimulator.platform/Developer/ Applications for the iPhone Simulator application. Figure 5-13 shows how the résumé example looks in the simulator.

If you are not using Mac OS X, there are alternatives. The Google Android SDK runs on Windows, Mac, and Linux, and is available at http://code.google.com/android/. This SDK includes an Android simulator, including the Android version of WebKit. Another advantage to running the Android SDK is that it is an approximately 90MB download, which is compelling considering the iPhone SDK is a hefty 1.56GB. Both the iPhone SDK and Android SDK will work fine for these examples.

Figure 5-13. The résumé page as it renders in the iPhone Simulator prior to WebKit CSS treatment

175

Basic layout properties

The screen of WebKit-enabled devices such as an iPhone or iPod touch is going to be much smaller than desktop browsers, but for the most part WebKit on these devices will be comparable in terms of capability. Mobile Safari on the iPhone and iPod Touch assumes by default a width of 980 pixels for the web sites it visits. It then automatically converts this width to a scaled-down level that fits on the devices' actual 320-pixel-wide display. It does the same thing for the height, shrinking the assumed 1091-pixel-high web site into the physical 480-pixel-high rendering.

Setting the viewport

The iPhone and iPod Touch assume a 980-pixel-wide page and then try to crunch the view of the resulting page into the 320-pixel-wide viewport of said device. This can result in some pretty tiny text. It is resizable a bit if you tilt the unit 90 degrees, but this can be considered another user inconvenience and it doesn't always do the trick.

This behavior is controllable via a special `<meta>` element that you can place into iPhone-optimized pages. For instance, if your web site is not 980 pixels wide but is instead 640 pixels wide, use `<meta name="viewport" content="width=640" />`. `<meta name="viewport" content="device-width">` is the default that's assumed if a `<meta name="viewport" ... />` element is not found.

On the iPhone and iPod Touch, and likely on most other WebKit-enabled devices, the user can scale the screen view to zoom in on particular elements. This is a useful feature for sites that aren't already optimized for mobile, but perhaps you've done the legwork to make your site as friendly as possible to the WebKit users and zooming would just throw the layout off. In these cases, use user-scalable=false: `<meta name="viewport" content="width=640; `**`user-scalable=false`**`" />`.

"But wait," the inner Standardista in you says, "this isn't CSS! Isn't this just presentational cruft being added to our markup?" True; establishing a viewport value via a metatag is not very flexible and this would probably be cleaner in a style sheet, but regardless this is an important aspect of mobile WebKit design and we have to leverage it if we want to benefit from this effect.

For our example, let's fix the width of the viewport to our screen layout `<div>`. The layout `<div>` was set to 60% in our screen style sheet, and we know that the iPhone assumes pages to be 980 pixels wide. So let's shoot for setting the viewport to 60% of the 980 pixels, which comes out to 588, reset the layout `<div>` to 100%, and see where that gets us (check out Figure 5-14):

Figure 5-14. Setting the viewport width

```
<meta name="viewport" content="width=588; user-scalable=false" />
<style type="text/css" media="only screen and ➡
(max-device-width: 480px)">
    div.layout {
        width:100%;
    }
</style>
```

This by itself doesn't look too bad. But by resetting the width of our layout `<div>` using the `screen` media type, we've broken our layout in the desktop browsers. We need to style the WebKit view separately, and this will be accomplished using a CSS3 media query.

Using media queries

Media queries are part of the CSS3 specification, and are gaining wider support in the modern mobile web browser scene. They provide more fine-grained control over what style sheets are served to what types of browsers and devices, and the scope goes way beyond the mobile web browser world. Media queries are recommended by Apple to apply style to Mobile Safari.

As mentioned earlier, WebKit and the latest versions of the Opera browser on mobile devices default to show the `screen` media type. On Opera there is an option to switch the default back to `mobile`, but on WebKit it is locked down and `handheld` is completely ignored. Using media queries is the recommended CSS mechanism to direct style sheets toward WebKit, and it will get picked up by Opera in the process.

So far, our small little change has yielded a layout that isn't too bad as viewed in the iPhone Simulator, but as mentioned earlier, we've broken the desktop view. Let's fix that by introducing a media query:

```
<meta name="viewport" content="width=588; user-scalable=false" />
<style type="text/css" ➡
media="only screen and (max-device-width: 480px)">
    div.layout {
        width:100%;
    }
</style>
```

This change adds some conditions to our media value, and may be read as "these styles are only for screen media where the maximum device width is 480 pixels." If you preview the page now in a desktop browser, you should see the same original design. And in a mobile version of WebKit, you should see the optimized width of the page.

Styling links to be touch-friendly

WebKit is prevalent on the iPhone OS and Android OS devices, both of which feature touch screen capability. But the finger, while *far* more convenient than toting a stylus or reaching for a mouse, is not a very precise pointing device. We need to make our page controls friendly to our fingertips, and this invariably means increasing the surface area of what is clickable.

For navigation buttons, it works well to make buttons approximately 1 centimeter wide and at least half a centimeter high. This creates a finger-selectable area that is pretty easy to target for most people. However, don't stop there if you feel like going larger. It is quite common to make navigation buttons and similar controls 100 percent of the width of the viewport. Let's see what we can do with our page to make it more usable on WebKit for finger selection (see Figure 5-15):

```
<style type="text/css" ➥
media="only screen and (max-device-width: 480px)">
    body {
        margin:0;
        padding:0;
    }
    div.layout {
        width:100%;
        margin:0;
        border:0;
    }
    #sitenav {
        margin-left:-12px;
    }
    div#sitenav a {
        width:97.7%;
        font-size:2em;
        margin:0;
        border:1px solid #333;
        text-align:center;
    }
</style>
```

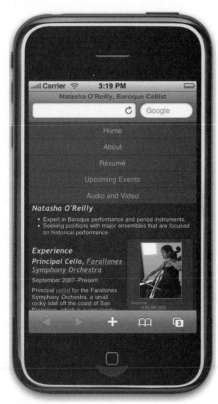

Figure 5-15. Styling buttons to be more touch-friendly

We have enlarged the text size and made our buttons wide enough to fill the width of the viewport. We had to zero out margin and padding on the body element to get rid of the browser defaults and make our interface fit more neatly on the screen. Now our buttons are easier to use with a fingertip, but we are missing our nice banner background image and the page looks a little plain now. As Figure 5-16 shows, we can bring that back, and solve a usability issue at the same time, by adding the following code beneath the div#sitenav a rule:

```
div#sitenav a[href="http://natasha.example.com/"] {
    background-image:url(bak.tif);
    background-position:top right;
    color:#000;
    font-family:"Trebuchet MS", sans-serif;
    font-style:italic;
    font-weight:bold;
}
div#sitenav a[href="http://natasha.example.com/"]:before {
    content: "Natasha O'Reilly, Baroque Cellist (";
}
```

```
div#sitenav a[href="http://natasha.example.com/"]:after {
    content: ")";
}
```

This nifty bit of code reuses some of our existing assets such as the background nav bar image and repurposes the home button to be a bit more descriptive. The attribute selector a[href="http://www.natasha.example.com/"] specifically selects our home link so we can treat it with special care. Then rather than making some new background image, we simply reuse the old banner bak.tif image, but this time we position it to the right. The reason we're using it right here is because the banner image had a bit of an angle along the bottom edge, turning the shape into more of a trapezoid than a rectangle. Using the wide part of the image, we hide most of the taper, except for a tiny bit remaining on the left side of our button. To remove that extra taper, reduce the font size on div#sitenav a from 2em down to 1.9em and it should look perfect. (When more of the CSS3 spec is supported by WebKit in the future, background-size may also become useful for attaining an optimal placement in conjunction with background-position for this background image without having to compromise on button size.)

The original button name of "Home" wasn't terribly flattering to this page. Now that the home button is the top visual element in our layout, it doesn't really help the site user orient them as to where they are. Using the :before and :after pseudo-selectors, we have placed a bit of extra content to the left and right of the word "Home" to make the full string read "Natasha O'Reilly, Baroque Cellist (Home)." The button now serves as a sort of masthead as well, and it remains a helpful beacon if the user wishes to tap back to the home page.

The next item to tackle is the definition list that contains the photo, email, and web address. The resolution of this section looks a little small in this layout, although it might still work as a floated element. Let's improve the size of the image and the text in this box:

```
dl {
    padding: 0;
    width: 48%;
}
dt, dd {
    margin: 0;
    text-align: center;
    font-size: 1.5em;
}
dd a {
    height: 2em;
```

Figure 5-16. Styling the home button to also function as the site banner

```
    display: block;
    padding-bottom: 0.5em;
}
.photo {
    width: 234px;
    height: 312px;
    margin: 1em auto;
    display: block;
    border: 1px solid #111;
}
```

The <dl> element could be a bit wider, so the width here has been increased to 48%. Padding was applied on the other screen style sheet, and we've zeroed that out here. The <dt> and <dd> elements have also had their margins reset, which really only applies to WebKit's default left margin placed on the <dd> element. The text has been centered, and the font sized increased to 1.5em. The <a> elements that are <dd> children have been given some extra height to make them more tappable and to provide some distinction, and an extra 0.5em of padding has been added to the bottom of these elements to further improve the usability and visual separation.

For the image, we set the width to 234px and the height to 312px, which is a proportional reduction from the photo's native 300×400 size. The image is set to display:block, the top and bottom margins are set to be 1em, and the auto keyword is used on the left and right margins to center the image. The border is set to a medium gray value of #111 to finish the trimming, and we're done with this floated section.

If you look at the space after the navigation button where the body of the page begins, you'll see the heading is a little too close in proportion to the rest of the headings. Also, the hyperlinks embedded within the copy look like they might be a little hard to execute with a finger tap and might be better if there were more surface area. Let's fix both of those problems:

```
p a, #interests a {
    padding-top:0.5em;
    padding-bottom:0.5em;
}
#interests li {
    line-height:2;
}
h1#bw-name {
    padding-top:1em;
}
```

The first rule selects all <a> elements that are children of either paragraph elements or the element with the ID of #interests, and it sets half an em of padding above and below the link. This makes the item a bit easier to hit with a fingertip. The next rule selects all <li> children of the #interests <div> and increases the line height to 2. This again will make our links easier to access with the finger, and we've already provided a slightly larger surface area for tapping. Finally, we fixed the spacing problem at the top of the page by giving it 1 em of padding on the <h1> element with the ID of #bw-name.

Another Mobile Safari–specific optimization is to ensure that, when you zoom by double-tapping onto an element (which Mobile Safari interprets as "find the nearest *replaced element* as defined by CSS and zoom so that this element's entire width is displayed in the viewport") is to use the vendor extension called -webkit-text-size-adjust. This property takes any value you can give line-height and adjusts the line height by that scale factor accordingly. This ensures that when you double-click to zoom onto a paragraph that stretches pretty wide, for example, the text itself is scaled up an appropriate amount so that it becomes readable. Therefore, you definitely want to ensure that you give this property a *relative* unit value!

Two more ways to customize tap behavior on Mobile Safari on the iPhone and iPod touch are to use -webkit-touch-callout and -webkit-tap-highlight-color. The -webkit-touch-callout property can use a value of none to disable the bubble that appears when you tap and hold a link on iPhone OS. The only allowable values are none or inherit (which is the default, and basically means "on"). The -webkit-tap-highlight-color property takes a CSS3-style rgba() value and customizes the color and transparency values of the highlight box that appears behind a link when you tap it (similar to the :active pseudo-class, which applies to the anchor text itself rather than this iPhone-added background box). To disable the background box entirely, use an Alpha value of 0, such as rgba(0, 0, 0, 0).

In this example, there is no reason to disable the callout bubble, but perhaps we might try styling that highlight color a bit. Let's make that background highlight a subdued shade of orange to match the site design:

```
a {
    -webkit-tap-highlight-color:rgba(255,128,0,0.2);
}
```

Now if you tap and hold on a link using WebKit on the iPhone OS, you will get an orange background with an opacity of 0.2 (or 20 percent if that helps).

> The iPhone and iPod touch browsers allow users to "bookmark" a web site by adding it as an icon to the device's home screen. Normally a simple "screenshot" of the web page in the state it is in when this bookmark is added is used as the graphical icon to represent that web application. However, you can specify a custom icon to use by placing a Tif image file called apple-touch-icon.tif at the root of your site. If found, this icon works much like a favicon.ico image in that it automatically becomes the icon used for the device's home screen when it is "added to home screen" by a user. You can customize where this file is searched for by Mobile Safari with a <link> element:
>
> ```
> <link  rel="apple-touch-icon"  href="http://example.com/iphone-
> icon.tif" />
> ```
>
> If you use the custom <link> element, your Tif icon needs to be precomposed, that is, look exactly like the finished product that will appear on the iPhone's home screen, rounded corners and all. On the other hand, if you use the canonical file location that Apple will check automatically, make sure that the Tif icon you use does not include the rounded corners or the shine—these effects are added by the iPhone OS itself for consistency. For a nice, crisp image, use one that is 60×60 pixels.

Using CSS selectors in JavaScript

It is worth mentioning here that Mobile Safari allows a couple of interesting selectors that will be very useful to experienced CSS developers: querySelector() and querySelectorAll(). These are both part of the emerging CSS3 specification and allow us to intuitively use CSS selectors in JavaScript calls.

querySelector() will return the first match:

```
var cellosOrBasses = document.querySelector("#cellos, #basses");
```

In this example, the first element containing an ID of either cellos or basses will be returned. If <div id="cellos"> comes before <div id="basses"> in the HTML document, then the returned value from the call would be just the <div id="cellos"> part.

querySelectorAll() will return all matching elements as an array:

```
var strings = document.querySelectorAll("div.strings");
```

This would gather all the <div class="strings"> elements into an array variable called strings.

WebKit CSS transforms and transitions

The WebKit team has come up with a set of DHTML-like functions to allow developers to manipulate objects on a page using transformations as the elements are rendered (such as skewing or rotating an object), or even transitioning or animating the element over time, purely in CSS alone. These are currently vendor additions, but Apple has pitched these extensions to the W3C as additional CSS3 modules and they became W3C Working Drafts as of March 2009. These functions are available to use today in Mobile Safari, and are hardware-accelerated on the iPhone and iPod Touch, making such transitions appear very fast and smooth on these devices.

To gain a little exposure to these new tools and get a flavor for the possibilities, let's experiment with some of these new constructs in our style sheet:

```
/* Webkit-specific rules */
a {
    -webkit-tap-highlight-color:rgba(255,128,0,0.2);
}
dl {
    opacity:0.25;
    -webkit-transform:skew(-30deg) rotate(-8deg) ➡
translate(-5em,-10em) scale(1.5);
    -webkit-box-shadow:2px 10px 13px rgba(0,0,0,0.5);
    -webkit-transition-duration:2s;
    -webkit-transition-timing-function:ease-in;
}
dl:hover {
    -webkit-transform: skew(0deg) rotate(0deg) translate(0,0) ➡
scale(1);
    opacity:1;
    -webkit-border-radius: 20px;
}
```

One of the easiest ways to develop iPhone-specific web sites is to use the Apple-provided Dashcode.app IDE as your development environment. Its preview pane is useful for testing how web applications built for Mobile Safari will look and function. Typically, when using Dashcode, you're better off getting your user interface laid out first, since many UI changes that you make via the drag-and-drop interface change code values underneath. If you make changes to the code itself in source view mode and then make additional changes with the drag-and-drop interface, your manual code changes will likely be overridden by the IDE.

You can make web applications run in full-screen mode! That's right; you can completely remove the Mobile Safari browser chrome from appearing when you launch a web app from the iPhone's home screen button. To do this, simply provide another special <meta> element like so:

```
<meta name="apple-mobile-web-app-capable" content="yes" />
```

If your users launch your application from the device home screen (instead of navigating to it directly from the Safari application's address bar), adding this line of HTML code will cause the application to launch in "full screen mode"—that is, sans browser chrome! It should be noted that this "full screen" behavior is only supported while the iPhone is in portrait (not landscape) orientation. You can also query full-screen state with a JavaScript one-liner:

```
window.navigator.standalone
```

This code returns true if the web app is in "full screen" mode (i.e., if it was launched via the home screen). Doing this does not remove the iPhone's "status bar" however. However, you can customize the coloring and style of the status bar with some built-in styles. Again, this is performed via a special <meta> element. The default style that you see on the home screen is the equivalent of this HTML command:

```
<meta name="apple-mobile-web-app-status-bar-style" content="black" />
```

Your other option for the status bar style is gray or black translucent.

You will notice that these are metatags with design elements baked in to the attributes. It is unfortunate that these elements are implemented as presentational markup instead of CSS, but they still could prove to be useful design tools in some instances. Use with caution.

Why is all this Mobile Safari stuff cool? Because you can use web-based content in native iPhone apps, too. Therefore, if you only know HTML/CSS but you want to build a native iPhone app, the only thing you need to do is create one large UIWebView window and the rest of your app can be embedded in it. You can even go so far as executing JavaScript from Cocoa applications as well as calling native Cocoa code from JavaScript.

Mobile Safari adds an entire JavaScript-based gesture API called DOM Touch so that your web applications can detect one- and two-finger gestures like pinch and zoom. This topic is beyond the scope of this book, but it's useful to note and we encourage you to learn more about it.

---

18. To call native Cocoa code from your HTML, CSS, and JavaScript code, register a custom URI scheme and construct a URI that the Cocoa code will catch, parse, and then execute. For example, calling a URI such as myapp://somefunction/parameter1/parameter2 inside your UIWebView will pass parameter1 and parameter2 to somefunction, assuming that the application that has been registered to handle the myapp scheme reacts appropriately, perhaps using the native NSURL class methods available to all Cocoa applications.

You can see the result of these code changes in Figure 5-17 and Figure 5-18.

Take a look at the `<dl>` rule first. The `-webkit-transform` property has four values after it: skew, rotate, translate, and scale. Skew and rotate are almost self-explanatory; they each perform skew and rotate operations based on the degrees (deg) value that you input. In this case, the -30deg will skew the top edge to the right and the bottom edge to the left, and a positive 30 would have the exact opposite effect. For rotate, we chose a value of -8deg because it looked nice for the effect we were going for, but try a value of 180deg and see what happens! The image will be upside down in the initial state.

The translate value is similar to relative positioning. The first number is the horizontal axis offset, and the second number is the vertical offset. A negative vertical offset will move the object higher, while a positive number will move it lower. For the horizontal plane, positive numbers will move the object to the right, and negative numbers to the left. Our example moves the object to the left 5 ems and up 10 ems.

It's also fairly simple to guess what scale does. The scale value can effectively be any number greater than or equal to 0. Here we've set the scale value to 1.5, or about 50 percent larger than the original.

Figure 5-17. The initial state of the iPhone page with the info box and portrait faded, skewed, and enlarged. Tap on the image to activate the animation sequence.

Figure 5-18. After tapping on the area where the picture appears, the objects animate and settle into the position shown.

The -webkit-box-shadow property gives us the ability to control shadows (such as the ubiquitous drop shadow) on any box object. The first value of 2px is the horizontal offset. In this case, the shadow is being shifted 2 pixels to the right (a negative value would shift it the other direction.) The second value is the vertical offset, and this value drops our shadow 10 pixels below the affected object. The third value is the critical blur radius value. A value of 0 would yield a crisp line. In this case, we've set it to 13 pixels, giving it a nice, soft blur. Finally, the last value is the color of our blur. We are able to use the CSS3-style RGBA value, set it to black with all zeroes for the R, G, and B spots, and take advantage of 0.5 for the alpha transparency spot to allow the shadow effect to blend in with the background color better.

Up to now we've described the transformations in CSS that affect our object's initial state. Now let's talk animation.

The -webkit-transition-duration value establishes timing for the transition effect. In this case, we've set it to 2s, or 2 seconds. This works in conjunction with the -webkit-transition-timing-function property to describe how this animation will flow. We have some default keyword values to play with such as linear, ease-in, and ease-out. Or we could define a custom value using the format cubic-bezier(x1, y1, x2, y2), and the four values represented would be used to compute a cubic Bezier curve. We're going to take the easy route and use the keyword ease-in, which gives a nice acceleration and snap at the end of the animation.

To trigger this animation, we are using dl:hover. On the iPhone and most other mobile devices that wield WebKit, there is no hover. However, the tap event works to execute this control and that's how we'll use it here. Within this rule we've simply reset the skew, rotate, translate, and scale values to their initial state. You could choose to tweak it the other direction or any which way you please, and we encourage you to experiment with these values to see what happens. We also have set opacity back to 1, and when the animation is triggered by a tap event, the whole box will snap back into place after 2 seconds. Try it by tapping on the image or anywhere within the border of the info box.

Speaking of borders, what would Web 2.0 be without rounded corners? We've added them here using the -webkit-border-radius property. You can get even more specific than that. Try -webkit-border-top-left-radius:20px; instead. Then add different border values to the other three corners. You can even add a 20 pixel rounded border to the bottom-left and bottom-right corners of the Audio and Video button to finish off the design (see Figure 5-19):

Figure 5-19. Rounding the bottom corners of the Audio and Video button

```
div#sitenav a[href="http://natasha.example.com/av/"] {
    -webkit-border-bottom-left-radius:55px;
    -webkit-border-bottom-right-radius:55px;
}
```

The final step of course is to extract our embedded styles and place them properly into an external style sheet. Copy everything in between the <style> tags into a new file titled webkit.css, add the highlighted line shown in the next code example to your HTML, and delete the old style tags. Here's how the <head> element should look now:

```
<head>
<title>Natasha O'Reilly, Baroque Cellist</title>
<meta http-equiv="Content-type" content="text/html; charset=utf-8" />
<link rel="stylesheet" href="screen.css" type="text/css" ➥
media="screen" />
<link rel="stylesheet" href="print.css" type="text/css" ➥
media="print" />
<link rel="stylesheet" href="handheld.css" type="text/css" ➥
media="handheld" />
<link rel="stylesheet" href="webkit.css" type="text/css" media="only ➥
screen and (max-device-width: 480px)" />
<meta name="viewport" content="width=588; user-scalable=false" />
</head>
```

And there you have it. We've styled our site to be very friendly to the WebKit browsers, and we've explored the future of CSS3. The WebKit platform is a growing market and worth paying attention to as other browsers will surely follow over time.

Summary

Earlier in this chapter we touched on the constraints we are faced with when developing for mobile devices. These issues can make or break a mobile design, so be sure you've considered and tested for them in your designs.

Bandwidth and processing capability are perpetual limitations for mobile devices, so you must follow good coding practices with the mobile set in mind. Use good markup practices: remove any presentational data from your HTML, use descendant selectors and classes in the broadest terms, and keep your code lightweight and optimized.

The mobile web is the fastest-growing area for web development. Since the release of the iPhone in summer 2007, mobile web use has exploded across all platforms, as have the number of pages that have begun to be optimized for handheld screens. Major web sites including Digg.com, Wikipedia, and the New York Times have all launched major efforts to make their web content more accessible to the handheld screen. As more and more people start to use mobile browsers to access your web content, don't miss the opportunity to make the adjustments to your site that may be necessary for keeping your pages attractive and accessible on the small screen. A small amount of effort in the mobile department can return large numbers of mobile users hungry for handheld-accessible web content.

Chapter 6

MANAGING AND ORGANIZING STYLE SHEETS

It is usual and customary for web authors to combine multiple style sheets that work together to style a web page. We have several reasons for doing so. One style sheet might be for typography, another for layout, and yet another for color. There may be one style sheet specifically designed to handle print output, and one or more possibly to deal with the explosion of mobile devices hitting the Web lately. Some of these may be architected to work so that there are various forms of failover for user agents that support this or that part of the CSS specifications. Applying multiple style sheets to a web site is quite common, and in fact encouraged, and in this chapter we will discuss various methodologies and techniques for putting your style sheets together.

Our primary goal is to support the widest range of browsers as possible—every one of the browsers would be perfect. A close second might be the maintainability of our site's CSS. Both of these goals can be served by an organized and functional set of style sheets and organization practices that follow a plan.

The need for organization

Sure, you could go and write that style sheet from scratch and dump everything all into one large file. You know what you are doing, and the tendency is to write one style after another as you construct your CSS from a design comp. But then what? How are you going to organize and manage your code over the life cycle of your web site? Who will work on it in the future? How will your code grow over time? How will your style sheets be handled by older browsers? By newer ones? By alternative media such as cell phones and printers? Will your users have any preferential control over the style sheets themselves?

If you've done any code development of any sort, then you know it is almost inevitable the code will tend to expand in size over time. Putting aside code optimization techniques (which we will discuss later), we know that we'll find new features to add, new bugs to fix, and new (or old) browsers to code around.

What organization looks like

Before we can be successful, we have to know what success is. An organized style sheet model is going to have the following characteristics:

- It is going to have a logical, hierarchical structure. Things will tend to be organized in a certain way: from large-scale layout to minute detail, or from broad selections such as redefinitions of HTML elements to nested descendant selectors for specific IDs, or ordered from low specificity to high according to the rules of specificity and the cascade.

- It is going to be a standardized pattern for organization and naming conventions that your shop, and dare we say the greater community, is following or able to follow.

- It allows for flexibility and is customized to make sense for the project you are working on. Trying to shoehorn everything into a rigid framework is going to be more work than it is worth. The best strategies are the ones that allow the greatest and easiest levels of customization.

- The code itself is organized: line breaks, braces, whitespace, and indentations are *consistent* throughout the entire set of style sheets. The code is easy to read. Helpful, concise comments are placed throughout the style sheet outlining major areas of concern, and are not overly detailed or verbose.

- One document is being served by multiple style sheets. Instead of forking your site for mobile, print, and IE, you have one site and one set of style sheets to handle the differences and serve progressive enhancement depending on the client capabilities.

Like good markup, good style sheets are self-documenting. The selectors should use the semantic structure of the markup it represents, without being too verbose or overly specific. Rules should be organized in a way that makes sense, with like rules grouped together and ordered in a way that makes sense for readability as well as for supporting the cascade and inheritance. It should be obvious to any developer coming across your code to see how this style sheet is being applied to the given site. This can be achieved through organization, good commenting, and good attention to the formatting of your code. Let's look at a few things inherent in CSS such as specificity that will help you get organized right away.

Using CSS features as architecture

Although it's not often talked about explicitly, CSS code has two very different functions. On the one hand, parts of style sheets are intended to be generic, while on the other hand, other parts define extremely specific things about various design components. One of the most powerful organizational techniques is to be able to extract the generic from the specific. This enables you to architect your CSS code in ways that are more modular and more easily understood.

Understanding specificity

In our experience, CSS works best if code is organized generally from low specificity to high. This makes it easier to override the more general selectors with more specific ones later on in our style sheets. Placing high specificity rules before low ones will result in those later and lower rules just not working if there's any kind of conflict, and putting things in the proper order from low to high makes it easier to add progressive fine-tuned enhancements to rules as they get more specific. Understand how specificity works, and use specificity and the cascade to your advantage in organizing and optimizing your CSS. See the upcoming section "Organizing from broad to specific" to dive further into how specificity can work in the scheme of how your code is organized.

Applying multiple style sheets to a page

When you apply multiple style sheets to a page, think about how these style sheets work together. You are likely going to want to start with a style sheet that covers any rules that would be common throughout the various media types and conditions. Then you will want to add style sheets for specific media types, and alternate style sheets below that. Finally, you will want to remember that any styles in style sheets linked or imported below another style sheet with the same selectors or basic specificity instructions will override earlier ones.

The grand order of at-rules

Use @charset rules at the very top of your style sheets to define what character set your style sheet is defined as. This will usually be ISO-8859-1 (Western European) or UTF-8 (Unicode), but might also be some other character set such as the likes of Big-5 (Traditional Chinese), ISO-8859-2 (Central European), or Windows-1252. It is especially important to indicate the character set being used in your style sheet if there is a mismatch between it and the master HTML or XML file—if they're different, the style sheet may fail by having the style sheet be unrecognized by the browser and ignored. An @charset rule denoting the use of Unicode would look this at the top of your linked or imported style sheet:

```
@charset "UTF-8";
```

As we mentioned in Chapter 2 and discussed further in Chapter 4, @import rules allow you to attach multiple style sheets from within a style sheet itself. These rules may appear in embedded or linked style sheets, and they must appear *before any other rule* in a style sheet, except for @charset rules.

Imported style sheets may be assigned media types. Usually you will want to import style sheets in the same way that you want to write CSS rules—from broad to specific. A style sheet with a media type of all or no media type specified will probably be best placed at the top of your import listing before any styles appearing later on.

The @namespace rules are used in XML contexts to handle selecting namespaced elements that might have a prefix, such as <dc:title>. The @namespace rules must appear after any @charset and @import rules. We discuss how to use @namespace in detail in Chapter 10.

The @media rules that we discussed in Chapter 2 are used to target sections of a style sheet to a set of given media types and may appear anywhere within the content of a style sheet, after any of the items that might appear above. Again, position these the same way you would treat linked and imported style sheets, with general rules appearing before the more specific ones.

The @font-face construct is a new recommendation in CSS3. This lets you add your own font resources to a page. Any @font-face declarations must appear before any rules that use the imported font. Other than that condition, @font-face may appear anywhere within a style sheet.

The @page construct handles styling for the page box in printed media. The @page constructs will contain rules for page margins and page breaks, and may appear anywhere in a style sheet after the required at-rules. Since they are more specific in affecting only paged media, they will likely be best presented further down in your rule hierarchy.

Classical inheritance schemes for style sheets

If you're familiar with object-oriented programming, you'll recognize the term "classical inheritance" as a technique by which subclasses inherit methods and members from their parent classes. Thanks to CSS's natural cascade, CSS authors can learn a lot from the principles of object-oriented programming. Managing multiple style sheets in a project is one such example.

One style sheet, let's call it base.css, is like the base class, which defines generic properties for generic elements. Then, a second style sheet, let's call it theme.css (which is still pretty generic), extends the design with additional properties specific to the current theme. In this example, theme.css is like a subclass of base.css.

Defining design relationships using selector groups

One of the most pressing issues in CSS-based development is how to write your declarations with the lowest edit-per-change ratio. Design is entirely about relationships that one element has to other elements. Your CSS should encode these relationships as best as possible, such as by using selector groups.

For example, absolute positioning is a great opportunity to use selector groups to encode visual relationships. If all three of your columns in your three-column layout begin at exactly 150 pixels from the top of their containing block, you should use a grouped CSS rule like this:

```
#MainColumn,
#ArticleSideBar,
#SiteSideBar { position: absolute; top: 150px; }
```

instead of three separate CSS rules like this:

```
#MainColumn, #ArticleSideBar, #SiteSideBar { position: absolute; }
#MainColumn { top: 150px; }
#ArticleSideBar { top: 150px; }
#SiteSideBar { top: 150px; }
```

Why? Beyond the fact that the first is less redundant, it also encodes the visual relationship of the position between the three elements in the selector group. This is the real reason to group the elements in this example.

Good coding principles

Neatness counts. Seriously. You should get in the habit of keeping a clean house when it comes to code. Have you ever tried to find a pen on your desk that you haven't tidied up in the past six months? What about that car registration renewal that you thought was due next week? Yes, you know who you are out there . . . Well, think of that pen as a class in CSS, and think of that DMV renewal form as an ID, and imagine you fresh on the job as the web designer for a major web operation. Your boss just stormed in and said we need to change all pen classes to have red borders, and the DMV renewal box needs to be moved to the right side of the page instead of the left. The style sheet is six printed pages long and is such a mess that you have no idea where to begin because you took this job only a month ago and haven't looked at the site style sheet much since then.

Organized code to the rescue. Let's look at some methods for improving our own lives and the lives of others through cleaner and more organized CSS.

Taking advantage of inheritance

At this point it would be a good idea to point out the issue of inheritance. If you return to Chapter 2 and look at Figure 2-4 and its accompanying code example, you'll see that the <body> element was set to reduce the font size to 80 percent of the default and to use a sans-serif font family. The styles font-family and font-size were assigned to the <body> element and yet the entire document seems to take on these values. This is extremely important because, along with the cascade, CSS inheritance is equally effective at transferring errors and discrepancies "downstream" (to child nodes) as it is at transferring correct CSS declarations.

In Figure 6-1, we can see how this has been rendered using a web browser. Interestingly, all of the elements have this sans-serif font treatment, and while you may have to take our word for it regarding the image rendering, the font sizes overall have been shrunk by the specified amount relative to their user agent defaults. This is made more obvious by the following code example as rendered in Figure 6-1:

```
<!DOCTYPE html PUBLIC "-//W3C//DTD XHTML 1.0 Strict//EN"
    "http://www.w3.org/TR/xhtml1/DTD/xhtml1-strict.dtd">
<html xmlns="http://www.w3.org/1999/xhtml" xml:lang="en" lang="en">
    <head>
        <title>Inheritance</title>
        <style type="text/css" media="screen">
            div {
                border:1px solid #777;
                font-style:italic;
                padding:12px;
            }
            p {
                border:inherit;
```

```
            }
        </style>
    </head>
    <body>
        <div>
            This is text inside the div. The div has a border.
            <p>This paragraph inherited a border.</p>
            <p>As did this one.</p>
            <p>This is because we specified p { border:inherit; }</p>
        </div>
    </body>
</html>
```

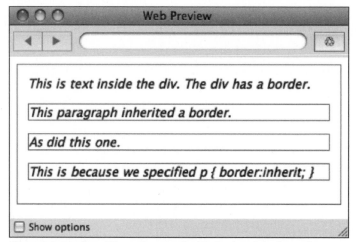

Figure 6-1. Preview of the code example showing how inheritance is propagated through the display of the page

Let's look at what happened here. The most obvious thing we can see is that all the paragraphs have inherited the border value from the <div> rule, and they should because that is exactly what we had told them to do. Normally, the border value is not inherited, so to get this to happen we had to write p { border:inherit; }. In addition to that, we can see that the italic typeface was inherited. Some properties are inherited from parent elements by default, while others are not. We did not specify font-style:italic in our paragraph rule, and yet italics appear here. The font-style property is one of those items inherited by default. Finally, we can see that the parent element was instructed to have 12 pixels of padding. Since padding is not inherited by default, the paragraphs do not render the parent's padding.

Organizing from broad to specific

As we just discussed, a selector can override another rule if the specificity of the first rule's selector is higher. The more specific a selector is, the more difficult it is to override it. Furthermore, a rule appearing later (further down) in a style sheet will override an earlier rule if both have the same specificity value. Therefore, it is a good idea to put your more general rules toward the top of your style sheets, and the more specific ones toward the bottom. This will make it easier to maintain your style sheets by reducing the number of things that can override specificity unexpectedly—low specificity will tend to be at the top and high specificity at the bottom, making it less likely that a high-specificity rule will be causing you lots of confusion and trouble throughout later parts of your style sheet.

Organizing from low specificity to high specificity means, in the broadest terms, placing your simple selector rules toward the top, class selectors toward the middle, and ID selectors toward the end of your style sheets. However, it is also highly likely that one of the first things you will do in your style sheet is to establish sections based on the structural, semantic ID elements that define the major sections of the markup, so within each section there might be its own hierarchical order of rules as well. As usual, an example will help illustrate the concept:

```
/* Basic rules */

body {
    margin:0;
    padding:0;
    font-family:Helvetica, Arial, sans-serif;
}
p, li, td {
    font-size:12px;
    color:#8567ae;
}

/* General class declarations */
.warning {
    border:1px solid #b73500;
    color:#f00;
    padding:2px;
    background-color:#ffdcde;
    font-weight:bold;
}

/* layout sections */
#header {
    height:180px;
    border-bottom:1px solid black;
}
#header h1 {
    text-indent: -9000px;
    background: url(coolbackground.png);
}
#header .search {
    width:200px;
    height:50px;
    float:right;
}
#content {
    width:400px;
    background-color:#e6e6e6;
```

```
    }
    #footer {
        border-top:1px solid black;
        padding-top:0.5em;
        font-size:80%;
    }
```

In this example, we started broad and moved toward specific. The broadest selector is the <body> element rule. <p>, <li>, and <td> elements follow as they are descendants of the <body> element. These simple selectors are followed by a section defining broad classes that could exist anywhere in the document. Following that, we have the selectors that define our document structure following the IDs laid out in our HTML. Even these follow a broad to specific pattern, and are organized in the order that the elements would appear in the HTML.

Avoid overusing arbitrary <div> elements, IDs, or classes

"Classitis" and "divitis" are terms that are commonly used to describe a chronic inflammatory condition whereby your markup contains an overgrowth of unnecessary <div> elements and class attributes. Your document structure should be defined using some elegantly placed elements with a sparse but effective use of IDs and a minimum of classes that will enable rich styling based on the semantics of the document itself. Resist the urge to add extra <div> elements or classes just because you think it will make your style sheets work. Use descendant selectors whenever possible. This will typically reduce the overall size of your code base, improve load times through reduced file sizes and cached style sheets, make your markup far easier to read and manage, and turn you into a magician in the eyes of your peers.

In fact, avoiding adding extra <div> elements and classes completely can be very educational. If your markup is well structured, then you can likely complete all of your design needs using the humble descendant combinator. As support for CSS selectors that use structural context improves (such as :last-child, and :only-child), the need for arbitrary styling hooks will become that much simpler.

Dividing style sheets into logical sections

Just as well-structured markup is considered easy to read and maintain, the same may be regarded for well-structured style sheets. Different sections of a page can be organized into different sections of a CSS file: page navigation rules go in one section, content rules go into another, the footer goes into a third, and so forth. If it's a blog or any kind of news site, there is likely a comments feature, and CSS rules for the comments section will probably have their own styles. Your style sheets will be best structured if the organization more or less follows the semantics, structure, and flow of your markup.

There are of course some pros and cons to such a practice. In the "pro" corner, it is easy to find and change properties that are within these sections on the page. If you're trying to make a change in the footer section of your web site, you would likely find the correct styles in the CSS file's "footer" section.

On the other hand, it is harder to see and manage all styles that apply to a specific element that happens to fall into more than one category. For example, <p> elements may be styled differently in the footer than they are in the content area or a section that might function as sidebar content. Fortunately with some tools such as the Firebug extension for Firefox, Adobe's Dreamweaver CS4, dedicated CSS editing software such as TopStyle or CSSEdit, or a good code-oriented text editor such as TextMate, such organizational issues can be simplified.

Dividing design principles into files

Dividing your CSS into separate files is where you organize your design methodology into distinct CSS files or sections within one or more style sheet files as discussed in the previous section. For instance, you have all your CSS positioning and layout declarations defined in a layout.css style sheet. Your typography declarations, such as text color and size and font choices and so forth, go into typography.css.

What are the pros and cons of this technique?

Placing styles into organized, hierarchical style sheets can be made to borrow from the classical inheritance model of object-oriented programming, such that each style sheet is easy to extend or replace. You create a plug-and-play architecture of style sheets that are each smaller chunks of a bigger design, leading to greater modularity and theoretically less coupling between CSS rules.

On the other hand, this is a somewhat heavier-weight technique since each new style sheet brings with it an additional HTTP request, causing optimization problems for large-scale sites. Additionally, a single element's properties are often scattered in multiple places, causing potential headaches for the CSS's maintainers, who sometimes need to hunt through many files to change an element's many properties. But is this really that bad? Once style sheets are downloaded, they are likely going to exist in the browser's cache, making subsequent page loads only responsible for downloading the markup, not the shared style sheet assets; and again with using tools such as the Inspect Element feature in the Firebug plug-in for Firefox, TextMate's CSS Preview feature (Bundles ➤ CSS ➤ Preview), or the Dreamweaver CSS Styles panel, it is easy to find out what styles might be affecting a given element.

Use the shortest URL that works

As we discussed in the earlier chapter about CSS values, URL references in style sheets are always relative to the style sheet itself, not the document that the style sheets reference. This means that you can create more modular style sheets by using the shortest possible URL you can get away with.

Quoting from Douglas Bowman's blog post at http://stopdesign.com/archive/2002/09/04/ relative-uris-within-css.html: "By changing the image and CSS file references to relative URIs— url("../images/logo.gif")—and ensuring that all images always live on the same server in the same relative location to the CSS files, we can avoid changing those references every time the Akamai image and CSS paths change."

Whenever you use a URL to point to another resource, should you use a relative URL (a path relative to the source file, such as ../images/tuba.gif), an absolute one (relative to the server root, such as /images/tuba.gif), or a fully qualified URL (such as http://example.com/images.gif)? Variations of URLs schemes are wildly inconsistent, and it is common to wonder which one is best to use. Here are some examples to take into consideration:

```
background-image: url("http://www.example.com/omg/img/ponies.jpg");
background-image: url("/omg/img/ponies.jpg");
background-image: url("../img/ponies.jpg");
background-image: url(../img/ponies.jpg);
```

Take a look at these examples and think about which one is shortest and most portable. The answer might be the most obvious one. Probably the last example with the relative path, right? Shorter URLs are likely to be more versatile and they have the obvious optimization benefits, too. Every byte counts when you're compressing and optimizing files. There's little reason to write a URL such as http://www.example.com/violas/ when /violas/ will do. Ultimately in most cases, a relative path will be the most versatile and briefest version of a path to use. If your domain name changes in the future and you've used a fully qualified URL, you'll end up with a broken link. If you're linking to a remote domain, then unless your own content will be published over multiple protocols (like HTTPS in addition to HTTP), you can even safely omit the scheme portion of a URL. Often server-side code can be made to handle these complexities for you, but even in these contexts it may be worthwhile to program the automated generation of a path to be relative.

Good code formatting conventions

Code formatting is important. Code authors should be careful to keep curly braces aligned and indentations consistent, and use whitespace and line breaks consistently. This makes code far easier for you and others to read, will make it easier to make batch changes across multiple properties or rules, and provides a certain pleasing sense of aesthetic that your inner geek will learn to appreciate.

As they say on the WordPress project, "Code is Poetry." And with that note in mind, go and look at a few poems yourself. Try some e. e. cummings, a little William Butler Yeats, and maybe some Charles Bukowski. Then look at a work or two by Shel Silverstein, or maybe some haiku. Look at the typography—the way the words are spaced and laid out. Each poet has his or her style, whether they follow convention or not, and this makes the poem more interesting and more readable. Each space is as important as each letter. Treat your code with a similar level of reverence and you'll be going in the right direction.

So what does CSS convention look like? One of the most common formatting patterns is as follows:

```
selector decendantSelector {
    property:value;
    property2:value;
}
```

The first line lists selectors on a single line, followed by a curly brace. The subsequent property/value pairs are each on their own line and indented. The rule closes with a final curly brace on the last line, with no indentation. This pattern is considered readable and is very common among developers in the CSS community. Using this convention, it is common to see rules with only one property displayed on a single line:

```
selector decendantSelector { property:value; }
```

These two basic formatting rules can serve the majority of your code formatting needs. Each property is on its own line, making it easy to pick out what things might have been changed using diff tools and source code management systems. Figure 6-2 shows an example of a program called FileMerge, illustrating the differences between two files. Note the visual advantage of having new properties appear each on their own line.

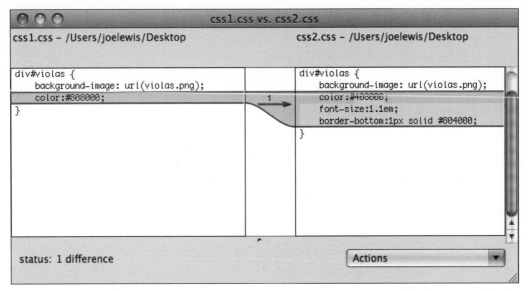

Figure 6-2. Keeping declarations on individual lines makes it easier for programs like FileMerge to show the differences between two CSS files visually.

For many cases, leaving your code in a readable format will be a good strategy. However, in high-traffic or mobile sites where bandwidth is an issue, you may wish to optimize your code to keep files as compact as possible. We discuss optimizing CSS in Chapter 10.

Alphabetize your declarations

In many cases it may be helpful to alphabetize the list of CSS declarations within a given rule. Of course, you would need to be careful not to mess up any cascade or inheritance issues with this practice, so use it as a guideline rather than a rule. At any rate, if you have a long list of declarations, it will be easier to scan through the list if they are more or less ordered alphabetically. For instance, examine the following rule:

```
#footer {
    text-align: center;
    border:0;
    color: #B6CCED;
    width: 760px;
    font-variant: small-caps;
    letter-spacing: 0.1em;
    border-top: 1px solid #999;
    font-size: .80em;
    clear: both;
    background-attachment: url(footer.jpg);
    text-shadow: none;
    word-spacing: normal;
    font-weight: normal;
    margin: 13px auto;
```

```
    font-family: Helvetica, sans-serif;
    font-style: italic;
    padding: 0;
    background-color: #e9eaea;
}
```

Compare this rule with the following one, which has been alphabetized:

```
#footer {
    background-attachment: url(footer.jpg);
    background-color: #e9eaea;
    border:0;
    border-top: 1px solid #999;
    clear: both;
    color: #B6CCED;
    font-family: Helvetica, sans-serif;
    font-size: .80em;
    font-style: italic;
    font-variant: small-caps;
    font-weight: normal;
    letter-spacing: 0.1em;
    margin: 13px auto;
    padding: 0;
    text-align: center;
    text-shadow: none;
    width: 760px;
    word-spacing: normal;
}
```

Because the second rule has been alphabetized, it should be easier to pick out, say, the font-variant rule, or any other choice, with a quick scan down the list in alphabetical order. One thing to notice is that the border-top: 1px solid #999; declaration must appear lower than the border:0; declaration; otherwise, you will probably come up with unexpected results.

Consistency is your ally

One of the most important things for organization is consistency. This is true when you author markup and it is also true when you author CSS. Consistency in how you write rules and what patterns you use to name and group elements gives you the ability to build on your own work.

For example, you can write CSS declarations one per line or all in one line. You can do the same thing with selectors in a selector group. Here are two ways to write the same thing:

```
h1, h2, h3, h4, h5, h6 { font-weight: bold; }
h1,
h2,
h3,
h4,
h5,
h6 { font-weight: bold; }
```

Is one rule (on the first line) better than the other (on the lines after it)? Not necessarily, but what is important is that you use one pattern and stick with it. This not only makes it much more readable, but it also gives you the ability to easily search through style sheets automatically.

Another example is in how you name classes and IDs. You can use these hooks to provide signposts to yourself or other readers of your code about the purpose of the element. In our work, we typically use CamelCase names for generic elements that are not project or site-specific. These include things like Header and Footer, GlobalNavigation or MainMenu. All sites tend to have these elements, and even if they don't, they are clearly not site-specific.

In contrast, we use dashed-names for elements that are site specific. So, for instance, bargain-basement might be the name of a particular sale of a particular store or newhaven-branch might be the ID for the list item that marks up the company's New Haven office.

Since computers were designed for it, the most reliable way to ensure consistency is to use a tool to aid you. This can come in many forms, such as writing macros in your favorite text editor, but one of the easiest is available at the Styleneat.com web site, which encodes some of these best practices into an automated style sheet organizer that can safely reformat your CSS code.

These stylistic choices make little technical difference beyond the issues of keeping things in order with inheritance and the cascade, but they can greatly improve the readability of your code when used consistently and communicated to the rest of your team. Perhaps the most obvious way of communicating these things to others is to keep your code well commented, which we discuss next.

Techniques for intra-team communication

It's extremely rare for a web project to be implemented by a single developer. This means you'll have to routinely communicate with other developers on your team. More often than people would like to admit, communication or the lack thereof between developers working together will make or break a project. And even if it doesn't make or break the project's launch, it will absolutely make a huge impact—for better or worse—on the organization of a code base.

These tips, while not technical, are nevertheless extremely important when you're working with others. Although you're not required to use *specifically these tips* in your project, we encourage you to come up with *some* method for communicating about code across team members.

CSS comments

CSS commenting is simple enough, but what to write? Good code should be self-documenting—easy to read, organized, and semantically structured. And using CSS comments should fill in the blanks. Adding a few succinct comments in key places where it might not be entirely obvious to the next person working on your code will help extend the value of your CSS while making life easier for others. Having a documentation strategy that includes structured and consistent use of comments in your code will set up your project for success.

Comments begin with a slash/asterisk and end with an asterisk/slash—the same as is found in multiline C++:

```
/* Here is a comment */
```

201

The comment can appear on multiple lines as well. The line breaks and whitespace are ignored:

```
/*

    "In the Land of The Dark,
    The Ship of The Sun
    is pulled by The Grateful Dead."

    --Egyptian Book of The Dead

*/
```

But clearly neither of those comment examples are of much use. Let's look at some methods for creating useful comments in our CSS files.

Comment headers

Comment headers are a common documentation feature throughout all forms of code, and CSS is no exception. Use comment headers at the top of CSS files to identify the author of a style sheet, a summary of intent, source repository URLs, or whatever is relevant to the file or project. Here is an example of an expanded comment header, to illustrate some of the possibilities. It should be noted that using intelligent build systems and proper development tools, it's possible to automate much of this in larger projects:

```
/*
Project:
    Title: Natasha O'Reilly's Cello Website
    URL: http://natasha.example.com/
    Created: 2008-10-21
    Repo: git://natasha.example.com/dev/site.git

File:
    Filename: main.css
    Location: /assets/css/
    Created: 2008-10-21

Developers:
  - Name: Joseph R. Lewis
    Last_Edit: 2009-01-31
  - Name: Meitar Moscovitz
    Last_Edit: 2009-01-22

Contents:
  - Section: branding
    Comments: Sets masthead image & typography.
  - Section: sidebars
    Comments: Set right column, convert links to buttons.
  - Section: content
    Comments: Styles for content type, images, & tables.
  - Section: footer
    Comments: Legal mumbo-jumbo.
```

```
Palette:
  - Color: #220000
    Uses: borders
  - Color: #770000
    Uses: shadows, table borders
  - Color: #cc2200
    Uses: visited links
  - Color: #ff9900
    Uses: type
  - Color: #ffff88
    Uses: headings, highlghts
*/
```

This example covers several areas of interest for the project and makes it obvious up front at the top of the file what it is for, where it should go, who has worked on it, and what sorts of things will be expressed in the contents. Coming up with a consistent pattern for CSS comments is a good plan for any development shop, be it a large group of in-house developers, an open source project, or just you alone. This particular example leveraged the YAML (http://yaml.org/) format to organize the comment data, which works great because it is a structured and descriptive text pattern that is easy for humans as well as machines to read. You don't have to use YAML, but you will definitely benefit from choosing some sort of structured pattern.

In the previous example, we outlined several important bits of information. The first section outlines the project metadata—what project this is for, where the source code repository is, when it was created, and of course the title of the project. It then goes on to describe the basics of the file—the file name and where it goes in the project. These bits of information so far will be very helpful if something gets misplaced, or if you're working and have a lot of files open at the same time and need to keep track of which is which.

Next up we added some information about the developers—in this case your authors—and showed when each of us last edited this file. Although it's certainly possible for each developer to keep these sorts of things up to date manually, it makes much more sense to let an automated tool handle this. Such a tool could be a homegrown shell script, part of a build system, or even your version control system. The takeaway is that such information can be added to your project automatically and could be useful as part of reporting systems or in a pipeline for other kinds of postprocessing tools.

Finally, the file wraps up with some information about the contents of the file and a color scheme. Having this basic information about the intent of the design and an overview of the file structure helps other developers get oriented, and it also helps you up front establish an organization structure for your code in this file. Describing how colors are used can save future developers (or yourself) the trouble of having to sift through a lot of code just to find out what the proper color is that should be used in some future CSS rule.

How you structure your CSS comment headers is up to you. You might choose a bit of basic information, or you might be verbose about it and use a structured format such as found in the previous example. Get into the habit of keeping comment headers present and up-to-date in your code, and see if it helps you down the road.

Comment signposts

In a long style sheet, it can be hard to find a particular point. Is the declaration you wanted at line 300 or line 600? It takes ages to search through the document manually. Moreover, if you're new to a project, you don't even necessarily know what you're searching for. This is where comment signposts (also referred to as "flags" or "milestones") can come in very useful.

A CSS comment signpost is simply a unique and easily searchable string of characters inside a CSS comment that the team uses to demarcate the important sections of a style sheet. These sections are arbitrary, of course. A developer can then use their text editor's search feature to locate the signpost comment, and then jump to each additional signpost after that. This way, becoming familiar with a long style sheet becomes far less of a chore.

One common example of a signpost is a comment such as this:

```
/*= Signpost name here */
```

In this example, the sequence /*= can be searched for. If you know what point in the style sheet you want to jump to, you can search for the sequence /*= Signpost name here.

Some programs interpret specially formatted comment patterns as section signposts and allow the developer to quickly find the given section through some feature of the software user interface. Let's look at some examples.

CSSEdit

CSSEdit (http://www.macrabbit.com/cssedit/) will create sections in between comments starting with a @group comment and closing with an @end comment. The section will appear as a folder in the left column, which can be expanded to show the styles contained within. The name of the section is taken from the text that appears to the right of @group, as shown in Figure 6-3.

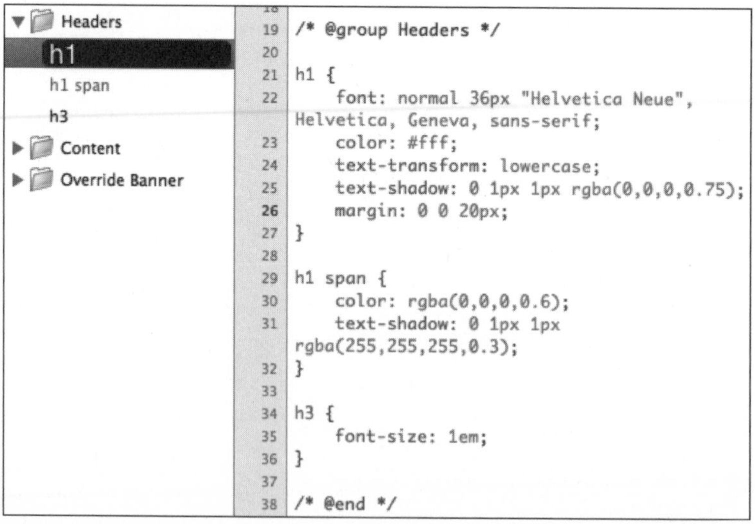

```
18
19   /* @group Headers */
20
21   h1 {
22       font: normal 36px "Helvetica Neue",
     Helvetica, Geneva, sans-serif;
23       color: #fff;
24       text-transform: lowercase;
25       text-shadow: 0 1px 1px rgba(0,0,0,0.75);
26       margin: 0 0 20px;
27   }
28
29   h1 span {
30       color: rgba(0,0,0,0.6);
31       text-shadow: 0 1px 1px
     rgba(255,255,255,0.3);
32   }
33
34   h3 {
35       font-size: 1em;
36   }
37
38   /* @end */
```

Figure 6-3. CSSEdit groups CSS rules in the left column between an @group and an @end comment.

TextMate

In TextMate, if you add a second asterisk to the comment opening (/**), the Symbol pop-up menu will be populated with the text of your comments. Select Navigation ➤ Go to Symbol to bring up the Symbol palette (Figure 6-4), or use the menu at the bottom right of a TextMate window status bar (Figure 6-5). The comment text will appear with two asterisks on either side, as shown in the following CSS code:

```
/** Header */
#header { background-color:blue; }
/** Body */
#body { background-color:green; }
/** Footer */
#footer { background-color:purple; }
```

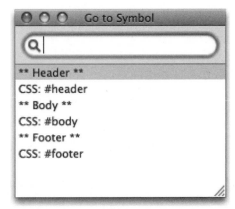

Figure 6-4. The TextMate symbol palette showing how comments appear in the list

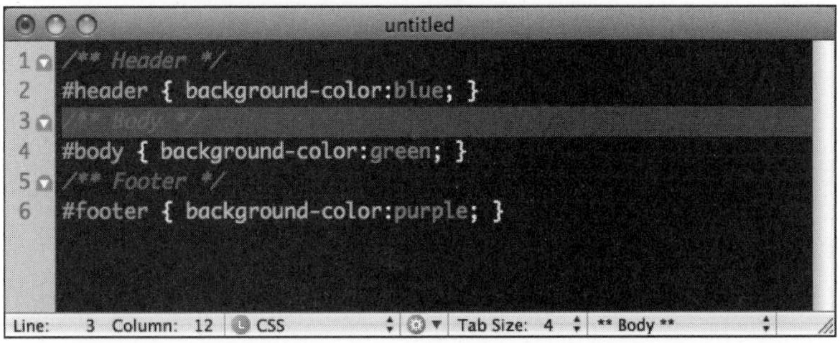

Figure 6.5. The TextMate status bar's Symbol menu on the far right indicating the highlighted Body comment

Using comment techniques such as these will help show exactly how your CSS files should be structured and organized, helping both you and your collaborators find what you need and keep things tidy. Next, we discuss how linking style sheets affects code organization and functionality.

205

Persistent, preferred, and alternate style sheets

Using the `<link>` element to point to external CSS files, we can define style sheets as being persistent, preferred, or alternate.

A persistent style sheet is one that holds common styles for a given media type. Some styles might be persistent throughout your site in any given media type. Let's say for every media type, we want the legal disclaimer to be in italics. So you could write

```
div.legal { font-style:italic; }
```

This would be placed in an external style sheet; let's call it `common.css`, and link to that style sheet like so:

```
<link rel="stylesheet" type="text/css" href="common.css" />
```

By simply omitting the `title` attribute, this style sheet is said to be persistent. If we add the `title` attribute, the style sheet becomes preferred:

```
<link rel="stylesheet" type="text/css" href="common.css"
    title="Common Styles" />
```

The differences between persistent and preferred style sheets are subtle, but can be important from an organizational standpoint. There is some impact with regard to how the style sheets are interpreted. A persistent style sheet is intended to be interpreted throughout a site regardless of preference or grouping. Preferred style sheets, on the other hand, will be interpreted together if they share a common title attribute:

```
<link rel="stylesheet" type="text/css" href="common.css" />
<link rel="stylesheet" type="text/css" href="viola-layout.css"➥
    title="Viola Theme" />
<link rel="stylesheet" type="text/css" href="viola-color.css"➥
    title="Viola Theme" />
<link rel="stylesheet" type="text/css" href="bass-layout.css"➥
    title="Bass Theme" />
<link rel="stylesheet" type="text/css" href="bass-color.css"➥
    title="Bass Theme" />
```

For this example, `common.css` is interpreted throughout the site. The `viola-layout.css` and `viola-color.css` style sheets are processed together when the Viola theme is selected. The `bass-layout.css` and `bass-color.css` style sheets are processed together if the Bass theme is selected. Style sheet switching is supported in Firefox and Opera browsers.[1] In Firefox, you can select a style sheet by using View ➤ Page Style, and in Opera the command is View ➤ Style.

---

1. Style sheet switching can be accomplished in other browsers by providing your own code to manage the functions of switching the groups of active CSS files. A number of easily deployable JavaScript solutions already exist for this purpose; perhaps the most well-known is published by A List Apart at http://www.alistapart.com/articles/alternate/.

Styling for media

You have already seen media types in action in Chapters 4 and 5. Let's dig a bit deeper into media types and learn how CSS3 media queries come into play.

Using media types, you can further refine how styles are applied based on the type of expected output. For instance, we will probably have a style sheet that defines how the page appears on a computer screen. We might then have another style sheet to handle our printed pages and another for handheld devices. Finally, we might want one style sheet to set some global precedents—containing rules such as how the <strong> element should be rendered with an italic and slightly larger typeface than the surrounding text for all media that can handle this case. Commonly we might see a suite of linked style sheets that look somewhat like the following:

```
<link rel="stylesheet" type="text/css" media="all" href="global.css" />
<link rel="stylesheet" type="text/css" media="screen"➡
    href="screen.css" />
<link rel="stylesheet" type="text/css" media="handheld"➡
    href="mobile.css" />
<link rel="stylesheet" type="text/css" media="print"➡
    href="print.css" />
```

In this case, each media type will be affected by the first linked style—global.css—because the media type here is set to all. In other words, printers will use styles from the global style sheet as well as the print style sheet. Handheld devices (well, most of them anyway) will also check with the global style sheet before adding handheld-specific styles from mobile.css. The same pattern follows for rendering on full-sized computer displays using the screen styles.

CSS3 media queries

We touched on the use of media queries in the last chapter on mobile web development. The good news is that media queries are not limited in application simply to styling for mobile devices—there's a whole range of neat ways we can apply media queries to get around some of the sticky issues that are involved with targeted media platforms.

Targeting a media *type* gives you some say as to how style might be applied based on the media in question, but that's it. It does not give you any say as to what additional environmental parameters might be involved. If the styled content is going to be printed, is the printer capable of color, or is it black and white? How are styles applied if the screen width is only 480 pixels wide? How about 640 pixels? Is the output orientation in landscape or portrait mode? With media queries, we can drill down even deeper into these conditions and produce more finely tailored output.

A media query builds on the media type construction by adding some conditional statements. If the statement is true, then the style sheet is evaluated; otherwise the style sheet is ignored. Media queries may be added to a media attribute of an HTML link element, or as part of a @media or an @import statement.

The W3C defines a media query as consisting of "a media type and zero or more expressions involving media features."[2] Essentially we are building on the existing media type construction, so this should look familiar. For example:

```
<link rel="stylesheet" media="print and (color)"➡
    href="colorprint.css" />
```

This example expands the traditional media type of print and asks whether or not color is supported. If it is, the style sheet colorprint.css is interpreted. If not, the style sheet is ignored. The and keyword is used to join the media type to a media query argument. Multiple arguments may be strung together via the and keyword:

```
<link rel="stylesheet" media="print and (color) and➡
    (device-width:12in)" href="color-letter.css" />
```

Here the example targets color-leter.css for media output that supports color and is 12 inches wide—your typical US Letter page. This example also introduces a new yet familiar construction: a property type (device-width) and a property value (12in). Several media features can be defined in this way:

- width: The width of the targeted display. Includes variants min-width and max-width.
- height: The height of the targeted display. Includes variants min-height and max-height.
- device-width: The width of the rendering surface, such as the screen or the paper. Includes variants min-device-width and max-device-width.
- device-height: The height of the rendering surface, such as the screen or the sheet of paper. Includes variants min-device-width and max-device-width.
- orientation: If the width of the viewport is wider than the height, the orientation value is landscape. Otherwise, the value is portrait.
- aspect-ratio: A pair of numbers that together divide a viewport's horizontal length by its vertical length, such as 16/9 or 4/3. Includes variants min-aspect-ratio and max-aspect-ratio.
- device-aspect-ratio: Same as aspect-ratio, but applied to the output device instead of the viewport. Includes variants min-device-aspect-ratio and max-device-aspect-ratio.
- color: The number of bits supported in the output's color component. Includes the variants min-color and max-color. Simply stating color implies all color devices, and this is likely to be your most commonly used value. Using media="handheld and (min-color: 2)" would target any handheld device that supported a minimum of two bits in the red, green, or blue components.
- color-index: The number of colors supported. A property of media="screen and (max-color-index: 256)" would target a screen that supported 256 colors or less.
- monochrome: Works similar to the color feature, but in a grayscale space. Use (monochrome) alone to specify any target relegated to black and white output. Includes min-monochrome and max-monochrome variants similar to color, but applied to the singular grayscale space.

---

2. As of this writing, this description is sourced from the abstract in the CSS Media Queries Candidate Recommendation, available at http://www.w3.org/TR/2009/CR-css3-mediaqueries-20090423/.

- resolution: Describes pixel density. For instance, media="print and (min-resolution: 150dpi)" would target print output with a minimum resolution capability of 150 dots per inch. Includes variants min-resolution and max-resolution.

- scan: Used to describe scanning output of televisions. For instance, media="tv and (scan: progressive)" would select TVs supporting progressive scanning. interlaced is another option.

- grid: Used to determine between grid and bitmap output systems. Examples include teletype devices for the deaf, or phones with a single line of fixed-width LED display (like we had in the old days...).

Developing a mobile strategy

In the previous chapter, we went into some detail about developing CSS for the mobile Web, and we mentioned how this was still new frontier for the web design world. There are many browsers, many screen sizes, many platforms, and little consistency. How can we target the mobile world and still keep our sanity as web professionals? What flavors of XHTML do we use? What CSS will work? What won't work? As Apple cofounder Steve Wozniak once said, "Never trust a computer you can't throw out a window." If nothing else, at least mobile devices are easily pitched...

In most cases there should be an opportunity to construct lean and semantic XHTML that can be repurposed with a variety of CSS techniques, so traditional XHTML is a fine choice for an all-purpose web page targeting multiple media. More advanced and usable devices and browsers will get significantly more use, and most all of these should support XHTML. All you really need to do is consider your rendering strategy and then test markup compatibility to the best of your abilities.

Our strategy for developing CSS on the mobile Web can be broken down into two main parts: design one style sheet for the handheld media type, and design another for media queries. This should cover most of the medium- to high-capability handsets fairly well. The handheld style sheet will cover all your traditional browsers on mobile handsets such as Opera and NetFront. You then design a style sheet that covers the media query–enabled user agents, such as those based on WebKit. To go any further, you'd need to use a script to sense which user agent and device is showing up at the door of your web server and serve trimmed markup such as Wireless Markup Language (WML). Our goal is to stick with our original markup and have it work on as many mobile devices as possible, and deliver style sheets by the handheld media type method and the media query method.

Now we have a bit of a dilemma. Mobile WebKit browsers will ignore the media type handheld and instead look for media queries to add style sheets. Newer versions of Opera understand both but default to screen and won't show handheld unless the user chooses the preference. The good news is, if you have implemented a strategy of using a handheld style sheet and a media query style sheet for the more advanced mobile devices, the Opera users will get one or the other. The user has made their preference and as a standards-savvy developer it is a fine option to respect that decision, but if you really wanted to alert the user that a more optimized view was available you might have something like this in the HTML:

```
<p class="operausers">Opera users may wish to try this page using➥
    screen rendering instead of handheld rendering.</p>
```

And then add a bit of style in your handheld style sheet to hide this information from users viewing the superior screen CSS:

```
p.operausers { display:none; }
```

But this sort of thing can be regarded as unnecessary cruft (see the discussion of "classitis" earlier) and is arguably best left out of your code.

In short, as mobile devices continue to gain in popularity for the purpose of using the Web, you should consider developing some kind of mobile strategy to start improving the availability of your site's content to the handheld device set. Put a stake in the ground, as these users are only going to increase in number over time.

Summary

In this chapter you learned several strategies for organizing your code for maintainability and efficient development. Keeping things organized will make life easier for you and for anyone else who comes across your code. In fact, you should assume that someone else is going to work on your code or examine it in some way, even if you are the only person you think is working on the given site. This is because it is trivial for anyone viewing a web site to use the browser's View Source command and look at your code, download your style sheets, and pick them apart. To make it even more trivial, installing things like the Web Developer Toolbar or Firebug on Firefox make picking apart your code a matter of choosing a menu command. More important, in a professional situation, it is highly likely and probably expected that you as a CSS developer will hand off your work to someone else at some point. You may have already inherited code yourself—clean it up if you can. As we say at the beach: leave it cleaner than when you arrived.

Good organization is greatly enhanced by good comment strategies. Keep your comments succinct—use a comment header at the top of your code to set some basic bits of information regarding where your CSS fits into your project. Use comments to indicate any CSS hacks you may left in there, as those may become issues later on as new browsers appear on the market. Use comment signposts to make your code more searchable and to work better with your code editors if they support such a feature.

This chapter covered the important issues of persistent, preferred, and alternate style sheets, and described the mechanisms for how media types and CSS3's media queries come into play, both from a functionality standpoint as well as for organization's sake. Using these constructs in tandem can serve your organization strategy well.

In summary, a little planning will go a long way. Think of it as writing an essay, where you stub out the major headings first and then fill in the content. Take some time up front to sketch out your CSS sections and files at the beginning of your project, and use that outline to develop your organized and well-formed code. Treat the formatting of your code like poetry, and strive for the most organized and clear way to express your intentions in how you organize your rules and your selectors, and how you write your comments.

CSS PATTERNS AND ADVANCED TECHNIQUES

As you saw in the earlier chapters of this book, much of what CSS is capable of depends heavily on organized and well-formed HTML or XML that's largely self-describing by working in concert with the semantic structure of the markup. Starting out this way, the markup itself functions as a sort of application programming interface (API) for other purposes. One common purpose for such semantic markup is to ease transformations from one format to another or extract data from it, as microformats and RDFa can do today.

In much the same way, CSS itself can benefit from being equally "self-describing." Writing CSS that is not merely readable but *meaningful* creates additional patterns and improves the reusability of CSS code whether the goal is to create rules for a set of web sites, user style sheets, JavaScript widgets, or other resources. Style sheets written in this way are then able to more freely move and mirror the semantic structures that they're applied to.

In this part of the book, you'll see how writing meaningful, reusable, modular style sheets can result in better CSS as well as other content when combined with appropriately semantic markup.

Chapter 7

SEMANTIC PATTERNS FOR STYLING COMMON DESIGN COMPONENTS

When developers talk about patterns, they are really talking about tasks, or things they have to do often. In the case of a CSS developer, common tasks might be creating a sidebar, styling a footer, skinning a navigation bar, or creating a mobile- or print-ready layout from an existing design. In turn, each of these tasks can be broken up into smaller chunks of work, where each chunk can be encoded into a particular CSS rule or groups of rules. The goal of creating patterns is to make these rules generic enough that they can be used with minimal modifications in more than one place.

Patterns can also be thought of as conventions, or—to use a linguistic phrase—idioms. As they do in human languages, conventions help ease interoperability among various components. When people talk about burning the midnight oil, we know they're not literally igniting a canister of fuel at midnight, but rather that they are working hard late into the night. Since this is a well-known phrase, communication between people usually runs smoothly. However, if some people weren't familiar with that phrase, then an explanation would be needed. Thus, being familiar with the idioms of a particular language helps you interface with its native speakers.

This phenomenon holds true for markup and CSS code as well. In this chapter, we'll introduce you to two major ways you can add semantics and functionality to your markup: microformats, and RDFa. Next, we'll show you how you can use CSS to style markup that uses these techniques effectively, as well as explain how taking advantage of these markup techniques makes your CSS easier to write and reuse much more logically. Finally, we'll show you how to take what you've learned about code reuse in the form of patterns in your markup and CSS and use it to make everyday tasks like styling various common interface elements a breeze regardless of what project you're working on now or in the future.

Markup patterns and common authoring conventions

Not surprisingly, being able to create CSS patterns depends on already having specific patterns in your markup. Thankfully, patterns are a naturally occurring phenomenon. This happens for a number of reasons; due to the simplicity of HTML and CSS, much of today's web content is created by people copying and pasting code that already exists and then modifying it to suit their needs; web sites with similar needs often have similar implementations. While much variation exists, there begins to emerge a semantic structure to your garden-variety HTML document.

Both of these evolved from the simplest of HTML patterns, so before all that, let's start at the beginning.

The evolution of markup conventions

HTML is a relatively simple language. It has a limited number of elements that represent function (that is, structure), and it used to have a number of elements that depicted form. As you know, the elements depicting form were deprecated and replaced with CSS. What was left were the structural elements, and while the needs of web developers evolved, the language itself stagnated for years.

The most recent incarnation of the HTML language is HTML 4.01, and it includes several "semantically meaningless" structural elements that are routinely overloaded with semantics in particular ways by developers today. For example, consider a fragment of HTML such as the following:

```
<body>
    <div id="page-wrapper">
        <div id="header">
            <h1>My Header</h1>
        </div>
        <div id="main">
            <div class="section">
                <!-- Other content here. -->
            </div>
            <!-- More sections here. -->
        </div>
        <div id="sidebar">
            <!-- Sidebar content here. -->
        </div>
    </div>
</body>
```

This is a common pattern that's almost second nature to many web authors today. It describes a document's major sections by providing structural differentiation between the content components in the document. This particular structure, with a "main" area, a "header," and a "sidebar" is so familiar, in fact, that you could even call it an HTML idiom.

These conventions are also noteworthy for how they've influenced HTML5, which is the version of HTML currently under development as of this writing. In this next major version of HTML, we have full-fledged elements like <section> and <header>. In other words, where authors commonly used markup such as <div class="section">, using HTML5 we will be able to more simply do things like this:

```
<header>
    <h1>My Header</h1>
</header>
<div id="main">
    <section>
        <!-- Other content here. -->
    </section>
</div>
```

This is no coincidence; the authors of the HTML5 specification purposefully used common authoring patterns to make decisions about what elements to add or remove from the language, and why. Such convention and consistency is thus an integral part of the evolution of web technology.

Markup patterns can be spread across entire document structures, such as the header-and-section pattern just shown (we call these "wide" patterns), or as small as single attribute and value pairs ("narrow" patterns). Here's another pattern that's even narrower, affecting an individual component on a page, a navigation list in this case:

```
<div id="main-navigation">
    <ul>
        <li class="selected">
            <a href="/">Home</a>
        </li>
        <!-- More list items here. -->
        <li>
            <a href="/contact/">Contact Us</a>
        </li>
    </ul>
</div>
```

This pattern—a <div> element containing a single <ul> element, which itself contains <li>s with <a> elements within them—is also a familiar HTML idiom to many developers. What's more, it's actually composed of several nested subpatterns, each level of nesting narrower than its ancestor's. For example, note that one of the list items has a class value of selected. This class name could indicate that the item in the list is the one the user is currently browsing.

The existence of these patterns allows you to create the simple but powerful rules that can apply to large numbers of documents at once. Indeed, some of the most powerful patterns are composed of the most humble parts. HTML5's addition of a <section> element, for instance, is likely to improve CSS because it means that more developers will more consistently use that element for demarcating the structural pieces of their documents, making style sheets that style such "sections" reusable across more published content.

Microformats: reusing markup patterns and adding semantics

The power in reusing existing design patterns and the reuse of conventions into attribute names like this is a central focus for the microformats community. By analyzing common use cases and breaking them down into constituent parts, markup patterns are developed for conveying different semantic meaning. These can be even nested inside one another, and when evolved to a particular degree are ultimately able to suggest the structure of a document based on its content.

Microformats are a community-driven effort to analyze and encode common HTML authoring conventions into specifications of patterns of element, attribute, and attribute values that add semantics and functionality to your markup. These patterns are widely adopted because they are simple and powerful; elemental microformats are atomic semantic building blocks from which compound microformats are built. In turn, compound microformats can be grouped, nested inside other microformats formats, or seamlessly integrated with custom markup without losing either the semantic fidelity acquired by using the microformat or—more to our purposes in this chapter—the styling potential.

In fact, this powerful framework of patterns-inside-patterns offers an incredibly rich array of styling hooks, and its implicit structural support makes CSS more readable, too.

How microformats work

The class attribute holds special meaning to CSS; it's one mechanism by which you can target markup elements with your CSS selectors.

Limitations to regular web development imposed by using microformats are worth mentioning. The fact is that microformats make use of core HTML properties in a way that the designers of the language never envisioned. This means that while microformats can provide unmatched benefits, they have some drawbacks and limitations that you may run into when you work with them.

The most obvious limitation is that, since many microformats rely heavily on class attribute values, you need to be cautious that the class names you choose to use do not clash with class names that are used in microformats on your pages. If such a clash occurs, you may find your CSS rules applying to elements you didn't intend, which can cause layout issues or other design problems. Thankfully, these issues are relatively easy to spot with a good inspector tool such as Firebug.

With recent surges in the adoption of semantic markup techniques like microformats, developers are running into naming collisions more and more frequently. Some developers are of the opinion that microformat values should be given "pseudo-namespaces" to avoid such class name collisions.[1] Of course, one easy way to work around the problem is to give your own class names a prefix or suffix, a technique heavily promoted as a best practice in JavaScript development already. This can be cumbersome, but at least this practice is effective and would help keep your custom classes distinct from commonly used vocabularies.

For example, one property of the hCard microformat is declared with a class attribute value of photo. There are lots of situations where such a class name could be used, both on <img> elements and on others, such as in the following example fragment:

---

1. Jens Meiert wrote more about this interesting topic on a blog post published at http://meiert.com/en/blog/20070913/microformats-and-pseudo-namespaces/.

```
<div class="photo">
<img src="/raven.jpg"➡
    alt="A black raven stands perched on a tree branch." />
    <p class="caption">
        The blackness of a Raven often symbolized darkness and night.
    </p>
</div>
```

This is where descendant selectors and specificity really come in handy. Simply using a .photo selector may target too many subjects, so if you know that all of your hCard's photographs use an <img> (and not, say, an <object>) element, it's safer to use img.photo as your selector. An even better selector would take advantage of the hierarchical HTML structure, and could therefore look like .vcard .photo img.

There are already some projects that are making use of these ideas on a large scale. The Oomph Microformats Toolkit[2] is a recent example, providing plug-and-play style sheets that attach themselves to microformatted content in your pages. Well before that in 2006, however, Jon Hicks was one of the first to provide a downloadable user style sheet that visibly highlighted microformats on web pages[3] and in the same year, John Allsopp demonstrated how designers could make use of CSS in conjunction with hCard microformats[4] for simple, logical styling. More recently, these ideas have also been used to style XFN and rel-license links.[5]

Despite their benefits, since microformats rely on embedding specific patterns inside of ordinary markup, they have some severe limitations: they can accomplish only what the markup itself will permit, they have few mechanisms for extensibility, and they can impinge upon other uses of the same markup (or class names). Due in part to these dangers, microformats can take a long time to mature and build functionality on top of. The microformats community is strictly focused on creating building blocks in markup that solves the most generic problems with the most broadly applicable solutions—the so-called 80 percent of the challenge with 20 percent of the complexity.

A full discussion of microformats is beyond the scope of this book, but thankfully there are some excellent resources available for you to learn more. As microformats are a semantic technique as well as a solid engineering practice, we strongly encourage you to pick up a copy of John Allsopp's book *Microformats: Empowering Your Markup for Web 2.0*.[6]

RDFa: adding extensible vocabularies to semantic markup

Since microformats typically don't try to solve specific cases for niche fields, RDFa picks up where microformats leave off by adding an open-ended mechanism for extending the semantics of markup without limitations from the host markup language itself. In other words, RDFa is a simple and, more

---

2. The Oomph Microformats Toolkit actually provides additional tools and widgets that work with microformats. You can learn more about the CSS portions of the toolkit at http://visitmix.com/Lab/Oomph#Style.
3. Jon Hicks's user style sheet can be downloaded from http://hicksdesign.co.uk/journal/highlight-microformats-with-css.
4. John Allsopp's article was published at http://24ways.org/2006/styling-hcards-with-css.
5. Christopher Schmitt shows several additional illustrative examples on an Opera Developer Community blog post at http://dev.opera.com/articles/view/styling-xfn-and-rel-license-links/.
6. John Allsopp's book (friends of ED, 2007) also has a useful free companion web site available at http://microformatique.com.

important, language-agnostic way of giving documents the means to be self-describing. RDFa uses a set of attributes (hence the trailing "a") that can be attached to any element whose values reference other elements in the same or other documents.

Recall from our discussion of the linguistics of markup languages in Chapter 1 that markup languages contain rudimentary but powerful grammars in three major forms: which elements are being used, which attributes and attribute values those elements have, and the hierarchical context of elements in relation to one another. The ability to nest one element within another creates implicit relationships between different elements, but is structurally limiting. If elements are required to be nested to reference one another, neither the document itself nor the rest of the Web can be flexibly structured.

RDFa adds a fourth grammatical form by allowing one element, via an attribute and value pair, to reference any other element anywhere else on the Web by way of its unique web address or URI. Rather than referring to a document, now the reference actually refers to an object—a person, idea, place, event, book, or some other thing. The attribute used to do this is the about attribute. For example, given a transcript of a speech we can now explicitly refer to and describe it without requiring that the two pieces of markup be structurally attached to one another.

```
<blockquote cite="http://example.com/myspeech" id="my-speech">
    <p>Once upon a time[...]</p>
</blockquote>
```

By giving this speech an explicit id attribute and unique value, we then use this value in a different element's about attribute:

```
<p>
    The speech was written by
    <a about="#my-speech" property="dc:creator"
        href="http://example.com/~bobsmith/">
        Bob Smith
    </a>
</p>
```

Here, we've described the speech as being created by Bob Smith. RDFa gets its name from the fact that it borrows a concept from the W3C's Resource Description Framework (RDF) called a **triple**, itself merely a way of describing two objects (two "things") with a relationship to one another. In the prior example, the quoted speech is one object (the subject), Bob Smith is the other (the predicate), and the fact that Bob wrote the speech (that is, he is the **creator**) is the relationship. The only magic here is that the meaning of a "creator" has already been defined by a vocabulary we're referring to as "dc" (short for Dublin Core[7]).

In addition to the attributes already present in XHTML that RDFa makes use of such as rel and rev, RDFa adds the following attributes:

---

7. The Dublin Core Metadata Initiative is an open industry collaboration that attempts to provide standardized and general metadata vocabularies useful for describing documents on the Web. Learn more at http://dublincore.org/.

- property: Specifies a URI (or CURIE, simply a more compact URI) that references a particular term in a given vocabulary; the marked-up content is then known to be that "thing." For instance, while blogging about this book, we might mark up its title like this: `<cite property="dc:title">AdvancED CSS</cite>`.

- about: Optionally provides an explicit reference to a second object that the current element describes.

- content: Optionally used with the property attribute to provide an explicit, machine-readable interpretation of the content of an element. For example, an element such as `<span property="dc:date" content="2009-05-17">May 17, 2009</span>` reads to humans as "May 17, 2009" but reads as 2009-05-17 to machines.

- datatype: Optional CURIE that specifies the data type of text specified for use with the property attribute (for example, string or integer, useful for ensuring data integrity for machine processing).

- typeof: Optional CURIE value that declares a new data item.

- resource: A URI or CURIE, which expresses the resource of a relationship.

It's this flexibility with the RDF triple and the extensible, highly specific capabilities that RDFa brings to markup languages that distinguishes it and makes it infinitely more scalable than the microformats initiative. Some might consider these two technologies in competition, but really they are not; both are simply differing approaches to solving the same challenge of having a more semantic and understandable markup framework on the Web. Some crossover exists, but both microformats and RDFa can coexist within the same markup.[8]

Although not new, RDFa is seeing greater adoption very recently than ever before. Notably, several of the redesigned web sites of the US government now sprinkle RDFa in their Creative Commons–licensed copyright statements.[9]

Opportunities and benefits of semantics for CSS developers

Whether semantic markup is in the form of microformats, RDFa, or some other construction, it is guaranteed to have some specific benefits for CSS developers. Patterns make it easier for multiple people working on the same code to work together, because they each have a sort of reference to follow in their work. Furthermore, when patterns become well known within a team or a community, the code itself becomes easier to grok for newer team members or contributors in the wider community (in the case of an open source project). Additionally, as we saw in the previous chapter, having consistency in your code increases reuse and optimization opportunities.

Another benefit of semantic markup is the fact that additional meaning exists in the content itself, and you can expose this extra meaning to end users with visual signals and cues. When your markup is smart enough to understand that a particular block is about a person, a visual symbol such as an icon or avatar can more easily be placed next to that block of text.

---

8. Toby Inkster provides a great example of mixing complex markup that uses both an hCard microformat and various aspects of RDFa at http://examples.tobyinkster.co.uk/hcard.

9. David Peterson was one of the earliest people to notice and publicize this on a blog post at http://www.sitepoint.com/blogs/2009/01/29/president-obama-uses-rdfa/.

In other words, when it comes to semantics, you should be thinking in terms of things, or objects. To do this, you must have a fair amount of familiarity with the content you have. Are you marking up a speech? The "thing" is the speech; it has properties you should describe in the markup you use, such as the date and time the speech was delivered, the name of the orator, a reference to the source where you got it, and so forth.

Encoding semantics naturally leads to creating patterns because there are, for instance, many speeches being given around the world and many of them share the same sorts of properties. Such patterns build on one another; the orator of the speech is a person, and if you've already got CSS rules that apply to "markup that describes people," this can be plugged into the details of the speech to highlight the orator. So it's not the semantics per se that you leverage with CSS, but rather the semantic patterns that emerge within one another like building blocks.

These building block patterns can be evident on a single page (often on "archive" or other sorts of pages that list collections of things), across a whole site, or—most interestingly—across the entire Web. With web-wide patterns, CSS becomes even more powerful. As it turns out, such patterns are appearing more frequently, and what's more, CSS that takes advantage of them is also appearing. Next, let's examine how you can write this sort of CSS yourself.

Styling microformats with CSS

Most microformats overload the use of the class attribute in order to imbue the markup with the necessary semantics to produce functional applications. However, not all microformats use the class attribute, and other microformats use a combination of attributes and elements in sequence (known as patterns). In theory, styling microformats with CSS shouldn't be too hard, since CSS 2.1 gives us all the mechanisms we need to do so in the form of its attribute selectors.

Unfortunately, not all mainstream browsers today support the attribute selector syntaxes, and as a result this throws a monkey wrench into the straightforwardness of styling microformats that don't use the class attribute. However, simple solutions—relying on additional site-specific structural markup patterns, or adding your own class names into the mix for the purposes of explicit CSS hooks—can be used to great effect to work around the problems in these cases.

Styling rel-tag links

A tag is a short, descriptive word or phrase that provides a moniker to describe piece of content. By using the rel attribute inside a link, you can more fully describe the kind of content that the link points to. When the rel attribute has a value of tag, the markup indicates that the destination of the link is a page about a particular subject. For example, here's a rel-tag link pointing to a page that lists blog posts about CSS:

```
<a href="http://technorati.com/tag/css" rel="tag">Cascading Style➡
    Sheets</a>
```

In this markup, the entirety of the microformat is the pattern of using the rel attribute with a value of tag, no more and no less.

Ordinarily, this should be as easy as

```
[rel=tag] { /* declarations for a tag; perhaps a background image? */ }
```

Unfortunately, this attribute selector syntax doesn't always work. Instead, we recommend you use an easily recognizable class name, perhaps, say, rel-tag? So, with your own class attribute here, we use this HTML, which is still a valid rel-tag microformat:

```
<a href="http://technorati.com/tag/css" rel="tag" class="rel-tag">➡
    Cascading Style Sheets</a>
```

with this CSS:

```
[rel=tag], .rel-tag {
    /* declarations for a tag; perhaps a background image? */
}
```

This will group both selectors with the same declarations, and voilà: mostly painless backward compatibility ahoy.

Styling an hCard

An hCard is modeled after the ISO's vCard standard for electronic business cards. This microformat is used for encoding contact information for people or places. This is a compound microformat that can make use of several elemental microformats, such as adr for encoding addresses and geo for encoding latitude and longitude coordinates. However, these are optional and so an hCard can be incredibly simple. Here's a simple paragraph that mentions Tim Berners-Lee, the director of the W3C:

```
<p>
    Tim Berners-Lee is the Director of the World Wide Web Consortium.
</p>
```

This is simple enough, but this information could be encoded in a machine-readable hCard microformat with nary much effort at all. hCards rely on nested HTML structures, the outermost element of which contains the class name vcard. In the simplest case, an hCard need only contain one additional element, with a class name of fn (standing for "formatted name"). A full, but simple, hCard microformat thus looks like

```
<p class="vcard">
    <span class="fn">Tim Berners-Lee</span>
    is the Director of the World Wide Web Consortium.
</p>
```

Since the attributes (in this case, class names) are what encode the semantics, the HTML itself can be altered. We can turn Tim Berners-Lee's name into a link to his homepage at the W3C:

```
<p class="vcard">
    <a class="fn" href="http://www.w3.org/People/Berners-Lee/">
        Tim Berners-Lee
    </a>
    is the Director of the World Wide Web Consortium.
</p>
```

With homepage information, it now becomes trivial to encode this into the hCard itself:

```
<p class="vcard">
    <a class="fn url" href="http://www.w3.org/People/Berners-Lee/">
        Tim Berners-Lee
    </a>
    is the Director of the World Wide Web Consortium.
</p>
```

The simple addition of the url class to the link signifies that the value of this link's href attribute should be used as the web address on this particular hCard. Also note that we've still got more information in this paragraph that describes Tim Berners-Lee. We can add this to the hCard as well:

```
<p class="vcard">
    <a class="fn url" href="http://www.w3.org/People/Berners-Lee/">
        Tim Berners-Lee
    </a>
    is the <span class="role">Director</span> of the
    <span class="org">World Wide Web Consortium</span>.
</p>
```

When you style microformats with nested HTML structures, it's safest to use descendant selectors in order to increase readability and decrease the chance for collisions in common class names. Therefore, for hCards, all your selectors should start with .vcard.

One way to think about this is to read CSS selectors as though they were English. In the first selector, we are saying, "Style all tags within an hCard..." whereas in the second selector we are saying, "Style all tags..." Naturally, CSS's specificity rules let us create two distinct looks for rel-tag microformats that exist inside or outside of hCards:

```
.vcard [rel=tag] { /* "Style all tags inside of an hCard… "*/ }
[rel=tag] { /* "Style all tags…" */ }
```

Using descendant selectors in this way is arguably the single most powerful technique for creating plug-and-play style sheets. As you develop styles for markup patterns that are building blocks such as these microformats, it behooves you to start with specific selectors over more general ones instead of the typical CSS workflow that favors generality and inheritance over specifics. This way, you can be assured that your styles will only apply to the appropriate parts, or components, on the page.

Styling an hCalendar

An hCalendar microformat is another compound microformat that encodes information about events, such as the time and date they occur, where they take place, what they're about, and so forth. hCalendars are composed of a number of elemental microformats just like hCards, including adr for addresses, and can even contain hCards for describing attendees, contact information, and organizers. In its simplest form, an hCalendar event only needs to contain a start time and a summary, so it can also remain pretty simple. Here's a note about an upcoming "unconference" (a conference-like but ad hoc and informal gathering of like-minded folk):

```
<p>
    On March 8<sup>th</sup>, I will be participating in the next local
    BarCamp!
    John Smith has put lots of time into (un)organizing it, and I am
    really excited to meet
    Jane Doe and her brother, Joe, when I attend.
</p>
```

Turning this into an hCalendar is just as straightforward as it was for an hCard. We merely mark the date and the topic with appropriate markup:

```
<p class="vevent">
    On <abbr title="2009-03-08" class="dtstart"> March 8<sup>th</sup>➥
    </abbr>, I will be participating
    in the next local <span class="summary">BarCamp</span>!
    John Smith has put lots of time into (un)organizing it, and I am
    really excited to meet
    Jane Doe and her brother, Joe, when I attend.
</p>
```

As before, we still have plenty of additional information we could add here. For instance, let's turn the BarCamp text into a link to the BarCamp homepage. By doing this and adding the url class, the href value becomes the web address of the event:

```
<p class="vevent">
    On <abbr title="2009-03-08" class="dtstart">March 8<sup>th</sup>➥
    </abbr>, I will be participating
    in the next local
    <a class="summary url" href="http://barcamp.org/">BarCamp</a>!
    John Smith has put lots of time into (un)organizing it, and I am
    really excited to meet
    Jane Doe and her brother, Joe, when I attend.
</p>
```

Of course, we also have a bunch more information about the event that may be plain for you to see but that a computer can't quite make out nearly as easily. We know that John Smith has helped organized the event, and that Jane and Joe Doe will both be in attendance. We can mark this information up as well:

```
<p class="vevent">
    On <abbr title="2009-03-08" class="dtstart">March 8<sup>th</sup>➥
    </abbr>, I will be participating
    in the next local
    <a class="summary url" href="http://barcamp.org/">BarCamp</a>!
    <span class="vcard fn organizer">John Smith</span>
    has put lots of time into (un)organizing it,
    and I am really excited to meet
    <span class="vcard fn attendee">Jane Doe</span> and her brother,
    <span class="vcard fn attendee">Joe</span>, when I attend.
</p>
```

As you can see, we've used hCards to encode the names of the people organizing and attending the event, although we didn't have to. This single block of HTML markup now has four distinct microformats inside it (actually, five, if you count the datetime design pattern being used in the <abbr> element).

As before, the CSS selectors for styling such a microformat should mirror the markup's structure. You can also use the element itself to create visual differentiation in how to display such embedded event information. For example, you might want to display a list of events as square blocks, and you can accomplish this by floating them all. Events embedded as part of plain, inline text might be differently styled such that the date itself is called out with an icon. You can even be specific to the point of matching particular dates.

```
li.vevent {
    float: left;
    width: 250px;
    height: 250px;
    margin: 5px 10px;
}
/* ... */
.vevent abbr[title$="-03-08"] { /* match March 8th */
    padding-left: 20px;
    background-image: url(cal-03-08-inline.png);
    background-position: left middle;
    background-repeat: no-repeat;
}
```

Styling RDFa with CSS

As the "a" in RDFa stands for attributes, you can instantly see the direction with which your CSS selectors need to be written to style this code. Beyond the styling hooks that the RDFa attributes add to your document themselves, the values in these attributes are also structured in such a way as to make it possible to use CSS to target certain elements.

For instance, say you wanted to style all Dublin Core metadata in a particular way. Since RDFa is an extension to XHTML, and XHTML is itself an application of XML, you start by supplying a localized namespace for the Dublin Core properties. To make RDFa distillers happy, you need to use a modified DOCTYPE as well as add a few additional attributes to the root html and head elements of your document.

```
<!DOCTYPE html PUBLIC "-//W3C//DTD XHTML+RDFa 1.0//EN"
    "http://www.w3.org/MarkUp/DTD/xhtml-rdfa-1.dtd">
<html version="XHTML+RDFa 1.0"
    xmlns="http://www.w3.org/1999/xhtml"
    xmlns:dc="http://purl.org/dc/elements/1.1/">
    <head version="XHTML+RDFa 1.0"
        profile="http://www.w3.org/1999/xhtml/vocab">
```

In this code snippet, we've used the XHTML+RDFa document type declaration, and added the appropriate vocabulary profile to the head element. The part of this code that's relevant to the Dublin Core metadata we're going to style is in the xmlns:dc attribute:

```
xmlns:dc="http://purl.org/dc/elements/1.1/"
```

We'll discuss XML namespaces in more detail in Chapter 9, but for now it's important to recognize certain pieces of this attribute and value pair. We have the attribute itself, xmlns, followed by a colon (:), followed by a **CURIE prefix**. In this case, that prefix is dc. However, the document author defines what the prefix will be. In other words, we could also have used code like this:

```
xmlns:dublincore="http://purl.org/dc/elements/1.1/"
```

That's perfectly valid as well, although in practice many people tend to use the more compact dc prefix.

Now that we have access to the Dublin Core vocabulary in our document, we can use it in the values of the RDFa code we're going to add to our document. Take some HTML describing web browsers, for example:

```
<ul>
    <li id="InternetExplorer">
        Internet Explorer, by➡
        <span about="#InternetExplorer" property="dc:creator">Microsoft, Inc.
    </li>
    <li id="Safari">
        Safari, Mobile Safari, by➡
        <span about="#Safari" property="dc:creator">Apple, Inc.</span>
    </li>
</ul>
```

What we have, obviously, is a list of web browsers and their manufacturers. The manufacturing companies are marked up with the RDFa property attribute, and these attribute values are using the Dublin Core vocabulary to denote that they are the creators of the particular browsers.

The styling hook we can use here is the RDFa itself, and we can do so in several ways. If we want to style any of the Dublin Core metadata, we can use this:

```
[property^="dc:"]
```

In this selector, we use the CURIE prefix we defined earlier, dc, followed by a colon as part of an attribute matching CSS selector. However, if we're developing CSS and don't necessarily know what the CURIE prefix will be, in many situations we can also do something like this:

```
[property$=":creator"]
```

Here, we've just reversed the attribute matching selector so it matches a **CURIE reference** (the part after the colon) instead of the CURIE prefix. In both examples, the colon is included in the CSS selector in order to more precisely match CURIE values, and not just plain string values.

Although a reference only needs to be unique inside a particular vocabulary, and there may be some overlap of functionality in some vocabularies, in practice few documents make use of overlapping vocabularies so CURIE references are usually safe styling hooks. In documents with an abundance of CURIE references, using descendant, type, and longer chains of other simple selectors to increase the specificity of a rule's subjects is a natural way to create ever more precise CSS.

Summary

On today's Web, having a solid structure for your data is essential. As the Web evolved, patterns of structured markup emerged and became ubiquitous among many web pages. This consistency enabled developers to more easily share and manipulate the data being published. To encourage this consistency even further, future revisions to core web technologies such as HTML5 are embedding the patterns that have emerged naturally into the language of the Web itself.

Microformats and RDFa are similar evolutions that embed semantics into the highly structured markup of well-formed data. Both of them offer numerous styling hooks that allow you to expose the meaning of the content they describe. Microformats give you particular classes and nested element patterns, whereas RDFa gives you particular attributes and a structure for those attributes' values called CURIEs. By writing CSS in a specific-to-general way instead of the usual general-to-specific method, you can make style sheets that style blocks of structured markup as components, like specific people or events.

Lots of the discussion in this chapter focused on concepts of reuse in markup and how you can leverage these markup patterns employed by the wider development community in your CSS. However, there are also patterns that are specific to the visual aspects of CSS without as much reliance on the markup underpinning it. In the next chapter, we'll explore these other CSS patterns in more detail, and examine how the evolution of such patterns ultimately resulted in CSS frameworks.

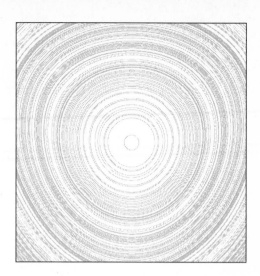

Chapter 8

USING A STYLE SHEET LIBRARY

In any journey where you go from novice to master, there comes a point where you've amassed enough knowledge and experience with the craft that you reach your own limitations. This is when you need to look beyond what you can do yourself and take stock of tools that can help you be more effective. If you were a carpenter, this is when you'd pick up an electric drill instead of using a manual screwdriver.

Throughout this book, you've thoroughly explored much of what can be accomplished using CSS you've written from scratch. In this chapter, we'll introduce you to the utility of using style sheet libraries and CSS frameworks built by others. You'll learn why style sheet libraries and frameworks are useful, and how they make solving particular tasks easier. You'll also learn how to compile your own style sheet library.

At first, libraries may sometimes appear as though they are silver bullets. Reality is, of course, far murkier, so we'll also discuss some of the drawbacks of using predeveloped frameworks since using such frameworks necessarily places constraints on your flexibility as a developer. Different frameworks are more useful for different tasks, so we'll also provide an overview of several of the most popular CSS frameworks, as well as highlighting their strengths and weaknesses.

Before we dive too deeply into the popular libraries used in development today, it's important to remind ourselves of why these frameworks came into being in the first place. For that, let's briefly refocus our attention on the challenges at hand rather than the potential solution libraries and frameworks aim to provide. We'll begin with the importance of leveling the playing field.

Leveling the playing field: "resetting CSS"

You'll recall from earlier in this book that the initial presentation given to documents in a web browser is actually sourced from the user agent's own baked-in style sheet. This default style sheet is what typically gives unordered list items a bullet, makes the sizes of headlines different, and changes the boldness or italicization of emphasized text. These initial CSS rules can be useful, but can also prove to be complications if you're unaware of them and how they interact with the CSS rules that you write yourself.

One nuisance is that these baked-in CSS rules are also subtly and frustratingly inconsistent across browsers. Since these initial CSS rules are inherited via the CSS cascade to your own style sheets, the inconsistencies present across various user agents means that your own style sheets need to deal with all the different default cases. As you can imagine, that's a lot of work. Thankfully, once a particular case is made consistent, the rules needed to accomplish that can be encoded in a style sheet and reused again on other pages or web sites, which is precisely what reset CSS style sheets do.

Resetting CSS nullifies the complications default browser styles bring with them by explicitly overriding all possible values to the same known defaults for every browser. As you know, the nature of CSS is such that the resultant output is an amalgamation of many input sources; declarations in a browser style sheet, a user style sheet, and your own multiple style sheets are all weighted against one another to produce a final result. Furthermore, thanks to inheritance, the effects of more general rules will trickle down into the deepest parts of your design, which means that if browser-level inconsistencies exist, they are propagated through much of your design. By adding your own style sheet that overrode the user agent's style sheet, you are assured a level playing field for your own, subsequent work.

Almost every CSS framework comes with a "CSS reset," and indeed, the earliest frameworks in widespread use were composed of *only* CSS reset libraries, since this was the most obvious shared task all designers faced on all projects. Generic selectors are used so that future styles may override these resetting rules. But why go through all the effort to "undress" your default presentation when you're just going to dress it up differently again?

One reason is because removing default styles makes you think more critically about the author styles you'll add later on. If you can avoid becoming accustomed to seeing boldfaced font when you add a <strong> element, you'll more likely remember that there needs to be a good reason why you're marking up a particular chunk of text using a <strong> element in the first place. Put another way, removing these initial visual cues can help you separate presentation from structure in your own mind as you work.

Although CSS resets can be used independently of a full-fledged framework, it can quickly become tedious to consistently reapply many of the more ubiquitous rules. Thankfully, again these rules can also be encoded in style sheets and reused many times over. Even better, not only can ubiquitous presentational styles be encoded in CSS, but so too can best practices regarding every aspect of visual presentation. In this sense, a style sheet library becomes much more like an actual brick-and-mortar library, housing the accumulated knowledge of thousands upon thousands of developers who have already previously struggled with and overcome the challenges you might face in your day-to-day development work.

Taking advantage of this awesome resource is another major reason to use CSS frameworks. For the inexperienced developer, they can serve as a useful guide for how to accomplish tasks in both technical and design challenges more effectively. It therefore comes as little surprise to us that the resurgence of grid-based design, which is a century-old typographical and layout concept, occurred simultaneously with the rise and development of CSS frameworks.

Before we dive too deeply into the technical aspects of CSS frameworks, let's first examine one of the best practice methodologies that such frameworks help enforce.

Designing to the grid

Grid-based design has its roots in twentieth-century graphic design. The primary concept behind the practice, "the grid," is to define page layout based on the size and ratios of the destination medium. In the 1900s, this medium was most commonly a piece of paper, and so early schools of thought applied grid-based design largely through typographic works.

Today, applying grid-based design concepts to web page layout has become popular and numerous frameworks have appeared to help implement the possibilities of grid-based web design. The frameworks are all tools that help simplify the mathematics behind finding the ratios of available space and how to divvy it up proportionally based on its surrounding dimensions. For instance, a page with a length-to-width ratio of 3:4 would be divided into a series of sections that are each based on the same 3:4 ratios. For a sheet of US Letter paper, the ratio would be 17:22 (or approximately 1:1.2941), so each of the grid divisions would be in some way based on this 17:22 ratio.

A grid is constructed by creating a sort of frame pattern for a given layout space, such as a sheet of paper or a computer screen. It doesn't matter so much how the grid is laid out for now, as long as there is some concept around the algorithm of ratios defined. Let's walk through an example of how we might construct a grid, just so that we can explore the concepts behind grid design. Using our earlier math with a 3:4 sheet of paper, we can create an initial grid with four rectangles of equal proportions to the page itself (Figure 8-1).

Figure 8-1. Adding rectangles to a 3:4 sheet of paper

These four rectangles are of equal size, and they share four corners that meet at the exact center of the page. This is the beginning of a symmetric treatment for our grid. Now we should be aware that there are two lines we might use to connect the diagonals on our sheet of paper (Figure 8-2).

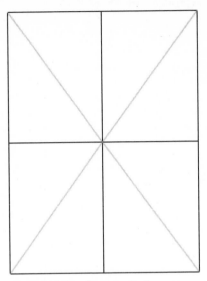

Figure 8-2. Diagonal lines on the paper also meet in the exact center of the page.

The next thing we might do is to add a rectangle, again in a 3:4 ratio, that connects with our diagonals (Figure 8-3).

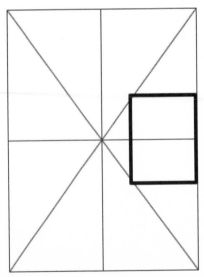

Figure 8-3. Inserting a rectangle that is dependent on the diagonals

Now just fill in the other three similar sections with similar rectangles (Figure 8-4).

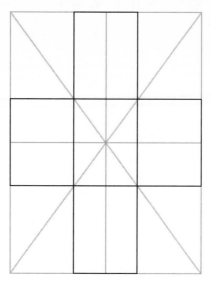

Figure 8-4. Filling out rectangles dependent on the diagonals

Next, we can add a rectangle in the center of the page, using a little artistic license (Figure 8-5).

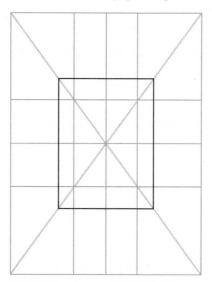

Figure 8-5. Adding a central rectangle

We can now fill out the space created by this rectangle by inserting proportional rectangles off the corners and extending them to the edge of the page (Figure 8-6).

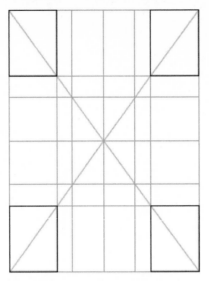

Figure 8-6. Filling out rectangles to the corners

We can now add more rectangles to create space for a margin and a central gutter (Figure 8-7). Keep in mind every one of these rectangles is using a 3:4 size ratio.

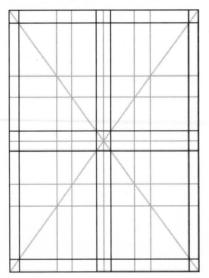

Figure 8-7. Adding margins and gutter to the grid layout

We can then add these graphic elements in arbitrary ways to our grid, snapping the elements to our lines we've created. The framework keeps things looking proportional and organized, even balanced, even though you won't see the grid in the final iteration (Figure 8-8).

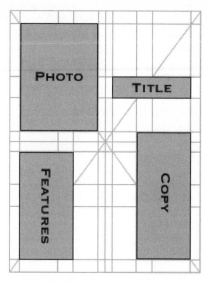

Figure 8-8. Adding content to our grid

This is of course a simplistic and watered-down idea of grid design, and we don't get into the finer nuances of the grid such as golden ratios or what constitutes a balanced page layout, but this discussion should give you a flavor for what grid design is all about.

The rigidity of attempting to fit design elements into some predefined grid system may seem constrictive and uncreative, but such grid design isn't actually arbitrary at all. Grid frameworks provide a subconscious sense of symmetry, and might be thought of as being analogous to the notes of a scale in music. The 12 notes in western harmonic theory provide an effective framework for the vast majority of music that we listen to, and for good reason: they tend to sound pleasant to our ears—at least more so than pitches with completely random frequencies would. This is because they themselves are based on the same proportional ratios. Two notes of an octave may be expressed as having a frequency ratio of 2:1 while a fifth has a ratio of 3:2.

Proportional values like these, whether auditory such as in the case of music or visual such as in the case of grid-based design, provide a certain aesthetic pleasure to the human brain. Our brains are built to sense the harmonies implied by these constructions, recognizing proportional values like balanced visual design and the fundamentals of music as aesthetically pleasing. Incorporating grid-based design into your work lets you align, manipulate, and stress those harmonic balances to greatly appreciative effects and simply result in better work.

Naturally, screen-based media is completely different from media in printed form, mostly because it's difficult to predetermine the conditions of the screen environment. You have many possibilities of screen resolutions, dot pitches, browser viewport sizes, color depths, available fonts, user preferences, and so on, to deal with in web design. As the screen environment is different, so too are the rules for grid layouts different here. As you may have guessed by now, you're going to be better off making use of relative units when dealing with the variables and unpredictability associated with screen-based media, and indeed, this is exactly what most frameworks are built to do.

Tools for grid diagnostics

There are plenty of tools that you can use to in your work that help with understanding and visualizing the grid. These tools can be used stand-alone, without the use of a framework, and they range from low-tech background images you can easily make yourself to high-tech widgets that provide JavaScript-powered overlays on your web pages.

Perhaps the simplest and most natural tool for a CSS developer to use is a background image with visible lines at the points of your grid. This can be a single, large background image attached to the body element during development, or it can be a smaller repeatable chunk of the grid that you can tile using the repeat-x and repeat-y properties, such as Andy Budd's Layout Grid Bookmarklet tool.[1] Either way, the result is that you'll be able to see actual grid lines on your page, much like Photoshop's "show grid" display.

Another grid visualizing tool is the TypoGridder,[2] which also works by overlaying a grid background image using the repeat-y property. Instead of visualizing a layout grid, however, its intent is to show you the typographic grid, as shown in Figure 8-9. It displays where the text of your page should align to the typographic grid's baseline, mean line, and other points. Other tools include online grid calculators to help you determine appropriate grid ratios, such as Grid Designer[3] and the CSS Grid Calculator.[4]

There are even grid-based design tools built to complement specific frameworks. Naturally, those tools require you to be familiar with the framework they supplement. Let's take the opportunity to begin our examination of some of CSS frameworks available to you today.

---

1. The Layout Grid Bookmarklet tool can be found at http://www.andybudd.com/archives/2006/07/layout_grid_ bookmarklet/.
2. TypoGridder can be found at http://milianw.de/projects/typogridder/.
3. The second version of the Grid Designer tool can be found at http://grid.mindplay.dk/.
4. The CSS Grid Calculator can be found at http://www.gwhite.us/downloads/css_grid_calc.html.

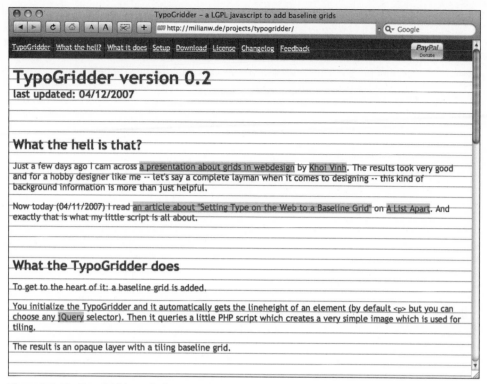

Figure 8-9. The TypoGridder web site eating its own dog food; the red lines are a tiled background image that reveals the typographic grid.

CSS frameworks

Like other computing frameworks, CSS frameworks aim to ease the development of web pages by providing reusable functionality in a modular way and with a flexible baseline. Some frameworks contain multiple library files, each with a specific purpose. For example, typographic CSS declarations might be in one style sheet while reset rules might be in another. This modularity lets you as the developer pick and choose the parts of a framework you want to use.

Although each CSS framework works slightly differently, they all guide you to a certain set of best practices and, because the CSS needed to implement these best practices are encoded in the library file itself, all a developer needs to do is understand how to interface with the library. This abstraction can reduce the amount of development time you might need to spend to overcome a particular hurdle, but it can also make you feel like you're working with the library instead of working with CSS. Indeed, much of the time when you work with CSS frameworks you rarely need to edit CSS code, focusing instead on HTML patterns that the pre-coded CSS will just pick up all on its own.

Nevertheless, many developers like to use CSS frameworks because they can be used to simplify your own efforts to manage and organize your CSS code. They can "hide" chunks of code, such as layout declarations, in their own library files. This allows the CSS you write to focus purely on "skinning" the content (adding colors, backgrounds, and so forth).

Another argument in favor of frameworks is that the very nature of a framework means a certain kind of reusability—as long as you play along with the rules of the framework, of course. Whether this comes in the form of microformat-like patterns of HTML, `class` attribute names, or other styling hooks, the framework's conventions create a well-known baseline that can make it easier to work in development teams. Other people familiar with the framework you're using will be more likely to grok your code than if you used your own code with your own unique class names or other conventions.

Perhaps the biggest benefit to using a framework isn't that your resulting production code will use the framework itself, but rather that the *development* effort you put into the design will be faster. Remember that you can always swap out a framework's own, potentially nonsemantic class names and other hooks with your own code later on. This is especially true if you've been building your own library of CSS code along the way. That said, CSS frameworks are fully functional, reliable, and production-ready libraries that many sites use on production servers every day.

CSS frameworks also place certain constraints upon developers, and different frameworks impose different sets of constraints. There isn't a silver bullet in the form of a CSS framework for every problem. Moreover, many problems can be solved in many different ways. The result is a kaleidoscope of problem-and-solution, cat-and-mouse situations; you can use one library to solve more than one problem, and some libraries may be better at solving problems than others will be.

Although there are some general principles that we'll cover here, the best way to know whether a certain framework will work for your design is to try it and see. Creating prototypes like this are not only extremely fast to construct with frameworks, they are often extremely useful for many additional reasons anyway. As long as you don't marry yourself to prototype code and don't worry about spending too much time correcting trivial details at the early stages of prototype development, you can often produce multiple prototypes for a single project and approach the project's challenges from multiple angles.

When you are working with CSS frameworks written by others, do not edit their code directly but rather import it and then use selector specificity to override aspects you don't like. This is like dealing with vendor code in a programming context; you don't want to be modifying a vendor library because if the library ever changes it becomes painful to make sure all of your modifications are applied in the same way.

YUI CSS Foundation

The YUI CSS Foundation, created and provided to CSS developers for free by Yahoo!, is a modular library composed of four different style sheets that build on one another. The complete library includes the following components:

- Reset CSS (http://developer.yahoo.com/yui/reset/): This component provides a clean foundation for "leveling the playing field" by overriding the built-in browser styles.

- Fonts CSS (http://developer.yahoo.com/yui/fonts/): This component provides typographical control and consistency. Lots of research went into em-based typographic sizing. It's recommend that you use percentages that map to eventual pixel renderings. These are very precise sizes that evaluate to specific pixel sizes: 123.1% evaluates to 16 pixels. The YUI CSS Cheatsheet[5] is almost a necessity here.

---

5. A printable YUI CSS Foundation Cheatsheet is available at http://yuiblog.com/assets/pdf/cheatsheets/css.pdf.

- Grids CSS (http://developer.yahoo.com/yui/grids/): This is the primary layout component of the framework. It allows you to build structures and define a layout for the overall design using markup patterns. The layouts are all based on em units internally, while the inner grid divisions are based on percentage lengths.

- Base CSS (http://developer.yahoo.com/yui/base/; optional): This is a standard helper file for consistency across elements. It puts back what Reset CSS takes away, but this isn't recommended for use in production code because you'd be removing the browser default only to add it again. Not only is this somewhat wasteful, but you may also need to then override these Base CSS rules yet again in your own code. For instance, <li> elements can be tabs and bullets, so why not provide the CSS you want? Say what you mean, and be explicit—it's good coding style!

Most of the functionality in the YUI CSS Foundation that you often interact with is in the Grids component because it provides page-level width and centering easily, as well as letting you create nested grids that allow you to arbitrarily create multicolumn layouts. You interact with the file by writing microformat-like HTML patterns, not by writing your own overriding CSS.[6]

YUI Grids CSS offers four common templates out of the box, selectable by assigning a particular ID value on the outermost <div> element of your page: 750px centered (doc), 950px centered (doc2), 974px centered (doc4), or 100 percent fluid (doc3). It is also possible to customize them, although that's not often required. Yahoo! strongly recommends sticking with these standards.

```
<body>
    <div id="doc"><!-- This is a 750px centered layout. --></div>
</body>
```

Page widths are actually defined behind-the-scenes using em units, which lets the page scale when users scale their text sizes. If for some reason you don't want this behavior, YUI CSS makes it easy to lock the layout's width using a CSS override in your own style sheets:

```
#doc2 { width: 950px; } /* lock to this width, without text resizing */
```

Grids CSS provides six basic templates that accommodate specific IAB advertising sizes. You set the template at the root node, the div#doc; this gives YUI source-order independence so that the narrower column can be either first or second without changing the layout—it'll still work.

Grids CSS templates make use of a "block" in the sense that each region of the page is grouped with a particular YUI class: yui-b (b for block). If you want to create two main regions, a sidebar and a main column perhaps, you need two such YUI blocks:

```
<body>
    <div id="doc">
        <div class="yui-b"></div>
        <div class="yui-b"></div>
    </div>
</body>
```

6. As it happens, this is a common interaction paradigm CSS frameworks use and is one of the most frequently cited criticisms for using CSS frameworks in the first place.

Then you identify which block is the block for the "main column" with a wrapper <div>:

```
<body>
    <div id="doc">
        <div id="yui-main">
            <div class="yui-b"></div>
        </div>
        <div class="yui-b"></div>
    </div>
</body>
```

Finally, you choose which Grids CSS template you want to use:

```
<body>
    <div id="doc" class="yui-t3">
        <div id="yui-main">
            <div class="yui-b"></div>
        </div>
        <div class="yui-b"></div>
    </div>
</body>
```

You can then subdivide these YUI block regions by using another microformat-like markup pattern. To do this, you use "grid holders" (yui-g) and "grid units" (yui-u), which equally divide a block region in half:

```
<body>
    <div id="doc" class="yui-t3">
        <div id="yui-main">
            <div class="yui-b"></div>
        </div>
        <div class="yui-b">
            <div class="yui-g">
                <div class="yui-u first">
                    <!-- The left ('first') sub-column. -->
                </div>
                <div class="yui-u ">
                    <!-- The right sub-column. -->
                </div>
            </div>
        </div>
    </div>
</body>
```

If you want to have uneven distributions of space within a grid holder or if you want an uneven number of columns within a single grid holder, different grid holders are available to you. These are applied using the same microformat-like pattern as ordinary grid holders, but with a different class name. Grid holders with a class of yui-gb give you three columns that equally share the available space, while yui-gc through yui-gf give you alternate distributions of space using a two-unit grid. The former gives you ⅔ and ⅓, while the latter gives you ¼ and ¾.

All grids are based on percentages, so they subdivide the available space. This lets you stack and nest grid units and grid holders pretty much to your heart's content—but there are limits. Deeply nested and odd distributions of space are atypical in the vast majority of designs, but if you run into them you may need to provide your own CSS overrides to adjust some of the deeply nested YUI CSS.

There's also a handy tool called the YUI Grid Builder[7] that can help you get started using YUI Grids CSS. Using the YUI Grid Builder, you can graphically design a grid-based page layout and then retrieve the necessary HTML via copy-and-paste. The YUI Grid Builder exposes most of the functionality from Grids CSS, including setting a custom page width and choosing different-sized rows, as shown in Figure 8-10, but it won't let you graphically nest grids within grids.

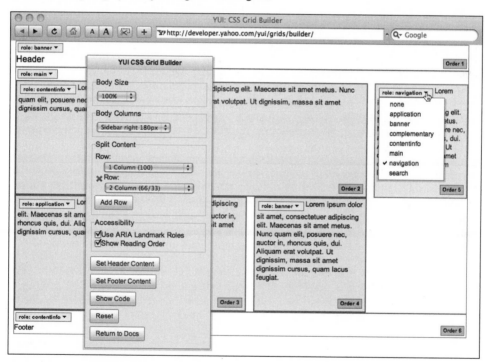

Figure 8-10. The YUI Grids Builder is a graphical tool that lets you easily create a page layout using the YUI Grids CSS framework. Once you create it, you can click the Show Code button to copy and paste the resulting HTML and CSS code into your editor.

---

7. The YUI Grid Builder can be found at http://developer.yahoo.com/yui/grids/builder/.

Criticisms of YUI are that it's very "divitis"-heavy, that is, it uses wrapping <div> elements relatively frequently that may feel "bloated" to some developers. On the other hand, the YUI CSS Foundation has been praised for the way it keeps itself self-contained; its CSS hooks (class and ID names) use a "pseudo-namespace" (a prefix) of yui- so as to avoid conflicts. For more information on the YUI CSS Foundation, Nate Koechley's YUI Theatre talk is very helpful.[8]

960 Grid System

The 960 Grid System CSS framework[9] is based entirely on grid layouts and as long as your design is intended to be laid onto a grid may prove to be another helpful tool. However, one of the potential drawbacks to using the 960 Grid System is that the resulting page design will be very rigid. Due to the limited nature of the framework—which gives you only a certain number of columns and a set of specific widths for each of these columns—changing these defined sizes can cause problems for designs that need to be wider than the allowed size.

Although 960-pixel-wide designs are considered standard for many web sites today, the future is still undetermined and wider sizes may prove more useful. Our hope is that the community of 960 Grid System users will update the framework to accommodate these changes in the future, but even beyond that there are still plenty of circumstances today when a strict 960-pixel width is suboptimal.

A great example of sites that may not want to use a 960-pixel-wide design are web applications that require dynamic resizing (think GMail). Interaction-heavy designs, compared to content-heavy designs, may not be happy with the strict widths imposed by the 960.gs framework. Another example is the many new devices that require a lower screen resolution, such as handheld and other mobile devices. Even desktop browsers that make use of much wider designs may not actually want to do so. The notion of keeping several browser windows open to do multitasking with may not be quite as passé as many people seem to think.

Once you write code that uses a framework, it can become very difficult to break free of the constraints imposed by the framework. Such is the case for the 960 Grid System, which creates page layouts that are a maximum of 960 pixels wide (hence the name). If you want to make a page design that's wider than this but that still uses the 960 Grid System, you'll find that you'll put a lot of extra work into changing your code to accommodate this, and the extra effort can become tiresome when a framework is ostensibly intended to reduce the amount of up-front work you need to do.

Furthermore, in reality design changes can come in from a variety of sources at a variety of times. Although we like to believe that a design is conceived, coded, and then launched, this is rarely the case in reality. In fact, a design is much like a code—it comes out in versions and sweeping changes are rarely self-contained within one or two versions. Design, much like code, changes iteratively, and so you may find yourself in a situation where your design utilizes only "half" of a framework. This is tricky, because it's the point at which your code is the most susceptible to breakage on two fronts: your customizations and interference from the framework.

---

8. Nate Koechley's YUI Theatre talk can be seen at http://video.yahoo.com/watch/1373808/4732784.
9. The home page for the 960 Grid System CSS framework is at http://960.gs/.

Another issue specifically with the 960 Grid System is that since it relies heavily on exactingly sized elements, adding your own padding or margins to the layout elements themselves breaks your pixel-perfect grid. The tempting solution to this is to explicitly override the width of the grid element, but this turns out to be dreadful for maintainability; now you have to deal with maintaining the width of a single element in two places in your code, which is precarious at best. Instead, you're much better off thinking about how you can restructure your markup to give yourself an extra box and give the padding or margins, leaving the elements that the 960 Grid System relies on alone.

Blueprint CSS

The Blueprint CSS framework[10] takes a similar approach to the YUI CSS Foundation framework. Blueprint CSS is composed of a set of style sheets that work together to provide a foundational layer for a grid-based design. The framework provides 24 columns to use, which is more than most (more than 960.gs's 12 at least).

The Blueprint CSS framework is a little different from some other frameworks in that it bills itself not merely as a prototyping or rapid application development (RAD) tool, but also as a foundation or "blueprint" (hence the name) for building production-quality releases and other tools to work with CSS on top of. The Blueprint CSS wiki lists a number of these tools,[11] which include code generators, WYSIWYG layout editors, and more.

Another distinction is that the Blueprint CSS framework comes equipped with a style sheet intended for print, which saves you some work on that front, too. All of these distinctions combined make Blueprint CSS feel a lot more like a design methodology suite whereas many of the other systems feel more like tools in a toolset. Each model has their pros and cons and which you choose can be largely a matter of style.

Like other frameworks, the Blueprint CSS framework offers a quick way to create grid-based layouts using certain markup patterns. In this case, we use an outermost `<div>` element with a class (not an ID) of container to hold the grid regions:

```
<body>
    <div class="container">
        <!-- Blueprint CSS markup patterns will go here. -->
    </div>
    <div>
        <!--
            You can still use custom HTML/CSS code
            outside of a Blueprint Container.
        -->
    </div>
</body>
```

---

10. The Blueprint CSS framework's home page is at http://blueprintcss.org.
11. The Blueprint CSS wiki page at http://wiki.github.com/joshuaclayton/blueprint-css/tools-and-resources links to tools built on top of the framework.

243

By default, this will provide an invisible grid within the container element that spans 950 pixels wide, equally divided among those 24 columns. The grid's "columns" can be thought of as "snap-to" guides, since they are not real columns themselves but behave more like rows. Each invisible grid column spans 30 pixels wide with a 10-pixel margin between columns, giving you an easy way to create real columns of particular widths by declaring how many grid columns wide the real column should be.

For instance, in the following example we create a two-column page where each column's width is equally divided within the available 950-pixel total container width. To do this, we give each <div> element to a class of span-12 (12 is half of the available 24 columns), and then add an additional class value of last to the final column:

```
<div class="container">
    <div class="span-12">
        <!-- Left column. -->
    </div>
    <div class="span-12 last">
        <!-- Right column. Note added 'last' class value. -->
    </div>
</div>
```

Columns can be nested, further subdividing the available space within each one. This is accomplished in exactly the same way as before. Let's further subdivide the left column into three narrower columns:

```
<div class="container">
    <div class="span-12">
        <!-- Left column. -->
        <div class="span-4">
            <!-- A left sidebar. -->
        </div>
        <div class="span-8 last">
            <!-- The left main column. -->
        </div>
    </div>
    <div class="span-12 last">
        <!-- Right column. Note added 'last' class value. -->
    </div>
</div>
```

Note that the new columns are given .span-x classes so that they add up to the available space in the larger column. In this way, you can quickly create consistent, cross-browser layouts that always snap to a grid dimensions.

Summary

We began this chapter by discussing the challenge of a browser's default style sheet and how to level the playing field when writing cross-browser compatible code. As this was a common challenge for web developers, libraries called "CSS resets" were developed that encoded the knowledge of how to do this inside a single reusable style sheet. This practice of creating modular, pluggable style sheets should sound familiar to you by now because it applies the knowledge you gained from previous chapters on an ever-widening scale.

Next, we looked at some of the other benefits of CSS frameworks, and you saw how they could be used to more quickly get up to speed with a project. You learned about grid-based design and the fundamental mathematics behind the proportions and spatial ratios embedded into the most popular CSS libraries. You also learned about grid-based design in terms of typography and saw a number of tools that could help you while developing.

CSS frameworks provide a lot of bang for your buck, so to speak, because they let you take advantage of the work of other developers. You saw how some of the more popular CSS frameworks actually worked. Most of them come with a CSS reset file, and then progressively build on the consistent foundation they provide to enable more complex functionality. The YUI CSS Foundation framework is an example of a modular framework from which you can elect to use one, some, or all of its parts. Blueprint CSS is another popular framework that comes with several components, including a print style sheet. The jQuery UI CSS Framework takes modularity to the component level, providing a CSS library with which you can easily style widgets and other individual blocks of content.

So far, we've been exploring CSS in the context of HTML pages. However, as you'll recall from the first chapter, CSS can be used in many more places than simple web pages. In the next chapter, we'll break free from the constraints of HTML and learn how to use CSS effectively in conjunction with true XML documents.

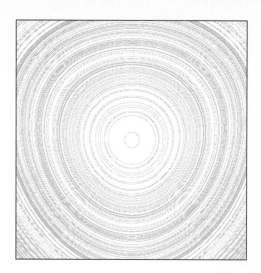

Chapter 9

STYLING XML WITH CSS

Throughout this book, we've explored both markup and CSS and how to develop patterns to leverage one from the other. We also discussed the various forms that your projects might take, such as traditional on-screen display, print, and mobile media. However, in all this time we've not yet explored the versatility and extensibility that we alluded to as being possible with XML in the beginning of this book.

In this chapter, you'll break free of styling HTML and spread your wings to include other forms of content, such as Atom feeds, SVG images, and your own custom XML applications. You'll see that many mainstream browsers support non-HTML-based web content very nicely, and you'll learn how to deal with some of the remaining browser quirks that styling client-side XML produces.

Using XML for your markup

HTML and XHTML are commonly used throughout the Web for marking up web pages. XML is not nearly as common for this use, but the good news is that it is for the most part supported by all major modern browsers. If you wish to dabble in XML or rebel against the HTML establishment, you can go right ahead.

CSS can be used to style much more than HTML or XHTML. If you are willing to adhere to the stricter rules of XML and aren't afraid of defining your own markup, XML may be a viable alternative for marking up your site. Or you may have reasons for styling existing XML sources: a data report in XML format, an SVG image, or an existing RSS feed are all candidates for XML sources that might be improved with a little CSS. Using CSS with XML can be liberating compared to dealing with HTML's constraints, but there are pros and cons with either approach.

Problems with POSH

Plain Old Semantic HTML (POSH) is a wonderful construct for the Web. It has proven time and time again to be a simple and effective format for delivering vast quantities of information over the Internet in a lightweight and easy-to-understand format. But there are some shortcomings. For one, HTML only tells us the format of a document—it does not tell us much about the content itself. Another problem is the legacy baggage that comes with HTML—all those browser bugs, and those varying opinions as to how elements are handled.

XHTML was intended to be a reformulation of HTML into XML, a path forward to advance the capability of web authors by providing the tools and extensibility of XML in an HTML framework. It was a great idea in theory—if only browsers would have played along.

Freedom from HTML

Casting aside the shackles of HTML can be liberating. Styling XML will free you from the default browser styles and implied meanings that come with HTML. You can make your own rules—define your own set of tags and attributes that more closely match the need in question. And then if you do choose XML, you have the full power of the Turing-complete XSL suite of technologies at your disposal too.

In HTML, web browsers treat certain elements in certain ways in all cases, and there's little you can do to get around that. For one, the <body> element is going to be the part of the document that appears in the viewport. Everything else going into the viewport is going to be a child of the <body> element. On the other hand, none of what is placed in the <head> section of your HTML can be styled. (Not that you'd likely need to—but say you wanted to extract attributes from meta elements using attr() and have them show up somewhere?) Nor can the overall <html> element be styled (except for specifying the behavior of its children that might appear at <body> and below).

Oh yeah? Well, XML sucks!

That isn't to say XML is without its own failings. Sometimes being too perfect is a burden in and of itself.

XML documents optionally begin with an XML prolog. The prolog may consist of two parts: the XML declaration and the document type definition (DTD). The DTD is very common in HTML and XHTML contexts. But with the XML declaration, it's not so common. It is this declaration that causes Internet Explorer 6 to trip and use quirksmode instead of standards mode rendering. The XML declaration looks like this:

```
<?xml version="1.0"?>
```

In conjunction with a DTD it might look like this:

```
<?xml version="1.0"?>
<!DOCTYPE html PUBLIC "-//W3C//DTD XHTML 1.0 Transitional//EN"
"http://www.w3.org/TR/xhtml1/DTD/xhtml1-transitional.dtd">
```

Another IE6 bug is the fact that web servers are supposed to serve XHTML using a special MIME type—specifically, `application/xhtml+xml`. If a page is served using this MIME type, IE will try to download the page as a text file instead of rendering it. For this reason, XHTML is often simply served as `text/html`. This works great for user agents that don't yet support the MIME type. But serving pages as `text/html` limits the benefit of having all this great XML at our fingertips. Browsers will continue to treat your well-formed and validating XHTML as plain-old HTML. It is nice-looking HTML, but it's not being honored with the full power of the XML juggernaut. In other words, XSL isn't going to work. No XPath for you. (On the plus side, IE will not throw up its arms and give up when one tiny mistake in your markup creeps through.)

> *According to the spec (`http://www.w3.org/TR/xhtml-media-types/#media-types`), you're supposed to serve XHTML as XML to those browsers that declare their support for it and as text to those that don't. So although the W3C also says that the `text/html` MIME type isn't suitable for XHTML, they don't explicitly forbid its usage, due to legacy user agents. As of this writing, XHTML 1.1 is the only version of XHTML that the W3C insists should be served as XML.*

Another problem: XML is supposed to be fussy, but most browsers are far more forgiving than XML allows and let XHTML get away with crimes against XML by rendering pages that should have failed. This harkens back to the wild and wooly days of the early Web, when rules were few and it was still a free-for-all. Standards are a double-edged sword; they were created to end the problems associated with ensuring sites were functional in the popular browsers, but fussy XML parsing means a browser should fail to render a page if the XML is not valid. One of the things that let HTML flourish so fast and wide was the fact that it was forgiving: HTML authors could make mistakes and it wasn't the end of the world. Their pages would still work. Imagine if XML was the norm and the world tried to adopt it back in those early days—we'd have a much more pristine, and much smaller World Wide Web than we have today. Take that for what you will.

Search engines for the most part have been trained to pay particular attention to the structures and conventions of HTML semantics. With XML, you are potentially casting aside all this good Google-juice in favor of your ideals. That is not to say that XML won't get indexed, but certain tags such as `<h1>` and `<title>` have particular meaning when search engines are indexing your site.

Double the style sheet fun

There are not one but two types of style sheets in XML. We have our familiar and traditional CSS, which is going to work *mostly* the same as you would expect it to work in an XHTML context, and then we have the Extensible Style Sheet Language (XSL), which gives web authors a great deal of power in how XML documents are interpreted.

XSL is actually a suite of technologies, which includes Extensible Style Sheet Language Transformations (XSLT), XPath, and XSL Formatting Objects (XSL-FO). The XSL-FO component is sometimes itself referred to as XSL, but for the purposes of this book let's keep things separate for clarity: XSL will be used for the general context, and XSL-FO will be used for the specific component it refers to.

CSS vs. XSL

So which to use—CSS or XSL? That all depends on the complexity of what you want to accomplish. For most cases, CSS will probably be fine, and is going to be the likely candidate for styling your project. If you need to do significant filtering or rearranging of your XML, then XSL might be the way to go. Heck, you can probably justify using both in many contexts—transforming an XML document into the correct format before applying a little CSS might be just what the doctor ordered.

In choosing between CSS and XSL, consider the Rule of Least Power. This rule states that when designing computer systems, you are often faced with a choice between using a more or less powerful language for publishing information, for expressing constraints, or for solving some problem. This finding explores trade-offs involving the choice of language to reusability of information. The Rule of Least Power suggests choosing the least powerful language suitable for a given purpose.

Styling a simple XML file

Custom XML applications may appear in all sorts of contexts. Perhaps you've exported a load of data from some application and want to make it more readable through a style sheet. Or perhaps you've created your own markup scheme and are putting it to use for a web project. In any case, the rules for CSS in XML are largely similar to the HTML world, but with a few minor caveats, which we'll explain as we go through the remainder of this chapter.

Linking a style sheet

Linking style sheets to XML documents should look very familiar to you. This operation is largely the same whether you're linking a CSS style sheet or an XSL style sheet.

```
<?xml-style sheet type="text/css" href="xmlstyles.css"?>
```

The difference here is that the opening bracket must begin with `<?xml-style` sheet and the element must close with a `?>`. The rest of it is similar to what you will find in HTML.

Embedding a style sheet

Currently there is no generic mechanism for embedding CSS in XML documents; a `<style type="text/css">` has to be defined in the given application's DTD or schema. XHTML and SVG are examples of XML applications that do have provisions for embedding CSS in a `<style>` element.

There is a small difference in how you embed CSS between HTML and XML documents that you must be aware of: you must escape the contents of a style sheet element—the CSS rules—as unparsed character data (CDATA). The reason for this is so that any < and & characters that might be used in the style sheets are not interpreted as markup.

```
<style type="text/css"><![CDATA[
    giraffe {
        color: #FC6;
        background-image: url(giraffe_pattern.tif);
        border: none;
    }
]]></style>
```

The thing to remember about embedding CSS in an XML document is that you have to be sure that the `<style>` element is supported. Without support for `<style>` already defined, the style sheet content will not make sense.

Using external style sheets is the preferred method for applying style to XML. If your style sheet will contain the characters <, &,]]>, or --, you will definitely want to use an external style sheet, and embedded style sheets in XML still lack formal specification. Use the `xml-style` linking method whenever possible.

Putting the X back in eXtensible

Consider XHTML for a moment. The first word in that acronym is "extensible." What does that mean? You know XHTML like the back of your hand I bet, but have you ever extended it? How do you go about extending this markup language?

It is important to remember that XHTML is, by definition, an application of XML itself, and despite the problems mentioned earlier there is a good argument for allowing XHTML to be processed as an XML document. Even if it is being interpreted as `text/html`, a lot of this stuff will still work from a CSS/ display standpoint. You are not limited to those tired old `<h1>`s and `<p>` tags. Try a little `<dc:title>` (a Dublin Core title element) or `<ml:mo>` (a MathML mathematical operator) on for size and see how it fits into your XHTML document.

Extending XHTML through namespaces

XHTML is an application of XML, and is defined as such through its namespace and a DTD. In practice, the namespace is usually implied, but technically you should really define the namespace like this:

```
<!DOCTYPE html PUBLIC "-//W3C//DTD XHTML 1.1//EN"
    "http://www.w3.org/TR/xhtml11/DTD/xhtml11.dtd">
<html xmlns="http://www.w3.org/1999/xhtml">
    <head>
        <title>An XHTML 1.1 Document</title>
    </head>
    <body>
        <h1>XHTML is keen</h1>
        <p>This is an example of XHTML 1.1.</p>
    </body>
</html>
```

The namespace here is defined without a prefix. This means all of the elements in this document are going to appear as you would expect to see them in a standard HTML document. No surprises here. But how would it look if we added a second namespace? There can be only one default namespace, so any other namespaces added to our document are going to require prefixes:

```
<!DOCTYPE html PUBLIC "-//W3C//DTD XHTML 1.1//EN"
    "http://www.w3.org/TR/xhtml11/DTD/xhtml11.dtd">
<html xmlns="http://www.w3.org/1999/xhtml" ➡
xmlns:vla="http://natasha.example.com/ns/viola">
    <head>
```

251

```
                <title>XHTML + Viola</title>
        </head>
        <body>
            <h1>XHTML is keen</h1>
            <p>This is an example of XHTML 1.1, now with more viola.</p>
            <vla:viola>
                <vla:maker>Amati</vla:maker>
                <vla:year>1566</vla:year>
                <vla:value>$940,000</vla:value>
            </vla:viola>
        </body>
    </html>
```

We now have a hybrid piece of markup, with the default namespace being XHTML and the namespace prefixed with vla pointing to some custom XML definition based on violas.

Namespaces may be easily and arbitrarily added to XML documents, including XHTML. Each will require a unique prefix (with one being allowed no prefix as "the default namespace"), and the url property should have a unique URL placed in quotes. The URL itself is arbitrary—it can be any URL as long as it is treated as unique for the given document.

Styling namespaces

Styling XML namespaces is a bit different than what you would probably expect. Your intuition likely is telling you that simply writing the selector as it appears as a namespace would be good enough:

```
dc:title { color:blue; }
```

What do you think might be wrong with that rule? If you guessed that the colon character separating dc and title is the culprit, you'd be on the right track. Colons in selectors are for indicating pseudo-selectors. There is no :title pseudo-selector, nor is that what we want to imply here. Something else needs to be done.

To handle namespaces in CSS, you must first declare a namespace in your style sheet, and then you need to write selectors using the pipe character (|) to separate namespaces and selectors. Namespaces are declared using @namespace:

```
@namespace dc url ➥
(http://dublincore.org/documents/2007/07/02/dcmi-namespace/);
```

In this example, dc is the prefix that will be used throughout your style sheet for any rules using the namespace. The URL serves as a unique identifier—it can be any URL, although some organizations (such as the W3C or Dublin Core) recommend specific URLs. If you're defining a custom DTD, you might post that somewhere and use it as your URL choice. The important thing is that this URL be unique for the style sheet in question. All @namespace rules must come after any @import and @charset rules, and before the rest of the rules in the style sheet in which they appear. This is important—if the order is incorrect, your browsers may ignore the namespace rule and your styles won't work as expected.

Now that this preliminary business is taken care of, it is time to create a CSS rule. A rule for our <dc:title> element would look something like this:

```
dc|title { color:blue; }
```

The pipe character serves to separate the namespace prefix from the element in CSS. The rest of the rule may proceed as expected.

Styling namespaces in Internet Explorer

What would a killer web standards technique be without a corresponding IE failure? Rest assured, styling XML namespaces is no different.

Early on in the life of the XML specification, namespaces had yet to have a CSS construct defined that would handle them. Failing solid guidance in the specification and anxious to get things moving, Microsoft implemented namespaces in style sheets using the backslash character to escape the colon:

```
dc\:title { color:blue; }
```

With this pattern, you won't need to declare a @namespace for the IE set. In fact, @namespace isn't even supported in any version of Internet Explorer, and that includes IE8. Plan on using conditional comments to link to a dedicated style sheet for any IE-specific code:

```
<!--[if IE]>
<?xml-stylesheet type="text/css" href="msie.css"?>
<![endif]-->
```

To achieve the widest level of compatibility with current browsers when styling XML with namespaces, as well as to future-proof your work, you should first set your styles using the standards-based @namespace and prefix|element{} pattern. Then add your IE-specific styles using the conditional comment pattern as indicated earlier. As of this writing, @namespace support is still not planned for any future updates to IE8, but if IE9 rolls around with support for the correct implementation as defined in the specification, then your style sheets should continue to work.

Painting SVGs

Scalable vector graphics (SVG) is an open and standards-based way of describing two-dimensional images in XML. As of this writing, SVG 1.1 (http://www.w3.org/TR/SVG11/) and SVG Tiny 1.2 (targeted at mobile devices; http://www.w3.org/TR/SVGTiny12/) are the current W3C recommendations. Since SVG is simply a non–binary-text-based file format written in XML, it is possible to create and edit images manually using nothing but a text editor, and it is easy to generate and manipulate images programmatically using server-side programming languages like PHP or Ruby, or using desktop software programs such as Adobe Illustrator or Inkscape.

An interesting feature of SVG that sets it apart from several other file formats is the fact that it supports text and is itself a text-based format. This gives SVG the capability of providing easily searchable information baked right into the file format in a way that search engines are already fundamentally capable of and good at. Couple SVG with the idea of combining XML applications in one document (such as, say, an XHTML document) and you have an interesting opportunity for a more semantic and meaningful Web.

Realistically it may not be terribly practical to hand-code finely detailed SVG images. But since SVG is just XML for the most part, it is highly conducive to programmatic manipulation and even modification by hand through its styling constructs. For example, if you wanted to modify a map of the United

States to highlight the state of California, it would be easy for you to open the file in a text editor; find, say, the #california ID that the original developer used to define the state; and give the state a nice golden background color with a blue border with a bit of style property modification. Another example would be in producing statistical graphics generated from server-side code—you could generate rich and meaningful statistical charts from real-time data simply by programmatically modifying the variables in the SVG file.

SVG supports the styling of its markup using CSS. While SVG itself is a purely presentational language with its own constructs built in for drawing and manipulating graphics, CSS may be used with it as a styling mechanism, which opens the door for a number of interesting applications. Consider the fact that there is a vector-based image format that you can color and manipulate using a language you already know: CSS. Does that sound like something fun to play with? You betcha!

For this example, let's look at something simple—a three-bar flag. It is commonly used throughout the world as perhaps the most widely used layout for a national flag, and it is easy to write in SVG. For our XML, use the following:

```
<?xml version="1.0" standalone="no"?>
<?xml-stylesheet href="svgexample.css" type="text/css"?>
<!DOCTYPE svg PUBLIC "-//W3C//DTD SVG 1.1//EN" ➡
"http://www.w3.org/Graphics/SVG/1.1/DTD/svg11.dtd">
<svg xmlns="http://www.w3.org/2000/svg" version="1.1" ➡
width="900" height="600">
    <rect id="bar1" width="900" height="600"/>
    <rect id="bar2" width="600" height="600"/>
    <rect id="bar3" width="300" height="600"/>
</svg>
```

And for the flag design, let's use Ireland as the example:

```
#bar1 {
    fill:orange;
}
#bar2 {
    fill:white;
}
#bar3 {
    fill:green;
}
```

The result of this simple example is a nice approximation of the flag of the Emerald Isle. With a few changes, we can move a little farther south toward the mainland and try for France:

```
#bar1 {
    fill:red;
}
#bar2 {
    fill:white;
}
#bar3 {
    fill:blue;
}
```

Vive la différence! With a couple of switches, we can make our flag French, Irish, Italian, or whatever other country uses this layout by simply swapping out a few color values. You could even provide for a more versatile example by using descendant selectors. With the following example, Ireland and France are handled gracefully and all you would need to do is swap out the value of the ID in the parent element:

```
<?xml version="1.0" standalone="no"?>
<?xml-stylesheet href="svgexample.css" type="text/css"?>
<!DOCTYPE svg PUBLIC "-/W3C//DTD SVG 1.1//EN" ➡
"http://www.w3.org/Graphics/SVG/1.1/DTD/svg11.dtd">
<svg xmlns="http://www.w3.org/2000/svg" version="1.1" ➡
width="900" height="600" id="ireland">
    <rect id="bar1" width="900" height="600"/>
    <rect id="bar2" width="600" height="600"/>
    <rect id="bar3" width="300" height="600"/>
</svg>
```

And the CSS for our Irish flag would be

```
#france #bar1 {
    fill:red;
}
#ireland #bar1 {
    fill:orange;
}
#bar2 {
    fill:white;
}
#france #bar3 {
    fill:blue;
}
#ireland #bar3 {
    fill:green;
}
```

Just change the id value in your XML from ireland to france and back as needed. See if you can add styles for Italy to your style sheet! Hint: #bar1 would be green, and #bar3 would be red.

The SVG specification does include a definition for a <style> element. So if you needed to have a self-contained single file for your image, you could do so. In this case, the previous example would look like this:

```
<?xml version="1.0" standalone="no"?>
<!DOCTYPE svg PUBLIC "-//W3C//DTD SVG 1.1//EN" ➡
"http://www.w3.org/Graphics/SVG/1.1/DTD/svg11.dtd">
<svg xmlns="http://www.w3.org/2000/svg" version="1.1" ➡
width="900" height="600" id="ireland">
    <style type="text/css"><![CDATA[
    #france #bar1 {
        fill:red;
```

```
        }
        #ireland #bar1 {
            fill:orange;
        }
        #bar2 {
            fill:white;
        }
        #france #bar3 {
            fill:blue;
        }
        #ireland #bar3 {
            fill:green;
        }
        ]]></style>
        <rect id="bar1" width="900" height="600"/>
        <rect id="bar2" width="600" height="600"/>
        <rect id="bar3" width="300" height="600"/>
    </svg>
```

With this code, the image may be treated as a single file. This will be important if you want your SVGs to be easily ported or referenced as other image file formats can be, such as JPEG or PNG. For this reason, unlike most other styled markup, it is likely that most SVG files you encounter will probably be styled with embedded instead of external style sheets.

SVG and CSS2

Many of the SVG styles are unique to its specification. However, a subset of the CSS2 spec is available in SVG, which includes the following properties and at-rules:

- clip
- color
- cursor
- direction
- display
- font
- font-family
- font-size
- font-size-adjust
- font-stretch
- font-style
- font-variant
- font-weight
- letter-spacing
- overflow

- text-align
- text-decoration
- unicode-bidi
- vertical-align
- visibility
- word-spacing
- @charset
- @font-face
- @import
- @media

The color property as applied in CSS requires some special consideration. We will discuss how color works as part of the SVG-specific styling properties in the next section. The clip and overflow properties are only applied to the outermost <svg> element. Child elements of the <svg> element will ignore any clip or overflow property values. As you might notice from the preceding list, the majority of the CSS properties here are typography related, as are many of the other things you might expect to be available in CSS such as margin, padding, background-color, and border properties. In SVG, you need other constructs to style those elements, but fortunately things will look largely similar to what you're used to in the CSS world.

SVG-specific style

Since the CSS specification itself is inadequate to handle the complexities and specific requirements of styling images, SVG includes a number of style extensions. We have already seen some use of the fill property in our earlier examples.

SVG style property/value pairs may be presented directly within the content of the markup as attributes. At the same time, SVG style properties may be treated as part of style sheets in the same way CSS works.

Here are some more property options to help you code your next work of art, along with a brief description of the intent of each property's function:

- alignment-baseline: A text property that specifies alignment with respect to its parent element.
- baseline-shift: Repositions the baseline of text relative to its parent element, usually resulting in a subscript or superscript effect.
- clip-path: Points a URI to another SVG graphic to be used as a clipping path. This can be an ID reference (such as #someClippingPath) if the SVG is embedded within the same document.
- clip-rule: Takes one of three values: inherit, evenodd, or nonzero (default). Without getting too deep into the details, imagine two concentric circles, with a clip-rule applied to the outermost circle. With nonzero, both circles would be filled. With evenodd, the inner circle would not be filled, resulting in an annulus.

- color-interpolation: Specifies which color space interpolation should occur in, with auto, sRGB (default), and linearRGB as possible values.

- color-interpolation-filters: Similar to color-interpolation but applied to filter effects.

- color-profile: Defines a color profile description. Can be used like an at-rule (@color-profile) or as a property.

- color-rendering: Tells the user agent to optimize speed or quality using the optimizeSpeed or optimizeQuality property.

- dominant-baseline: In typography, used to determine the baseline of the script with the dominant run. Values could be alphabetic for Western contexts, mathematical for math formulas, and ideographic for the East Asian scripts Chinese, Japanese, Korean, and Vietnamese Chữ Nôm.

- enable-background: Describes how backgrounds are accumulated, using the property new or accumulate, or an x/y offset value.

- fill: Paints the interior of a given element.

- fill-opacity: Sets the opacity of the fill color.

- fill-rule: Similar to clip-rule, using evenodd or nonzero (default) to set the fill behavior.

- filter: Can set a URL to point to a filter that would be applied to an object.

- flood-color: Indicates a color value to use to flood a filter subregion.

- flood-opacity: Sets an opacity value to flood a filter subregion.

- glyph-orientation-horizontal: Controls glyph orientation when the inline-progression-direction (set by writing-mode) is vertical relative to the reference orientation.

- glyph-orientation-vertical: Controls glyph orientation when the inline-progression-direction (set by writing-mode) is horizontal relative to the reference orientation.

- image-rendering: Tells the user agent to optimize speed or quality using the optimizeSpeed or optimizeQuality property. (See color-rendering.)

- kerning: Adjusts length between glyphs.

- lighting-color: Defines a color for light sources that can be applied against SVG's <feDiffuseLighting> and <feSpecularLighting> elements.

- marker: Shorthand property for marker-end, marker-start, and marker-mid.

- marker-end: Defines a marker or an arrow at the end of a path.

- marker-mid: Defines markers at all vertices except for the beginning and end markers.

- marker-start: Defines a marker or an arrow at the beginning of a path.

- mask: References a <mask> element to implement a path used for generating a mask effect.

- opacity: Sets the opacity of an object, using decimal values from 0 (fully transparent) to 1 (fully opaque). A value of 0.5 would be 50 percent opacity.

- pointer-events: Controls under what circumstances an object can become the target of pointer events.

- shape-rendering: Tells the user agent to optimize speed or quality using the optimizeSpeed or crispEdges property.

- stop-color: Sets a color to use at a gradient stop.

- stop-opacity: Sets an opacity used at a gradient stop.

- stroke: Describes the stroke effect applied to an object.

- stroke-dasharray: Sets pattern of dashes and gaps in a stroke.

- stroke-dashoffset: Sets how far into a stroke the dash pattern will begin.

- stroke-linecap: Sets the shape used at the end of open subpaths, using the values butt, round, and square.

- stroke-linejoin: Sets the shape of corners, using the values miter, round, and bevel.

- stroke-miterlimit: Sets a limit on the ratio of the miter length to stroke-width.

- stroke-opacity: Sets the opacity of the stroke.

- stroke-width: Sets the width of a stroke.

- text-anchor: Aligns text to a specified point, using the values start, middle, and end.

- text-rendering: Tells the user agent to optimize speed or quality using the optimizeSpeed or optimizeLegibility property.

- writing-mode: Determines which direction text flows; left to right, right to left, and/or top to bottom.

Browser support for SVG

SVG enjoys at least partial native support in modern versions of Gecko-based browsers such as Firefox, WebKit-based browsers such as Safari, and the Opera line of browsers since version 8. As you probably guessed, there are no versions of Microsoft Internet Explorer, including version 8, that support SVG.

Fortunately for the IE users, there are excellent plug-ins that provide support for SVG. The Adobe SVG plug-in was under active development up until January 1, 2009, when active development was discontinued. The Adobe plug-in is still available for download from the Adobe web site. However, their motivations for discontinuing support included the fact that better options existed in the marketplace and that most browser vendors (save for the one big one) already feature native support for SVG. For IE users and developers who would like to recommend a plug-in, we suggest the excellent RENESIS Player, available from examotion at http://www.examotion.com/.

Making an Atom feed more presentable

The Atom Syndication Format is an XML application created to standardize web feeds, and is an alternative to RSS (although the two are largely similar). It is a proposed standard published under the Internet Engineering Task Force (IETF) as RFC 4287. RSS and Atom feeds are highly popular features of the modern Web, providing an XML-formatted feed of regularly updated content that may be subscribed to by feed reader software or consumed by software applications. Here is an example of what an Atom feed might look like:

```xml
<?xml version="1.0" encoding="utf-8"?>
<feed xmlns="http://www.w3.org/2005/Atom">
    <title>Viola Universe</title>
    <subtitle>More viola than you can shake a baton at.</subtitle>
    <link href="http://viola.example.org/feed/" rel="self"/>
    <link href="http://viola.example.org/"/>
    <updated>2009-02-28T17:31:05Z</updated>
```

259

```
<author>
    <name>Violaman</name>
    <email>violaman@viola.example.com</email>
</author>
<id>http://viola.example.org/feed/iri/</id>
<entry>
    <title>Violas Run Amok</title>
    <link href="http://viola.example.org/2009/02/28/violasrunamok/"/>
    <id>http://viola.example.org/2009/02/28/violasrunamok/id</id>
    <updated>2009-02-28T17:31:05Z</updated>
    <summary>In which the entire viola section loses all pretense ➥
of control.</summary>
    </entry>
</feed>
```

An integrated example

Let's look at a step-by-step examination of a single XML document founded on some custom markup. For our example, we'll use an XML document that describes a list of classical music composers, including information about the composer's dates of birth and death, what period they are categorized with (such as Baroque, Classical, Romantic), and some representative works. We'll use this markup to apply some CSS styles to make it more interesting and readable. The code here is truncated due to space constraints, but the full example may be found in the chapter 9 folder of the source code downloads. Here's the code we'll start with:

```
<?xml version="1.0" encoding="UTF-8" standalone="no"?>
<!DOCTYPE composers SYSTEM "composers.dtd">
<composers>
    <composer>
        <name>
            <givenname>Gustav</givenname>
            <surname>Mahler</surname>
        </name>
        <yearbirth>1860</yearbirth>
        <yeardeath>1911</yeardeath>
        <period>Post-Romantic</period>
        <favoriteworks>
            <work>
                <title>Symphony No.2</title>
                <date>1894</date>
                <instrumentation>Full orchestra</instrumentation>
            </work>
            <work>
                <title>Symphony No.6</title>
                <date>1906</date>
                <instrumentation>Full orchestra</instrumentation>
```

```
            </work>
        </favoriteworks>
    </composer>
    /* Code truncated here. See 09.2.1.composers.xml */
    <composer>
        <name>
            <givenname>Antonín</givenname>
            <surname>Dvo ák</surname>
        </name>
        <yearbirth>1841</yearbirth>
        <yeardeath>1904</yeardeath>
        <period>Romantic</period>
        <favoriteworks>
            <work>
                <title>Quintet</title>
                <date>1875</date>
                <instrumentation>2vl, vla, vc, db</instrumentation>
            </work>
            <work>
                <title>Symphony No. 9, in E Minor "From the New World" ➥
(Op. 95)</title>
                <date>1893</date>
                <instrumentation>Full orchestra</instrumentation>
            </work>
        </favoriteworks>
    </composer>
    <composer>
        <name>
            <givenname>Charles</givenname>
            <surname>Wuorinen</surname>
        </name>
        <yearbirth>1938</yearbirth>
        <period>Modern</period>
        <favoriteworks>
            <work>
                <title>Spinoff</title>
                <instrumentation>violin, bass, congas</instrumentation>
            </work>
        </favoriteworks>
    </composer>
</composers>
```

The raw and unstyled XML appears as a document tree in many user agents, such as Gecko-based browsers like Camino, as shown in Figure 9-1.

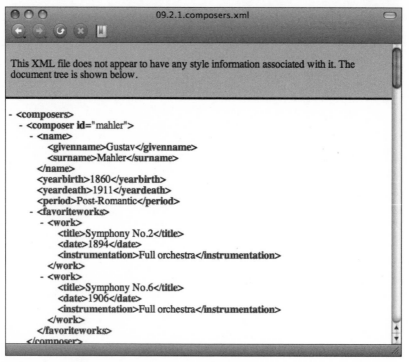

Figure 9-1. Unstyled XML displayed as a document tree

Try viewing this in a few browsers to get a feel for what raw, unstyled XML looks like. Firefox and Internet Explorer will render the previous code as a document tree, while Safari and Opera will render a clump of unformatted, inline text. Now let's add a style sheet. Create a file called `composers.css` in the same directory as the previous XML file. Insert the following line on line 2 of the XML file:

```
<?xml-stylesheet type="text/css" href="composers.css" ?>
```

Now check your browsers again; what do you see? All browsers should now be rendering that amorphous clump of text we saw earlier in Safari and Opera. Nothing really special has happened here, but you will note something of at least minor importance: all of our elements appear exactly the same. There is no variance in font sizing. There are no block elements—only inline. It is simply a shapeless stew of content.

The first step is to add some definition. Let's start by taking at the natural organization of our XML file. There are some high-level nodes in this file called <composer>, and they group the information for each composer that we have listed. This grouping is in fact defined and enforced by the referenced DTD file that is included. So the first thing we could do is to make that a block-level element in com-posers.css:

```
composer {
    display:block;
}
```

This sets each composer block to be rendered on its own line in the browser, as shown in Figure 9-2.

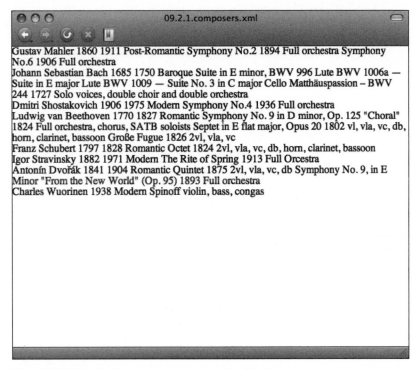

Figure 9-2. Displaying the <composer> element as blocks

Instantly our example makes more sense. Each composer begins on its own new line. However, with the wrapping that likely is occurring in your browser, it still might be a little confusing. Let's add some margin and borders too:

```
composer {
    display:block;
    margin-bottom:1em;
    border-bottom:1px dotted #ccc;
}
```

These changes are reflected in Figure 9-3.

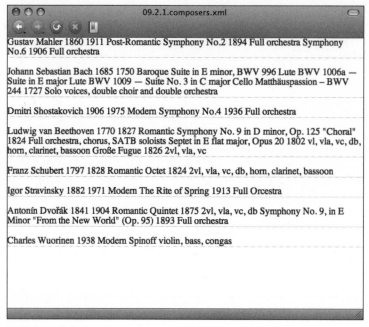

Figure 9-3. Adding a little visual separation to the block elements

Now things are becoming clearer. Let's further equalize the display of our information with a bit of work on the overall layout by establishing some margins and contrast on the viewport:

```
composers {
    background-color:#4C4C4C;
    padding-top:4em;
    font-family:Georgia, serif;
    font-size:0.95em;
}
composer {
    display:block;
    margin:0 auto 1em auto;
    padding:1em;
    background-color:#fff;
    width:50%;
    border-bottom:1px dotted #ccc;
}
```

These changes will provide some contrast and immediate visual layout benefits, as shown in Figure 9-4.

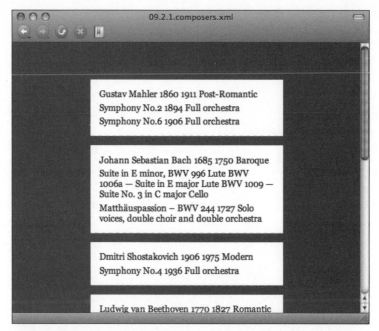

Figure 9-4. Establishing margins and contrast in the viewport

Now we've put our layout into clear and digestible bits of information. The outermost XML element <composers> works like our <body> and <html> elements in traditional HTML contexts, giving us a hook from which to apply global styles. Since the outermost element can set certain global properties in CSS that will be inherited, adding a font-family and font-size here makes sense. It is interesting to note here for a moment the difference between HTML and XML with respect to the <body> element. It is the <body> element that is visible to the viewport, and anything contained in the <head> is invisible. With stock XML formats, the outermost element is the default content for the viewport and hiding anything from it must be done manually.

Now that the large blocks of information make sense, we need to sort out the details of each composer in our list. Let's add a few more block-level elements and some typography to style things to be more organized:

```
composers {
    background-color:#4C4C4C;
    padding-top:4em;
    font-family:Georgia, serif;
    font-size:0.95em;
}
composer {
    display:block;
    margin:0 auto 1em auto;
```

265

```
    padding:1em;
    background-color:#fff;
    width:50%;
    border-bottom:1px dotted #ccc;
}
name {
    display:block;
    font-weight:bold;
}
work {
    display: list-item;
    list-style-type: square;
    margin-left:2em;
}
period {
    display:block;
    font-style:italic;
}
```

With just a few typographic changes, the content becomes instantly clearer on the page, as shown in Figure 9-5.

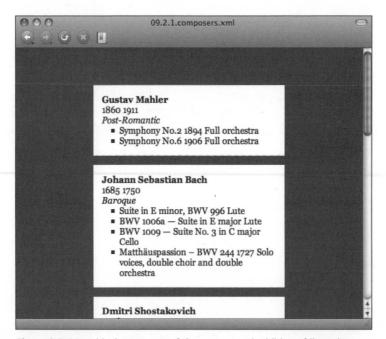

Figure 9-5. More block treatment of the content and addition of list styles

At this point, our information is displayed fairly well considering the meaning of the markup. We first added block-level treatment to the <name> and <period> elements, and set the <work> element to display as a list-item. How often do you get to do that? In XML, it is often that you will have list-like child elements, and using the list-item value for the display property becomes entirely appropriate for this need. If you want to see something interesting, try changing the list-style-type property value to decimal instead of list-item, and then reload your page in Safari or Opera. You now have ordered lists! This is a handy tool to have around when styling long chunks of XML data, but unfortunately your mileage may vary when it comes to browser support.

Now what would really help is some indication of what some of the data types are. First, the numbers that appear directly below the names are the birth and death dates for each composer. But these are formatted poorly at best, and for someone unfamiliar with music history this might be completely meaningless. Let's see what we can do with generated content:

```
composers {
    background-color:#4C4C4C;
    padding-top:4em;
      font-family:Georgia, serif;
    font-size:0.95em;
}
composer {
    display:block;
    margin:0 auto 1em auto;
    padding:1em;
    background-color:#fff;
    width:50%;
    border-bottom:1px dotted #ccc;
}
name {
    display:block;
    font-weight:bold;
}
work {
    display: list-item;
    list-style-type: decimal;
    margin-left:2em;
}
period {
    display:block;
    font-style:italic;
    margin-bottom:0.5em;
}
yearbirth:before {
    content: "b. ";
}
yeardeath:before {
    content: "- d.";
}
favoriteworks:before {
    content: "Favorite works";
    font-weight:bold;
}
```

We now have content that is more properly labeled and readable, as you can see in Figure 9-6.

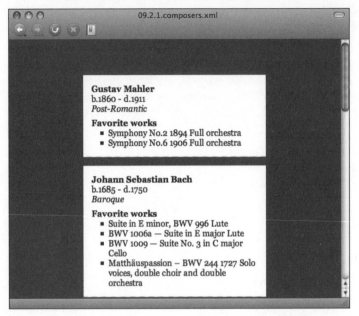

Figure 9-6. Using generated content to make the data more readable

Now we've used the :before pseudo-class and the content property to generate some meaningful labels to some of our markup. The dates are now labeled a bit better, with b. appearing before the birth year and - d. appearing if and when a year of death is indicated, directly preceding this date. We added a label of Favorite Works before the list of pieces. And finally, we wrap things up with a bit of margin on the bottom of the <period> element to create a little more visual distinction on the page. The rest is detail and polish at this point.

Really what this thing needs is some images to liven up the page and associate more of a visual identity with each composer. There is no equivalent to the <img> element in our XML document, but that's OK—we won't need it. We can use background images attached to the <composer> elements by leveraging their unique id properties:

```
composer {
    display:block;
    margin:0 auto 1em auto;
    padding:1em;
    padding-right:150px;
    background-color:#fff;
    width:40%;
    border-bottom:1px dotted #ccc;
    background-position:96% 1em;
    background-repeat:no-repeat;
}

composer[id="mahler"] { background-image: url(img/mahler.jpg); }
```

```
composer[id="bach"] { background-image: url(img/bach.jpg); }
composer[id="shostakovich"] { background-image: ➡
url(img/shostakovich.jpg); }
composer[id="beethoven"] { background-image: url(img/beethoven.jpg); }
composer[id="schubert"] { background-image: url(img/schubert.jpg); }
composer[id="stravinsky"] { background-image: ➡
url(img/stravinsky.jpg); }
composer[id="dvorak"] { background-image: url(img/dvorak.jpg); }
composer[id="wuorinen"] { background-image: url(img/wuorinen.jpg); }
```

As Figure 9-7 illustrates, pictures really help the display of our page and give it a more personal character.

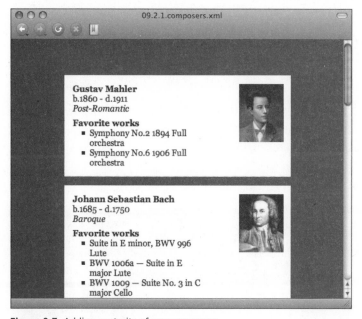

Figure 9-7. Adding portraits of our composers

It's looking good! We reduced the overall width to 40% since the extra padding was pushing our layout out a bit, and we positioned our background images to the right of each box with some padding applied to keep the content out of the way. Now with a couple of typographical tweaks we can probably wrap up this project. To these indicated rules, add the items in bold:

```
name {
    display:block;
    font-weight:bold;
    font-style:italic;
    font-size: 1.3em;
    font-family: "Trebuchet MS", Verdana, Helvetica, sans-serif;
    color:#333;
}
work {
    display: list-item;
```

```
        list-style-type: square;
        margin-left:2em;
    }
    title {
        font-style:italic;
        border-bottom:1px dotted #ccc;
    }
    period {
        display:block;
        font-style:italic;
        margin-bottom:0.5em;
    }
    instrumentation {
        text-transform: lowercase;
    }
    date:before {
        content: "(";
    }
    date:after {
        content: ")";
    }
    instrumentation:before {
        content: "for ";
    }
```

Our final touches to our style sheet will show up as shown in Figure 9-8.

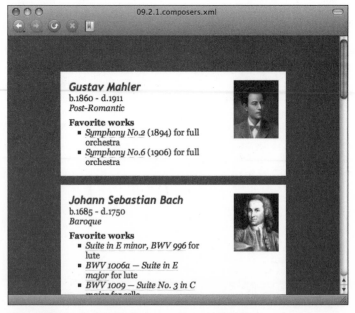

Figure 9-8. The final styling for our composers XML file

With those additions, we've finished up making a raw XML file turn into a rather attractive and readable page, which was our goal for this project. For the name of the composer, which includes the <givenname> and <surname> values, we styled it to be more of a heading-like object with a stylistic sans-serif font, slightly larger, and in a lighter shade. For the <instrumentation> element, we have to transform it to lower case, since some of the values have capitalization that doesn't look right in the final output. Here is our final style sheet in its entirety:

```css
composers {
    background-color:#4C4C4C;
    padding-top:4em;
    font-family:Georgia, serif;
    font-size:0.95em;
}
composer {
    display:block;
    margin:0 auto 1em auto;
    padding:1em;
    padding-right:150px;
    background-color:#fff;
    width:40%;
    border-bottom:1px dotted #ccc;
    background-position:96% 1em;
    background-repeat:no-repeat;
}

composer[id="mahler"] { background-image: url(img/mahler.jpg); }
composer[id="bach"] { background-image: url(img/bach.jpg); }
composer[id="shostakovich"] { ➡
    background-image: url(img/shostakovich.jpg); }
composer[id="beethoven"] { background-image: url(img/beethoven.jpg); }
composer[id="schubert"] { background-image: url(img/schubert.jpg); }
composer[id="stravinsky"] { ➡
    background-image: url(img/stravinsky.jpg); }
composer[id="dvorak"] { background-image: url(img/dvorak.jpg); }
composer[id="wuorinen"] { background-image: url(img/wuorinen.jpg); }

name {
    display:block;
    font-weight:bold;
    font-style:italic;
    font-size: 1.3em;
    font-family: "Trebuchet MS", Verdana, Helvetica, sans-serif;
    color:#333;
}
work {
    display: list-item;
    list-style-type: square;
    margin-left:2em;
}
```

```
title {
    font-style:italic;
    border-bottom:1px dotted #ccc;
}
period {
    display:block;
    font-style:italic;
    margin-bottom:0.5em;
}
instrumentation {
    text-transform: lowercase;
}
date:before {
    content: "(";
}
date:after {
    content: ")";
}
instrumentation:before {
    content: "for ";
}
yearbirth:before {
    content: "b.";
}
yeardeath:before {
    content: "- d.";
}
favoriteworks:before {
    content: "Favorite works";
    font-weight:bold;
}
```

Summary

XML is a largely untapped realm when it comes to applying CSS, making it an interesting area for exploration. More often an XSL transformation is applied and the document is made to produce good ol' HTML before applying any CSS, or the document is fully handled using XSL-FO. However, following the principles of using the Rule of Least Power that we discussed earlier, CSS may very well be a fine choice for a large number of jobs. It is a skill you're already familiar with by now, and it may warrant consideration should you ever be presented with the task of having to put some polish and shine on a piece of XML.

With good support for basic XML styling using CSS among most of the major browsers today, styling XML using CSS is certainly worthy of consideration for your projects. Use CSS to style your XML documents whenever possible, and use the simpler CSS option over the more complex process of XSL for styling your documents, if the former will suit the needs of the project.

Chapter 10

OPTIMIZING CSS FOR PERFORMANCE

There are many aspects to consider in appraising how well a tool accomplished the goal it was designed for. A web site is, in its base form, just such a tool. In previous chapters, we've discussed how web sites perform in accomplishing their goals in terms of technical capability (what CSS can do). In this chapter, we'll switch gears and discuss performance in terms of how efficiently and speedily CSS can do the things you want to do with it.

Indeed, performance is an important part of every web site and CSS developers are not excluded. There are many things to consider with regard to optimizing CSS for performance, including the number of style sheets you use, how you include them in your code, and even the specific rules they contain. To master CSS optimization, you need to think about your code from a web browser's point of view, not a human's.

Thankfully, optimization is one aspect of CSS development that is relatively browser-agnostic, since most CSS-capable user agents function in basically the same way. From a performance standpoint, each user agent has the same basic resources to consider: CPU speed and network connection speed.

Why optimize?

To be usable, web sites must be fast—very fast. Although optimizations are not typically considered part of the initial development process, optimizing your code and tuning it for performance is a big part of what defines professional-quality work. To separate the wheat from the chaff, so to speak, optimizations are a requirement because it is the optimization process that propels an implementation to the next level.

Optimize to increase speed

Visitors like pages that load quickly and work well. Studies have shown that web site users most often prefer sites that are (or at least *appear* to be) faster over sites that allow them to customize their experience.[1] In essence, a web site that doesn't respond quickly to your input is sometimes worse than not having a web site at all. Therefore, it behooves you as a professional developer to ensure that every aspect of your code is as optimized as can be, and CSS code is no exception to this rule.

An increase in web site response speed has also been shown to increase sales for e-commerce sites. Speed is so important because the maximum amount of time users can wait in order to remain focused on steps between a task is 10 seconds.[2] Despite broadband connections becoming more common, other factors such as low-power mobile devices and ever more demanding technical challenges are always pushing the envelope of what we can accomplish, and how quickly we can do so.

Even today, many web users have limited connections to the Internet, and a typical 500KB page can take up to a minute and 10 seconds to download for these users. If this lag time happens in the middle of multipage form purchase, then you have a serious usability problem. Moreover, Jens Meiert estimates that the typical web page increases in size by 20KB per year,[3] so producing code optimized for speed actually provides cumulative gains to performance over time.

A snappier user experience is a more usable and a higher-quality experience. A faster user experience has some pretty obvious benefits, but they all amount to an improvement in the way your quality is perceived by users. Speeding up your web site will make you look better to your visitors because the speed at which your pages display affects the perceived quality, reliability, and credibility of your product or service. In fact, a lack of speed is the most common complaint among web surfers because user satisfaction is directly proportionate to web site response time.

---

1. Articles about web site optimization as a broader topic than purely CSS are plentiful, and one of the best resources is WebSiteOptimization.com, which publishes their results of a study researching the relative importance of interface design features at http://www.websiteoptimization.com/speed/tweak/design-factors/. In this study, speed was shown to be the most important factor of an interface's design.
2. This human-computer interaction principle has remained the same for about 30 years, as Jakob Nielsen reports in the findings of one of his many usability studies. You can check out this one at http://www.useit.com/papers/responsetime.html.
3. Jens Meiert's blog post discussing interface load times discusses increasing page bloat over the years: http://meiert.com/en/blog/20070621/load-time-the-ux-factor-facts-and-measures/.

Optimize to lower bandwidth usage and costs

Each CSS rule needs to be transferred over the wire to the browser before it can be used, unless it is already cached locally.[4] There is some cost both in terms of speed and in terms of physical resources such as electricity when this happens. How many actual bytes of data are sent over the wire can be reduced without degrading the final result in a number of ways.

One obvious way to do this is to make use of shorthand CSS properties when they make sense (for example, when they consist of fewer characters to type). Another is to compress the style sheet with GZip and decompress it on the client side. Both of these techniques shrink the physical payload that needs to be communicated from server to client. Not only does this use less bandwidth, it can speed up the transfer itself, which in turn contributes to an overall speed boost.

Moreover, reducing bandwidth usage can also save money for both content producer and consumer. In many parts of the world, bandwidth is still capped or throttled to avoid overuse, and despite claims of "unlimited" bandwidth by major Internet service providers, bandwidth is still a limited resource. Further, the increase of mobile use puts additional importance on bandwidth optimization as cellular networks charge a per-megabyte fee for bandwidth use. Users who visit a bloated site may receive not only a poor experience, but also a frighteningly high telephone bill.

Optimization vs. organization

Some of the optimization tips in this chapter go against the grain of the organization tips in Chapter 6. Sometimes, organization for humans, such as code formatting conventions and whitespace indentation, is less than ideally optimized code. It's important to strike a balance between broad-scale organization in an architectural sense so that the code is something you and your fellow humans can work with, and targeted optimizations in a technical sense so the code is optimally performant.

Indeed, even some features of CSS itself are not beneficial from a technical optimization standpoint. In particular, the @import statement is a notorious culprit, as the more imports you have, the more HTTP requests you're making, which can slow things down. However, as discussed previously, the @import rule is useful for creating modular sets of style sheet files that are easier for people to work with, or more logically organized in a file system on disk. To get the best of both worlds, many sites use specific, possibly automated build steps that take a collection of source files (of which CSS is just one kind in a web site) and put them together in a particular, distributable way, akin to a compilation step in traditional software development. The details of how to create such build systems are beyond the scope of this book, but there are a number of useful tools, regardless of whether you create a build system, that should become a familiar part of your optimization repertoire.

---

4. Actually, caching is one of the best things you can do to mitigate download costs, and is sadly underutilized. To learn more about caching, which is beyond the scope of this book, be sure to read Mark Nottingham's Caching Tutorial at http://www.mnot.net/cache_docs/.

There's also been some great research into CSS selector optimization and performance done by Steve Souders[5] and others. Largely, the conclusion this research has reached is that optimizing CSS selectors gives you only a very small performance boost, and that the effort required to do so is not a good place to spend your time. This brings up what is perhaps the most important point regarding optimization: there is always more that can be done, but many things that can be done often shouldn't be.

When you think of optimizing code, there are a number of factors you need to consider beyond simple performance tests. These factors include many of the things we've already discussed, such as code readability, maintainability, organization, effectiveness, and reusability. Micro-optimizations like CSS selectors can easily slip into doing more harm than good for your web site when such work is taken out of the context of a sterile speed test. In other words, know what's vital, know what's trivial, and measure whether a change of your code is "good" or not by factoring in *all* aspects of the change, not just performance. Such optimizations are only "good" if the net benefit is positive—something you need to decide for yourself.

Optimization techniques

In this section, we'll look at a number of web site optimization techniques. Some of these are ways to make your CSS more performant, and others are ways to use CSS to improve other potential optimization bottlenecks.

There are a number of things that you can do to quickly and easily make the CSS you write speedier in web browsers today. In any optimization effort, these are the things you want to tackle first because they will give you the most reward for the least amount of effort. They are also good things to keep in mind for new projects; if you write new code with these fruits already harvested, you'll find optimization concerns are further down the road.

When optimizing CSS code for performance, you have two main challenges. First is getting the CSS to load in the browser as quickly as possible by reducing download times and style sheet size. Second is ensuring that the CSS itself helps efficient rendering. The second concern is one that screen-based media is especially susceptible to, as browser windows on the desktop are highly dynamic objects; changing the size of the browser viewport causes something called a **reflow** and possibly also a **repaint**. Reflows and repaints are costly from a performance standpoint because they require that certain elements be rendered again.[6] A reflow is triggered whenever the browser needs to reevaluate the layout of an element,[7] while a repaint is triggered whenever the browser needs to reevaluate the visual appearance of an element (but not its layout).

When appraising CSS optimizations, consider which of these optimization goals you are working toward. If you are trying to achieve faster download times, it is not unwise to be willing to rework a block of code that renders quickly but is larger than it might otherwise need to be.

---

5. Steve wrote a very interesting blog post on the subject available at http://www.stevesouders.com/blog/2009/03/10/performance-impact-of-css-selectors/.
6. Nicole Sullivan has a fantastic blog post discussing reflows and repaints specifically in the context of CSS at http://www.stubbornella.org/content/2009/03/27/reflows-repaints-css-performance-making-your-javascript-slow/.
7. Mozilla documentation about reflows is particularly explanatory, and can be found at http://www.mozilla.org/newlayout/doc/reflow.html.

Optimizing with CSS shorthand, selector groups, and inheritance

Perhaps the most obvious optimization technique is simply to write less CSS code. The CSS language offers a number of ways to declare rules that are operationally equivalent but syntactically different. Taking full advantage of these turns out to be a good thing not only for organizing your CSS in logical chunks, but also for optimizing it since it also often results in physically shorter, and thus often also simpler, style sheets.

The simplest example is the use of CSS shorthand, which can be used to define a number of distinct properties using just one. The border property is an excellent example of this, as it expands to 12 related properties: border-top-width, border-top-style, border-top-color, border-right-width, border-right-style, border-right-color, and so on. Some graphical CSS editors will produce code like this:

```
#example {
    border-top-width: 5px;
    border-top-style: solid;
    border-top-color: black;
    border-right-width: 5px;
    border-right-style: solid;
    border-right-color: black;
    /* and so on... */
}
```

This is a dramatic situation, but many similar examples are prevalent in style sheets that haven't been optimized or have not been written by hand. In this case, the multiple repetitive declarations in the previous declaration block can be shortened to simply one declaration using the border shorthand property:

```
#example { border: 5px solid black; }
```

CSS shorthand can be exceptionally useful for shortening style sheets, but it shouldn't be thought of solely as an optimization technique. Using CSS shorthand properties can sometimes be operationally different than using the precise property. It's also not the only tool in the drawer of its type.

Another common and very simple optimization is to eliminate repetitive declarations by combining them into a single new block with a selector group. For example, many style sheets declare fonts explicitly for many different portions of a web page along with other declarations, like this:

```
#example-meta-content {
    font-family: Helvetica;
    width: 70%;
}
#example-sidebar {
    font-family: Helvetica;
    width: 50%;
}
#example-navbar {
    font-family: Helvetica;
    width: 85%;
}
```

We can collate all the font-family declarations into a new single block, like this:

```
#example-sidebar, ➡
#example-meta-content, ➡
#example-navbar { font-family: Helvetica; }
```

Like shorthand, this isn't solely an optimization technique but it can be used that way. Organizationally speaking, it groups related design choices by encoding them in a single place. Creating logical groupings in this way helps maintain organizational consistency because it reduces the number of different edits required to make a single logical change.

A third best practice that keeps the size of CSS code down is making the most of inheritance. Given the earlier example with font choices, we can presume that the majority of the web page is to be typeset using Helvetica. In such a case, it makes more sense to allow inheritance to define the general case because that results in a shorter style sheet:

```
body { font-family: Helvetica; }
```

Then, defining the exceptions adds negligible weight to your code:

```
#footer { font-family: "Times New Roman"; }
```

Avoid universal selectors or lengthy descendant selectors

When crafting CSS selectors, use brevity whenever possible. However, don't sacrifice precision in order to do so, because being precise is just as important to the browser as being brief is.

Using the universal or "star" selector (*) can slow down some browsers' performance. While the effect may not be noticeable to all users, be mindful that such a selector will apply the same declarations to every single element in your markup. The more markup you have, the longer it'll take the CPU to process all that information and style it. Ultimately, some or all of this effort may even be for naught if other declarations override major portions of these styles later on. This is yet another reason why taking advantage of inheritance for more generally applicable rules saves time both for you as the developer and for the user.

A similar issue exists when using lengthy descendant selectors. For instance, a selector such as body div#content div#post div.metadata p#author { ... } degrades performance and increases download times unnecessarily if a simpler selector like #author { ... } would have sufficed. In situations where more precision is necessary—perhaps because there are many author elements on the page as opposed to just one and so you're using a class selector (.author) instead of an ID selector (#author)—it's still important to keep the selector brief. Use only the parts of the document hierarchy that are relevant:

```
/* Too verbose. */
div#content div#post div.metadata .author { color: red; }

/* Usually suffices, is faster and clearer. */
#content .author { color: red; }
```

Lengthy descendant selectors usually appear because each additional simple selector added to the chain of simple selectors gives the rule more specificity in the cascade. To override the red text in the previous example code, you might write a new rule such as

```
#content #post .author { color: blue; }
```

Although it's not a common technique today primarily due to a lack of support by Internet Explorer 6, the child combinator (>) can also be used to keep descendant selectors short. Instead of adding to the growing chain of simple selectors, consider replacing the descendant combinator with a child combinator instead:

```
#content > .author { color: blue; }
```

Using the child combinator not only reduces selector length, but also limits the scope of the selector's subjects, which reduces processing time. That is, rather than asking the browser to find all elements descended from another element, you're only asking the browser to find that element's children, thus avoiding the need to access or address quite as many elements.

Put CSS at the top

As we noted earlier, sometimes performance is as much about perception as it is about technical measurement. One of the best ways to improve the perception of performance is to place your style sheets early in the <head> element of your HTML document. This enables browsers to display whatever content they get as early as possible, complete with visual styling.

Providing this quick, early visual feedback to a user effectively transforms the HTML page itself into a load progress indicator. This also follows the principle of progressive enhancement by applying it to how the page renders. Progressive rendering may not reduce the total render time of the entire page, but it can significantly improve the user experience by creating a situation in which discrete chunks of the page, such as the header and other content above the fold, are rendered earlier in comparison to how they might have rendered otherwise.

Putting CSS at the top of your page also helps reduce the occurrence of a flash of unstyled content or, worse, simply a blank white screen upon first page load. The former may appear if the HTML content of your pages completes loading significantly ahead of the styles. The latter may appear if some part of the page load causes the rendering thread in the browser to block, such as downloading scripts might.

Prefer <link> elements over @import rules

Using <link> elements to reference style sheets almost always results in a faster page load time than using @import statements will. This happens because CSS referenced using <link> elements are more reliably downloaded in parallel by web browsers today, whereas style sheets that are imported using @import are requested by the browser sequentially. Using @import requires an additional round-trip to the server because the browser has to first fetch the CSS, then parse it and fetch the rest. Further, Internet Explorer behaves undesirably when style sheets are included using @import and JavaScripts are also present; it fetches the scripts before completing to fetch the style sheets, regardless of the order <script> or style sheet references are placed in the document's <head>.[8]

---

8. This is demonstrated in one of Steve Souders' blog posts on the topic at http://www.stevesouders.com/blog/2009/04/09/dont-use-import/.

Since @import rules can cause such performance headaches, a common solution to this is to merge all imported style sheets into one file that gets delivered to the browser in one go. There are a number of ways to do this, but in all cases, doing so dynamically allows you to remain architecturally modular with CSS files without adversely affecting performance. Often, concatenating multiple CSS files can be easily automated, so you might even consider merging every one of your style sheets, not just your imported ones, as we discuss in the next section.

Compressing, combining, and minifying style sheets

Another way to optimize CSS is to compress it in a number of ways. The objective here is to reduce a style sheet's file size so that the user downloads the CSS as quickly as possible and so that the file can be read by software quicker. Unfortunately, in this context the term *compressing* is ambiguous because it can refer both to the raw CSS code as well as to the HTTP transfer that needs to occur. The former is more precisely referred to as minimizing and the latter as "GZipping."

CSS minimizers are like strainers that remove extraneous whitespace, comments, and other unnecessary data bytes (such as a trailing semicolon at the end of a declaration block from a style sheet file). An automated build system is a great place for a CSS minimizer. Yahoo! created a minification tool called YUI Compressor for this purpose.[9] Using Compressor, you can quickly and easily minify your CSS code one style sheet at a time, or you can use it as part of an automation pipeline that can create a single, minimized CSS file out of any CSS files you give it. Here is a simple shell loop to do just that:

```
find . -name '*.css' -print | while read file; do
    java -jar \
        /path/to/yuicompressor-2.4.2/build/yuicompressor-2.4.2.jar \
            "$file" >> all-min.css
done;
```

This loop first searches for all the files in the current directory that end in .css and sends the resulting list of file names through to the YUI Compressor. The output from the compressor is then concatenated into a single file—in this case, all-min.css. Combining multiple style sheets is a further optimization in the same vein. However, note that minification tools like the YUI Compressor don't actually parse CSS, so if you do combine all your style sheets into a single file you should strip out any @import declarations before you do the minification. Also, if the CSS files are scattered in multiple directories and reference resources such as background images in relative paths, concatenation may result in 404 errors. To work around this, simply use server-relative URIs to reference other resources from your CSS code.

An array of other, similar minification tools exist as well. The CSS Formatter and Optimiser[10] is a web-based tool that does for individual style sheets a lot of what the YUI Compressor does. Minification of CSS code can turn readable code into an extreme eyesore. The good news is that just as minification can be automated, so too can expansion.[11]

---

9. Actually, the YUI Compressor was originally created to minify JavaScript. However, recent versions do a great job of minifying CSS as well.
10. The CSS Formatter and Optimiser also has options for organizing CSS code, such as sorting properties alphabetically within declaration blocks. You can find it at http://floele.flyspray.org/csstidy/css_optimiser.php.
11. An online tool called Styleneat, accessible at http://styleneat.com/, can un-minify CSS and return it to a readable state.

Another area where you can get some transfer savings is in the case where CSS rules are targeted for a particular media. Rather than using an entirely separate style sheet, you may consider using a @media block. This is especially useful in situations where few other media CSS rules are needed, or on sites where you expect the user to switch from one media to another often, such as in the case of cooking blogs where recipes are very often printed. Since it's just another CSS rule, the @media block itself can also be minimized and concatenated with the rest of the style sheets.

However, for each addition to the CSS code itself, you require that these additional bytes be downloaded. At some point, you need to balance the size of a single file with how likely it is to be used. In the case of alternate style sheets for a mobile version of a web site, you probably want to avoid using a @media block or combining the mobile rules with the rest of the styles because only one set of rules are likely to be used. This is why we recommend that you use the <link> element and create multiple style sheets to modularize the CSS itself.

By using HTTP compression—a capability built into both web servers and web browsers that uses a compression algorithm such as GZip for transferring resources transparently—you can also mitigate the amount of code users need to download. GZipping style sheets usually involves configuring the web server you use to automatically compress CSS files on the fly, although you can also create server-side scripts in languages such as PHP to do this for you if other options aren't available. Since CSS is plain text, it compresses in this fashion very effectively (typically anywhere from 60 percent to 80 percent), although since well-written CSS is often very short, the optimization benefits of using HTTP compression on style sheets are not often pursued except by extremely large-scale installations.

For the Apache web server, two modules can be used to accomplish HTTP compression: mod_gzip[12] and mod_deflate.[13] Both modules function by examining the HTTP headers sent to the server by the user agent. If these headers include the Accept-Encoding header and specify an encoding that the server knows how to provide (most commonly, gzip), then Apache will invoke one of these modules to work its magic.

Both options require that the server be precompiled with the module's presence. If it's not, and you have access to your own web server, you can compile the source code yourself as either a dynamic or static module. Once available, setting up the module merely involves editing a few configuration lines. For mod_gzip, here's a sample configuration that will handle CSS files:

```
mod_gzip_item_include  file   \.css$
mod_gzip_item_include  mime   ^text/css$
```

If you're using mod_deflate, then here's a simple minimum configuration you can use:

```
AddOutputFilterByType DEFLATE text/html text/plain text/xml text/css
```

Another option for taking advantage of HTTP compression is using a server-side scripting language.[14] These options are typically a bit messier because they require more code and create additional indirection. However, they may be more portable or even required in your particular hosting environment.

---

12. mod_gzip is an open source project hosted by SourceForge at http://sourceforge.net/projects/mod-gzip/.
13. Ample documentation on mod_deflate exists on the Apache web site at http://httpd.apache.org/docs/2.0/mod/mod_deflate.html.
14. Mike Papageorge maintains a fantastic overview of HTTP compression methods specifically for CSS on his blog post at http://www.fiftyfoureleven.com/weblog/web-development/css/the-definitive-css-gzip-method.

Avoid CSS expressions and filters

CSS expressions offer developers a way to dynamically script style rules within style sheets and are a feature of Internet Explorer. As they are nonstandard, other browsers will ignore their declarations, so they are usually harmless (although they will prevent your style sheet from validating). Sometimes they are useful for working around limitations or bugs in Internet Explorer's support for CSS. However, they are a double-edged sword because they are also incredibly resource intensive.

Much of the time, it is better to avoid CSS expressions altogether. When you can't, it's important to keep in mind that the expressions you write may get evaluated by Internet Explorer many more times than expected. This is because every UI change, including moving the mouse around the page, causes Internet Explorer to reevaluate the expression, eating up processor cycles. It's far better to use JavaScript as part of a script than to use a CSS expression in this case.

Filters create a similar situation. They are useful for providing interface enhancements such as opacity in Internet Explorer, but block rendering and should ultimately simply be avoided in favor of gracefully degrading fallbacks.

As Internet Explorer improves, another issue is that future versions offer support for both the standard and nonstandard methods of using CSS. In IE7, in particular, the alpha channel that provides PNG images with a measure of opacity can be used much like it can in other browsers, making obsolete some uses of its proprietary opacity filters. However, the filters are still there and so you may need to find yourself using a CSS hack to hide the `filter` rule from IE7 and IE8 while still showing it to earlier versions of the browser.

Reference external CSS instead of inline styles

To avoid reflows and repaints, you should write CSS for the resultant design and then reference it all at once when changing dynamically, rather than adding it all at once. Encapsulating the design in a single class name also brings you closer to "object-oriented" CSS.

Use absolute or fixed positioning on animated elements

Since absolute and fixed positioning create new document flows, CSS boxes positioned using those schemes do not affect the layout of nearby elements. Animations, which often change layout dimensions of elements, are guaranteed to cause both reflows and repaints, so isolating their effects within an absolute or fixed position document flow limits the scope of the DOM to which the reflow applies.

Diagnostic tools for CSS performance

Performance optimizations require exact measurements and lots of testing. Optimizations like these are much more of a science than an art. To effectively optimize CSS code, you need to measure the before and after states of the changes you make. To this end, you'll find it incredibly helpful to use some if not all of the tools we'll discuss in this section. Also, we recommend using a version control system to maintain multiple different versions of your code and compare the variations between them.[15]

---

15. If you've never used a version control system before, we recommend that you give git a try. Its simple and offline administration makes it ideally suited for front-end developers and web designers, since it requires no special server or system administration skills to use. A good beginning tutorial is Git for Designers, available at http://hoth.entp.com/output/git_for_designers.html.

The Firebug Net panel

Among the most useful tools for web developers is, of course, Firebug. This Firefox extension includes a Net panel that draws waterfall speed graphs of how quickly resources are requested and downloaded by the browser. As you can see in Figure 10-1, the Firebug Net panel shows you the amount of time each resource took to download in milliseconds as well as a waterfall chart of when it began. This can let you see blocks and help you to parallelize the downloading of resources referenced on your page.

Figure 10-1. The Firebug Net panel provides copious information relating to the downloading and rendering time, parellelism, and other details of web pages.

YSlow Firebug plug-in

YSlow (see Figure 10-2) is specifically a speed testing plug-in for Firebug. It uses Yahoo!'s front-end engineering guidelines[16] as a means to evaluate a page's performance. It also shows you download time estimates with both primed and empty caches.

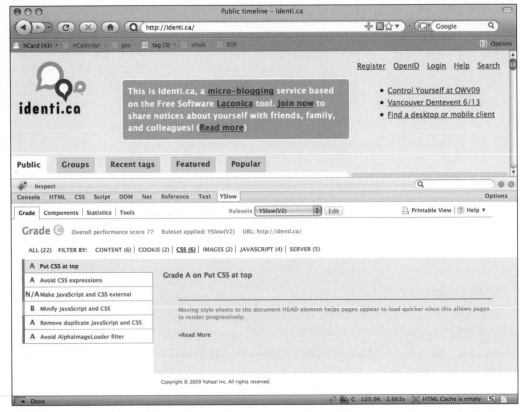

Figure 10-2. The YSlow plug-in for Firebug analyzes page performance across a number of facets and provides an in-browser interface for viewing and printing the results of its tests.

---

16. Yahoo!'s front-end engineering guidelines are published on the Yahoo! Developer Network at http://developer.
yahoo.com/performance/rules.html.

WebKit Web Inspector network timeline

Safari 3 and later provides an option called Show the Develop Menu. Enabling this option also provides access to the WebKit Web Inspector, a window that exposes the HTML, CSS, and JavaScript code behind a web page. One of the visible panes in the Web Inspector is the network timeline (see Figure 10-3), which provides a waterfall chart of load times of all the resources on a page, broken down by type (HTML page, images, style sheets, scripts, and so on).

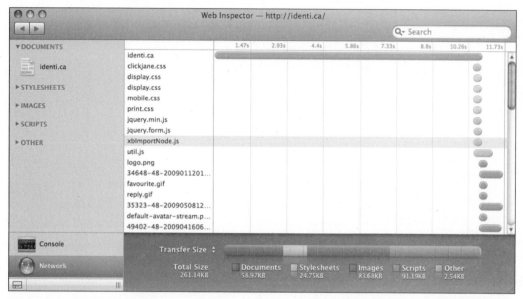

Figure 10-3. WebKit's Web Inspector (available as part of the Safari web browser) offers a network timeline that lets you examine all the resources from a page and view when and how quickly they were downloaded.

Reflow and repaint timers and visualizers

As reflows and repaints are so important to optimizing the efficiency of CSS, a number of timers and visualizers have been created very recently that can help you measure the effects of changes to your style sheets. As of this writing, some of these tools only function in the latest nightly builds of browsers.

One such tool is a cross-browser bookmarklet that times reflows on pages called Reflowr.[17] Run interactively as shown in Figure 10-4, this tool gives you a number of buttons that time changes in a particular area of rendering.

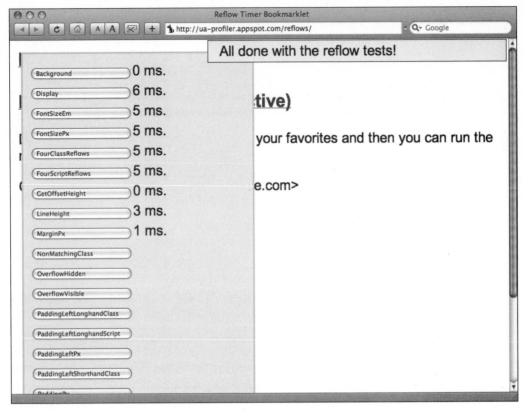

Figure 10-4. Reflowr's interactive mode gives you buttons to run its individual tests, times them, and then displays a result measured in milliseconds (ms).

Another similar tool is John Resig's repaint tracker for Mozilla Firefox.[18] It uses a new developer feature of Mozilla's most recent Firefox 3.1 nightly build[19] that allows JavaScript to detect paint events triggered by the browser itself.

---

17. You can download the Reflowr bookmarklet from http://reflowr.appspot.com/.
18. You can learn more about and download John Resig's repaint tracker at http://ejohn.org/blog/browser-paint-events/.
19. The Firefox nightly builds can be downloaded from http://ftp.mozilla.org/pub/mozilla.org/firefox/nightly/latest-trunk/.

Summary

Web site optimization is a big topic and optimizing CSS code is only one aspect of it. Nevertheless, optimizing CSS code itself is an important aspect of implementing projects. Moreover, CSS techniques can be useful in optimizing other areas of a web site's performance because the capabilities that style sheets offer often streamline the process of getting something done.

Optimized CSS code is fundamentally well-architected code. Do not try to optimize CSS that isn't first written in a logical, consistent, and well-organized manner. Doing the initial legwork of ensuring your style sheets make sense is a prerequisite to creating highly optimized style sheets, and techniques such as CSS shorthand properties, selector groups, and inheritance are all built-in features of the language that provide both power and eloquence—the goals of optimization in the first place.

Next, be certain to target as much low-hanging fruit as you can, because these easy-to-do things will net you the majority of the performance gains that will result from your efforts. They include things like simply putting CSS code near the top of the <head> element, using <link> elements over @import statements when possible, and avoiding CSS expressions and filters.

With Ajax becoming an ever more commonplace occurrence, CSS is also being used dynamically after the initial page load. This brings new optimization challenges because reflows and repaints become an increasing concern, which can be costly in terms of CPU cycles with complicated page layouts. Some ways to mitigate the effects of reflows is to position elements that will be animated in their own document flow using absolute or fixed positioning. Similarly, repaints should be handled in an all-at-once fashion by encapsulating the desired visual result with CSS that is already written in an external style sheet and switching a class name once, rather than writing out individual CSS rule changes one at a time in your JavaScript.

There are also a number of tools, some still very new as of this writing, that are available to you to measure CSS performance. They include tools for measuring download speed as well as reflow and repaint events. These are areas where CSS is still developing quickly and in which we expect advancements from CSS3 will begin to play a major role. As we'll see in the next chapter, capabilities like animations and simple transformations, once the sole domain of JavaScript or SVG, are now being integrated directly into CSS, and some browsers, notably Apple's Safari, show promise of making such effects hardware accelerated for even faster performance.

Part 4

THE FUTURE OF CSS

We have come far from the early, heady days of CSS 1.0 and the initial implementations scattered about in browsers that attempted to support it. With the completion of CSS2.1 support in Internet Explorer 8, the major browsers now feature solid support for this version of Cascading Style Sheets.

That is *so* 2009. Browsers are already experimenting with implementing features of the emerging version of the specification, CSS3. Now let us look to the future of CSS and take a peek at what's in store in the coming months and years.

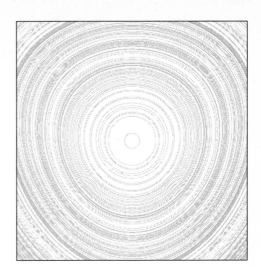

Chapter 11

EXPLORING THE EMERGENCE OF CSS3

Because of the scope and complexity of the CSS3 efforts, the specification has been organized into multiple modules. Previous editions of the CSS specification were written as single entities, but with so much more being added to CSS3 it made sense to bring certain sections of the spec online as modules. That way, a spec could be developed, ratified, and implemented more quickly than if everything had to be in place in a single document. These modules are organized into specific topics such as color, media queries, paged media, text, and multicolumn layout.

Additionally, the W3C categorizes CSS projects according to priority: high, medium, or low. As of this writing, there are four publications classified as "high priority," 27 classified as "medium priority," and 19 classified as "low priority." See `http://www.w3.org/Style/CSS/current-work` for the latest list of publications.

In this chapter, we will focus on CSS3 modules that have made solid progress in their publication development and have had experimental features implemented or scheduled to be implemented in at least one of the major web browsers. For the purposes of this discussion, we consider "major" web browsers to be using one of the four most widely used rendering engines: Trident-based browsers such as Internet Explorer, Gecko-based browsers such as Firefox, WebKit-based browsers such as Safari, and Presto-based browsers such as Opera.

When will it be done?

The list of CSS3 modules is a moving target. The modules are continually in flux and more modules are being added all the time. Just during the writing of this very chapter, four new modules were added (as of March 20, 2009): CSS 2D Transforms Module (http://www.w3.org/TR/css3-2d-transforms), CSS 3D Transforms Module (http://www.w3.org/TR/css3-3d-transforms), CSS Transitions Module Level 3 (http://www.w3.org/TR/css3-transitions), and CSS Animations Module Level 3 (http://www.w3.org/TR/css3-animations).

With that said, each module can have various levels of completion. Some may be classified as "candidate recommendations," others as "working drafts," and so on. The final status is called "recommendation," but in practical terms many of these features in the precursory drafts may already be implemented in several browsers, while other components that make it all the way to final status may be ignored by most or all of the browser market indefinitely.

Using CSS3 today

We have already touched on several CSS3 features throughout this book and illustrated where they might be effective. For instance, in Chapter 4 we mentioned how CSS3 is set to transform everyday web pages into a powerful print platform using @page. When we discussed mobile web design, we looked at media queries for more fine-grained targeting of user agent environmental conditions, and took a stab at working with box positioning features that haven't even made it into the emerging specs yet.

Using vendor extensions and "beta" features

The convention with vendor extensions and features that aren't fully baked yet is to include a dash at the beginning of the rule. This dash immediately identifies rules that will be outside of the specifications, and will likely only work in one browser. Be prepared to write multiple lines for the same thing. This is not necessarily a bad thing—it's experimental territory and browser vendors will have different ideas on how to implement a feature that is still in flux in the specification.

Browser support

This is an interesting time in the browser market. New advanced features are being added to browsers all the time, and especially interesting for our purposes, that includes features borrowed from the emerging CSS3 specification. After years of just trying to get to where we felt safe writing CSS2.1, along come all these shiny new CSS3 toys that we can actually play with. What's an easily distracted web developer to do? That's right—play along, experiment, and see what works.

Many of the new CSS3 features have already made their way into today's web browsers. The fun thing with all of this is that if something doesn't work, your site likely won't collapse in on itself. If a browser doesn't recognize a feature and you've architected your CSS accordingly, the site should still work. Write your code to the principles of progressive enhancement and watch the cool kids flock to your site with their shiny new browsers to see it in action!

Opera (Presto)

Opera is often the first to adopt many of the CSS3 specifications and can be a great place to start experimenting with new CSS features. Opera is also the most widely deployed browser on mobile handsets and can be useful when designing for modern mobile devices. The Opera browser is built on Opera's own Presto rendering engine, which also drives output for Nintendo's DS and Wii browsers and a few other specialized mobile browsers.

The bleeding-edge version of the Opera browser as of this writing is beta version 10, and this should be at general release by the time you read this. Opera 10 includes numerous improvements to CSS3, including string support for CSS3 selectors and most new declarations, but no support yet for certain declarations such as transitions, transformations, and animations, `border-radius`, or `box-shadow`.

Safari (WebKit)

WebKit is the rendering engine behind Apple's Safari browser, and is used as the rendering engine for many other third-party web browsers such as OmniWeb and Google Chrome. Many mobile platforms such as Google's Android, Nokia's S60, and of course the iPhone OS base their default web browsers on WebKit. WebKit is often on the cutting edge for supporting CSS3 features, and what is especially compelling about this platform is the large number of iPhone OS mobile users who can use these features right away. (Whereas Opera is the most widely deployed browser on mobile, WebKit is the most widely used.) When designing mobile sites, pay attention to this platform.

As of this writing, Safari 4.0 is the latest release. Safari 4 and current versions of WebKit include excellent support for CSS3 selectors and declarations. WebKit is the only platform so far to have implemented CSS3 transitions, transformations, and animations.

Firefox (Gecko)

Firefox and other up-to-date Gecko-based browsers have strong support for emerging CSS3 features. And since Firefox is the second most widely used web browser platform after Internet Explorer, this makes a good initial platform target for incorporating those new CSS3 features that you'd like to give some attention to.

Firefox 3.5 is currently in beta and should be generally available by the time you read this. Firefox and other browsers that use the latest versions of Gecko have strong support for CSS3 selectors and declarations.

Internet Explorer (Trident)

Internet Explorer 7 greatly improves support for the CSS specs over its predecessors, but where you really want to pay attention is IE8 and beyond. IE8 does make great strides toward better support for CSS and has begun implementation of a few CSS3 features that you can use today.

Unfortunately, while the Internet Explorer browser still leads in terms of market share, it has had the least support for the CSS3 features as of this writing. The goal of IE8 was to complete CSS2.1 support. However, there are a couple of CSS3 features such as substring matching selectors that have made their way in to the IE browser platform, and for some of the other features there are workarounds.

Using new CSS3 features

Now that we've illustrated what you might be able to expect from browsers, let's look at some of the new features of CSS3 in practice. The principle for using any of these techniques is to understand that it is probable that not all browsers will have implemented the given technique you wish to use, and that these should be used for progressive enhancement and not for mission-critical design elements until the browser market has for the most part universally implemented these features.

CSS3 color units and opacity

CSS3 adds several new ways to write color values. You can now write color values using HSL values (similar to HSB for you Photoshop buffs) and add the idea of transparency via a new opacity property. Opacity can be further incorporated as alpha values in the HSLA and RGBA color declaration constructs.

HSL is composed of three values: hue, saturation, and lightness. If you can imagine a color circle, the hue value represents a degree on that circle—a value between 0 and 360. The specification defines 0 and 360 (which would be the same position on a circle) as equal to the color red. Saturation is a percentage, with 100% indicating full color and 0% indicating gray. Lightness is also represented as a percentage, with 50% the normal value (consider this your default for most cases), 100% fully washed out to white, and 0% completely black. To illustrate, a few examples are in order. The following code demonstrates how some of these values would look in code, and Figure 11-1 shows what you can expect when the code is rendered in a supporting browser:

```
<!DOCTYPE html PUBLIC "-//W3C//DTD XHTML 1.1//EN" ➥
"http://www.w3.org/TR/xhtml11/DTD/xhtml11.dtd">
<html xmlns="http://www.w3.org/1999/xhtml" xml:lang="en">
<head>
    <meta http-equiv="content-type" content="text/html; ➥
charset=utf-8" />
    <title>HSL Color Boxes</title>
    <style type="text/css">
        div {
            width:30px;
            height:60px;
            float:left;
            border:2px outset #666;
        }
        div#red { background-color: hsl(0, 100%, 50%) }
        div#green { background-color: hsl(120, 100%, 50%) }
        div#blue { background-color: hsl(240, 100%, 50%) }
        div#black { background-color: hsl(0, 100%, 0%) }
        div#maroon { background-color: hsl(0, 100%, 35%) }
        div#pink { background-color: hsl(0, 100%, 80%) }
        div#white { background-color: hsl(0, 100%, 100%) }
    </style>
</head>
<body>
    <div id="red"></div>
```

```
            <div id="green"></div>
            <div id="blue"></div>
            <div id="black"></div>
            <div id="maroon"></div>
            <div id="pink"></div>
            <div id="white"></div>
        </body>
        </html>
```

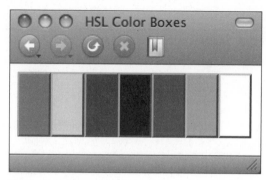

Figure 11-1. Boxes using HSL color values

Try experimenting with your own HSL color values without relying on an editor and see if you can get the hang of it. Try making a deep purple, a pale violet, or a nice shade of ocher. Many believe that the HSL scheme is easier to work with because you have more intuitive control over the hue in one value rather than having to mix three separate values. Also, you can control those saturation and lightness values directly, which can be simpler to visualize than getting the balance right when mixing three buckets of paint.

opacity is a stand-alone property for enabling some transparency when coloring an element. To get some use out of opacity, it helps to have text or an image underneath to illustrate the effect. opacity may have a value from 0 to 1, where 1 is fully opaque (think 100 percent) and 0 is fully transparent. A value of 0.5 would mean 50 percent transparent. To illustrate this, let's add the opacity property to our <div> elements in the previous example. But simply changing the opacity of an element on a white background isn't going to give us the full picture here—visually all we'll see is faded pastel versions of our original color bars. To show how the opacity change lets background items appear, we'll throw in a background image on the <body> element, the output of which is shown in Figure 11-2:

```
        body { background: url(eagbd.gif) no-repeat; }
        div {
            width:30px;
            height:60px;
            float:left;
            border:2px outset #666;
            opacity: 0.7;
        }
        div#red { background-color: hsl(0, 100%, 50%) }
        div#green { background-color: hsl(120, 100%, 50%) }
        div#blue { background-color: hsl(240, 100%, 50%) }
```

```
div#black { background-color: hsl(0, 100%, 0%) }
div#maroon { background-color: hsl(0, 100%, 35%) }
div#pink { background-color: hsl(0, 100%, 80%) }
div#white { background-color: hsl(0, 100%, 100%) }
```

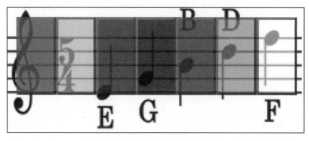

Figure 11-2. Transparency allows objects beneath to show through.

Internet Explorer browsers prior to version 8 in strict mode do not support the opacity property, but there is a workaround. Use `filter:alpha(opacity=70)` alongside our `opacity:0.7` declaration to get the same effect in IE6 and IE7. IE8 still doesn't support the opacity property, and has replaced their old proprietary filter with a new one: `-ms-filter: "progid:DXImageTransform.Microsoft.Alpha(Opacity=70)";`. Think of the filter values for Internet Explorer as percentages, where 70 = 70 percent or 0.7, 40 = 40 percent or 0.4, 100 = 100 percent or 1, and so on.

opacity can further be incorporated into HSL and RGB color properties by adding a fourth value, alpha, to the rule. The opacity-supporting versions of HSL and RGB are known as HSLA and RGBA, respectively. alpha works in exactly the same way as the opacity property, where 1 is opaque and 0 is transparent, and levels in between will show transparency accordingly. Here is CSS code for the same example illustrated in Figure 11-2, but with alternating HSLA and RGB values instead:

```
body { background: url(eagbd.gif) no-repeat; }
div {
    width:30px;
    height:60px;
    float:left;
    border:2px outset #666;
}
div#red { background-color: hsla(0, 100%, 50%, 0.7) }
div#green { background-color: rgba(0, 255, 0, 0.7) }
div#blue { background-color: hsla(240, 100%, 50%, 0.7) }
div#black { background-color: rgba(0, 0, 0, 0.7) }
div#maroon { background-color: hsla(0, 100%, 35%, 0.7) }
div#pink { background-color: rgba(255, 153, 153, 0.7) }
div#white { background-color: hsla(0, 100%, 100%, 0.7) }
```

General sibling combinators

The General Sibling Combinator (GSC) is a mouthful of a name, but it does have some simple yet powerful functionality. The GSC performs the function of selecting a specified element that is at the same node level after another specified element appears in the order of your markup. The following example and Figure 11-3 will help clarify:

```
<!DOCTYPE html PUBLIC "-//W3C//DTD XHTML 1.1//EN" "http://www.w3.org/TR/xhtml11/
DTD/xhtml11.dtd">
<html xmlns="http://www.w3.org/1999/xhtml" xml:lang="en">
<head>
    <meta http-equiv="content-type" content="text/html; ➡
charset=utf-8" />
    <title>The Violas of Rome</title>
    <style type="text/css">
        h1 ~ p {
            font-weight: bold;
        }
        h2 ~ p {
            font-style: italic;
            font-weight: normal;
        }
    </style>
</head>
<body>
    <h1>The Violas of Rome</h1>
    <p>It was the best of times, it was the worst of times. It was a ➡
dark and stormy night.</p>
    <p>Her heart was racing as she walked towards the stairs. No one ➡
would play her viola again. The nightmares would end - tonight.</p>
    <h2>A soldier's tale</h2>
    <p>It all began many years ago, in a small hamlet by the seaside. ➡
Her cousins would knock at the door and they'd go into the village to ➡
see their aunt at the shop. Never in her life would she suspect that ➡
the hamlet would be the very place that they would come first - the ➡
druids that came in from the sea.</p>
    <p>That Saturday was Salame and Cheese night. Would she be able ➡
to tell her girlfriends the sad truth about her nightmares?</p>
    <div class="aside">
        <p>As an aside, we should note that one should never trouble ➡
trouble unless trouble troubles you.</p>
    </div>
</body>
</html>
```

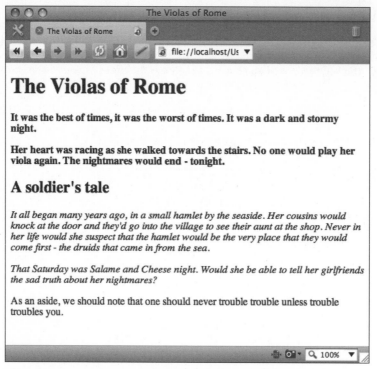

Figure 11-3. Using the GSC to differentiate between content after the first-level heading and after the second-level heading

In this example, the markup contains a first-level heading followed by two paragraphs, and then a second-level heading followed by two paragraphs. Finally, there is a paragraph contained within a <div>, nested at a nonadjacent level from the other paragraph elements in this document.

For the styling, we've created two GSCs: one for general siblings of the <h1> element, and one for the general siblings of the <h2> element. For the <h1> siblings, we have set the font weight to bold. For the <h2> siblings we have set the font style to italic, and in addition to that we have set the font weight back to normal. We just wanted italics—not bold italics—so we had to reset this property. This property is reset to normal because the font-weight property still would apply for the rest of the document, as long as a paragraph element were at the same hierarchical level in the node tree as the <h1> elements, including any <p> elements occurring after the <h2>.

The great thing about using the GSC is that all of the major browsers now support it, including IE7 and higher. If you can live without IE6 support, this is a CSS3 feature you may start implementing in your web page designs right away.

CSS3 attribute matching selectors

Attribute matching selectors are a useful method for pinpointing specific elements based on their attribute values, and CSS3 lets you take things a step further by allowing you to match substrings of attribute values. You can match the beginning, end, or any substring within. The following is a list of the new CSS3 attribute selectors (where "E" is an HTML or XML element or equivalent selector):

- E[instrument^="bass"]: Selects any attribute beginning with the string "bass". Given a list of standard orchestral instruments, "bassoon", "bass clarinet", "basset_clarinet", "basset_horn", and "bass_drum" would be matches. Other instruments containing the string "bass", such as "contrabassoon" and "double_bass", would be omitted.

- E[instrument$="bass"]: Selects any attribute ending with the string "bass". Going back to our list of orchestral instruments, "double_bass" would be a match and the rest would be skipped.

- E[instrument*="bass"]: Selects any attribute beginning with the string "bass". This time the entire list of instruments from the first example containing the string "bass" would be matches.

CSS3 pseudo-classes

CSS3 adds a lot of new pseudo-classes. These pseudo-classes were designed to further target the nodes of an XML or HTML document tree with increased flexibility and precision. The names assigned to these pseudo-selectors are more or less intuitive as to what the function is that they represent, so they shouldn't be too hard to learn, understand, and begin implementing in your own code.

CSS3 pseudo-classes have been implemented in major web browsers as of Safari 3.1, Firefox 3.5, IE8 in standards mode, and even partial support in IE7 if you don't need generated content. They are usable today in your own designs.

E:root

E:root selects the root element of a document. In your typical HTML cases, this will be the <html> element. For XML documents, this would be the outermost element node. In HTML contexts, this pseudo-selector is nearly useless since you can be certain that <html> is going to be the root. But in XML it can be valuable for web developers to be able to select the root element with no prior knowledge of the markup structure's actual root element name.

E:nth-child(n)

E:nth-child(n) selects the "nth" child of the given element's parent. The (n) part is an expression with a prototype of an+b, in which the an part defines the frequency of any repeating that may occur, and the +b part is a modifier that indicates on which order of the nodes the counting begins. The an part or the +b part may each exist on their own, and the operator in between the two may be a plus or minus symbol. The keywords odd and even may be used as well.

Got all that? Neither do we—but the premise is quite simple if you visualize it. Let's look at some examples and things will become clearer in the following code example and in Figure 11-4:

```
<!DOCTYPE html PUBLIC "-//W3C//DTD XHTML 1.0 Transitional//EN"
    "http://www.w3.org/TR/xhtml1/DTD/xhtml1-transitional.dtd">
<html>
    <head>
        <title>nth child</title>
    </head>
    <style type="text/css">
        p {
            height:30px;
            width:110px;
            margin:0;
            padding:2px;
            float:left;
        }
        p:nth-child(3n+1) { background-color: #6CF; }
        p:nth-child(3n+2) { background-color: #6FC; }
        p:nth-child(3n+3) { background-color: #FC6; }
        p:nth-child(7) {
            font-size:1.8em;
            font-weight:bold;
            text-align:center;
            color:#e00000;
        }
        p:nth-child(even) { color:#fff; }
        p:nth-child(5n) { font-style:italic; }
    </style>
    <body>
        <div id="string_instruments">
            <p>Violin</p>
            <p>Viola</p>
            <p>Cello</p>
            <p>Double Bass</p>
            <p>Viola da Gamba</p>
            <p>Guitar</p>
            <p>Banjo</p>
            <p>Mandolin</p>
            <p>Mandola</p>
            <p>Mandocello </p>
            <p>Lute</p>
            <p>Theorbo</p>
            <p>Erhu</p>
            <p>Pipa</p>
            <p>Guzheng</p>
            <p>Sitar</p>
        </div>
    </body>
</html>
```

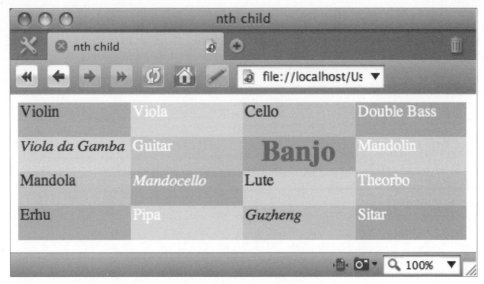

Figure 11-4. Various methods of using nth child pseudo-selectors

In this example, the first three nth-child declarations set three alternating background colors for the <div> elements. The first nth-child declaration is passed a value of p:nth-child(3n+1), which might be read in English as "select every third sibling paragraph, starting with the first one." The next one, p:nth-child(3n+2), selects every third paragraph element starting with the second one, and p:nth-child(3n+3) does the same starting with the third one. The result is alternating background colors. The same treatment might be applied to conveniently create zebra-striped table rows, for instance.

The next selector, p:nth-child(7), targets the seventh sibling paragraph. In this case, we are highlighting the node with the string "Banjo" in the content (although why anyone would want to highlight the banjo is beyond us). If the an value of the argument is absent, the b component is used to select a node.

After that, the p:nth-child(even) is next, and this selector illustrates the ability to use a keyword instead of a set of numeric values as the argument. In this case, we set the text color for all even-numbered nodes to white. An equivalent way to represent (even) in our code would be (2n), while (odd) is equivalent to (2n+1). Finally, the p:nth-child(5n) selector is used to set every fifth sibling in italics.

All this should illustrate the an+b pattern. To recap, an sets the repeating property, while b modifies where the repeats start or selects a single node. We will use this construct again in the next three pseudo-selectors, so it is important to understand how this pattern works.

The E:nth-last-child(n) pseudo-selector works just like the previous example in reverse, counting back from the last child. To illustrate this, try replacing every instance of nth-child in the previous example with nth-last-child and observe what happens:

```
p {
    height:30px;
    width:110px;
```

```
        margin:0;
        padding:2px;
        float:left;
    }
    p:nth-last-child(3n+1) { background-color: #6CF; }
    p:nth-last-child(3n+2) { background-color: #6FC; }
    p:nth-last-child(3n+3) { background-color: #FC6; }
    p:nth-last-child(7) {
        font-size:1.8em;
        font-weight:bold;
        text-align:center;
        color:#e00000;
    }
    p:nth-last-child(even) { color:#fff; }
    p:nth-last-child(5n) { font-style:italic; }
```

The elements become colorized in an order that begins from the last element ("Sitar"), the seventh element from the last node containing the word "Mandolin" is highlighted in red, the selection of even elements to be colored white begins from the last node, and the fifth and tenth nodes containing the strings "Theorbo" and "Viola" are italicized, as shown in Figure 11-5.

Figure 11-5. Demonstrating how :nth-last-child selects elements starting from the last node

E:nth-of-type(n)

This pseudo-selector works similar to :nth-child, but only selects elements that are of the same type. This can be particularly useful if you have images in a storyline and want to alternate floats left or right, which is a common algorithm used when embedding multiple images in a story. Again, the following example will help clarify, which is illustrated in Figure 11-6:

```
<!DOCTYPE html PUBLIC "-//W3C//DTD XHTML 1.0 Transitional//EN"
    "http://www.w3.org/TR/xhtml1/DTD/xhtml1-transitional.dtd">
<html>
    <head>
        <title>nth child</title>
    </head>
    <style type="text/css">
        img {
            margin-bottom:2em;
        }
```

```
        img:nth-of-type(2n+1) {
            float: right;
            margin-left:2em;
        }
        img:nth-of-type(2n) {
            float: left;
            margin-right:2em;
        }
    </style>
    <body>
        <div id="string_instruments">
            <img src="violin.gif" alt="violin" />
            <p>Lorem ipsum dolor sit amet, consectetur adipisicing ➥
elit, sed do eiusmod tempor incididunt ut labore et dolore magna ➥
aliqua. Ut enim ad minim veniam, quis nostrud exercitation ➥
ullamco laboris nisi ut aliquip ex ea commodo consequat. Duis ➥
aute irure dolor in reprehenderit in voluptate velit esse cillum ➥
dolore eu fugiat nulla pariatur. Excepteur sint occaecat cupidatat ➥
non proident, sunt in culpa qui officia deserunt mollit anim id est ➥
laborum.</p>
            <img src="cello.gif" alt="cello" />
            <p>Lorem ipsum dolor sit amet, consectetur adipisicing ➥
elit, sed do eiusmod tempor incididunt ut labore et dolore magna ➥
aliqua. Ut enim ad minim veniam, quis nostrud exercitation ➥
ullamco laboris nisi ut aliquip ex ea commodo consequat. Duis ➥
aute irure dolor in reprehenderit in voluptate velit esse cillum ➥
dolore eu fugiat nulla pariatur. Excepteur sint occaecat cupidatat ➥
non proident, sunt in culpa qui officia deserunt mollit anim id est ➥
laborum.</p>
            <img src="bugle.gif" alt="bugle" />
            <p>Lorem ipsum dolor sit amet, consectetur adipisicing ➥
elit, sed do eiusmod tempor incididunt ut labore et dolore magna ➥
aliqua. Ut enim ad minim veniam, quis nostrud exercitation ➥
ullamco laboris nisi ut aliquip ex ea commodo consequat. Duis ➥
aute irure dolor in reprehenderit in voluptate velit esse cillum ➥
dolore eu fugiat nulla pariatur. Excepteur sint occaecat cupidatat ➥
non proident, sunt in culpa qui officia deserunt mollit anim id est ➥
laborum.</p>
            <img src="romanbugle.gif" alt="roman bugle" />
            <p>Lorem ipsum dolor sit amet, consectetur adipisicing ➥
elit, sed do eiusmod tempor incididunt ut labore et dolore magna ➥
aliqua. Ut enim ad minim veniam, quis nostrud exercitation ➥
ullamco laboris nisi ut aliquip ex ea commodo consequat. Duis ➥
aute irure dolor in reprehenderit in voluptate velit esse cillum ➥
dolore eu fugiat nulla pariatur. Excepteur sint occaecat cupidatat ➥
non proident, sunt in culpa qui officia deserunt mollit anim id est ➥
laborum.</p>
        </div>
    </body>
</html>
```

305

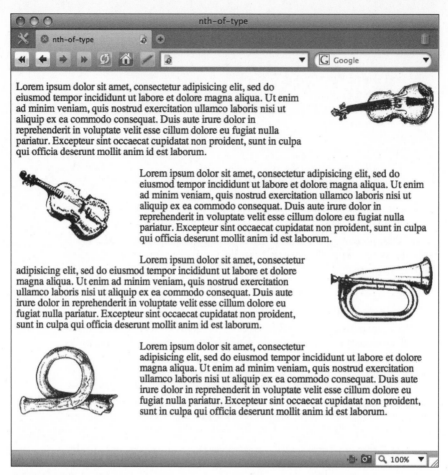

Figure 11-6. Demonstrating nth-of-type to float images in a story alternating from right to left

E:nth-last-of-type(n)

This pseudo-selector works like E:nth-of-type(n) but counting from the last sibling instead of the first. Using the previous XHTML example, try using this CSS instead:

```
<style type="text/css">
    img {
        margin-bottom:2em;
        float:right;
    }
    img:nth-last-of-type(-n+2) {
        float:left;
        margin-right:2em;
    }
    img:nth-last-of-type(1) {
        float:none;
```

```
        display:block;
        margin:0 auto;
    }
</style>
```

These changes are reflected in Figure 11-7.

Lorem ipsum dolor sit amet, consectetur adipisicing elit, sed do eiusmod tempor incididunt ut labore et dolore magna aliqua. Ut enim ad minim veniam, quis nostrud exercitation ullamco laboris nisi ut aliquip ex ea commodo consequat. Duis aute irure dolor in reprehenderit in voluptate velit esse cillum dolore eu fugiat nulla pariatur. Excepteur sint occaecat cupidatat non proident, sunt in culpa qui officia deserunt mollit anim id est laborum.

Lorem ipsum dolor sit amet, consectetur adipisicing elit, sed do eiusmod tempor incididunt ut labore et dolore magna aliqua. Ut enim ad minim veniam, quis nostrud exercitation ullamco laboris nisi ut aliquip ex ea commodo consequat. Duis aute irure dolor in reprehenderit in voluptate velit esse cillum dolore eu fugiat nulla pariatur. Excepteur sint occaecat cupidatat non proident, sunt in culpa qui officia deserunt mollit anim id est laborum.

Lorem ipsum dolor sit amet, consectetur adipisicing elit, sed do eiusmod tempor incididunt ut labore et dolore magna aliqua. Ut enim ad minim veniam, quis nostrud exercitation ullamco laboris nisi ut aliquip ex ea commodo consequat. Duis aute irure dolor in reprehenderit in voluptate velit esse cillum dolore eu fugiat nulla pariatur. Excepteur sint occaecat cupidatat non proident, sunt in culpa qui officia deserunt mollit anim id est laborum.

Figure 11-7. Showing :nth-last-of-type being used to target the last two image elements in the document

The rule selecting img:nth-last-of-type(-n+2) will select the second <img> element from the last one, floating the image to the left. The img:nth-last-of-type(1) selects the last <img> element. Try changing the values here to see how things move about. This construct would be very useful for conclusions, special treatment of lists, and so on where the ending needs some special emphasis or style treatment.

E:last-child

This is the same as writing :nth-last-child(1) and is the corresponding -last pseudo-selector to CSS2.1's E:first-child. It selects the last child of the element in question. To illustrate this, add italics to the last paragraph of the preceding example:

```
<style type="text/css">
    img {
        margin-bottom:2em;
        float:right;
    }
```

```
        img:nth-last-of-type(-n+2) {
            float:left;
            margin-right:2em;
        }
        img:nth-last-of-type(1) {
            float:none;
            display:block;
            margin:0 auto;
        }
        p:last-child { font-style:italic; }
    </style>
```

Now, the last paragraph will appear italicized, as shown in Figure 11-8.

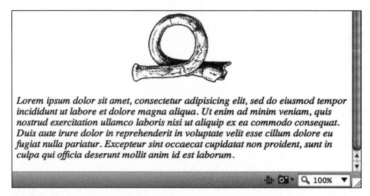

Figure 11-8. The last paragraph of the previous code example now has italicized text using the :last-child pseudo-selector.

E:first-of-type

This selector is a pseudonym for E:nth-of-type(1), and selects the first child of the indicated element. Again using the previous HTML example, modify the CSS as shown:

```
    <style type="text/css">
        img {
            margin-bottom:2em;
            float:right;
        }
        p:first-of-type { font-style:italic; }
    </style>
```

This should result in a rendering similar to Figure 11-9.

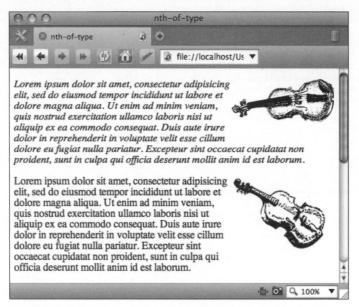

Figure 11-9. Using p:first-of-type to select the first paragraph and convert it to italics

E:last-of-type

The :last-of-type pseudo-selector targets the last sibling of the indicated element's parent. The following code will select the last <img> element in the document and float it to the right, which is illustrated in Figure 11-10:

```
<style type="text/css">
    img {
        margin-bottom:2em;
        float:right;
    }
    img:last-of-type {
        margin-right:2em;
        float:left;
    }
</style>
```

Figure 11-10. Using :last-of-type to float the last image in another direction

E:only-child

The :only-child pseudo-selector will target the indicated sibling elements when there is only one child element and there are no more element children:

```
<!DOCTYPE html PUBLIC "-//W3C//DTD XHTML 1.0 Transitional//EN"
    "http://www.w3.org/TR/xhtml1/DTD/xhtml1-transitional.dtd">
<html>
    <head>
        <title>only-child</title>
    </head>
    <style type="text/css">
        p:only-child
        {
          font-weight:bold;
          font-style:italic;
        }
    </style>
    <body>
        <h1>Trout Quintet - Instruments</h1>
        <div id="string_instruments">
            <p>Violin</p>
            <p>Viola</p>
            <p>Cello</p>
            <p>Double Bass</p>
        </div>
        <div id="keyboards">
            <p>Piano</p>
        </div>
    </body>
</html>
```

There is only one `<p>` element under the `<div id="keyboards">` hierarchy, so that is what will be selected, which in this case emphasizes the word "Piano," as shown in Figure 11-11.

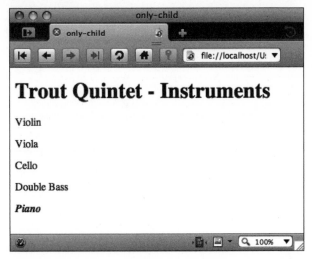

Figure 11-11. Using the :only-child pseudo-selector to target the only child of the `<div id="keyboards">` element

E:only-of-type

The `:only-of-type` will select children of the parent element where there is only one of the given element type:

```
<!DOCTYPE html PUBLIC "-//W3C//DTD XHTML 1.0 Transitional//EN"
    "http://www.w3.org/TR/xhtml1/DTD/xhtml1-transitional.dtd">
<html>
    <head>
        <title>only-of-type</title>
    </head>
    <style type="text/css">
        div:only-of-type
        {
          font-weight:bold;
          font-style:italic;
        }
    </style>
    <body>
        <h1>Trout Quintet - Instruments</h1>
        <div id="string_instruments">
            <p>Violin</p>
            <p>Viola</p>
            <p>Cello</p>
            <div>Double Bass</div>
        </div>
        <div id="keyboards">
```

311

```
            <p>Piano</p>
        </div>
    </body>
</html>
```

In this case, the words "Double Bass" are wrapped by a <div> instead of a <p>, so they become the only element of their type within the sibling group, as shown in Figure 11-12.

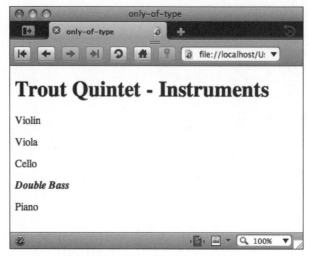

Figure 11-12. Highlighting the unique element within a node using :only-of-type

E:empty

E:empty selects an empty node, where there are no child elements or even text content. This example selects any empty paragraph elements and instructs the browser to show them as red boxes (as shown in Figure 11-13), perhaps for the purpose of cleaning up any extraneous markup:

```
<!DOCTYPE html PUBLIC "-//W3C//DTD XHTML 1.0 Transitional//EN"
    "http://www.w3.org/TR/xhtml1/DTD/xhtml1-transitional.dtd">
<html>
    <head>
        <title>only-of-type</title>
    </head>
    <style type="text/css">
        p:empty {
            background-color:#f00;
            display:block;
            border:1px solid black;
            width:200px;
            height:20px;
        }
    </style>
    <body>
```

```
<h1>Trout Quintet - Instruments</h1>
<div id="string_instruments">
    <p>Violin</p>
    <p>Viola</p>
    <p>Cello</p>
    <p>Double Bass</p>
    <p></p>
</div>
<div id="keyboards">
    <p>Piano</p>
</div>
</body>
</html>
```

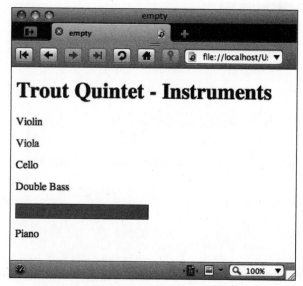

Figure 11-13. Using :empty to highlight elements with no content

E:target

The :target pseudo-class will select the target of referring URIs. This is especially useful to modify ID elements on a given page after clicking on a link:

```
<!DOCTYPE html PUBLIC "-//W3C//DTD XHTML 1.0 Transitional//EN"
    "http://www.w3.org/TR/xhtml1/DTD/xhtml1-transitional.dtd">
<html>
    <head>
        <title>target</title>
    </head>
    <style type="text/css">
        div:target {
            background-color:#F66;
            border:1px solid black;
```

```
        }
    </style>
    <body>
        <h1>Trout Quintet - Instruments</h1>
        <a href="#string_instruments">Strings</a> | ➡
<a href="#keyboards">Keyboards</a>
        <div id="string_instruments">
            <p>Violin</p>
            <p>Viola</p>
            <p>Cello</p>
            <p>Double Bass</p>
            <p></p>
        </div>
        <div id="keyboards">
            <p>Piano</p>
        </div>
    </body>
</html>
```

Figure 11-14 illustrates what the user would see when the Strings link is clicked.

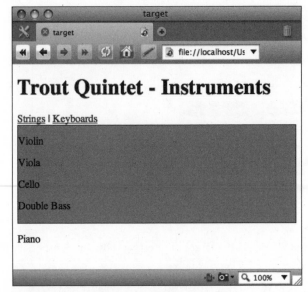

Figure 11-14. The string section is highlighted after clicking the Strings link, thanks to the :target pseudo-selector.

E:enabled, E:disabled, and E:checked

The E:enabled, E:disabled, and E:checked pseudo-elements are used for form input elements such as text fields, radio buttons, and any other form element that supports the disabled property. As we will see from the example, certain elements are not very conducive to styling in CSS using the current array of modern browsers, and are often best left alone. This is especially true of browsers that use native form elements such as the Mac OS X Aqua themed check box of browsers such as Safari. Here to compensate we've implemented a margin-left property to illustrate support of the element in Safari and other browsers that use Aqua for the check box and radio button elements:

```
<!DOCTYPE html PUBLIC "-//W3C//DTD XHTML 1.0 Transitional//EN"
    "http://www.w3.org/TR/xhtml1/DTD/xhtml1-transitional.dtd">
<html>
<head>
<title>enabled, disabled, and checked</title>
</head>
<style type="text/css">
  label {
    display:block;
    margin-top:1em;
  }
  input:enabled {
    border:2px solid green;
    font-weight:bold;
    background-color:#edfdda;
  }
  input:disabled {
    font-weight:normal;
    border:2px solid #666;
    background-color:#ddd;
  }
  input[type="radio"], input[type="checkbox"] { border:none; }
  input[type="radio"]:disabled, input[type="checkbox"]:disabled { ➡
visibility:hidden; }
  input:checked {
    background-color:#edfdda;
    color:#800000;
    border:2px solid blue;
    margin-left:4em;
  }
}
</style>
<body>
<form action="193232.11.16.html" method="post">
  <label for="instrument_name">Instrument Name</label>
  <input type="text" name="instrument_name" id="instrument_name" />
  <label for="instrument_name">Legacy Instrument Name</label>
  <input type="text" name="legacy_name" id="legacy_name" ➡
disabled="disabled" />
  <p>
    <label>
    <input type="radio" name="category" value="strings" />
    strings</label>
    <label>
    <input type="radio" name="category" value="woodwinds" />
    woodwinds</label>
```

```
      <label>
      <input type="radio" name="category" value="brass" />
      brass</label>
      <label>
      <input type="radio" name="category" value="percussion" ➥
disabled="disabled" />
      percussion</label>
      <label>
      <input name="nonstandard" type="checkbox" disabled="disabled" ➥
value="true" />
      Non-standard instrument</label>
      <label>
      <input name="nonstandard" type="checkbox" checked="checked" ➥
value="true" />
      Modern instrument</label>
    </p>
    <p>
      <input type="submit" value="Continue &rarr;">
    </p>
  </form>
</body>
</html>
```

These form element treatments are illustrated in Figure 11-15.

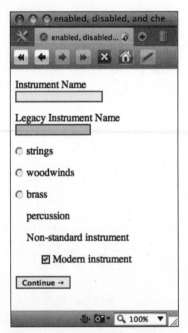

Figure 11-15. Demonstrating the
:enabled, :disabled, and :checked
pseudo-selectors in a form

Remember to keep accessibility in mind when modifying the display of form elements. If you change the selection color to a combination with low contrast to the nonselected text, it may be harder for some users to see the edges of their selection.

E::selection

The `E::selection` pseudo-selector actively targets the text being selected, allowing the web author to specify things like background colors and font colors for the selection:

```
<!DOCTYPE html PUBLIC "-//W3C//DTD XHTML 1.0 Transitional//EN"
    "http://www.w3.org/TR/xhtml1/DTD/xhtml1-transitional.dtd">
<html>
    <head>
        <title>::select</title>
    </head>
    <style type="text/css">
        p::selection {
            color: purple;
            background: yellow;
        }
    </style>
    <body>
        <p>Select some text! Lorem ipsum dolor sit amet, consectetur ➥
adipisicing elit, sed do eiusmod tempor incididunt ut labore et ➥
dolore magna aliqua. Ut enim ad minim veniam, quis nostrud ➥
exercitation ullamco laboris nisi ut aliquip ex ea commodo ➥
consequat. Duis aute irure dolor in reprehenderit in voluptate velit ➥
esse cillum dolore eu fugiat nulla pariatur. Excepteur sint occaecat ➥
cupidatat non proident, sunt in culpa qui officia deserunt mollit ➥
anim id est laborum.</p>
    </body>
</html>
```

Using the mouse to select some text in the paragraph will result in output similar to Figure 11-16.

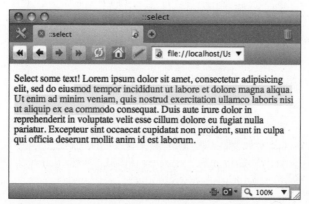

Figure 11-16. Using ::selection to modify the text color and background color of selected text

317

E:not(s)

E:not(s) selects all elements except the one specified in the argument. This example, which is illustrated in Figure 11-17, selects all <div>s that are not using id="keyboards" to be italicized:

```
<!DOCTYPE html PUBLIC "-//W3C//DTD XHTML 1.0 Transitional//EN"
    "http://www.w3.org/TR/xhtml1/DTD/xhtml1-transitional.dtd">
<html>
    <head>
        <title>empty</title>
    </head>
    <style type="text/css">
        div:not(#keyboards) { font-style:italic; }
    </style>
    <body>
        <h1>Trout Quintet - Instruments</h1>
        <div id="string_instruments">
            <p>Violin</p>
            <p>Viola</p>
            <p>Cello</p>
            <p>Double Bass</p>
        </div>
        <div id="keyboards">
            <p>Piano</p>
        </div>
    </body>
</html>
```

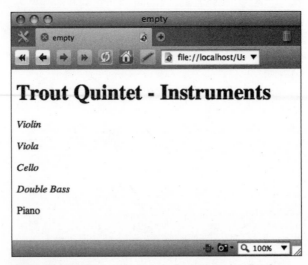

Figure 11-17. Using :not to exclude the keyboards <div> from being italicized

Typographic effects and web fonts

CSS3 includes three modules for dealing with text-related styling. The first one, which will be the most familiar, is the CSS Fonts module (http://www.w3.org/TR/css3-fonts/). This module includes, for the most part, the familiar text-oriented CSS properties that you are already familiar with by now, such as font-size and font-family. CSS Text (http://www.w3.org/TR/css3-text/) again should be mostly familiar to you; this module deals with text-based attributes such as alignment, word wrapping, justification, letter spacing, and so on. CSS Web Fonts (http://www.w3.org/TR/css3-webfonts/), on the other hand, is for the most part completely new, and designed to cover a new set of functionalities around the concept of being able to download more specialized fonts that might not necessarily exist on the client. This frees us from the constraints of having to guess an array of possible acceptable typefaces using the font-family declaration. Let's look at some of the more interesting typographic features of CSS3: the new word wrap and text shadow properties, and the web fonts module.

Word wrap

In the normal text flow of an HTML block, words will invariably run up against the edge of the box that contains them. At that point, the text has to do something—it gets clipped off, it flows past the box, or it wraps to the next line. The word-wrap property aims to tackle some of these issues by governing how a long word gets broken, or not, when it is displayed within a box that is too narrow to contain all of the characters on one line. As we see in the following example, word-wrap:break-word will cause long words to wrap within their containing element (where the default is to not break and have the word extend past the box). This is illustrated in the following code example and in Figure 11-18:

```
<!DOCTYPE html PUBLIC "-//W3C//DTD XHTML 1.0 Transitional//EN"
    "http://www.w3.org/TR/xhtml1/DTD/xhtml1-transitional.dtd">
<html>
    <head>
        <title>word-wrap</title>
    </head>
    <style type="text/css">
        li {
            width: 10em;
            border: 2px dashed #aaa;
            padding:0.4em;
            margin-bottom:0.5em;
        }
        .broken { word-wrap:break-word; }
        .unbroken { word-wrap:normal; }
    </style>
    <body>
        Long words, like rules, were meant to be broken:
        <ul class="broken">
            <li>Antidisestablishmentarianism</li>
            <li>Supercalifragilisticexpialidocious</li>
            <li>Aequeosalinocalcalinoceraceoaluminosocupreovitriolic ➡
</li>
        </ul>
        On the other hand, why break up a good thing?
        <ul class="unbroken">
```

```
            <li>Floccinaucinihilipilification</li>
            <li>Honorificabilitudinitatibus</li>
            <li>Chargoggagoggmanchauggagoggchaubunagungamaugg ➡
        </li>
            </ul>
        </body>
</html>
```

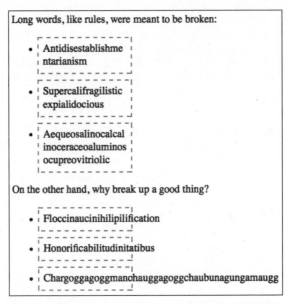

Figure 11-18. A list styled with word-wrap:break-word, followed by a list styled with word-wrap:normal as rendered in
Firefox 3.5

In most Western scripts, hyphens are needed to properly break a word as is done in the first example. However, this construct might be particularly useful in the context of handling the breaking or preservation of long strings such as URLs or code examples where the hyphen is not typically used.

Text shadow

A number of cool and interesting effects may be applied to text using the text-shadow property. This property can take four values: a color value and three dimensional values. The dimensional values are, in order, an X offset coordinate, a Y offset coordinate, and a blur radius. Sets of these shadow values may be concatenated together to apply multiple shadows to the same element, which can create some interesting effects, such as the ones that appear in Figure 11-19:

```
<!DOCTYPE html PUBLIC "-//W3C//DTD XHTML 1.0 Transitional//EN"
    "http://www.w3.org/TR/xhtml1/DTD/xhtml1-transitional.dtd">
<html>
    <head>
        <title>word-wrap</title>
    </head>
```

```
<style type="text/css">
    .quote {
        text-shadow: 2px 2px 4px #666;
        font-size:1.4em;
    }
    p.author {
        font-style:italic;
        text-shadow:
            hsl(280,100%,50%) 2px 2px 4px,
            orange 10px 6px 12px,
            hsla(140,100%,50%,0.6) -5px -3px 12px;
    }
    .author::before { content:"\2014"; }
</style>
<body>
    <div class="quote">
        <p>A painter paints pictures on canvas.  But musicians ➡
paint their pictures on silence.</p>
        <p class="author">Leopold Stokowski</p>
    </div>
    <div class="quote">
        <p>You must play the violin so that fathers will want to ➡
keep you away from their daughters.</p>
        <p class="author">Eric Rosenblith</p>
    </div>
</body>
</html>
```

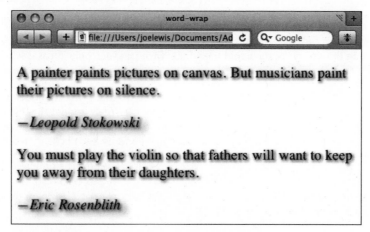

Figure 11-19. Using text-shadow on quotations in Safari 4

Here's an exercise to try making your own text-shadow effects: make it so that three instances of the text appear that are progressively each 5 pixels higher in their x, y values; 1 pixel higher in the blur radius values; and 25 percent lighter in their color values. Using HSL color values might be particularly useful for this need.

Web fonts

The CSS3 Web Fonts module is often touted as the way that web authors can finally specify font varieties that venture beyond the usual Verdana/Arial/Courier/Helvetica/Georgia/Times suspects, and this is indeed the most widely anticipated feature. But there is a bit more to the web fonts module. It includes descriptions about how to match a font (based on properties such as the x-height, serif treatment, slant, and so on). It also includes a mechanism to generate fonts on the fly based on the appearance and metrics of the requested font.

Before we go any further, we should mention a bit of history here: web fonts are not new to the CSS3 spec. They were first proposed in CSS2, and have had varying degrees of support in some older browsers. But today, with a reinvigorated CSS3 module and shiny new web browsers that support this feature, it is now possible to use web fonts in a more or less interesting and reliable way. And hey, if the browser doesn't support your specified downloadable font choice, give them something nice to look at in the font-family anyway.

Web fonts are initiated by the @font-face at-rule. The @font-face rules set up a definition within a style sheet for the name of a font, which can be used elsewhere in the style sheet as part of a font-family or shorthand font rule. Such a rule might look like the following:

```
@font-face {
    font-family: "BiauKai";
    src: url("http://www.example.com/assets/fonts/BiauKai.ttf");
}
```

This in turn makes it possible for us to write "BiauKai" as part of another font-family or font short-hand rule later in the style sheet:

```
html:lang(zh-tw) div.post { font-family: BiauKai, serif }
```

What happens behind the scenes here isn't just a simple routine of looking on the client to see if the BiauKai font exists. In this case the user agent should go one step further and download the font from the URL indicated in the src property within the @font-face rule, but only in cases where the specified font does not exist already on the client.

It is important to note right up front that most fonts are intellectual property under some form of copyright and should be treated as such. Do not assume you can freely and legally distribute any old font on your system as uploaded to a web server. Be sure to check the license carefully first. Public domain fonts or licenses where distribution via embedded web fonts is explicitly granted are the way to go. The Open Font Library (http://openfontlibrary.org/) is one of many sites that caters to just this need.

Using our previous markup example with the music quotes, let's try out applying a web font to the style sheet and see how that looks in Figure 11-20:

```
<style type="text/css">
    @font-face {
        font-family: "Ink Calligraphy";
        src:url(ZemusuInkCalligraphy.ttf);
        /* public domain font by zeimusu @ Open Font Library
           from http://openfontlibrary.org/media/files/zeimusu/15
```

```
            please visit and support the Open Font Library at
            http://openfontlibrary.org/
        */
    }
    .quote {
        text-shadow: 2px 2px 4px #666;
        font-size:1.4em;
        font-family:"Ink Calligraphy", sans-serif;
    }
    p.author {
        font-style:italic;
        text-shadow:
            hsl(280,100%,50%) 2px 2px 4px,
            orange 10px 6px 12px,
            hsla(140,100%,50%,0.6) -5px -3px 12px;
    }
    .author::before { content:"\2014"; }
</style>
```

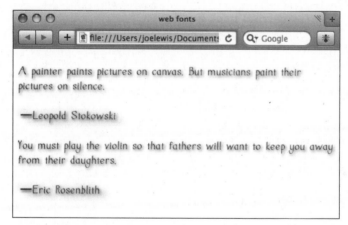

Figure 11-20. Using @font-face to import a specific font into the quotations page, as shown in Safari 4

Here we've defined a font called "Ink Calligraphy" in the @font-face rule, linked it to a local source file, and called it on the .quote rule. How cool is that? Try finding some of your own fonts with open licensing and experiment with this technique in your own pages.

Border and background effects

Box borders and backgrounds are fundamental concepts behind web page layout. We discuss box properties in terms of padding, margin, and content as well as boxes and borders, but it is the borders and backgrounds that we see as visual manifestations of the box itself. CSS3 includes several features to ease and improve our ability to manipulate background and border properties.

Rounded corners

Ninety-degree angles abound in the older generations of the Web. And then it became cool to break that cycle and design using rounded corners. But before browsers supported anything remotely resembling a rounded-corner CSS rule, web authors were forced to achieve this technique through contrived hacking of inserting up to four correctly shaped images into the corner of the box in question. This was no small feat since browsers and the CSS spec also lacked the ability to display more than one background image at a time! Clearly there should be an easier way.

And so there is: using border-radius, web authors can bend the borders of their box elements to their will. As of this writing, all implementations of it (Mozilla, WebKit) use vendor extensions. Let's use those for now with the expectation that this will be sorted out sometime in the next decade, again building on our previous markup example and just modifying the style sheet:

```
<style type="text/css">
    @font-face {
        font-family: "Ink Calligraphy";
        src:url(ZemusuInkCalligraphy.ttf);
        /* public domain font by zeimusu @ Open Font Library
            from http://openfontlibrary.org/media/files/zeimusu/15
            please visit and support the Open Font Library at
            http://openfontlibrary.org/
        */
    }
    div {
        width:50%;
        background-color: #FFFEEA;
        -moz-border-radius:20px;
        -webkit-border-radius:20px;
        border-radius:20px;
        border:1px solid red;
        padding:1em;
        margin-bottom:1em;
    }
    .quote {
        text-shadow: 2px 2px 4px #666;
        font-size:1.4em;
        font-family:"Ink Calligraphy", sans-serif;
    }
    p.author {
        font-style:italic;
        text-shadow:
            hsl(280,100%,50%) 2px 2px 4px,
            orange 10px 6px 12px,
            hsla(140,100%,50%,0.6) -5px -3px 12px;
    }
    .author::before { content:"\2014"; }
</style>
```

Figure 11-21 shows how these borders will now appear in a supporting browser.

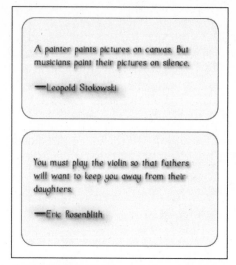

Figure 11-21. Rounded corners in our music quotes example

The things to pay attention to here in this example are the -moz-border-radius, -webkit-border-radius, and of course border-radius declarations. The two vendor-specific properties are required at this point since the specification isn't fully baked as of this writing, and the border-radius rule is included with the expectation that this will be in the final specification.

Individual corners may be further targeted by using specific properties. This is where the browser vendors begin to really show their differences. Try modifying the following code on the above <div> rule as shown:

```
div {
    width:50%;
    background-color: #FFFEEA;
    -moz-border-radius-topleft: none;
    -webkit-border-top-left-radius: none;
    -moz-border-radius-topright: 10px;
    -webkit-border-top-right-radius: 10px;
    -moz-border-radius-bottomleft: 20px;
    -webkit-border-bottom-left-radius: 20px;
    -moz-border-radius-bottomright: 80px;
    -webkit-border-bottom-right-radius: 80px;
    border-radius:20px;
    border:1px solid red;
    padding:1em;
    margin-bottom:1em;
}
```

Now observe in Figure 11-22 how this changes the appearance of the quotation borders.

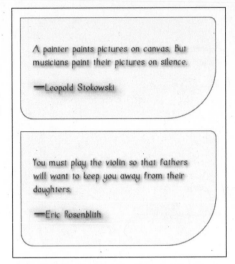

Figure 11-22. Targeting specific corners using border-radius

Be sure to check the latest version of the specification and the current state of web browsers as things unfold in the future. The details of this one in particular are sure to change.

Box shadow

The box-shadow property declarations are constructed in a similar way as the text-shadow properties we saw earlier, using values for x-offset, y-offset, blur radius, and color. This can make for a nice drop shadow effect on boxes such as images and pull-quote boxes. Again using the markup and style sheet from the previous example, set the <div> back to use a 20-pixel border radius on all the corners and set a drop shadow using the highlighted code:

```
div {
    width:50%;
    background-color: #FFFEEA;
    -moz-border-radius: 20px;
    -webkit-border-radius: 20px;
    border-radius:20px;
    border:1px solid red;
    -moz-box-shadow: 6px 6px 14px #999;
    -webkit-box-shadow: 6px 6px 14px #999;
    box-shadow: 6px 6px 14px #999;
    padding:1em;
    margin-bottom:1em;
}
```

Figure 11-23 shows how these box shadows should appear.

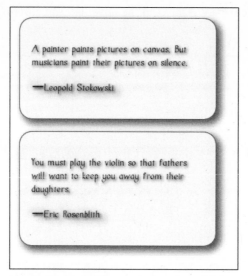

Figure 11-23. Using box-shadow on the musical quotes example

Multiple backgrounds

It has long been a desire of CSS developers to have the ability to place more than one background image on an element. Enter multiple backgrounds and background resizing. The capability prior to these features was limited to a single background image and the ability to position it vertically and horizontally, and the option to tile the images (or not). This resulted in some creative solutions to achieve complete coverage of a designer's goals, but they often involved extra markup or larger-than-necessary images.

For achieving multiple backgrounds in CSS3, the developer simply separates the standard background shorthand value sets with commas. Try modifying the previous example by inserting the highlighted code into the <div> rule:

```
div {
    width:50%;
    background: url(openquote.tif) 1% 5% no-repeat, ➡
url(closequote.tif) 99% 96% no-repeat;
    background-color: #FFFEEA;
    -moz-border-radius: 20px;
    -webkit-border-radius: 20px;
    border-radius:20px;
    border:1px solid red;
    -moz-box-shadow: 6px 6px 14px #999;
    -webkit-box-shadow: 6px 6px 14px #999;
    box-shadow: 6px 6px 14px #999;
    padding:1em;
    margin-bottom:1em;
    opacity: 1;
    -webkit-transition: opacity 2s linear;
}
```

327

This will result in having quote mark graphics in the upper-left and lower-right corners of the <div> elements, as shown in Figure 11-24.

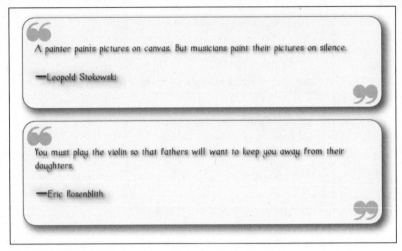

Figure 11-24. Quote marks using multiple background images

Background image resizing

The other side of this background image coin is the ability to resize a background image. In olden times, developers were stuck with the native pixel resolution of an image for display as a background image in a given element. But with the ability to resize this image using the background-size property, you may now let an image fill the space of a given <div>, or resize it to any number of ways depending on your design requirements.

The background-image property can accept percentage values, length units (such as px or em), and the keywords auto, cover, and contain. The auto property works to automatically resize if, say, the width was set to 15em while preserving the aspect ratio of the image. The contain keyword scales an image proportionally to fit inside an element, while the cover keyword proportionally scales an element to completely cover the element.

In addition to the background-image property, developers may use the background-origin property to specify which box the background image is being positioned against using the value padding-box, border-box, or content-box.

Animations, transitions, and transforms

We saw a few of these cutting-edge features when we were looking at styling for mobile Safari browsers on devices such as the iPhone earlier in this book. These visual effect features were introduced as proposed recommendations to the CSS3 specification in March 2009, and pose some really interesting and easily implemented alternatives compared to prior methods such as JavaScript or Flash. Let's touch on some of these new features, keeping in mind that these are proposals and may change over time.

Transitions

Transitions allow CSS properties to change from one value to another over a period of time. The two key properties introduced to enable transitions are transition-property (used to define which property is affected), transition-duration (used to set the duration of the transition effect), and timing-function (used to set how the timing will accelerate, decelerate, or otherwise change during the transition effect). These can be combined in a shorthand property called transition.

Try using the previous example and modifying the CSS as shown. This will create the effect of having each <div> element slowly disappear when you move the mouse over it. Currently Safari and other browsers using current versions of WebKit are the only ones that will support this, using the -webkit- prefix:

```
div {
    width:50%;
    background-color: #FFFEEA;
    -moz-border-radius: 20px;
    -webkit-border-radius: 20px;
    border-radius:20px;
    border:1px solid red;
    -moz-box-shadow: 6px 6px 14px #999;
    -webkit-box-shadow: 6px 6px 14px #999;
    box-shadow: 6px 6px 14px #999;
    padding:1em;
    margin-bottom:1em;
    opacity: 1;
    -webkit-transition-property: opacity;
    -webkit-transition-duration: 2s;
    -webkit-timing-function: linear;
}
div:hover {
    opacity: 0;
}
```

Now test it in Safari 4. Each <div> should fade gradually as you move the mouse in front of it. If desired, you might choose to write the previous transition statements using a single line of shorthand:

```
-webkit-transition: opacity 2s linear;
```

Transforms

Transforms allow you to perform things like size, rotation, and positioning changes. There is a 2D version of the Transforms module, and another for 3D.

A 2D transform might be written like this (using the -webkit- prefix if you would like to try this in Safari):

```
img {
    -webkit-transform: translate(20px, 80px) scale(2.5, 2.5) ➡
rotate(20deg);
  }
```

This transform takes an image and offsets it using the `translate` function 20 pixels to the right and 80 pixels down, uses the `scale` function to increase the size by 2.5 times the native size, and rotates it clockwise 20 degrees with the `rotate` function. This is a simple way to add much more capability to your page layout using one simple property. Arguably the `translate` and `scale` functions could be achieved by manipulation of other CSS properties such as with typical CSS positioning techniques and the `width` and `height` properties. But `rotate` does add a new and powerful feature, and it is very convenient to keep all of them in one concise and well-organized construction.

Animation

Animation in CSS introduces the concept of keyframes. If you've done any animation work in, say, Adobe Flash, then the concept of keyframes will be familiar to you. Animation is in fact similar to transitions, but they differ in that the animation effects are more specific about when and where things happen and allow for greater flexibility and precise timing, while transitions pretty much just get you from one state to the next. Animation has not yet been implemented in WebKit, but you can read the specification at `http://www.w3.org/TR/css3-animations/` and keep an eye on some of the sites mentioned in the chapter summary to find out when this might become available for tinkering.

Summary

In this chapter we looked at the emerging features of CSS3 and explored ways to experiment and incorporate these tools into your own code. Many of the features discussed in this chapter are still evolving, but they are quickly making their way into browsers in one form or another and are becoming available for you to try out. We suggest you take advantage of them whenever you can—perhaps to provide a little extra polish for your advanced browser users if you don't have to worry too much about legacy browser support.

Keep on top of the developments in CSS3 as they unfold by reading web sites that discuss such issues. Great places to look for this information include (but are by no means limited to)

- **IEBlog**: `http://blogs.msdn.com/ie/`
- **Surfin' Safari**: `http://webkit.org/blog/`
- **Opera Desktop Team**: `http://my.opera.com/desktopteam/blog/`
- **The Mozilla Blog**: `http://blog.mozilla.com/`
- **A List Apart**: `http://www.alistapart.com/`
- **CSS3.info**: `http://www.css3.info/`
- **W3C CSS home page**: `http://www.w3.org/Style/CSS/`

When you write emerging CSS3 features that rely on vendor extensions into your production code and release style sheets into the wild, it may be a good idea to give your best guess as to what the final declaration might be and include that in your code as well. On the chance that it does become more widely accepted, your designs will continue to work as new browsers adopt the feature.

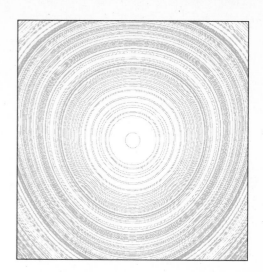

Chapter 12

THE FUTURE OF CSS AND THE WEB

Throughout this book, you've been shown advanced concepts, up to the cutting edge of CSS development. You are now well equipped with tools that you'll be using for years to come. But what will you build? How can you keep innovating? What other sources might you look toward to find inspiration? In this chapter, we invite you to imagine the future with us. From here on out, the Web is going to be whatever you make it.

There is a remarkable amount of room in which to grow and develop new techniques and technologies today and in the years to come. Remember that, in historical terms, the Web is an exceptionally young medium. As of this writing, if you consider that Tim Berners-Lee launched the World Wide Web by publishing his summary of the fundamental technologies to the `alt.hypertext` newsgroup on August 6, 1991, the Web is just over 17 years old. Television by comparison has been around for 80 years; the telephone for over 130 years; the telegraph, since the early 1800s; and the printing press emerged around the year 1450.

Considering these media, the Web is still in its infancy. Imagine where we'll be ten years from now, or even in a hundred years. In this chapter, as a way to tie up some of the ideas we have learned in this book, we will briefly explore some of the things that you might come to expect from CSS and the web development platform in the future, and we ask you, the reader, to consider some of the questions posed here and to think about where all this might be going next.

The bright future of the Web

Even as you read this book, the CSS specifications are evolving. Whether or not you realize it, everyone who works with these technologies plays a role in the development of the Web. Regardless of whether you are writing specifications, implementing technologies in a browser, or using emerging CSS techniques in your own web designs—as you should now be now well equipped to do after studying the subjects within this book—you are blazing trails for things that will be used decades from now.

If you wish to make history, then make history by doing: push that envelope. We encourage you to see what is possible, or at least what you can get away with during your daily grind. As you work, look for opportunities to sprinkle CSS enhancements for modern browsers in your projects in spite of a lack of support from older browsers (opacity, text-shadow, box-shadow, and any of the standard properties implemented only as with vendor-specific prefixes are great examples); this is how you push the Web forward.

Expanding CSS in print

Although CSS currently predominates on computer screens of various shapes and sizes, print is still the most widely deployed medium for human communication. Despite the predominance of gadgetry that replaces print—such as the Amazon Kindle, smartphones with screens large enough to keep you from going blind, and of course the "good old-fashioned computer screen"—print will be around for some time to come. Print has some advantages compared to electronic media: it doesn't require electricity, it is comfortable to read, and it can be constructed with physical dimensions such as die cutting, natural handmade paper, pop-ups, and other specialized ornamentation that transcend the two-dimensional world of the computer screen. And in most cases, a nice, hardbound printed book makes a much more meaningful gift than the intangible e-book equivalent.

Therefore, the biggest potential area where CSS usage will expand is very likely in the area of print, especially as CSS3 begins to solve many of the shortcomings earlier CSS specifications had with regard to flexibly addressing printable portions of paper that we discussed back in Chapter 4. It's also possible that support for CSS in areas such as Braille and aural content will see improvements in future applications, as CSS already contains a growing wealth of possibilities for those media types.

As you know, the possibility of easily repurposing a single body of content for multiple formats is an extremely attractive proposition both for content producers and publishers alike. For instance, say a symphony orchestra produced some promotional material and wanted to target it to four different page layout scenarios: one for a CD booklet, one for a concert program, one for a promotional page on their website, and one as a section for a printed annual yearbook containing a compilation of works. With the right content in the right markup (either HTML or some form of XML), this is an achievable task with today's CSS implementations, and yet only one of the four options mentioned involves a computer display as final distribution medium.

To do something like that today, you might spend a great deal of time developing a style sheet by using the typical code-load-refresh methodology inside a web browser. However, we believe that as the usefulness of CSS makes itself evident on the Web, we'll see more applications that treat CSS for printed and other media as first-class citizens. One such notable product today is PrinceXML, a CSS-capable XML and HTML to PDF transformer.[1] With good parsing clients for print like this appearing

---

1. PrinceXML (http://www.princexml.com/) is a product created by YesLogic Pty Ltd of Melbourne, Australia.

and support for the improvements in CSS3 for print media, CSS becomes a powerful print publishing platform.

There's also no technical reason why end users should need to learn how to write a markup language or CSS themselves. Even today, desktop and online word processors alike such as Microsoft Word and Google Docs are capable of producing files that combine some form of XML with an embedded style sheet for presentation. These are essentially crude graphical user interfaces for working with CSS in a particular context—text. Since we have CSS, we're simply missing a similar graphical user interface that generates CSS for its aural or other contexts.

XSL Formatting Objects (XSL-FO) is a markup language used most often for creating print document formats. Might CSS replace current use of XSL-FO someday? We know CSS is great for print and CSS3 makes things that much better, so what can CSS do in place of XSL-FO for the publishing community, and would that be easier or better? XSL-FO is an intermediary step between an XML document and ultimately what is likely a print format such as PDF. If CSS were refined enough to the point that we could achieve parity in print output between CSS and XSL-FO, then really XSL-FO becomes an unnecessary step.

How much of this print-on-demand stuff can we democratize? CSS is much more widely known by developers than XSL-FO and sites like Lulu (http://www.lulu.com/) let authors self-publish books. Can we envision a situation in which these authors also provide Lulu with a CSS file to style their book, rather than using PDFs? Would this be a benefit to web designers, Lulu, consumers, some of these, or all three, and why?

Audible CSS

Yet another idea would be reformulating a blog into a podcast simply by using a speech media style sheet. With today's publishing platforms improving their support to output semantically rich pages and with voice synthesis technologies improving, it may not be quite so far a leap to imagine a system that can take this output and automatically speak it. In such a system, a CSS file might be used to describe the ways that different parts of the text would be verbalized.

On the same note, imagine a system that can also work in the reverse way; taking an audio recording or audio input and automatically transcribing it to a file that contains semantically rich markup. Although it's not quite this sophisticated yet, Google's new "Google Voice" can automatically transcribe aural messages to real text and can even email you the result. Could CSS be used more than to give those transcriptions a bit of typographic style, perhaps doing so much for author customizations as describing what "air quotes" sound like when particular individuals pause dramatically enough when they use them in speech? Sure, this seems far-out today, and perhaps it won't ultimately be possible for CSS to provide such a capability, but the influence of what CSS has accomplished is already visible in numerous other systems and technologies related to semantic encoding.[2]

Ultimately, CSS is computer code for style. So what can be styled via a computer? Ask yourself this question and you will likely find opportunities for future directions in CSS.

---

2. One notable example of this is RDF-EASE, which is a CSS-like language for describing the RDF vocabularies in XML documents. Think RDFa, but inside of "semantic style sheets" instead of coupled to the markup itself. The RDF-EASE draft specification, which is not an official draft by any means, is available at http://buzzword.org.uk/2008/rdf-ease/.

HTML5 and CSS

The last published recommendations for HTML were under the 4.01 version, adopted as of December 24, 1999. Subsequent markup efforts were then focused on the XML variants of HTML, such as XHTML1, XHTML1.1, and current work going on for XHTML2.

Recently, a new effort originally started under a group called the Web Hypertext Application Technology Working Group (WHATWG) decided to work on an upgrade to the HTML specification under the guises that the XML parsing requirements of XHTML were too strict and poorly enforced, and that the beauty of the success of the Web was the ease of use and forgivingness of good old HTML. Why not improve on those aspects of it? From that effort, what is now HTML5 was born.

HTML5 comes in two flavors, one of the plain-old HTML variety, and one that is an XHTML-like version that borrows XHTML's self-closing tag syntax. The XHTML-compatible version aims to maintain markup's ability to be extended, which the HTML version also benefits from. Developing a version of HTML5 that uses XML syntax in parallel with the more forgiving traditional HTML parsing rules continues to steer the future of markup toward well-formed, semantic structures. HTML5 has strong backing from developers and technology vendors alike. Despite early fireworks, it has become a W3C project and can already be used and validated against from the W3C's markup validation service.

The new elements in HTML5 include the following (as of this writing):

- **Structural, block-level elements**: <section>, <header>, <footer>, <nav>, and <article>
- **Block-level semantic elements**: <aside>, <figure>, and <dialog>
- **Inline semantic elements**: <mark>, <time>, <meter>, and <progress>
- **Multimedia elements**: <audio> and <video>
- **Interactive elements**: <details>, <datagrid>, <menu>, <command>

In addition to the new elements, new rules will apply. For instance, in HTML5 you can wrap an <a> element around an <h1> and additional elements after that. Here's a block of markup that will be a single link, with a little CSS to illustrate the point:

```
<!DOCTYPE HTML PUBLIC "-//W3C//DTD HTML 4.01//EN"
  "http://www.w3.org/TR/html4/strict.dtd">
<html>
  <head>
    <title>A Hover of Many</title>
    <style type="text/css" media="screen">
      a[href="/2009/seattle/"]:hover {
        color:red;
      }
    </style>
  </head>
  <body>
    <a href="/2009/seattle/">
      <h1>Welcome to Viola World</h1>
      <img src="violaplayer.jpg" ➡
```

```
    alt="A viola player trying to count to four." />
        <p>Where all your viola needs are met!</p>
      </a>
    </body>
  </html>
  </a>
```

Yes, Virginia, this is legal markup in HTML5, and why not? We would like to link a bunch of elements in an <a> element. It will save developers time, and more easily generalizes what an HTML "anchor" was intended to be in the first place. The anchor-wrapping example will also affect CSS: you'll have the ability to select new descendants of <a> elements, including the <h1> and <p> elements. For those of us who have been coding HTML for a long time and were taught that inline elements such as the <a> were never allowed to have block-level elements within, this might seem unnatural at first. But there's no technical reason why the rules can't be changed to make our lives as web developers a little easier, and it makes perfect sense.

CSS remains the core styling language for HTML5, and HTML5 introduces a lot of new markup and new rules into the mix. With that in mind, we now have a new suite of tags to style, complete with a whole new world of opportunities for styling our web sites, and a new suite of potential browser bugs to battle. How will CSS fit in with the HTML5 enhancements? How will CSS3—and even CSS4 when that comes about one day—be affected by the core markup trends of the Web such as HTML5? What opportunities do they present from the perspective of a CSS developer? These questions are open-ended—ask yourself these from time to time as the specifications continue to evolve.

Influences, tensions, and competitors to CSS

One of the amazing things about the development of web technologies is that they were relatively anarchic. Unlike the development of traditional GUI systems, which were created behind the closed doors of academic institutions like Xerox's PARC and later developed further by products such as Apple's original Macintosh, the Web evolved in an open and, for lack of a better term, amateurish fashion. Although we can debate the benefits of one form of evolution over another, few argue that the Web isn't a platform for incredible innovation, proving that either evolutionary method can push the development of such technologies in interesting and useful new directions.

As with all technologies, CSS is designed to solve a particular use case: separating the presentation of content from the structure of the content itself and reforming it to new presentations easily. However, CSS is not the only technology designed to solve this same use case. As we briefly mentioned in the previous section, one notable competitor is XSL-FO, heavily used in the publishing industries for print layouts.[3]

XSL-FO is a self-contained, unified, presentational markup language. This means that an XSL-FO document does not require external style sheets, scripts, or other apparatus to work as expected, and it

---

3. A 2005 article published on XML.com by Michael Day and Håkon Wium Lie, one of the creators of CSS, compared and contrasted XSL-FO with CSS when used for printing XML documents. Perhaps unsurprisingly, the article, which can be found at http://www.xml.com/lpt/a/1527, concluded that CSS is the simpler choice.

is not considered semantically structured the way HTML or XHTML is. It is most often used to create print documents and is specifically tailored for paged media. A typical workflow involving XSL-FO would look something like this:

1. The XML document (such as DocBook, used in publishing contexts) is created.

2. The XML document is passed through an Extensible Style Sheet Transformation (XSLT) to convert the XML into XSL-FO.

3. The XSL-FO is passed through an "FO Processor"—software intended to convert the presentational document to another (potentially binary) format. The usual output is some press-ready format, such as PDF or PostScript.

XSL-FO contrasts with CSS in that it is a markup language, and all of the presentational data is contained within element attributes. It is not semantic at all, nor is it modular. It is a transition format between XML and some other format, and isn't intended to be worked with by itself without some sort of programmatic capabilities on either end of the process (such as XSLT and software to convert to PDF).

The question—as we alluded to earlier—is at what point in the advancement of CSS does XSL-FO become obsolete? With improvements in the specification around web fonts and print media, all the components for a full-featured print styling mechanism are coming into place. All that remains is a parser to convert your markup into a press-ready format such as PDF or PostScript. Printing your markup directly from a CSS style sheet instead of doing all that XSL-FO transformation means one less step in the process, and it leverages the opportunity to use external style sheets and skills that you already know to write manually, if that is needed or desired.

Another open question among web technologists concerns the CSS selection model. In CSS3, the ways in which elements can be targeted by CSS rules has been extracted into its own module called CSS3 Selectors.[4] As you know, CSS's notion of selectors originated in the first version of the specification, first published in 1996. However, in 1999 the W3C standardized a similar technology intended to be used to address parts of an XML document that provided much more granular control over which parts of the document were selected. This technology is called the XML Path Language, or XPath.

Today, the earliest versions of XPath still give XPath authors greater specificity over which parts of an XML document they wish to address than even the latest CSS3 Selectors draft. Many developers wonder, then, if such a precise language exists already, why is the CSS3 Selectors draft not incorporating more of it?

Some believe that XPath's syntax is too complicated. A common selection such as "all <p> elements" is extremely intuitive using CSS (the selector is simply a p) and in XPath it is not (to achieve the same effect, the *XPath expression* you need to use is //p).

On the other hand, with new CSS constructions such as div#content > div:not(p:nth-of-type(3) a[href]), CSS Selectors can become frustratingly complex as well. What is an appropriate balance between simplicity and power? This is a debate that rages on to this day.

---

4. As of this writing, the CSS3 Selectors module specification is still in Working Draft state and can be found at http://www.w3.org/TR/css3-selectors/.

Other parts of CSS are taking the opposite route; rather than developing their own syntax and capabilities, they are taking on the behavior and terminology of other technologies. At the time of this writing, the proposed CSS3 modules for CSS Animations and Transitions was accepted to the standards track by the W3C. These modules (discussed in Chapter 11, with examples of these techniques presented in Chapter 5) incorporate SVG-like capabilities. More to the point, they are so similar that they can be thought of as a CSS interface to SVG graphical capability. Of course, CSS can be applied to SVG markup, so clearly there is some opportunity there for web authors to leverage their CSS skills in SVG elements.

In this case, the ubiquity of CSS is helping to promote and standardize the capabilities developed by other technologies. Since there are so many more knowledgeable CSS developers than there are SVG developers, it makes sense to utilize your existing familiarity to push the envelope of what is technically possible.[5]

However, this path is not without its concerns. Although some would argue that creating more than one way to do something is a good thing, others argue that creating too many different ways to accomplish the same task fragments a standard and undermines its usefulness. Since many modern browsers support SVG today, the question becomes why not promote its use as is?

A further question that comes up is related to the technicality of the implementation itself. SVG is, as mentioned as early as Chapter 1 in this book, a "thing" that can be referenced and repurposed as a form of content. It is ultimately a language that describes building blocks of visual things. When you put the pieces together, you can create ever more complex graphical objects. On the other hand, CSS requires the use of a different thing; by itself, a style sheet doesn't do anything.

These examples are the product of nothing more magical than developers like you playing around with the building blocks that we have today; such academic experimentation is the best thing you can do to expand your skills. When you run into a problem, ask yourself if you can use an existing building block—a CSS property or particular browser feature—to solve it, or if you need a new building block altogether. If you do need to create something new, since you've now imagined what it might be, tell other people what you need or, if you can, build it yourself.

Keeping up-to-date = getting involved

Since you're reading this book, you're likely interested in keeping your skills up-to-date. You are probably interested in being a better web developer, and it is arguable that you might want to display that skill by being able to tackle whatever the latest trends and implementations have emerged in the web browser market. These skills make you marketable.

One of the beautiful things about the World Wide Web and related Internet-based technological marvels is that they are built on open standards and proven techniques that are created by global networks of industry experts, enthusiasts, and journeymen. These people are computer scientists, web developers, graphic designers, accessibility experts, networking professionals, students, interns, software developers, and so on. In other words, people a lot like yourself!

---

5. John Allsopp argues this point eloquently in the comments on his post "Shiny Happy Buttons" at http://24ways.org/ 2008/shiny-happy-buttons#c002096.

Web specifications such as CSS, HTML, XML, and others are all deliberated around some kind of organization, such as the World Wide Web Consortium (W3C), the Internet Engineering Task Force (IETF), ECMA International, and others. They are debated in discussion forums, weblogs, and industry articles. Want to join in the party? The good news is, for most aspects of these organizations, participation is free. As designers and CSS coders, you are encouraged to participate. These specifications can all use more end-user input.

Participating in the W3C

The CSS specification is a recommendation published by the W3C. While there is a core group of contributors, the specifications are up for review and open to debate via a mailing list.

There are three ways that an individual can directly participate in the W3C specifications: by joining a mailing list and participating in the dialogue, by joining as part of a parent organization such as your company or school, or by becoming an invited expert. There is no mechanism for individual membership in the W3C, but that is probably unnecessary for the average individual and participation in the email discussion forums will usually suffice. To get on the CSS discussion, send an email to www-style-request@w3.org with the word *subscribe* in the subject line. For more information on the subject of participating in the W3C discussion groups, please visit http://www.w3.org/Mail/.

The Web Standards Project

The Web Standards Project (http://www.webstandards.org/) began in 1998 to take on social and industry change in how web pages were coded and how browsers interpreted our code. Back then, the problem was that web browser vendors, notably Netscape and Microsoft, were implementing proprietary features and interpreting code in ways that were different enough to often warrant the creation of two or more code bases for any single given web page, site, or application. Needless to say, this was nuts and made web developers crazy. It was primarily through the efforts of the Web Standards Project that browser manufacturers eventually agreed to implement "standards mode."

These efforts continue today. While most modern browsers do support web standards to some degree, the levels of compliance vary greatly. Internet Explorer, even at version 8, with vastly improved support for CSS and other specifications, still has a great many issues when it comes to things like XML support or CSS3. Furthermore, there is an ongoing effort to promote web standards in the tools that build the Web. Tools from companies such as Adobe and Microsoft have an enormous impact on how web pages are built with the tools they provide—notably Adobe Dreamweaver and Microsoft Visual Studio. Check out the projects at the Web Standards Project; monitor the issues and trends. And if you feel inspired, get involved!

Exchanging ideas

An excellent way to keep on top of this stuff is to pay attention to the weblogs, microblogs (such as Twitter.com and Laconi.ca) and other information streams that have been known to disseminate these tidbits of information as soon as they are available. Find some CSS gurus who keep their blogs up-to-date with new and interesting CSS techniques, commentary on emerging specifications, and examples of how to implement new CSS features in the latest web browsers.

Often when we are writing a blog post on something about CSS or other web technologies, we are opening up the floor for comment. Here as well is a good opportunity to participate. Let's say I write something about how best to style for aural user agents. But it's a first cut—a strawman—and there are still some problems with how to handle some aspect of it. Perhaps you have an idea for the answer. You post a comment, and the dialogue begins.

Even faster—or lazier as the case may be—might be the use of microblogging platforms such as Twitter. Pose a question to the hive mind of the Internet and see what comes back. Use search features (such as hashtags—perhaps #css3 for instance) to see what the community is wrestling with, what people are chatting about, and what might be on the horizon.

Consider starting a weblog about your ideas on web development, or adding such content to an existing blog if you have one. If you don't have a blog yet, they are easy to set up and free in most cases. Even if you're the only one reading it, there is a benefit: writing about the things you learn helps you acquire knowledge, and keeping a blog can serve for many of us as a kind of knowledgebase for ourselves and perhaps our colleagues as well. Writing things down helps you acquire and remember these issues.

Summary

Today, CSS continues to obtain increasing traction. In addition to solidifying support for long-awaited capabilities, this also means that brand-new capabilities are being developed all the time. These emerging capabilities are the newest, furthest edge of that envelope, and as such are a part of our collective and continuing mission as web developers to boldly go where no browser has gone before.

In this chapter, we wanted to touch on some possibilities for future developments and trends in CSS and what it means for the future of web. But the future is largely up to you—how you code your sites, how you push the envelope and test the edges of what we are capable of. We hope that we have pointed you in the right general direction and created some food for thought, and that you have new ideas to explore.

The future is yours. The best way to face that future is with eyes and ears open, feet forward, boots on, and ready to march bravely into the unknown.

INDEX

C